LAW'S EMPIRE

Ronald Dworkin is Professor of Jurisprudence at Oxford University and Professor of Law at New York University. He is the author of *Taking Rights Seriously* and *A Matter of Principle*.

Fontana Masterguides

Robert A. Hinde
Ethology

Leszek Kolakowski
Religion

Edmund Leach
Social Anthropology

Wynne Godley and Francis Cripps
Macroeconomics

Bernard Williams
Ethics and the Limits of Philosophy

Joseph Kerman
Musicology

Ronald Dworkin

LAW'S EMPIRE

Fontana Press

First published in 1986 by Fontana Paperbacks,
8 Grafton Street, London W1X 3LA
Second impression October 1986

Copyright © Ronald Dworkin 1986

Fontana Press is an imprint of
Fontana Paperbacks, part of
the Collins Publishing Group

A hardback edition is available from Harvard University Press

Typeset in the United States of America
Printed and bound in Great Britain by
William Collins Sons & Co. Ltd, Glasgow

FOR BETSY

We live in and by the law. It makes us what we are: citizens and employees and doctors and spouses and people who own things. It is sword, shield, and menace: we insist on our wage, or refuse to pay our rent, or are forced to forfeit penalties, or are closed up in jail, all in the name of what our abstract and ethereal sovereign, the law, has decreed. And we *argue* about what it has decreed, even when the books that are supposed to record its commands and directions are silent; we act then as if law had muttered its doom, too low to be heard distinctly. We are subjects of law's empire, liegemen to its methods and ideals, bound in spirit while we debate what we must therefore do.

What sense does this make? How can the law command when the law books are silent or unclear or ambiguous? This book sets out in full-length form an answer I have been developing piecemeal, in fits and starts, for several years: that legal reasoning is an exercise in constructive interpretation, that our law consists in the best justification of our legal practices as a whole, that it consists in the narrative story that makes of these practices the best they can be. The distinctive structure and constraints of legal argument emerge, on this view, only when we identify and distinguish the diverse and often competitive dimensions of political value, the different strands woven together in the complex judgment that one interpretation makes law's story better on the whole, all things considered, than any other can. This book refines and expands and illustrates that conception of law. It excavates its foundations in a more general politics of integrity, community, and fraternity. It tracks its consequences for abstract legal theory and then for a series of concrete cases arising under the common law, statutes, and the Constitution.

I use several arguments, devices, and examples that I have used before, though in each case in different and, I hope, improved form. That repetition is deliberate: it allows many discussions and examples to be briefer here, since readers who wish to pursue them in greater detail, beyond the level necessary for this book's argument, may consult the references I provide to fuller treatment. (Many of these longer discussions are available in *A Matter of Principle*, Cambridge, Mass., and London, 1985.) This book touches, as any general book on legal theory must, on a number of intricate and much-studied issues in general philosophy. I have not wanted to interrupt the general argument by any excursion into these issues, and so I have, whenever possible, taken them up in long textual notes. I have also used long notes for extended discussions of certain arguments particular legal scholars have made.

I have made no effort to discover how far this book alters or replaces positions I defended in earlier work. It might be helpful to notice in advance, however, how it treats two positions that have been much commented upon. In *Taking Rights Seriously* I offered arguments against legal positivism that emphasized the phenomenology of adjudication: I said that judges characteristically feel an obligation to give what I call "gravitational force" to past decisions, and that this felt obligation contradicts the positivist's doctrine of judicial discretion. The present book, particularly in Chapter 4, emphasizes the interpretive rather than the phenomenological defects of positivism, but these are, at bottom, the same failures. I have also argued for many years against the positivist's claim that there cannot be "right" answers to controversial legal questions, but only "different" answers; I have insisted that in most hard cases there are right answers to be hunted by reason and imagination. Some critics have thought I meant that in these cases one answer could be *proved* right to the satisfaction of everyone, even though I insisted from the start that this is not what I meant, that the question whether we can have reason to think an answer right is different from the question whether it can be demonstrated to be right. In this book I argue that the critics fail to understand what the controversy about right answers is really about—what it must be about if the skeptical thesis, that there are no right answers, is to count as any argument against the theory of law I defend. I claim the controversy is really about morality, not metaphysics, and the no-right-answer thesis, understood as a moral claim, is deeply unpersuasive in morality as well as in law.

I have not tried generally to compare my views with those of other legal and political philosophers, either classical or contemporary, or to point out how far I have been influenced by or have drawn from their work. Nor is this book a survey of recent ideas in jurisprudence. I do discuss at length several fashionable views in legal theory, including "soft" legal positivism, the economic analysis of law, the critical legal studies movement, and the "passive" and "framers' intention" theories of American constitutional law. I discuss these, however, because their claims fall across the argument I am making, and I entirely neglect many legal philosophers whose work is of equal or greater importance.

Frank Kermode, Sheldon Leader, Roy McLees, and John Oakley each read a draft of a substantial part of the book and offered extensive comments. Their help was invaluable: each saved me from serious mistakes, contributed important examples, saw issues that had eluded me, and made me rethink certain arguments. Jeremy Waldron read and improved Chapter 6, and Tom Grey did that for Chapter 2. Most of the notes, though not the long textual ones, were prepared by William Ewald, William Riesman, and, especially, Roy McLees; any value the book has as a source of references is entirely to their credit. I acknowledge the generous support of the Filomen D'Agostino and Max E. Greenberg Research Fund of New York University School of Law. I am grateful to David Erikson of Xyquest, Inc., who volunteered to make special adaptations to that firm's remarkable word-processing program, XyWrite III, so that I could use it for this book. Peg Anderson of Harvard University Press was exceptionally helpful and long-suffering in tolerating changes beyond the last moment.

I owe more diffuse debts. My colleagues in the jurisprudential community of Great Britain, particularly John Finnis, H. L. A. Hart, Neil MacCormick, Joseph Raz, and William Twining, have been patient tutors to a dense pupil, and my friends at New York University Law School, especially Lewis Kornhauser, William Nelson, David Richards, and Laurence Sager, have been a steady source of imaginative insight and advice. I am grateful, above all, to the powerful critics I have been lucky enough to attract in the past; this book might have been dedicated to them. Replying to criticism has been, for me, the most productive of all work. I hope I shall be lucky again.

. CONTENTS .

ONE · WHAT IS LAW? 1

    Why It Matters   Disagreement about Law
    The Plain-Fact View   A Threshold Objection
    The Real World   Semantic Theories of Law
    The Real Argument for Semantic Theories

TWO · INTERPRETIVE CONCEPTS 45

    The Semantic Sting   An Imaginary Example
    A First Look at Interpretation
    Interpretation and Author's Intention
    Art and the Nature of Intention
    Intentions and Practices   Stages of
    Interpretation   Philosophers of Courtesy
    A Digression: Justice   Skepticism about
    Interpretation

THREE · JURISPRUDENCE REVISITED 87

    A New Picture   Concepts and Conceptions
    of Law   Skeptical Conceptions and Wicked
    Law   Grounds and Force of Law

FOUR · CONVENTIONALISM 114

    Its Structure   Its Appeal   Legal Conventions
    Two Kinds of Conventionalism
    Does Conventionalism Fit Our Practice?
    Does Conventionalism Justify Our Practice?

FIVE · PRAGMATISM AND PERSONIFICATION   151

A Skeptical Conception   Does Pragmatism
Fit?   Law without Rights   The Claims of
Integrity   Community Personified

SIX · INTEGRITY   176

Agenda   Does Integrity Fit?   Is Integrity
Attractive?   The Puzzle of Legitimacy
Obligations of Community
Fraternity and Political Community
Untidy Endnotes

SEVEN · INTEGRITY IN LAW   225

A Large View   The Chain of Law   Law: The
Question of Emotional Damages   A Provisional
Summary   Some Familiar Objections   Skepticism
in Law

EIGHT · THE COMMON LAW   276

The Economic Interpretation   Complexities
The Question of Justice   The Utilitarian Duty
The Egalitarian Interpretation   Equality and
Comparative Cost   Private People and Public
Bodies

NINE · STATUTES   313

Legislative Intention   Speaker's Meaning
Convictions   Hercules' Method
Legislative History   Statutes over Time
When Is the Language Clear?

TEN · THE CONSTITUTION   355

Is Constitutional Law Built on a Mistake?   Liberals
and Conservatives   Historicism   Passivism
Hercules on Olympus   Theories of Racial
Equality   Deciding *Brown*   Deciding *Bakke*
Is Hercules a Tyrant?

ELEVEN · LAW BEYOND LAW   400

Law Works Itself Pure   Law's Dreams
Epilogue: What Is Law?

Notes   417
Index   455

LAW'S EMPIRE

ONE

WHAT IS LAW?

WHY IT MATTERS

It matters how judges decide cases. It matters most to people unlucky or litigious or wicked or saintly enough to find themselves in court. Learned Hand, who was one of America's best and most famous judges, said he feared a lawsuit more than death or taxes. Criminal cases are the most frightening of all, and they are also the most fascinating to the public. But civil suits, in which one person asks compensation or protection from another for some past or threatened harm, are sometimes more consequential than all but the most momentous criminal trials. The difference between dignity and ruin may turn on a single argument that might not have struck another judge so forcefully, or even the same judge on another day. People often stand to gain or lose more by one judge's nod than they could by any general act of Congress or Parliament.

Lawsuits matter in another way that cannot be measured in money or even liberty. There is inevitably a moral dimension to an action at law, and so a standing risk of a distinct form of public injustice. A judge must decide not just who shall have what, but who has behaved well, who has met the responsibilities of citizenship, and who by design or greed or insensitivity has ignored his own responsibilities to others or exaggerated theirs to him. If this judgment is unfair, then the community has inflicted a moral injury on one of its members because it has stamped him in some degree or dimension an outlaw. The injury is gravest when an innocent person is convicted of a crime, but it is substantial enough when a plaintiff with a sound claim is turned away from court or a defendant leaves with an undeserved stigma.

These are the direct effects of a lawsuit on the parties and their dependents. In Britain and America, among other places, judicial decisions affect a great many other people as well, because the law often becomes what judges say it is. The decisions of the United States Supreme Court, for example, are famously important in this way. That Court has the power to overrule even the most deliberate and popular decisions of other departments of government if it believes they are contrary to the Constitution, and it therefore has the last word on whether and how the states may execute murderers or prohibit abortions or require prayers in the public schools, on whether Congress can draft soldiers to fight a war or force a president to make public the secrets of his office. When the Court decided in 1954 that no state had the right to segregate public schools by race, it took the nation into a social revolution more profound than any other political institution has, or could have, begun.[1]

The Supreme Court is the most dramatic witness for judicial power, but the decisions of other courts are often of great general importance as well. Here are two examples, chosen almost at random, from English legal history. In the nineteenth century English judges declared that a factory worker could not sue his employer for compensation if he was injured through the carelessness of another employee.[2] They said that a worker "assumes the risk" that his "fellow servants" might be careless, and anyway that the worker knows more than the employer about which other workers are careless and perhaps has more influence over them. This rule (which seemed less silly when Darwinian images of capitalism were more popular) much influenced the law of compensation for industrial accidents until it was finally abandoned.[3] In 1975 the House of Lords, the highest court in Britain, laid down rules stipulating how long a Cabinet officer must wait after leaving office to publish descriptions of confidential Cabinet meetings.[4] That decision fixed the official records that are available to journalists and contemporary historians criticizing a government, and so it affected how government behaves.

DISAGREEMENT ABOUT LAW

Since it matters in these different ways how judges decide cases, it also matters what they think the law is, and when they disagree about this, it matters what kind of disagreement they are having. Is there any mystery about that? Yes, but we need some distinctions to see what it is. Lawsuits always raise, at least in principle, three different kinds of issues: issues of fact, issues of law, and the twinned issues of political morality and fidelity. First, what happened? Did the man at the lathe really drop a wrench on his fellow worker's foot? Second, what is the pertinent law? Does the law allow an injured worker damages from his employer for that sort of injury? Third, if the law denies compensation, is that unjust? If so, should judges ignore the law and grant compensation anyway?

The first of these issues, the issue of fact, seems straightforward enough. If judges disagree over the actual, historical events in controversy, we know what they are disagreeing about and what kind of evidence would put the issue to rest if it were available. The third issue, of morality and fidelity, is very different but also familiar. People often disagree about moral right and wrong, and moral disagreement raises no special problems when it breaks out in court. But what about the second issue, the issue of law? Lawyers and judges seem to disagree very often about the law governing a case; they seem to disagree even about the right tests to use. One judge, proposing one set of tests, says the law favors the school district or the employer, and another, proposing a different set, that it favors the schoolchildren or the employee. If this is really a third, distinct kind of argument, different both from arguments over historical fact and from moral arguments, what kind of argument is it? What is the disagreement about?

Let us call "propositions of law" all the various statements and claims people make about what the law allows or prohibits or entitles them to have. Propositions of law can be very general—"the law forbids states to deny anyone equal protection within the meaning of the Fourteenth Amendment"—or much less general—"the law does not provide compensation for fellow-servant injuries"—or very concrete—"the law requires Acme Corporation to compensate John Smith for the injury he suffered in its employ last February." Lawyers and judges and ordinary people generally assume that some propositions of law, at least, can be true or false.[5] But no one thinks they report the declarations of some ghostly figure: they are not about what Law whispered to the planets. Lawyers, it is true, talk about what the law "says" or whether the law is "silent" about some issue or other. But these are just figures of speech.

Everyone thinks that propositions of law are true or false (or neither) in virtue of other, more familiar kinds of propositions on which these propositions of law are (as we might put it) parasitic. These more familiar propositions furnish what I shall call the "grounds" of law. The proposition that no one may drive over 55 miles an hour in California is true, most people think, because a majority of that state's legislators said "aye" or raised their hands when a text to that effect lay on their desks. It could not be true if nothing of that sort had ever happened; it could not then be true just in virtue of what some ghostly figure had said or what was found on transcendental tablets in the sky.

Now we can distinguish two ways in which lawyers and judges might disagree about the truth of a proposition of law. They might agree about the grounds of law—about when the truth or falsity of other, more familiar propositions makes a particular proposition of law true or false—but disagree about whether those grounds are in fact satisfied in a particular case. Lawyers and judges might agree, for example, that the speed limit is 55 in California if the official California statute book contains a law to that effect, but disagree about whether that is the speed limit because they disagree about whether, in fact, the book does contain such a law. We might call this an empirical disagreement about law. Or they might disagree about the grounds of law, about which other kinds of propositions, when true, make a particular proposition of law true. They might agree, in the empirical way, about what the statute books and past judicial decisions have to say about compensation for fellow-servant injuries, but disagree about what the law of compensation actually is because they disagree about whether statute books and judicial decisions exhaust the pertinent grounds of law. We might call that a "theoretical" disagreement about the law.

Empirical disagreement about law is hardly mysterious. People can disagree about what words are in the statute books in the same way they disagree about any other matter of fact. But theoretical disagreement in law, disagreement about law's grounds, is more problematic. Later in this chapter we shall see that lawyers and judges do disagree theoretically. They disagree about what the law really is, on the question of racial segregation or industrial accidents, for example, even when they agree about what statutes have been enacted and what legal officials have said and thought in the past. What kind of disagreement is this? How would we ourselves judge who has the better of the argument?

The general public seems mainly unaware of that problem; indeed it seems mainly unaware of theoretical disagreement about law. The public is much more occupied with the issue of fidelity. Politicians and editorial writers and ordinary citizens argue, sometimes with great passion, about whether judges in the great cases that draw public attention "discover" the law they announce or "invent" it and whether "inventing" law is statecraft or tyranny. But the issue of fidelity is almost never a live one in Anglo-American courts; our judges rarely consider whether they should follow the law once they have settled what it really is, and the public debate is actually an example, though a heavily disguised one, of theoretical disagreement about law.

In a trivial sense judges unquestionably "make new law" every time they decide an important case. They announce a rule or principle or qualification or elaboration—that segregation is unconstitutional or that workmen cannot recover for fellow-servant injuries, for example—that has never been officially declared before. But they generally offer these "new" statements of law as improved reports of what the law, properly understood, already is. They claim, in other words, that the new statement is required by a correct perception of the true grounds of law even though this has not been recognized previously, or has even been denied. So the public debate about whether judges "discover" or "invent" law is really about whether and when that ambitious claim is true. If someone says the judges discovered the illegality of school segregation, he believes segregation was in fact illegal before the decision that said it was, even though no court had said so before. If he says they invented that piece of law, he means segregation was not illegal before, that the judges changed the law in their decision. This debate would be clear enough—and could easily be settled, at least case by case—if everyone agreed about what law is, if there were no theoretical disagreement about the grounds of law. Then it would be easy to check whether the law before the Supreme Court's decision was indeed what that decision said it was. But since lawyers and judges do disagree in the theoretical way, the debate about whether judges make or find law is part of that disagreement, though it contributes nothing to resolving it because the real issue never rises to the surface.

THE PLAIN-FACT VIEW

Incredibly, our jurisprudence has no plausible theory of theoretical disagreement in law. Legal philosophers are of course aware that theoretical disagreement is problematic, that it is not immediately clear what kind of disagreement it is. But most of them have settled on what we shall soon see is an evasion rather than an answer. They say that theoretical disagreement is an illusion, that lawyers and judges all actually agree about the grounds of law. I shall call this the "plain fact" view of the grounds of law; here is a preliminary statement of its main claims. The law is only a matter of what legal institutions, like legislatures and city councils and courts, have decided in the past. If some body of that sort has decided that workmen can recover compensation for injuries by fellow workmen, then that is the law. If it has decided the other way, then that is the law. So questions of law can always be answered by looking in the books where the records of institutional decisions are kept. Of course it takes special training to know where to look and how to understand the arcane vocabulary in which the decisions are written. The layman does not have this training or vocabulary, but lawyers do, and it therefore cannot be controversial among them whether the law allows compensation for fellow-servant injuries, for example, unless some of them have made an empirical mistake about what actually was decided in the past. "Law exists as a plain fact, in other words, and what the law is in no way depends on what it should be. Why then do lawyers and judges sometimes appear to be having a theoretical disagreement about the law? Because when they appear to be disagreeing in the theoretical way about what the law is, they are really disagreeing about what it should be. Their disagreement is really over issues of morality and fidelity, not law."

The popularity of this view among legal theorists helps explain why laymen, when they think about courts, are more concerned with fidelity to law than with what law is. If judges divide in some great case, and their disagreement cannot be over any question of law because law is a matter of plain fact easily settled among knowledgeable lawyers, one side must be disobeying or ignoring the law, and this must be the side supporting a decision that is novel in the trivial sense. So the question of fidelity is the question that demands public discussion and the attention of the watchful citizen. The most popular opinion, in Britain and the United States, insists that judges should always, in every decision, follow the law rather than try to improve upon it. They may not like the law they find—it may require them to evict a widow on Christmas eve in a snowstorm—but they must enforce it nevertheless. Unfortunately, according to this popular opinion, some judges do not accept that wise constraint; covertly or even nakedly, they bend the law to their own purposes or politics. These are the bad judges, the usurpers, destroyers of democracy.

That is the most popular answer to the question of fidelity, but it is not the only one. Some people take the contrary view, that judges should try to improve the law whenever they can, that they should always be political in the way the first answer deplores. The bad judge, on the minority view, is the rigid "mechanical" judge who enforces the law for its own sake with no care for the misery or injustice or inefficiency that follows. The good judge prefers justice to law.

Both versions of the layman's view, the "conservative" and the "progressive," draw on the academic thesis that law is a matter of plain fact, but in certain ways the academic thesis is more sophisticated. Most laymen assume that there is law in the books decisive of every issue that might come before a judge. The academic version of the plain-fact view denies this. The law may be silent on the issue in play, it insists, because no past institutional decision speaks to it either way. Perhaps no competent institution has ever decided either that workmen can recover for fellow-servant injuries or that they cannot. Or the law may be silent because the pertinent institutional decision stipulated only vague guidelines by declaring, for example, that a landlord must give a widow a "reasonable" time to pay her rent. In these circumstances, according to the academic version, no way of deciding can count as enforcing rather than changing the law. Then the judge has no option but to exercise a discretion to make new law by filling gaps where the law is silent and making it more precise where it is vague.

None of this qualifies the plain-fact view that law is always a matter of historical fact and never depends on morality. It only adds that on some occasions trained lawyers may discover that there is no law at all. Every question about what the law is still has a flat historical answer, though some have negative answers. Then the question of fidelity is replaced with a different question, equally distinct from the question of law, which we may call the question of repair. What should judges do in the absence of law? This new political question leaves room for a division of opinion very like the original division over the question of fidelity. For judges who have no choice but to make new law may bring different ambitions to that enterprise. Should they fill gaps cautiously, preserving as much of the spirit of the surrounding law as possible? Or should they do so democratically, trying to reach the result they believe represents the will of the people? Or adventurously, trying to make the resulting law as fair and wise as possible, in their opinion? Each of these very different attitudes has its partisans in law school classrooms and after-dinner speeches at professional organizations. These are the banners, frayed with service, of jurisprudential crusades.

Some academic lawyers draw especially radical conclusions from the sophisticated version of the plain-fact view of law.[6] They say that past institutional decisions are not just occasionally but almost always vague or ambiguous or incomplete, and that they are often inconsistent or even incoherent as well. They conclude that there is never really law on any topic or issue, but only rhetoric judges use to dress up decisions actually dictated by ideological or class preference. The career I have described, from the layman's trusting belief that law is everywhere to the cynic's mocking discovery that it is nowhere at all, is the natural course of conviction once we accept the plain-fact view of law and its consequent claim that theoretical disagreement is only disguised politics. For the more we learn about law, the more we grow convinced that nothing important about it is wholly uncontroversial.

The plain-fact view is not, I must add, accepted by everyone. It is very popular among laymen and academic writers whose specialty is the philosophy of law. But it is rejected in the accounts thoughtful working lawyers and judges give of their work. They may endorse the plain-fact picture as a piece of formal jurisprudence when asked in properly grave tones what law is. But in less guarded moments they tell a different and more romantic story. They say that law is instinct rather than explicit in doctrine, that it can be identified only by special techniques best described impressionistically, even mysteriously. They say that judging is an art not a science, that the good judge blends analogy, craft, political wisdom, and a sense of his role into an intuitive decision, that he "sees" law better than he can explain it, so his written opinion, however carefully reasoned, never captures his full insight.[7]

Very often they add what they believe is a modest disclaimer. They say there are no right answers but only different answers to hard questions of law, that insight is finally subjective, that it is only what seems right, for better or worse, to the particular judge on the day. But this modesty in fact contradicts what they say first, for when judges finally decide one way or another they think their arguments better than, not merely different from, arguments the other way; though they may think this with humility, wishing their confidence were greater or their time for decision longer, this is nevertheless their belief. In that and other ways the romantic "craft" view is unsatisfactory; it is too unstructured, too content with the mysteries it savors, to count as any developed theory of what legal argument is about. We need to throw discipline over the idea of law as craft, to see how the structure of judicial instinct is different from other convictions people have about government and justice.

I have not yet offered reasons for my claim that the academically dominant plain-fact view of law is an evasion rather than a theory. We need actual examples of theoretical disagreement, which I shall soon supply. But if I am right, we are in poor case. If laymen, teachers of jurisprudence, working lawyers, and judges have no good answer to the question how theoretical disagreement is possible and what it is about, we lack the essentials of a decent apparatus for intelligent and constructive criticism of what our judges do. No department of state is more important than our courts, and none is so thoroughly misunderstood by the governed. Most people have fairly clear opinions about how congressmen or prime ministers or presidents or foreign secretaries should carry out their duties, and shrewd opinions about how most of these officials actually do behave. But popular opinion about judges and judging is a sad affair of empty slogans, and I include the opinions of many working lawyers and judges when they are writing or talking about what they do. All this is a shame, and it is only part of the damage. For we take an interest in law not only because we use it for our own purposes, selfish or noble, but because law is our most structured and revealing social institution. If we understand the nature of our legal argument better, we know better what kind of people we are.

A THRESHOLD OBJECTION

This book is about theoretical disagreement in law. It aims to understand what kind of disagreement this is and then to construct and defend a particular theory about the proper grounds of law. But of course there is more to legal practice than arguments about law, and this book neglects much that legal theory also studies. There is very little here about issues

of fact, for example. It is important how judges decide
whether a workman has a legal right to damages when a fellow employee drops a wrench on his foot, but it is also important how a judge or a jury decides whether the workman
(as his employer claims) dropped the wrench on his own foot
instead. Nor do I discuss the practical politics of adjudication, the compromises judges must sometimes accept, stating
the law in a somewhat different way than they think most
accurate in order to attract the votes of other judges, for instance. I am concerned with the issue of law, not with the
reasons judges may have for tempering their statements of
what it is. My project is narrow in a different way as well. It
centers on formal adjudication, on judges in black robes, but
these are not the only or even the most important actors in
the legal drama. A more complete study of legal practice
would attend to legislators, policemen, district attorneys,
welfare officers, school board chairmen, a great variety of
other officials, and to people like bankers and managers and
union officers, who are not called public officials but whose
decisions also affect the legal rights of their fellow citizens.

Some critics will be anxious to say at this point that our
project is not only partial in these various ways but wrong,
that we will misunderstand legal process if we pay special
attention to lawyers' doctrinal arguments about what the
law is. They say these arguments obscure—perhaps they aim
to obscure—the important social function of law as ideological force and witness. A proper understanding of law as a social phenomenon demands, these critics say, a more
scientific or sociological or historical approach that pays no
or little attention to jurisprudential puzzles over the correct
characterization of legal argument. We should pursue, they
think, very different questions, like these: How far, and in
what way, are judges influenced by class consciousness or
economic circumstance? Did the judicial decisions of nineteenth-century America play an important part in forming
the distinctive American version of capitalism? Or were
those decisions only mirrors reflecting change and conflict,

but neither promoting the one nor resolving the other? We will be diverted from these serious questions, the critics warn, if we are drawn into philosophical arguments about whether and why propositions of law can be controversial, like anthropologists sucked into the theological disputes of some ancient and primitive culture.

This objection fails by its own standards. It asks for social realism, but the kind of theory it recommends is unable to provide it. Of course, law is a social phenomenon. But its complexity, function, and consequence all depend on one special feature of its structure. Legal practice, unlike many other social phenomena, is *argumentative*. Every actor in the practice understands that what it permits or requires depends on the truth of certain propositions that are given sense only by and within the practice; the practice consists in large part in deploying and arguing about these propositions. People who have law make and debate claims about what law permits or forbids that would be impossible—because senseless—without law and a good part of what their law reveals about them cannot be discovered except by noticing how they ground and defend these claims. This crucial argumentative aspect of legal practice can be studied in two ways or from two points of view. One is the external point of view of the sociologist or historian, who asks why certain patterns of legal argument develop in some periods or circumstances rather than others, for example. The other is the internal point of view of those who make the claims. Their interest is not finally historical, though they may think history relevant; it is practical, in exactly the way the present objection ridicules. They do not want predictions of the legal claims they will make but arguments about which of these claims is sound and why; they want theories not about how history and economics have shaped their consciousness but about the place of these disciplines in argument about what the law requires them to do or have.

Both perspectives on law, the external and the internal, are essential, and each must embrace or take account of the other. The participant's point of view envelops the historian's when some claim of law depends on a matter of historical fact: when the question whether segregation is illegal, for example, turns on the motives either of the statesmen who wrote the Constitution or of those who segregated the schools.[8] The historian's perspective includes the participant's more pervasively, because the historian cannot understand law as an argumentative social practice, even enough to reject it as deceptive, until he has a participant's understanding, until he has his own sense of what counts as a good or bad argument within that practice. We need a social theory of law, but it must be jurisprudential just for that reason. Theories that ignore the structure of legal argument for supposedly larger questions of history and society are therefore perverse. They ignore questions about the internal character of legal argument, so their explanations are impoverished and defective, like innumerate histories of mathematics, whether they are written in the language of Hegel or of Skinner. It was Oliver Wendell Holmes who argued most influentially, I think, for this kind of "external" legal theory;[9] the depressing history of social-theoretic jurisprudence in our century warns us how wrong he was. We wait still for illumination, and while we wait, the theories grow steadily more programmatic and less substantive, more radical in theory and less critical in practice.

This book takes up the internal, participants' point of view; it tries to grasp the argumentative character of our legal practice by joining that practice and struggling with the issues of soundness and truth participants face. We will study formal legal argument from the judge's viewpoint, not because only judges are important or because we understand everything about them by noticing what they say, but because judicial argument about claims of law is a useful paradigm for exploring the central, propositional aspect of legal practice. Citizens and politicians and law teachers also worry and argue about what the law is, and I might have taken their arguments as our paradigms rather than the judge's. But the structure of judicial argument is typically more explicit, and judicial reasoning has an influence over other forms of legal discourse that is not fully reciprocal.

THE REAL WORLD

We need relief from the daunting abstraction of these introductory remarks. I shall try to show how the plain-fact thesis distorts legal practice, and I begin by describing some actual cases decided by judges in the United States and Britain. These are all famous cases, at least among law students, and continue to be discussed in classes. I set them out here and together for several reasons. They introduce certain technical legal terms to readers who have had no legal training. They provide extended examples for the various arguments and discussions of later chapters. I hope they will provide, in a more general way, some sense of the actual tone and texture of legal argument. This last reason is the most important, for in the end all my arguments are hostage to each reader's sense of what does and can happen in court.

Elmer's Case

Elmer murdered his grandfather—he poisoned him—in New York in 1882.[10] He knew that his grandfather's existing will left him the bulk of the estate, and he suspected that the old man, who had recently remarried, would change the will and leave him nothing. Elmer's crime was discovered; he was convicted and sentenced to a term of years in jail. Was he legally entitled to the inheritance his grandfather's last will provided? The residuary legatees under the will, those entitled to inherit if Elmer had died before his grandfather, were the grandfather's daughters. Their first names are not reported, so I will call them Goneril and Regan. They sued the administrator of the will, demanding that the property now go to them instead of Elmer. They argued that since Elmer had murdered the testator, their father, the law entitled Elmer to nothing.

The law pertaining to wills is for the most part set out in special statutes, often called statutes of wills, which stipulate the form a will must take to be considered valid in law: how many and what kinds of witnesses must sign, what the mental state of the testator must be, how a valid will, once executed, may be revoked or changed by the testator, and so forth. The New York statute of wills, like most others in force at that time, said nothing explicit about whether someone named in a will could inherit according to its terms if he had murdered the testator. Elmer's lawyer argued that since the will violated none of the explicit provisions of the statute it was valid, and since Elmer was named in a valid will he must inherit. He said that if the court held for Goneril and Regan, it would be changing the will and substituting its own moral convictions for the law. The judges of the highest court of New York all agreed that their decision must be in accordance with the law. None denied that if the statute of wills, properly interpreted, gave the inheritance to Elmer, they must order the administrator to give it to him. None said that in that case the law must be reformed in the interests of justice. They disagreed about the correct result in the case, but their disagreement—or so it seems from reading the opinions they wrote—was about what the law actually was, about what the statute required when properly read.

How can people who have the text of a statute in front of them disagree about what it actually means, about what law it has made? We must draw a distinction between two senses of the word "statute." It can describe a physical entity of a certain type, a document with words printed on it, the very words congressmen or members of Parliament had in front of them when they voted to enact that document. But it can also be used to describe the law created by enacting that document, which may be a much more complex matter. Consider the difference between a poem conceived as a series of words that can be spoken or written and a poem conceived as the expression of a particular metaphysical theory or point of view. Literary critics all agree about what poem "Sailing to Byzantium" is in the first sense. They agree it is the series of words designated as that poem by W. B. Yeats. But they nevertheless disagree about what the poem is in the second sense, about what the poem really says or means. They disagree about how to construct the "real" poem, the poem in the second sense, from the text, the poem in the first sense.

In much the same way, judges before whom a statute is laid need to construct the "real" statute—a statement of what difference the statute makes to the legal rights of various people—from the text in the statute book. Just as literary critics need a working theory, or at least a style of interpretation, in order to construct the poem behind the text, so judges need something like a theory of legislation to do this for statutes. This may seem evident when the words in the statute book suffer from some semantic defect; when they are ambiguous or vague, for example. But a theory of legislation is also necessary when these words are, from the linguistic point of view, impeccable. The words of the statute of wills that figured in Elmer's case were neither vague nor ambiguous. The judges disagreed about the impact of these words on the legal rights of Elmer, Goneril, and Regan because they disagreed about how to construct the real statute in the special circumstances of that case.

The dissenting opinion, written by Judge Gray, argued for a theory of legislation more popular then than it is now. This is sometimes called a theory of "literal" interpretation, though that is not a particularly illuminating description. It proposes that the words of a statute be given what we might better call their acontextual meaning, that is, the meaning we would assign them if we had no special information about the context of their use or the intentions of their author. This method of interpretation requires that no context-dependent and unexpressed qualifications be made to

general language, so Judge Gray insisted that the real statute, constructed in the proper way, contained no exceptions
for murderers. He voted for Elmer.

Law students reading his opinion now are mostly con-
temptuous of that way of constructing a statute from a text;
they say it is an example of mechanical jurisprudence. But
there was nothing mechanical about Judge Gray's argument. There is much to be said (some of which he did say)
for his method of constructing a statute, at least in the case
of a statute of wills. Testators should know how their wills
will be treated when they are no longer alive to offer fresh
instructions. Perhaps Elmer's grandfather would have preferred his property to go to Goneril and Regan in the event
that Elmer poisoned him. But perhaps not: he might have
thought that Elmer, even with murder on his hands, was still
a better object for his generosity than his daughters. It might
be wiser in the long run for judges to assure testators that the
statute of wills will be interpreted in the so-called literal way,
so that testators can make any arrangements they wish, confident that their dispositions, however amusing, will be respected. Besides, if Elmer loses his inheritance just because
he is a murderer, then that is a further punishment, beyond
his term in jail, for his crime. It is an important principle of
justice that the punishment for a particular crime must be
set out in advance by the legislature and not increased by
judges after the crime has been committed. All this (and
more) can be said on behalf of Judge Gray's theory about
how to read a statute of wills.

Judge Earl, however, writing for the majority, used a very
different theory of legislation, which gives the legislators' *intentions* an important influence over the real statute. "It is a
familiar canon of construction," Earl wrote, "that a thing
which is within the intention of the makers of a statute is as
much within the statute as if it were within the letter; and a
thing which is within the letter of the statute is not within
the statute, unless it be within the intention of the makers."[11]
(Notice how he relies on the distinction between the text,

which he calls the "letter" of the statute, and the real statute, which he calls the "statute" itself.) It would be absurd, he thought, to suppose that the New York legislators who originally enacted the statute of wills intended murderers to inherit, and for that reason the real statute they enacted did not have that consequence.

We must take some care in stating what Judge Earl meant about the role intention should play in constructing statutes. He did not mean that a statute can have no consequence the legislators did not have in mind. This is plainly too strong as a general rule: no legislator can have in mind all the consequences of any statute he votes for. The New York legislators could not have contemplated that people might bequeath computers, but it would be absurd to conclude that the statute does not cover such bequests. Nor did he mean only that a statute can contain nothing that the legislators intended that it not contain. This seems more plausible, but it is too weak to be of any use in Elmer's case. For it seems likely that the New York legislators did not have the case of murderers in mind at all. They did not intend that murderers inherit, but neither did they intend that they should not. They had no active intention either way. Earl meant to rely on a principle we might call intermediate between these excessively strong and weak principles: he meant that a statute does not have any consequence the legislators would have rejected if they had contemplated it.[12]

Judge Earl did not rely only on his principle about legislative intention; his theory of legislation contained another relevant principle. He said that statutes should be constructed from texts not in historical isolation but against the background of what he called general principles of law: he meant that judges should construct a statute so as to make it conform as closely as possible to principles of justice assumed elsewhere in the law. He offered two reasons. First, it is sensible to assume that legislators have a general and diffuse intention to respect traditional principles of justice unless they clearly indicate the contrary. Second, since a statute forms part of a larger intellectual system, the law as a whole, it should be constructed so as to make that larger system coherent in principle. Earl argued that the law elsewhere respects the principle that no one should profit from his own wrong, so the statute of wills should be read to deny inheritance to someone who has murdered to obtain it.

Judge Earl's views prevailed. They attracted four other judges to his side, while Judge Gray was able to find only one ally. So Elmer did not receive his inheritance. I shall use this case as an illustration of many different points, in the argument that follows, but the most important is this: the dispute about Elmer was not about whether judges should follow the law or adjust it in the interests of justice. At least it was not if we take the opinions I described at face value and (as I shall argue later) we have no justification for taking them in any other way. It was a dispute about what the law was, about what the real statute the legislators enacted really said.

The Snail Darter Case

I now describe a much more recent case, though more briefly, in order to show that this kind of dispute continues to occupy judges.[13] In 1973, during a period of great national concern about conservation, the United States Congress enacted the Endangered Species Act. It empowers the secretary of the interior to designate species that would be endangered, in his opinion, by the destruction of some habitat he considers crucial to its survival and then requires all agencies and departments of the government to take "such action necessary to insure that actions authorized, funded, or carried out by them do not jeopardize the continued existence of such endangered species."[14]

A group of conservationists based in Tennessee had been opposing dam construction projects of the Tennessee Valley Authority, not because of any threat to species but because these projects were altering the geography of the area by converting free-flowing streams into narrow, ugly ditches to produce an unneeded increase (or so the conservationists believed) in hydroelectric power. The conservationists discovered that one almost finished TVA dam, costing over one hundred million dollars, would be likely to destroy the only habitat of the snail darter, a three-inch fish of no particular beauty or biological interest or general ecological importance. They persuaded the secretary to designate the snail darter as endangered and brought proceedings to stop the dam from being completed and used.

The authority argued that the statute should not be construed to prevent the completion or operation of any project substantially completed when the secretary made his order. It said the phrase "actions authorized, funded, or carried out" should be taken to refer to beginning a project, not completing projects begun earlier. It supported its claim by pointing to various acts of Congress, all taken after the secretary had declared that completing the dam would destroy the snail darter, which suggested that Congress wished the dam to be completed notwithstanding that declaration. Congress had specifically authorized funds for continuing the project after the secretary's designation, and various of its committees had specifically and repeatedly declared that they disagreed with the secretary, accepted the authority's interpretation of the statute, and wished the project to continue.

The Supreme Court nevertheless ordered that the dam be halted, in spite of the great waste of public funds. (Congress then enacted a further statute establishing a general procedure for exemption from the act, based on findings by a review board.)[15] Chief Justice Warren Burger wrote an opinion for the majority of the justices. He said, in words that recall Judge Gray's opinion in Elmer's case, that when the text is clear the Court has no right to refuse to apply it just because it believes the results silly. Times change, however, and the chief justice's opinion was in one respect very different from Judge Gray's. Burger recognized the relevance of congressional intention to the decision what statute Congress had made. But he did not accept Earl's principle about the *way* in which congressional intention is relevant. He refused to consider the counterfactual test that Earl's analysis made decisive. "It is not for us," he said, "to speculate, much less act, on whether Congress would have altered its stance had the specific events of this case been anticipated."[16]

Instead he adopted what I called, in discussing Earl's opinion, the excessively weak version of the idea that judges constructing a statute must respect the legislature's intentions. That version comes to this: if the acontextual meaning of the words in the text is clear—if the words "carry out" would normally include continuing as well as beginning a project—then the Court must assign those words that meaning unless it can be shown that the legislature actually intended the opposite result. The legislative history leading up to the enactment of the Endangered Species Act did not warrant that conclusion, he said, because Congress plainly wanted to give endangered species a high order of protection even at great cost to other social goals, and it is certainly possible, even if not probable, that legislators with that general aim would want the snail darter saved even at the amazing expense of a wasted dam. He rejected the evidence of the later committee reports and the actions of Congress in approving funding for the continuation of the dam, which might have been thought to indicate an actual intention not to sacrifice the dam to this particular species. The committees that had reported in favor of the dam were not the same as the committees that had sponsored the act in the first place, he said, and congressmen often vote on appropriations without fully considering whether the proposed expenditures are legal under past congressional decisions.

Justice Lewis Powell wrote a dissent for himself and one other justice. He said that the majority's decision constructed an absurd real statute from the text of the Endangered Species Act. "It is not our province," he said, "to rectify policy or political judgments by the Legislative Branch, however egregiously they may disserve the public interest. But where the statutory and legislative history, as in this case, need not be construed to reach such a result, I view it as the duty of this Court to adopt a permissible construction that accords with some modicum of common sense and the public weal."[17] This states yet another theory of legislation, another theory of how the legislature's intentions affect the statute behind the text, and it is very different from Burger's theory. Burger said that the acontextual meaning of the text should be enforced, no matter how odd or absurd the consequences, unless the court discovered strong evidence that Congress actually intended the opposite. Powell said that the courts should accept an absurd result only if they find compelling evidence that *it* was intended. Burger's theory is Gray's, though in a less rigid form that gives some role to legislative intention. Powell's theory is like Earl's, though in this case it substitutes common sense for the principles of justice found elsewhere in the law.

Once again, if we take the opinions of these two justices at face value, they did not disagree about any historical matters of fact. They did not disagree about the state of mind of the various congressmen who joined in enacting the Endangered Species Act. Both justices assumed that most congressmen had never considered whether the act might be used to halt an expensive dam almost completed. Nor did they disagree over the question of fidelity. Both accepted that the Court should follow the law. They disagreed about the question of law; they disagreed about how judges should decide what law is made by a particular text enacted by Congress when the congressmen had the kinds of beliefs and intentions both justices agreed they had in this instance.

McLoughlin

Elmer's case and the snail darter case both arose under a statute. The decision in each case depended upon the best construction of a real statute from a particular legislative text. In many lawsuits, however, the plaintiff appeals not to

any statute but to earlier decisions by courts. He argues that
the judge in his case should follow the rules laid down in
these earlier cases, which he claims require a verdict for him.
McLoughlin was of this sort.[18]

Mrs. McLoughlin's husband and four children were injured in an automobile accident in England at about 4 P.M.
on October 19, 1973. She heard about the accident at home
from a neighbor at about 6 P.M. and went immediately to
the hospital, where she learned that her daughter was dead
and saw the serious condition of her husband and other children. She suffered nervous shock and later sued the defendant driver, whose negligence had caused the accident, as
well as other parties who were in different ways involved, for
compensation for her emotional injuries. Her lawyer pointed
to several earlier decisions of English courts awarding compensation to people who had suffered emotional injury on
seeing serious injury to a close relative. But in all these cases
the plaintiff had either been at the scene of the accident or
had arrived within minutes. In a 1972 case, for example, a
wife recovered—won compensation—for emotional injury;
she had come upon the body of her husband immediately
after his fatal accident.[19] In 1967 a man who was not related
to any of the victims of a train crash worked for hours trying
to rescue victims and suffered nervous shock from the experience. He was allowed to recover.[20] Mrs. McLoughlin's lawyer relied on these cases as precedents, decisions which had
made it part of the law that people in her position are entitled to compensation.

British and American lawyers speak of the doctrine of
precedent; they mean the doctrine that decisions of earlier
cases sufficiently like a new case should be repeated in the
new case. They distinguish, however, between what we
might call a strict and a relaxed doctrine of precedent. The
strict doctrine *obliges* judges to follow the earlier decisions of
certain other courts (generally courts above them but sometimes at the same level in the hierarchy of courts in their
jurisdiction), even if they believe those decisions to have

been wrong. The exact form of the strict doctrine varies from place to place; it is different in the United States and Britain, and it differs from state to state within the United States. According to most lawyers' view of the strict doctrine in Britain, the Court of Appeals, which is just below the House of Lords in authority, has no choice but to follow its own past decisions, but American lawyers deny that the comparable courts in their hierarchy are constrained in this way. Lawyers within a particular jurisdiction sometimes disagree about the details, at least, of the strict doctrine as it applies to them: most American lawyers think that the lower federal courts are absolutely bound to follow past decisions of the Supreme Court, but that view is challenged by some.[21]

The relaxed doctrine of precedent, on the other hand, demands only that a judge give some weight to past decisions on the same issue, that he must follow these unless he thinks them sufficiently wrong to outweigh the initial presumption in their favor. This relaxed doctrine may embrace the past decisions not only of courts above him or at the same level in his jurisdiction but of courts in other states or countries. Obviously, much depends on how strong the initial presumption is taken to be. Once again, opinion varies among lawyers from jurisdiction to jurisdiction, but it is also likely to vary within a jurisdiction to a greater extent than opinion about the dimensions of the strict doctrine. Any judge is likely to give more weight to past decisions of higher than of lower courts in his own jurisdiction, however, and to past decisions of all these courts than to courts of other jurisdictions. He may well give more weight to recent decisions of any court than to earlier ones, more weight to decisions written by powerful or famous judges than to those written by mediocre judges, and so forth. Two decades ago the House of Lords declared that the strict doctrine of precedent does not require it to follow its own past decisions[22]—before that declaration British lawyers had assumed that the strict doctrine did require this—but the House nevertheless gives great weight to its own past decisions, more than it gives to past decisions of courts lower in the British hierarchy, and much more than it gives to decisions of American courts.

Differences of opinion about the character of the strict doctrine and the force of the relaxed doctrine explain why some lawsuits are controversial. Different judges in the same case disagree about whether they are obliged to follow some past decision on exactly the question of law they now face. That was not, however, the nerve of controversy in *McLoughlin*. Whatever view lawyers take of the character and force of precedent, the doctrine applies only to past decisions sufficiently like the present case to be, as lawyers say, "in point." Sometimes one side argues that certain past decisions are very much in point, but the other side replies that these decisions are "distinguishable," meaning they are different from the present case in some way that exempts them from the doctrine. The judge before whom Mrs. McLoughlin first brought her suit, the trial judge, decided that the precedents her lawyer cited, about others who had recovered compensation for emotional injury suffered when they saw accident victims, were distinguishable because in all those cases the shock had occurred at the scene of the accident while she was shocked some two hours later and in a different place. Of course not every difference in the facts of two cases makes the earlier one distinguishable: no one could think it mattered if Mrs. McLoughlin was younger than the plaintiffs in the earlier cases.

The trial judge thought that suffering injury away from the scene was an important difference because it meant that Mrs. McLoughlin's injury was not "foreseeable" in the way that the injury to the other plaintiffs had been. Judges in both Britain and America follow the common law principle that people who act carelessly are liable only for reasonably foreseeable injuries to others, injuries a reasonable person would anticipate if he reflected on the matter. The trial judge was bound by the doctrine of precedent to recognize that emotional injury to close relatives at the scene of an accident is reasonably foreseeable, but he said that injury to a mother who saw the results of the accident later is not. So he thought he could distinguish the putative precedents in that way and decided against Mrs. McLoughlin's claim.

She appealed his decision to the next highest court in the British hierarchy, the Court of Appeals.[23] That court affirmed the trial judge's decision—it refused her appeal and let his decision stand—but not on the argument he had used. The Court of Appeals said it *was* reasonably foreseeable that a mother would rush to the hospital to see her injured family and that she would suffer emotional shock from seeing them in the condition Mrs. McLoughlin found. That court distinguished the precedents not on that ground but for the very different reason that what it called "policy" justified a distinction. The precedents had established liability for emotional injury in certain restricted circumstances, but the Court of Appeals said that recognizing a larger area of liability, embracing injuries to relatives not at the scene, would have a variety of adverse consequences for the community as a whole. It would encourage many more lawsuits for emotional injuries, and this would exacerbate the problem of congestion in the courts. It would open new opportunities for fraudulent claims by people who had not really suffered serious emotional damage but could find doctors to testify that they had. It would increase the cost of liability insurance, making it more expensive to drive and perhaps preventing some poor people from driving at all. The claims of those who had suffered genuine emotional injury away from the scene would be harder to prove, and the uncertainties of litigation might complicate their condition and delay their recovery.

Mrs. McLoughlin appealed the decision once more, to the House of Lords, which reversed the Court of Appeals and ordered a new trial.[24] The decision was unanimous, but their lordships disagreed about what they called the true state of the law. Several of them said that policy reasons, of the sort described by the Court of Appeals, might in some circum-

stances be sufficient to distinguish a line of precedents and so
justify a judge's refusal to extend the principle of those cases
to a larger area of liability. But they did not think these policy reasons were of sufficient plausibility or merit in Mrs.
McLoughlin's case. They did not believe that the risk of a
"flood" of litigation was sufficiently grave, and they said the
courts should be able to distinguish genuine from fraudulent
claims even among those whose putative injury was suffered
several hours after the accident. They did not undertake to
say when good policy arguments might be available to limit
recovery for emotional injury; they left it an open question, for example, whether Mrs. McLoughlin's sister in Aus-
tralia (if she had one) could recover for the shock she might
have in reading about the accident weeks or months later in
a letter.

Two of their lordships took a very different view of the
law. They said it would be wrong for courts to deny recovery
to an otherwise meritorious plaintiff for the *kinds* of reasons
the Court of Appeals had mentioned and which the other
law lords had said might be sufficient in some circumstances.
The precedents should be regarded as distinguishable, they
said, only if the moral *principles* assumed in the earlier cases
for some reason did not apply to the plaintiff in the same
way. And once it is conceded that the damage to a mother in
the hospital hours after an accident is reasonably foreseeable
to a careless driver, then no difference in moral principle can
be found between the two cases. Congestion in the courts or
a rise in the price of automobile liability insurance, they
said, however inconvenient these might be to the community
as a whole, cannot justify refusing to enforce individual
rights and duties that have been recognized and enforced
before. They said these were the wrong sorts of arguments to
make to judges as arguments of law, however cogent they
might be if addressed to legislators as arguments for a
change in the law. (Lord Scarman's opinion was particularly
clear and strong on this point.) The argument among their

lordships revealed an important difference of opinion about the proper role of considerations of policy in deciding what result parties to a lawsuit are entitled to have.

Brown

After the American Civil War the victorious North amended the Constitution to end slavery and many of its incidents and consequences. One of these amendments, the Fourteenth, declared that no state might deny any person the "equal protection of the laws." After Reconstruction the southern states, once more in control of their own politics, segregated many public facilities by race. Blacks had to ride in the back of the bus and were allowed to attend only segregated schools with other blacks. In the famous case of *Plessy v. Ferguson*[25] the defendant argued, ultimately before the Supreme Court, that these practices of segregation automatically violated the equal protection clause. The Court rejected their claim; it said that the demands of that clause were satisfied if the states provided separate but equal facilities and that the fact of segregation alone did not make facilities automatically unequal.

In 1954 a group of black schoolchildren in Topeka, Kansas, raised the question again.[26] A great deal had happened to the United States in the meantime—a great many blacks had died for that country in a recent war, for example—and segregation seemed more deeply wrong to more people than it had when *Plessy* was decided. Nevertheless, the states that practiced segregation resisted integration fiercely, particularly in the schools. Their lawyers argued that since *Plessy* was a decision by the Supreme Court, that precedent had to be respected. This time the Court decided for the black plaintiffs. Its decision was unexpectedly unanimous, though the unanimity was purchased by an opinion, written by Chief Justice Earl Warren, that was in many ways a compromise. He did not reject the "separate but equal" formula outright; instead he relied on controversial sociological evidence to show that racially segregated schools could not be equal, for that reason alone. Nor did he say flatly that the Court was now overruling *Plessy*. He said only that *if* the present decision was inconsistent with *Plessy,* then that earlier decision was being overruled. The most important compromise, for practical purposes, was in the design of the remedy the opinion awarded the plaintiffs. It did not order the schools of the southern states to be desegregated immediately, but only, in a phrase that became an emblem of hypocrisy and delay, "with all deliberate speed."[27]

The decision was very controversial, the process of integration that followed was slow, and significant progress required many more legal, political, and even physical battles. Critics said that segregation, however deplorable as a matter of political morality, is not unconstitutional.[28] They pointed out that the phrase "equal protection" does not in itself decide whether segregation is forbidden or not, that the particular congressmen and state officials who drafted, enacted, and ratified the Fourteenth Amendment were well aware of segregated education and apparently thought their amendment left it perfectly legal, and that the Court's decision in *Plessy* was an important precedent of almost ancient lineage and ought not lightly be overturned. These were arguments about the proper grounds of constitutional law, not arguments of morality or repair: many who made them agreed that segregation was immoral and that the Constitution would be a better document if it had forbidden it. Nor were the arguments of those who agreed with the Court arguments of morality or repair. If the Constitution did not as a matter of law prohibit official racial segregation, then the decision in *Brown* was an illicit constitutional amendment, and few who supported the decision thought they were supporting that. This case, like our other sample cases, was fought over the question of law. Or so it seems from the opinion, and so it seemed to those who fought it.

SEMANTIC THEORIES OF LAW

Propositions and Grounds of Law

Earlier in this chapter I described what I called the plain-fact view of law. This holds that law depends only on matters of plain historical fact, that the only sensible disagreement about law is empirical disagreement about what legal institutions have actually decided in the past, that what I called theoretical disagreement is illusory and better understood as argument not about what law is but about what it should be. The sample cases seem counterexamples to the plain-fact view: the arguments in these cases seem to be about law, not morality or fidelity or repair. We must therefore put this challenge to the plain-fact view: why does it insist that appearance is here an illusion? Some legal philosophers offer a surprising answer. They say that theoretical disagreement about the grounds of law must be a pretense because the very meaning of the word "law" makes law depend on certain specific criteria, and that any lawyer who rejected or challenged those criteria would be speaking self-contradictory nonsense.

We follow shared rules, they say, in using any word: these rules set out criteria that supply the word's meaning. Our rules for using "law" tie law to plain historical fact. It does not follow that all lawyers are aware of these rules in the sense of being able to state them in some crisp and comprehensive form. For we all follow rules given by our common language of which we are not fully aware. We all use the word "cause," for example, in what seems to be roughly the same way—we agree about which physical events have caused others once we all know the pertinent facts—yet most of us have no idea of the criteria we use in making these judgments, or even of the sense in which we are using criteria at all. It falls to philosophy to explicate these for us. This may be a matter of some difficulty, and philosophers may

well disagree. Perhaps no set of criteria for using the word
"cause" fits ordinary practice exactly, and the question will
then be which set provides the overall best fit or best fits the
central cases of causation. A philosopher's account of the
concept of causation must not only fit, moreover, but must
also be philosophically respectable and attractive in other
respects. It must not explain our use of causation in a question-begging way, by using that very concept in its description of how we use it, and it must employ a sensible
ontology. We would not accept an account of the concept of
causation that appealed to causal gods resident in objects.
So, according to the view I am now describing, with the
concept of law. We all use the same factual criteria in framing, accepting, and rejecting statements about what the law
is, but we are ignorant of what these criteria are. Philosophers of law must elucidate them for us by a sensitive study
of how we speak. They may disagree among themselves, but
that alone casts no doubt on their common assumption,
which is that we do share some set of standards about how
"law" is to be used.

Philosophers who insist that lawyers all follow certain linguistic criteria for judging propositions of law, perhaps un-
awares, have produced theories identifying these criteria. I
shall call these theories collectively semantic theories of law,
but that name itself requires some elaboration. For a long
time philosophers of law packaged their products as definitions of law. John Austin, for example, whose theory I shall
shortly describe, said he was explicating the "meaning" of
law. When philosophers of language developed more sophisticated theories of meaning, legal philosophers became more
wary of definitions and said, instead, that they were describing the "use" of legal concepts, by which they meant, in our
vocabulary, the circumstances in which propositions of law
are regarded by all competent lawyers as true or as false. This
was little more than a change in packaging, I think; in any
case I mean to include "use" theories in the group of seman-

tic theories of law, as well as the earlier theories that were more candidly definitional.[29]

Legal Positivism

Semantic theories suppose that lawyers and judges use mainly the same criteria (though these are hidden and unrecognized) in deciding when propositions of law are true or false; they suppose that lawyers actually agree about the grounds of law. These theories disagree about which criteria lawyers do share and which grounds these criteria do stipulate. Law students are taught to classify semantic theories according to the following rough scheme. The semantic theories that have been most influential hold that the shared criteria make the truth of propositions of law turn on certain specified historical events. These positivist theories, as they are called, support the plain-fact view of law, that genuine disagreement about what the law is must be empirical disagreement about the history of legal institutions. Positivist theories differ from one another about which historical facts are crucial, however, and two versions have been particularly important in British jurisprudence.

John Austin, a nineteenth-century English lawyer and lecturer, said that a proposition of law is true within a particular political society if it correctly reports the past command of some person or group occupying the position of sovereign in that society. He defined a sovereign as some person or group whose commands are habitually obeyed and who is not in the habit of obeying anyone else.[30] This theory became the object of intense, and often scholastic, debate. Legal philosophers argued about whether certain obviously true propositions of law—propositions about the number of signatures necessary to make a will legally valid, for example—could really be said to be true in virtue of anyone's *command*. (After all, no one has commanded you or me to make any will at all, let alone to make a valid will.) They also debated whether any group could be said to be an Austinian sovereign in a democracy, like the United States, in which the people as a whole retain the power to alter the form of government radically by amending the constitution. But though Austin's theory was found defective in various matters of detail, and many repairs and improvements were suggested, his main idea, that law is a matter of historical decisions by people in positions of political power, has never wholly lost its grip on jurisprudence.

The most important and fundamental restatement of that idea is H. L. A. Hart's book, *The Concept of Law,* first published in 1961.[31] Hart rejected Austin's account of legal authority as a brute fact of habitual command and obedience. He said that the true grounds of law lie in the acceptance by the community as a whole of a fundamental master rule (he called this a "rule of recognition") that assigns to particular people or groups the authority to make law. So propositions of law are true not just in virtue of the commands of people who are habitually obeyed, but more fundamentally in virtue of social conventions that represent the community's acceptance of a scheme of rules empowering such people or groups to create valid law. For Austin the proposition that the speed limit in California is 55 is true just because the legislators who enacted that rule happen to be in control there; for Hart it is true because the people of California have accepted, and continue to accept, the scheme of authority deployed in the state and national constitutions. For Austin the proposition that careless drivers are required to compensate mothers who suffer emotional injury at the scene of an accident is true in Britain because people with political power have made the judges their lieutenants and tacitly adopt their commands as their own. For Hart that proposition is true because the rule of recognition accepted by the British people makes judges' declarations law subject to the powers of other officials—legislators—to repeal that law if they wish.

Hart's theory, like Austin's, has generated a good deal of

debate among those who are drawn to its basic idea. What does the "acceptance" of a rule of recognition consist in? Many officials of Nazi Germany obeyed Hitler's commands as law, but only out of fear. Does that mean they accepted a rule of recognition entitling him to make law? If so, then the difference between Hart's theory and Austin's becomes elusive, because there would then be no difference between a group of people accepting a rule of recognition and simply falling into a self-conscious pattern of obedience out of fear. If not, if acceptance requires more than mere obedience, then it seems to follow that there was no law in Nazi Germany, that no propositions of law were true there or in many other places where most people would say there is law, though bad or unpopular law. And then Hart's theory would not, after all, capture how all lawyers use the word "law." Scholars have worried about this and other aspects of Hart's theory, but once again his root idea, that the truth of propositions of law is in some important way dependent upon conventional patterns of recognizing law, has attracted wide support.

Other Semantic Theories

Positivist theories are not unchallenged in the classical literature of jurisprudence; I should mention two other groups of theories generally counted as their rivals. The first is usually called the school of natural law, though the various theories grouped under that title are remarkably different from one another, and the name suits none of them.[32] If we treat these as semantic theories (in Chapter 3 I describe a better way to understand them), they have this in common: they argue that lawyers follow criteria that are not entirely factual, but at least to some extent moral, for deciding which propositions of law are true. The most extreme theory of this kind insists that law and justice are identical, so that no unjust proposition of law can be true. This extreme theory is very implausible as a semantic theory because lawyers often

speak in a way that contradicts it. Many lawyers in both
Britain and the United States believe that the progressive
income tax is unjust, for example, but none of them doubts
that the law of these countries does impose tax at progressive
rates. Some less extreme "natural law" theories claim only
that morality is sometimes relevant to the truth of propositions of law. They suggest, for instance, that when a statute
is open to different interpretations, as in Elmer's case, or
when precedents are indecisive, as in Mrs. McLoughlin's
case, whichever interpretation is morally superior is the more
accurate statement of the law. But even this weaker version
of natural law is unpersuasive if we take it to be a semantic
theory about how all lawyers use the word "law"; Judge
Gray seems to have agreed with Judge Earl that the law
would be better if it denied Elmer his inheritance, but he did
not agree that the law therefore did deny it to him.

Students are taught that the second rival to positivism is
the school of legal realism. Realist theories were developed
early in this century, mainly in American law schools,
though the movement had branches elsewhere. If we treat
them as semantic theories, they argue that the linguistic
rules lawyers follow make propositions of law instrumental
and predictive. The best version suggests that the exact
meaning of a proposition of law—the conditions under
which lawyers will take the proposition to be true—depends
on context. If a lawyer advises a client that the law permits
murderers to inherit, for example, he must be understood as
predicting that this is what judges will decide when the
matter next comes to court. If a judge says this in the course
of his opinion, he is making a different sort of predictive hypothesis, about the general course or "path" the law is most
likely to take in the general area of his decision.[33] Some realists expressed these ideas in dramatically skeptical language.
They said there is no such thing as law, or that law is only a
matter of what the judge had for breakfast. They meant that
there can be no such thing as law apart from predictions of
these different sorts. But even understood in this way, real-

ism remains deeply implausible as a semantic theory. For it is hardly contradictory—indeed it is common—for lawyers to predict that judges will make a mistake about the law or for judges to state their view of the law and then add that they hope and expect that the law will be changed.

Defending Positivism

I shall concentrate on legal positivism because, as I just said, this is the semantic theory that supports the plain-fact view and the claim that genuine argument about law must be empirical rather than theoretical. If positivism is right, then the appearance of theoretical disagreement about the grounds of law, in Elmer's case and *McLoughlin* and the snail darter case and *Brown,* is in some way misleading. In these cases past legal institutions had not expressly decided the issue either way, so lawyers using the word "law" properly according to positivism would have agreed there was no law to discover. Their disagreement must therefore have been disguised argument about what the law should be. But we can restate that inference as an argument against positivism. For why should lawyers and judges pretend to theoretical disagreement in cases like these? Some positivists have a quick answer: judges pretend to be disagreeing about what the law is because the public believes there is always law and that judges should always follow it. On this view lawyers and judges systematically connive to keep the truth from the people so as not to disillusion them or arouse their ignorant anger.

This quick answer is unpersuasive. It is mysterious why the pretense should be necessary or how it could be successful. If lawyers all agree there is no decisive law in cases like our sample cases, then why has this view not become part of our popular political culture long ago? And if it has not—if most people still think there is always law for judges to follow—why should the profession fear to correct their error in the interests of a more honest judicial practice? In any case, how can the pretense work? Would it not be easy for the disappointed party to demonstrate that there really was no law according to the grounds everyone knows are the right grounds? And if the pretense is so easily exposed, why bother with the charade? Nor is there any evidence in our sample cases that any of the lawyers or judges actually believed what this defense attributes to them. Many of their arguments would be entirely inappropriate as arguments for either the repair or the improvement of law; they make sense only as arguments about what judges must do in virtue of their responsibility to enforce the law as it is. It seems odd to describe Gray or Burger as bent on reform or improvement, for example, for each conceded that what he took to be the law was open to serious objections of fairness or wisdom. They argued that the statute in question had to be interpreted in a certain way *in spite of* its evident defects so interpreted.

But once the positivist concedes that Gray was trying to state what the law was rather than what it should be, he must also concede that Gray's views about the grounds of law were controversial even within his own court. Earl's rival position must also be understood as a claim about what the law requires—a claim that Gray was wrong—not a disguised maneuver to repair or revise the law. In *McLoughlin* the judges of the Court of Appeal did seem to think that since the precedents were limited to emotional injury at the scene of an accident, there was no law either way on emotional injury away from the scene, and that their task was therefore one of repair, of developing the law in the best way, all things considered. But that was not the view of the House of Lords, and very much not the view of Lord Scarman, who thought he was bound by principles embedded in the precedents. For all we know, Lord Scarman agreed with the judges of the Court of Appeal that the community would be made worse off on the whole by allowing recovery in those circumstances. The various judges who adjudicated Mrs.

McLoughlin's case disagreed about the force and character of precedent as a source of law, and though the disagreement was subtle it was nevertheless a disagreement about what the law was, not about what should be done in the absence of law.

In fact there is no positive evidence of any kind that when lawyers and judges seem to be disagreeing about the law they are really keeping their fingers crossed. There is no argument for that view of the matter except the question-begging argument that if the plain-fact thesis is sound they just must be pretending. There is, however, a more sophisticated defense of positivism, which concedes that lawyers and judges in our sample cases thought they were disagreeing about the law but argues that for a somewhat different reason this self-description should not be taken at face value. This new argument stresses the importance of distinguishing between standard or core uses of the word "law" and borderline or penumbral uses of that word. It claims that lawyers and judges all follow what is mainly the same rule for using "law" and therefore all agree about, for example, the legal speed limit in California and the basic rate of tax in Britain. But because rules for using words are not precise and exact, they permit penumbral or borderline cases in which people speak somewhat differently from one another. So lawyers may use the word "law" differently in marginal cases when some but not all of the grounds specified in the main rule are satisfied. This explains, according to the present argument, why they disagree in hard cases like our sample cases. Each uses a slightly different version of the main rule, and the differences become manifest in these special cases.[34] In this respect, the argument continues, our use of "law" is no different from our use of many other words we find unproblematical. We all agree about the standard meaning of "house," for example. Someone who denies that the detached one-family residences on ordinary suburban streets are houses just does not understand the English language.

Nevertheless there are borderline cases. People do not all follow exactly the same rule; some would say that Buckingham Palace is a house while others would not.

This more sophisticated defense of positivism tells a somewhat different story about our sample cases from the "fingers-crossed" story. According to this new story, Earl and Gray and the other judges and lawyers were in no way pretending or trying to deceive the public. They were disagreeing about the state of the law, but their disagreement was a "merely verbal" one like a disagreement about whether Buckingham Palace is a house. From *our* standpoint as critics, according to this defense, it is better to think of their argument as one about repair, about what the law should be, because we will understand the legal process better if we use "law" only to describe what lies within the core of that concept, if we use it, that is, to cover only propositions of law true according to the central or main rule for using "law" that everyone accepts, like the propositions of the highway code. It would be better if lawyers and judges used "law" that way, just as it would be better if no one argued about the correct classification of Buckingham Palace but instead agreed to use "house" in the same way whenever they could. So positivism, defended in this different way, has a reforming as well as a descriptive character. In any case, the defense protects the plain-fact thesis. It treats the main question in each of our sample cases as a question of repair, even though the judges themselves might not have conceived it that way, and encourages us to evaluate their performance by asking how judges should develop new law when some case cannot be resolved by applying rules about the grounds of law that all lawyers accept.

The new story is in one way like the fingers-crossed story, however: it leaves wholly unexplained why the legal profession should have acted for so long in the way the story claims it has. For sensible people do not quarrel over whether Buckingham Palace is really a house; they understand at once that this is not a genuine issue but only a matter of how one chooses to use a word whose meaning is not fixed at its boundaries. If "law" is really like "house," why should lawyers argue for so long about whether the law really gives the secretary of the interior power to stop an almost finished dam to save a small fish, or whether the law forbids racially segregated schools? How could they think they had arguments for the essentially arbitrary decision to use the word one way rather than another? How could they think that important decisions about the use of state power should turn on a quibble? It does not help to say that lawyers and judges are able to deceive themselves because they are actually arguing about a different issue, the political issue whether the secretary should have that power or whether states should be forbidden to segregate their schools. We have already noticed that many of the arguments judges make to support their controversial claims of law are not appropriate to those directly political issues. So the new defense of positivism is a more radical critique of professional practice than it might at first seem. The crossed-fingers defense shows judges as well-meaning liars; the borderline-case defense shows them as simpletons instead.

The borderline defense is worse than insulting, moreover, because it ignores an important distinction between two kinds of disagreements, the distinction between borderline cases and testing or pivotal cases. People sometimes do speak at cross-purposes in the way the borderline defense describes. They agree about the correct tests for applying some word in what they consider normal cases but use the word somewhat differently in what they all recognize to be marginal cases, like the case of a palace. Sometimes, however, they argue about the appropriateness of some word or description because they disagree about the correct tests for using the word or phrase on *any* occasion. We can see the difference by imagining two arguments among art critics about whether photography should be considered a form or branch of art. They might agree about exactly the ways in which photography is like and unlike activities they all recognize as "standard" uncontroversial examples of art like painting and sculpture. They might agree that photography is not fully or centrally an art form in the way these other activities are; they might agree, that is, that photography is at most a borderline case of an art. Then they would probably also agree that the decision whether to place photography within or outside that category is finally arbitrary, that it should be taken one way or another for convenience or ease of exposition, but that there is otherwise no genuine issue to debate whether photography is "really" an art. Now consider an entirely different kind of debate. One group argues that (whatever others think) photography is a central example of an art form, that any other view would show a deep misunderstanding of the essential nature of art. The other takes the contrary position that any sound understanding of the character of art shows photography to fall wholly outside it, that photographic techniques are deeply alien to the aims of art. It would be quite wrong in these circumstances to describe the argument as one over where some borderline should be drawn. The argument would be about what art, properly understood, really is; it would reveal that the two groups had very different ideas about why even standard **art** forms they both recognize—painting and sculpture—**can** claim that title.

You might think that the second argument I just described is silly, a corruption of scholarship. But whatever you think, arguments of that character do occur,[35] and they are different from arguments of the first kind. It would be a serious misunderstanding to conflate the two or to say that one is only a special case of the other. The "sophisticated" defense of positivism misunderstands judicial practice in just that way. The various judges and lawyers who argued our sample cases did not think they were defending marginal or borderline claims. Their disagreements about legislation and precedent were fundamental; their arguments showed that they disagreed not only about whether Elmer should have his inheritance, but about why any legislative act, even traffic codes and rates of taxation, impose the rights and obligations everyone agrees they do; not only about whether Mrs. McLoughlin should have her damages, but about how and why past judicial decisions change the law of the land. They disagreed about what makes a proposition of law true not just at the margin but in the core as well. Our sample cases were understood by those who argued about them in courtrooms and classrooms and law reviews as pivotal cases testing fundamental principles, not as borderline cases calling for some more or less arbitrary line to be drawn.

THE REAL ARGUMENT FOR SEMANTIC THEORIES

If legal argument is mainly or even partly about pivotal cases, then lawyers cannot all be using the same factual criteria for deciding when propositions of law are true and false. Their arguments would be mainly or partly about which criteria they should use. So the project of the semantic theories, the project of digging out shared rules from a careful study of what lawyers say and do, would be doomed to fail. The waiting challenge has now matured. Why are positivists so sure that legal argument is not what it seems to be? Why are they so sure, appearances to the contrary, that lawyers follow common rules for using "law"? It cannot be experience that convinces them of this, for experience teaches the contrary. They say judicial and legal practice is not what it seems. But then why not? The symptoms are classic and my diagnosis familiar. The philosophers of semantic theory suffer from some block. But what block is it?

Notice the following argument. If two lawyers are actually following *different* rules in using the word "law," using different factual criteria to decide when a proposition of law is true or false, then each must mean something different from the other when he says what the law is. Earl and Gray must mean different things when they claim or deny that the law permits murderers to inherit: Earl means that his grounds for law are or are not satisfied, and Gray has in mind his own grounds, not Earl's. So the two judges are not really disagreeing about anything when one denies and the other asserts this proposition. They are only talking past one another. Their arguments are pointless in the most trivial and irritating way, like an argument about banks when one person has in mind savings banks and the other riverbanks. Worse still, even when lawyers appear to agree about what the law is, their agreement turns out to be fake as well, as if the two people I just imagined thought they agreed that there are many banks in North America.

These bizarre conclusions must be wrong. Law is a flourishing practice, and though it may well be flawed, even fundamentally, it is not a grotesque joke. It means something to say that judges should enforce rather than ignore the law, that citizens should obey it except in rare cases, that officials are bound by its rule. It seems obtuse to deny all this just because we sometimes disagree about what the law actually is. So our legal philosophers try to save what they can. They grasp at straws: they say that judges in hard cases are only pretending to disagree about what the law is, or that hard cases are only borderline disputes at the margin of what is clear and shared. They think they must otherwise settle into some form of nihilism about law. The logic that wreaks this havoc is the logic just described, the argument that unless lawyers and judges share factual criteria about the grounds of law there can be no significant thought or debate about what the law is. We have no choice but to confront that argument. It is a philosophical argument, so the next stage of our project must be philosophical as well.

TWO

INTERPRETIVE CONCEPTS

THE SEMANTIC STING

I shall call the argument I have just described, which has caused such great mischief in legal philosophy, the semantic sting. People are its prey who hold a certain picture of what disagreement is like and when it is possible. They think we can argue sensibly with one another if, but only if, we all accept and follow the same criteria for deciding when our claims are sound, even if we cannot state exactly, as a philosopher might hope to do, what these criteria are. You and I can sensibly discuss how many books I have on my shelf, for example, only if we both agree, at least roughly, about what a book is. We can disagree over borderline cases: I may call something a slim book that you would call a pamphlet. But we cannot disagree over what I called pivotal cases. If you do not count my copy of *Moby-Dick* as a book because in your view novels are not books, any disagreement is bound to be senseless. If this simple picture of when genuine disagreement is possible exhausts all possibilities, it must apply to legal concepts, including the concept of law. Then the following dilemma takes hold. Either, in spite of first appearances, lawyers actually all do accept roughly the same criteria for deciding when a claim about the law is true or there can be no genuine agreement or disagreement about law at all, but only the idiocy of people thinking they disagree because they attach different meanings to the same sound. The second leg of this dilemma seems absurd. So legal philosophers embrace the first and try to identify the hidden ground rules that *must* be there, embedded, though unrecognized, in legal practice. They produce and debate semantic theories of law.

Unfortunately for these theories, this picture of what makes disagreement possible fits badly with the kinds of disagreements lawyers actually have. It is consistent with lawyers and judges disagreeing about historical or social facts, about what words are to be found in the text of some statute or what the facts were in some precedent judicial decision. But much disagreement in law is theoretical rather than empirical. Legal philosophers who think there must be common rules try to explain away the theoretical disagreement. They say that lawyers and judges are only pretending or that they disagree only because the case before them falls in some gray or borderline area of the common rules. In either case (they say) we do better to ignore the words judges use and to treat them as disagreeing about fidelity or repair, not about law. There is the sting: we are marked as its target by too crude a picture of what disagreement is or must be like.

AN IMAGINARY EXAMPLE

The Interpretive Attitude

Perhaps this picture of what makes disagreement possible is too crude to capture any disagreement, even one about books. But I shall argue only that it is not exhaustive and, in particular, that it does not hold in an important set of circumstances that includes theoretical argument in law. It does not hold when members of particular communities who share practices and traditions make and dispute claims about the best interpretation of these—when they disagree, that is, about what some tradition or practice actually requires in concrete circumstances. These claims are often controversial, and the disagreement is genuine even though people use different criteria in forming or framing these interpretations; it is genuine because the competing interpretations are directed toward the same objects or events of interpretation. I shall try to show how this model helps us to understand legal argument more thoroughly and to see the role of law in the larger culture more clearly. But first it will be useful to see how the model holds for a much simpler institution.

Imagine the following history of an invented community. Its members follow a set of rules, which they call "rules of courtesy," on a certain range of social occasions. They say, "Courtesy requires that peasants take off their hats to nobility," for example, and they urge and accept other propositions of that sort. For a time this practice has the character of taboo: the rules are just there and are neither questioned nor varied. But then, perhaps slowly, all this changes. Everyone develops a complex "interpretive" attitude toward the rules of courtesy, an attitude that has two components. The first is the assumption that the practice of courtesy does not simply exist but has value, that it serves some interest or purpose or enforces some principle—in short, that it has some point—that can be stated independently of just describing the rules that make up the practice. The second is the further assumption that the requirements of courtesy—the behavior it calls for or judgments it warrants—are not necessarily or exclusively what they have always been taken to be but are instead sensitive to its point, so that the strict rules must be understood or applied or extended or modified or qualified or limited by that point. Once this interpretive attitude takes hold, the institution of courtesy ceases to be mechanical; it is no longer unstudied deference to a runic order. People now try to impose *meaning* on the institution—to see it in its best light—and then to restructure it in the light of that meaning.

The two components of the interpretive attitude are independent of one another; we can take up the first component of the attitude toward some institution without also taking up the second. We do that in the case of games and contests. We appeal to the point of these practices in arguing about how their rules should be changed, but not (except in very limited cases)[1] about what their rules now are; that is fixed by history and convention. Interpretation therefore plays only an external role in games and contests. It is crucial to my story about courtesy, however, that the citizens of courtesy adopt the second component of the attitude as well as the first; for them interpretation decides not only why courtesy exists but also what, properly understood, it now requires. Value and content have become entangled.

How Courtesy Changes

Suppose that before the interpretive attitude takes hold in both its components, everyone assumes that the point of courtesy lies in the opportunity it provides to show respect to social superiors. No question arises whether the traditional forms of respect are really those the practice requires. These just *are* the forms of deference, and the available options are conformity or rebellion. When the full interpretive attitude develops, however, this assumed point acquires critical power, and people begin to demand, under the title of courtesy, forms of deference previously unknown or to spurn or refuse forms previously honored, with no sense of rebellion, claiming that true respect is better served by what they do than by what others did. Interpretation folds back into the practice, altering its shape, and the new shape encourages further reinterpretation, so the practice changes dramatically, though each step in the progress is interpretive of what the last achieved.

People's views about the proper grounds of respect, for example, may change from rank to age or gender or some other property. The main beneficiaries of respect would then be social superiors in one period, older people in another, women in a third, and so forth. Or opinions may change about the nature or quality of respect, from a view that external show constitutes respect to the opposite view, that respect is a matter of feelings only. Or opinions may change along a different dimension, about whether respect has any value when it is directed to groups or for natural properties rather than to individuals for individual achievement. If respect of the former sort no longer seems important, or even seems wrong, then a different interpretation of the practice will become necessary. People will come to see the point of courtesy as almost the converse of its original point, in the value of impersonal forms of social relation that, because of their impersonality, neither require nor deny any greater significance. Courtesy will then occupy a different and diminished place in social life, and the end of the story is in sight: the interpretive attitude will languish, and the practice will lapse back into the static and mechanical state in which it began.

A FIRST LOOK AT INTERPRETATION

That is a birds-eye view from the perspective of history of how the tradition of courtesy changes over time. We must now consider the dynamics of transformation from closer in, by noticing the kinds of judgments and decisions and arguments that produce each individual's response to the tradition, the responses that collectively, over long periods, produce the large changes we first noticed. We need some account of how the attitude I call interpretive works from the inside, from the point of view of interpreters. Unfortunately, even a preliminary account will be controversial, for if a community uses interpretive concepts at all, the concept of interpretation itself will be one of them: a theory of interpretation is an interpretation of the higher-order practice of using interpretive concepts. (So any adequate account of interpretation must hold true of itself.) In this chapter I offer a theoretical account particularly designed to explain interpreting social practices and structures like courtesy, and I defend that account against some fundamental and apparently powerful objections. The discussion will, I fear, take us far from law, into controversies about interpretation that have occupied mainly literary scholars, social scientists, and

philosophers. But if law is an interpretive concept, any jurisprudence worth having must be built on some view of what
interpretation is, and the analysis of interpretation I construct and defend in this chapter is the foundation of the rest
of the book. The detour is essential.

Interpreting a social practice is only one form or occasion
of interpretation. People interpret in many different contexts, and we should begin by seeking some sense of how
these contexts differ. The most familiar occasion of interpretation—so familiar that we hardly recognize it as such—is
conversation. We interpret the sounds or marks another person makes in order to decide what he has said. So-called scientific interpretation is another context: we say that a
scientist first collects data and then interprets them. Artistic
interpretation is yet another: critics interpret poems and
plays and paintings in order to defend some view of their
meaning or theme or point. The form of interpretation we
are studying—the interpretation of a social practice—is like
artistic interpretation in this way: both aim to interpret
something created by people as an entity distinct from them,
rather than what people say, as in conversational interpretation, or events not created by people, as in scientific interpretation. I shall capitalize on that similarity between artistic interpretation and the interpretation of social practice; I
shall call them both forms of "creative" interpretation to distinguish them from conversational and scientific interpretation.

Conversational interpretation is purposive rather than
causal in some more mechanical way. It does not aim to explain the sounds someone makes the way a biologist explains
a frog's croak. It assigns meaning in the light of the motives
and purposes and concerns it supposes the speaker to have,
and it reports its conclusions as statements about his "intention" in saying what he did. May we say that all forms of interpretation aim at purposive explanation in that way, and
that this aim distinguishes interpretation, as a type of explanation, from causal explanation more generally? That
description does not seem, at first blush, to fit scientific

interpretation, and we might feel compelled, if we are attracted to the idea that all genuine interpretation is purposive, to say that scientific interpretation is not really interpretation at all. The phrase "scientific interpretation," we might say, is only a metaphor, the metaphor of data "speaking to" the scientist in the way one person speaks to another; it pictures the scientist as straining to understand what the data try to tell him. We can dissolve the metaphor and speak accurately, we might well think, only by eliminating the idea of purpose from our final description of the scientific process.

Is creative interpretation also, then, only a metaphorical case of interpretation? We might say (to use the same metaphor) that when we speak of interpreting poems or social practices we are imagining that these speak to us, that they mean to tell us something just the way a person might. But we cannot then dissolve that metaphor, as we can in the scientific case, by explaining that we really have in mind an ordinary causal explanation, and that the metaphor of purpose and meaning is only decorative. For the interpretation of social practices and works of art is *essentially* concerned with purposes rather than mere causes. The citizens of courtesy do not aim to find, when they interpret their practice, the various economic or psychological or physiological determinants of their convergent behavior. Nor does a critic aim at a physiological account of how a poem was written. So we must find some way to replace the metaphor of practices and pictures speaking in their own voices that recognizes the fundamental place of purpose in creative interpretation.

One solution is very popular. It dissolves the metaphor of poems and pictures speaking to us by insisting that creative interpretation is only a special case of conversational interpretation. We listen, not to the works of art themselves as the metaphor suggests, but to their actual, human authors. Creative interpretation aims to decipher the authors' purposes or intentions in writing a particular novel or main-

taining a particular social tradition, just as we aim in conversation to grasp a friend's intentions in speaking as he
does.[2] I shall defend a different solution: that creative interpretation is not conversational but *constructive*. Interpretation
of works of art and social practices, I shall argue, is indeed
essentially concerned with purpose not cause. But the purposes in play are not (fundamentally) those of some author
but of the interpreter. Roughly, constructive interpretation
is a matter of imposing purpose on an object or practice in
order to make of it the best possible example of the form or
genre to which it is taken to belong. It does not follow, even
from that rough account, that an interpreter can make of a
practice or work of art anything he would have wanted it to
be, that a citizen of courtesy who is enthralled by equality,
for example, can in good faith claim that courtesy actually
requires the sharing of wealth. For the history or shape of a
practice or object constrains the available interpretations of
it, though the character of that constraint needs careful ac-
counting, as we shall see. Creative interpretation, on the
constructive view, is a matter of interaction between purpose
and object.

A participant interpreting a social practice, according to
that view, proposes value for the practice by describing some
scheme of interests or goals or principles the practice can be
taken to serve or express or exemplify. Very often, perhaps
even typically, the raw behavioral data of the practice—
what people do in what circumstances—will underdetermine
the ascription of value: those data will be consistent, that is,
with different and competing ascriptions. One person might
see in the practices of courtesy a device for ensuring that respect is paid to those who merit it because of social rank or
other status. Another might see, equally vividly, a device for
making social exchange more conventional and therefore *less*
indicative of differential judgments of respect. If the raw
data do not discriminate between these competing interpretations, each interpreter's choice must reflect his view of
which interpretation proposes the most value for the prac-

tice—which one shows it in the better light, all things considered.

I offer this constructive account as an analysis of creative interpretation only. But we should notice in passing how the constructive account might be elaborated to fit the other two contexts of interpretation I mentioned, and thus show a deep connection among all forms of interpretation. Understanding another person's conversation requires using devices and presumptions, like the so-called principle of charity, that have the effect in normal circumstances of making of what he says the best performance of communication it can be.[3] And the interpretation of data in science makes heavy use of standards of theory construction like simplicity and elegance and verifiability that reflect contestable and changing assumptions about paradigms of explanation, that is, about what features make one form of explanation superior to another.[4] The constructive account of creative interpretation, therefore, could perhaps provide a more general account of interpretation in all its forms. We would then say that all interpretation strives to make an object the best it can be, as an instance of some assumed enterprise, and that interpretation takes different forms in different contexts only because different enterprises engage different standards of value or success. Artistic interpretation differs from scientific interpretation, we would say, only because we judge success in works of art by standards different from those we use to judge explanations of physical phenomena.

INTERPRETATION AND AUTHOR'S INTENTION

The constructive account of interpretation will strike many readers as bizarre, however, even when it is limited to creative interpretation or, more narrowly still, to the interpretation of social practices like courtesy. They will object because they prefer the popular account of creative interpretation I mentioned: that creative interpretation is only conversational interpretation addressed to an author. Here is a representative statement of their complaint. "No doubt people can make claims of the sort you describe the citizens of courtesy making about social practices they share; no doubt they can propose and contest opinions about how these practices should be understood and continued. But it is a serious confusion to call this *interpretation,* or to suggest that this is in some way making sense of the practice *itself.* That is deeply misleading in two ways. First, interpreting means trying to understand something—a statement or gesture or text or poem or painting, for example—in a particular and special way. It means trying to discover the author's motives or intentions in speaking or acting or writing or painting as he did. So interpreting a social practice, like your practice of courtesy, can only mean discerning the intentions of its members, one by one. Second, interpretation tries to show the object of interpretation—the behavior or the poem or the painting or the text in question—*accurately,* as it really is, not as you suggest through rose-colored glasses or in its best light. That means retrieving the actual, historical intentions of its authors, not foisting the interpreter's values on what those authors created."

I shall confront this objection in stages, and the following advance outline of my argument might be helpful, though it is necessarily condensed. I shall argue, first, that even if we take the goal of artistic interpretation to be retrieving the intention of an author, as the objection recommends, we cannot escape using the strategies of constructive interpretation the objection condemns. We cannot avoid trying to make of the artistic object the best, in our opinion, it can be. I shall try to show, next, that if we do take the goal of artistic interpretation to be discovering an author's intention, this must be a *consequence* of having applied the methods of constructive interpretation to art, not of having rejected those methods. I shall argue, finally, that the techniques of ordinary conversational interpretation, in which the interpreter aims to discover the intentions or meanings of another person, would in any event be inappropriate for the interpretation of a social practice like courtesy because it is essential to the structure of such a practice that interpreting the practice be treated as different from understanding what other participants mean by the statements they make in its operation. It follows that a social scientist must participate in a social practice if he hopes to understand it, as distinguished from understanding its members.

ART AND THE NATURE OF INTENTION

Is artistic interpretation inevitably a matter of discovering some author's intentions? Is discovering an author's intentions a factual process independent of the interpreter's own values? We start with the first of these questions, and with a guarded claim. Artistic interpretation is not simply a matter of retrieving an author's intention if we understand "intention" to mean a conscious mental state, not if we take the claim to mean that artistic interpretation always aims to identify some particular conscious thought wielding its baton in an author's mind when he said or wrote or did what he did. Intention is always a more complex and problematical matter than that. So we must restate our first question. If someone wants to see interpretation in art as a matter of retrieving an author's intention, what must he understand by an intention? That revised first question will reshape the second. Is there really so sharp a distinction as the objection supposes between discovering an artist's intention and finding value in what he has done?

We must first notice Gadamer's crucial point, that interpretation must *apply* an intention.[5] The theater provides an illuminating example. Someone who produces *The Merchant of Venice* today must find a conception of Shylock that will evoke for a contemporary audience the complex sense that the figure of a Jew had for Shakespeare and his audience, so his interpretation must in some way unite two periods of "consciousness" by bringing Shakespeare's intentions forward into a very different culture located at the end of a very different history.[6] If he is successful in this, his reading of Shylock will probably be very different from Shakespeare's concrete vision of that character. It may in some respects be contrary, replacing contempt or irony with sympathy, for example, or it may change emphasis, perhaps seeing Shylock's relation to Jessica as much more important than Shakespeare, as director, would have seen it.[7] Artistic intention, that is, is complex and structured: different aspects or levels of intention may conflict in the following way. Fidelity to Shakespeare's more discrete and concrete opinions about Shylock, ignoring the effect his vision of that character would have on contemporary audiences, might be treachery to his more abstract artistic purpose.[8] And "applying" that abstract purpose to our situation is very far from a neutral, historical exercise in reconstructing a past mental state. It inevitably engages the interpreter's own artistic opinions in just the way the constructive account of creative interpretation suggests, because it seeks to find the best means to express, given the text in hand, large artistic ambitions that Shakespeare never stated or perhaps even consciously defined but that are produced for us by our asking how the play he wrote would have been most illuminating or powerful to his age.

Stanley Cavell adds further complexity by showing how even the concrete, detailed intentions of an artist can be problematic.[9] He notices that a character in Fellini's film *La Strada* can be seen as a reference to the Philomel legend, and he asks what we need to know about Fellini in order to say that the reference was intentional (or, what is different, not unintentional). He imagines a conversation with Fellini in which the filmmaker says that although he has never heard of the story before, it captures the feeling he had about his character while filming, that is, that he *now* accepts it as part of the film he made. Cavell says that he is inclined in these circumstances to treat the reference as intended. Cavell's analysis is important for us, not because anything now turns on whether it is right in detail, but because it suggests a conception of intention quite different from the crude conscious-mental-state conception. An insight belongs to an artist's intention, on this view, when it fits and illuminates his artistic purposes in a way he would recognize and endorse even though he has not already done so. (So the imagined-conversation test can be applied to authors long dead, as it must be if it is to be of general critical use.) This brings the interpreter's sense of artistic value into his reconstruction of the artist's intention in at least an evidential way, for the interpreter's judgment of what an author would have accepted will be guided by his sense of what the author should have accepted, that is, his sense of which readings would make the work better and which would make it worse.

Cavell's imagined conversation with Fellini begins in Cavell's finding the film better if it is read as including a reference to Philomel and in his supposing that Fellini could be brought to share that view, to *want* the film read that way, to see his ambitions better realized by embracing that intention. Most of the reasons Cavell is likely to have for supposing this are his reasons for preferring his own reading. I do not mean that this use of artistic intention is a kind of fraud, a disguise for the interpreter's own views. For the imagined conversation has an important negative role: in some circumstances an interpreter would have good reason to suppose that the artist would reject a reading that appeals to the interpreter. Nor do I mean that we must accept the general claim that interpretation is a matter of retrieving or reconstructing a particular author's intention once we abandon the crude conscious-mental-state view of intention. Many critics now reject the general claim even in a more subtle form, and in the next section we shall have to consider how this continuing quarrel should be understood. My present point is only that the author's-intention claim, when it becomes a method or a style of interpretation, itself engages an interpreter's artistic convictions: these will often be crucial in establishing what, for that interpreter, the developed artistic intention really is.

We can, if we wish, use Cavell's account to construct a new description of what the citizens of my imaginary community of courtesy are doing in interpreting their social practice, an account that might have seemed preposterous before this discussion. Each citizen, we might say, is trying to discover his own intention in maintaining and participating in that practice—not in the sense of retrieving his mental state when last he took off his cap to a lady but in the sense of finding a purposeful account of his behavior he is comfortable in ascribing to himself. This new description of social interpretation as a conversation with oneself, as joint author and critic, suggests the importance in social interpretation of the shock of recognition that plays such an important part in the conversations Cavell imagines with artists. ("Yes, that does make sense of what I have been doing in taking off my hat; it fits the sense I have of when it would be wrong to do this, a sense I have not been able to describe but can now." Or, "No, it does not.") Otherwise the new description adds nothing to my original description that will prove useful to us. It shows only that the language of intention, and at least some of the point in the idea that interpretation is a matter of intention, is available for social as well as artistic interpretation if we want it. There is nothing in the idea of intention that necessarily divides the two types of creative interpretation.

But now we reach a more important point: there is something in that idea that necessarily unites them. For even if we reject the thesis that creative interpretation aims to discover some actual historical intention, the concept of intention nevertheless provides the *formal* structure for all interpretive claims. I mean that an interpretation is by nature the report of a purpose; it proposes a way of seeing what is interpreted—a social practice or tradition as much as a text or painting—as if this were the product of a decision to pursue one set of themes or visions or purposes, one "point," rather than another. This structure is required of an interpretation even when the material to be interpreted is a social practice, even when there is no historical author whose historical mind can be plumbed. An interpretation of courtesy, in our imaginary history, will wear an intentional air even though the intention cannot belong to anyone in particular or even people in general. This structural requirement, taken to be independent of any further requirement tying interpretation to a particular author's intention, provides an exciting challenge, which will occupy us later, mainly in Chapter 6. What could be the point of insisting on the formal structure of purpose, in the way we explain texts or legal institutions, beyond the goal of retrieving some actual historical intention?

Intention and the Value of Art

I said, just now, that the author's-intention method of artistic interpretation is disputed even in its most plausible form. Many critics argue that literary interpretation should be sensitive to aspects of literature—the emotional effects it has on readers or the way its language escapes any reduction to one particular set of meanings or the possibility it creates for dialogue between artist and audience, for example— whether or not these are part of its author's intention even in the complex sense we have been noticing. And even those who still insist that the artist's intention must be decisive of what the "real" work is like disagree about how that intention should be reconstructed. These various disagreements about intention and art are important for us not because we should take sides—that is not necessary here—but because we should try to understand the character of the argument, what the disagreements are really about.

Here is one answer to that question. Works of art present themselves to us as having, or at least as claiming, value of the particular kind we call aesthetic: that mode of presentation is part of the very idea of an artistic tradition. But it is always a somewhat open question, particularly in the general critical tradition we call "modernist," where that value lies and how far it has been realized. General styles of interpretation are, or at least presuppose, general answers to the question thus left open. I suggest, then, that the academic argument about author's intention should be seen as a particularly abstract and theoretical argument about where value lies in art. In that way this argument plays its part, along with more concrete and valuable arguments more directed to particular objects, in the overarching practices that provide us with the aesthetic experience.

This way of seeing the debate among critics explains why some periods of literary practice have been more concerned with artistic intention than others: their intellectual culture ties value in art more firmly to the process of artistic creation. Cavell points out that "in modernist art the issue of the artist's intention . . . has taken on a more naked role in our acceptance of his works than in earlier periods," and that "the practice of poetry alters in the nineteenth and twentieth centuries, in such a way that issues of intention . . . are forced upon the reader by the poem itself."[10] That change reflects and contributes to the growth in those periods of the romantic conviction that art has the value it does, and realizes that value in particular objects and events, because and when it embodies individual creative genius. The dominance of that view of art's value in our culture explains not only our preoccupation with intention and sincerity but much else besides—our obsession with originality, for example. So our dominant style of interpretation fixes on authorial intention, and arguments within that style about what, more precisely, artistic intention is reflect more finely tuned doubt and disagreement about the character of creative genius, about the role of the conscious, the unconscious, and the instinctive in its composition and expression. Some critics who dissent from the authorial style more markedly, because they emphasize values of tradition and continuity in which an author's place shifts as tradition builds, argue for a retrospective interpretation that makes the best reading of his work depend on what was written a century later.[11] Still more radical challenges, which insist on the relevance of the social and political consequences of art or of structuralist or deconstructionist semantics, or insist on narrative constructed between author and reader, or seem to reject the enterprise of interpretation altogether, deploy very different conceptions of where the conceptually presupposed value of art really lies.

This is a frighteningly simplistic account of the complex interaction between interpretation and other aspects of culture; I mean only to suggest how the argument over intention in interpretation, located within the larger social practice of contesting the mode of art's value, itself assumes the more abstract goal of constructive interpretation, aiming to make the best of what is interpreted. I must be careful not to be misunderstood. I am not arguing that the author's intention theory of artistic interpretation is wrong (or right), but that whether it is wrong or right and what it means (so far as we can think about these issues at all within our own tradition of criticism) must turn on the plausibility of some more fundamental assumption about why works of art have the value their presentation presupposes. Nor do I mean that a critic who is concerned to reconstruct Fellini's intentions in making La Strada must have in mind as he works some theory that connects intention to aesthetic value: critical intention is no more a mental state than artistic intention. Nor do I mean that if he reports that intention as including a reworking of Philomel, though this was never recognized by Fellini, he must be conscious of having the thought that the film is a better film read that way. I mean only that in the usual critical circumstances we must be able to attribute some such view to him, in the way we normally attribute convictions to people, if we are to understand his claims as interpretive rather than, for example, mocking or deceitful.[12] I do not deny what is obvious, that interpreters think within a tradition of interpretation from which they cannot wholly escape. The interpretive situation is not an Archimedian point, nor is that suggested in the idea that interpretation aims to make what is interpreted the best it can seem. Once again I appeal to Gadamer, whose account of interpretation as recognizing, while struggling against, the constraints of history strikes the right note.[13]

INTENTIONS AND PRACTICES

In reply to the objection I set out at the beginning of this discussion, I claim that artistic interpretation in our culture is constructive interpretation. The large question how far the best interpretation of a work of art must be faithful to the author's intention turns on the constructive question whether accepting that requirement allows interpretation to make of the artistic object or experience the best it can be. Those who think it does, because they think genius is the nerve of art or for some other reason, must make more detailed judgments of artistic value in deciding what the pertinent intention of the author really is. We must now consider the objection as it applies specifically to the other form of creative interpretation, the interpretation of social practices and structures. How could that form of interpretation aim to discover anything like an author's intention? We noticed one sense in which someone might think it can. A member of a social practice might think interpreting his practice means discovering his own intentions in the sense I described. But that hypothesis offers no comfort to the objection, because the objection argues that interpretation must be neutral and therefore that the interpreter must aim to discover someone *else's* motives and purposes. What sense can we make of that suggestion in the context of social interpretation?

There are two possibilities. Someone might say that interpretation of a social practice means discovering the purposes or intentions of the other participants in the practice, the cit-

izens of courtesy for example. Or that it means discovering
the purposes of the community that houses the practice,
conceived as itself having some form of mental life or group
consciousness. The first of these suggestions seems more attractive because less mysterious. But it is ruled out by the internal structure of an argumentative social practice, because
it is a feature of such practices that an interpretive claim is
not just a claim about what other interpreters think. Social
practices are composed, of course, of individual acts. Many
of these acts aim at communication and so invite the question, "What did he mean by that?" or "Why did he say it
just then?" If one person in the community of courtesy tells
another that the institution requires taking off one's hat to
superiors, it makes perfect sense to ask these questions, and
answering them would mean trying to understand him in
the familiar way of conversational interpretation. But a social practice creates and assumes a crucial distinction between interpreting the acts and thoughts of participants one
by one, in that way, and interpreting the practice itself, that
is, interpreting what they do collectively. It assumes that
distinction because the claims and arguments participants
make, licensed and encouraged by the practice, are about
what *it* means, not what *they* mean.

That distinction would be unimportant for practical purposes if the participants in a practice always agreed about
the best interpretation of it. But they do not agree, at least in
detail, when the interpretive attitude is lively. They must, to
be sure, agree about a great deal in order to share a social
practice. They must share a vocabulary: they must have in
mind much the same thing when they mention hats or requirements. They must understand the world in sufficiently
similar ways and have interests and convictions sufficiently
similar to recognize the sense in each other's claims, to treat
these *as* claims rather than just noises. That means not just
using the same dictionary, but sharing what Wittgenstein
called a form of life sufficiently concrete so that the one can
recognize sense and purpose in what the other says and does,

see what sort of beliefs and motives would make sense of his diction, gesture, tone, and so forth. They must all "speak the same language" in both senses of that phrase. But this similarity of interests and convictions need hold only to a point: it must be sufficiently dense to permit genuine disagreement, but not so dense that disagreement cannot break out.

So each of the participants in a social practice must distinguish between trying to decide what other members of his community think the practice requires and trying to decide, for himself, what it really requires. Since these are different questions, the interpretive methods he uses to answer the latter question cannot be the methods of conversational interpretation, addressed to individuals one by one, that he would use to answer the former. A social scientist who offers to interpret the practice must make the same distinction. He can, if he wishes, undertake only to report the various opinions different individuals in the community have about what the practice demands. But that would not constitute an interpretation of the practice itself; if he undertakes that different project he must give up methodological individualism and use the methods his subjects use in forming their own opinions about what courtesy really requires. He must, that is, *join* the practice he proposes to understand; his conclusions are then not neutral reports about what the citizens of courtesy think but claims about courtesy *competitive* with theirs.[14]

What about the more ambitious suggestion that interpretation of a social practice is conversational interpretation addressed to the community as a whole conceived as some superentity? Philosophers have explored the idea of a collective or group consciousness for many reasons and in many contexts, some of them pertinent to interpretation; I discuss some of these in a note.[15] Even if we accept the difficult ontology of this suggestion, however, it is defeated by the same argument as is fatal to the less ambitious one. Conversational interpretation is inappropriate because the practice being interpreted sets the conditions of interpretation: courtesy insists that interpreting courtesy is not just a matter of discovering what any particular person thinks about it. So even if we assume that the community is a distinct person with opinions and convictions of its own, a group consciousness of some sort, that assumption only adds to the story a further person whose opinions an interpreter must judge and contest, not simply discover and report. He must still distinguish, that is, between the opinion the group consciousness has about what courtesy requires, which he thinks he can discover by reflecting on its distinct motives and purposes, and what he, the interpreter, thinks courtesy really requires. He still needs a kind of interpretive method he can use to test that entity's judgment once discovered, and this method cannot be a matter of conversation with that entity or anything else.

We began this long discussion provoked by an important objection: that the constructive account of creative interpretation is wrong because creative interpretation is always conversational interpretation. That objection fails for the interpretation of social practices even more dramatically than it fails for artistic interpretation. The constructive account must face other objections: in particular the objection I consider later in this chapter, that constructive interpretation cannot be objective. But we should study that mode of interpretation further before we test it again.

STAGES OF INTERPRETATION

We must begin to refine constructive interpretation into an instrument fit for the study of law as a social practice. We shall need an analytical distinction among the following three stages of an interpretation, noticing how different degrees of consensus within a community are needed for each stage if the interpretive attitude is to flourish there. First, there must be a "preinterpretive" stage in which the rules and standards taken to provide the tentative content of the practice are identified. (The equivalent stage in literary interpretation is the stage at which discrete novels, plays, and so forth are identified textually, that is, the stage at which the text of *Moby-Dick* is identified and distinguished from the text of other novels.) I enclose "preinterpretive" in quotes because some kind of interpretation is necessary even at this stage. Social rules do not carry identifying labels. But a very great degree of consensus is needed—perhaps an interpretive community is usefully defined as requiring consensus at this stage—if the interpretive attitude is to be fruitful, and we may therefore abstract from this stage in our analysis by presupposing that the classifications it yields are treated as given in day-to-day reflection and argument.

Second, there must be an interpretive stage at which the interpreter settles on some general justification for the main elements of the practice identified at the preinterpretive stage. This will consist of an argument why a practice of that general shape is worth pursuing, if it is. The justification need not fit every aspect or feature of the standing practice, but it must fit enough for the interpreter to be able to see himself as interpreting that practice, not inventing a new one.[16] Finally, there must be a postinterpretive or reforming stage, at which he adjusts his sense of what the practice "really" requires so as better to serve the justification he accepts at the interpretive stage. An interpreter of courtesy, for example, may come to think that a consistent enforcement of the best justification of that practice would require people to tip their caps to soldiers returning from a crucial war as well as to nobles. Or that it calls for a new exception to an established pattern of deference: making returning soldiers exempt from displays of courtesy, for example. Or perhaps even that an entire rule stipulating deference to an entire group or class or persons must be seen as a mistake in the light of that justification.[17]

Actual interpretation in my imaginary society would be much less deliberate and structured than this analytical structure suggests. People's interpretive judgments would be more a matter of "seeing" at once the dimensions of their practice, a purpose or aim in that practice, and the post-interpretive consequence of that purpose. And this "seeing" would ordinarily be no more insightful than just falling in with an interpretation then popular in some group whose point of view the interpreter takes up more or less automatically. Nevertheless there will be inevitable controversy, even among contemporaries, over the exact dimensions of the practice they all interpret, and still more controversy about the best justification of that practice. For we have already identified, in our preliminary account of what interpretation is like, a great many ways to disagree.

We can now look back through our analytical account to compose an inventory of the kind of convictions or beliefs or assumptions someone needs to interpret something. He needs assumptions or convictions about what counts as part of the practice in order to define the raw data of his interpretation at the preinterpretive stage; the interpretive attitude cannot survive unless members of the same interpretive community share at least roughly the same assumptions about this. He also needs convictions about how far the justification he proposes at the interpretive stage must fit the standing features of the practice to count as an interpretation of it rather than the invention of something new. Can the best justification of the practices of courtesy, which almost everyone else takes to be mainly about showing deference to social superiors, really be one that would require, at the reforming stage, no distinctions of social rank? Would this be too radical a reform, too ill-fitting a justification to count as an interpretation at all? Once again, there cannot be too great a disparity in different people's convictions about fit; but only history can teach us how much difference is too much. Finally, he will need more substantive convictions about which kinds of justification really would show the practice in the best light, judgments about whether social ranks are desirable or deplorable, for example. These substantive convictions must be independent of the convictions about fit just described, otherwise the latter could not constrain the former, and he could not, after all, distinguish interpretation from invention. But they need not be so much shared within his community, for the interpretive attitude to flourish, as his sense of preinterpretive boundaries or even his convictions about the required degree of fit.

PHILOSOPHERS OF COURTESY

Institutional Identity

In Chapter 1 we reviewed classical theories or philosophies of law, and I argued that, read in the way they usually are, these theories are unhelpful because paralyzed by the semantic sting. Now we can ask what kind of philosophical theories *would* be helpful to people who take the interpretive attitude I have been describing toward some social tradition. Suppose our imaginary community of courtesy boasts a philosopher who is asked, in the salad days of the interpretive attitude, to prepare a philosophical account of courtesy. He is given these instructions: "We do not want your own substantive views, which are of no more interest than those of anyone else, about what courtesy actually requires. We want a more conceptual theory about the nature of courtesy, about what courtesy is in virtue of the very meaning of the word. Your theory must be neutral about our day-to-day controversies; it should provide the conceptual background or rules governing these controversies rather than taking sides." What can he do or say in reply? He is in a position like that of the social scientist I cited, who must join the practices he describes. He cannot offer a set of semantic rules for proper use of the word "courtesy" like the rules he might offer for using "book." He cannot say that taking off one's hat to a lady is by definition a case of courtesy, the way *Moby-Dick* might be said to be a book by definition. Or that sending a thank-you note is a borderline case that can properly be treated as either falling under courtesy or not, as a large pamphlet can properly be treated either as a book or not. Any step he took in that direction would immediately cross the line the community drew around his assignment; he would have provided his own positive interpretation, not a piece of neutral background analysis. He is like a man at the North Pole who is told to go any way but south.

He complains about his assignment and is given new instructions. "At least you can answer this question. Our practices are now very different from what they were several generations ago, and different as well from the practices of courtesy in neighboring and distant societies. Yet we know the practice we have is the same *sort* of practice as those. There must therefore be some feature all these different practices have in common in virtue of which they are all versions of courtesy. This feature is surely neutral in the way we want, since it is shared by people with such different ideas of what courtesy actually requires. Please tell us what it is." He can indeed answer this question, though not in the way the instructions suggest.

His explanation of the sense in which courtesy remains the same institution throughout its career of changes and adaption and across different communities with very different rules will not appeal to any "defining feature" common to all instances or examples of that institution.[18] For by hypothesis there is no such feature: courtesy is at one stage regarded as a matter of respect, and at another as something very different. His explanation will be historical: the institution has the continuity—to use the familiar Wittgensteinian figure—of a rope composed of many strands no one of which runs for its entire length or across its entire width. It is only a historical fact that the present institution is the descendant, through interpretive adaptations of the sort we noticed, of earlier ones, and that foreign institutions are also descendants of similar earlier examples. The changes from one period to another, or the differences from one society to another, may be sufficiently great so that the continuity should be denied. Which changes are great enough to cut the thread of continuity? That itself is an interpretive question, and the answer would depend on why the question of continuity arises.[19] There is no feature that any stage or instance of the practice just must have, in virtue of the meaning of the word "courtesy," and the search for such a feature would be just another example of the lingering infection of the semantic sting.

Concept and Conception

Can the philosopher be less negative and more helpful? Can he provide something in the spirit of what his clients want: an account of courtesy more conceptual and less substantive than the theories they already have and use? Perhaps. It is not unlikely that the ordinary debates about courtesy in the imaginary community will have the following treelike structure. People by and large agree about the most general and abstract propositions about courtesy, which form the trunk of the tree, but they disagree about more concrete refinements or subinterpretations of these abstract propositions, about the branches of the tree. For example, at a certain stage in the development of the practice, everyone agrees that courtesy, described most abstractly, is a matter of respect. But there is a major division about the correct interpretation of the idea of respect. One party thinks respect, properly understood, should be shown to people of a certain rank or group more or less automatically, while the other thinks respect must be deserved person by person. The first of these parties subdivides further about which ranks or groups are entitled to respect; the second subdivides about what acts earn respect. And so on into further and further subdivisions of opinion.

In these circumstances the initial trunk of the tree—the presently uncontroversial tie between courtesy and respect—would act, in public argument as well as private rumination, as a kind of plateau on which further thought and argument are built. It would then be natural for people to regard that tie as special and in the way of conceptual, to say, for example, that respect is part of the "very meaning" of courtesy. They mean, not that anyone who denies this is guilty of self-contradiction or does not know how to use the word "courtesy," but only that what he says marks him as outside the community of useful or at least ordinary discourse about the institution. Our philosopher will serve his community if he can display this structure and isolate this "conceptual" connection between courtesy and respect. He can capture it in the proposition that, for this community, respect provides the *concept* of courtesy and that competing positions about what respect really requires are *conceptions* of that concept. The contrast between concept and conception is here a contrast between levels of abstraction at which the interpretation of the practice can be studied. At the first level agreement collects around discrete ideas that are uncontroversially employed in all interpretations; at the second the controversy latent in this abstraction is identified and taken up. Exposing this structure may help to sharpen argument and will in any case improve the community's understanding of its intellectual environment.

The distinction between concept and conception, understood in this spirit and made for these purposes, is very different from the more familiar distinction between the meaning of a word and its extension. Our philosopher has succeeded, we are supposing, in imposing a certain structure on his community's practice such that particular substantive theories can be identified and understood as subinterpretations of a more abstract idea. In one way his analysis, if successful, must also be uncontroversial, because his claim— that respect provides the concept of courtesy—fails unless people are by and large agreed that courtesy is a matter of respect. But though uncontroversial in this way, his claim is interpretive not semantic; it is not a claim about linguistic ground rules everyone must follow to make sense. Nor is his claim timeless: it holds in virtue of a pattern of agreement and disagreement that might, as in the story I told earlier, disappear tomorrow. And his claim can be challenged at any time; the challenger will seem eccentric but will be perfectly well understood. His challenge will mark the deepening of disagreement, not, as with someone who says *Moby-Dick* is not a book, its superficiality.

Paradigms

There is one more task—less challenging but no less important—the philosopher might perform for his constituents. At each historical stage of the development of the institution, certain concrete requirements of courtesy will strike almost everyone as paradigms, that is, as requirements of courtesy if anything is. The rule that men must rise when a woman enters the room, for example, might be taken as a paradigm for a certain season. The role these paradigms play in reasoning and argument will be even more crucial than any abstract agreement over a concept. For the paradigms will be treated as concrete examples any plausible interpretation must fit, and argument against an interpretation will take the form, whenever this is possible, of showing that it fails to include or account for a paradigm case.

The connection between the institution and the paradigms of the day will be so intimate, in virtue of this special role, as to provide another kind of conceptual flavor. Someone who rejects a paradigm will seem to be making an extraordinary kind of mistake. But once again there is an important difference between these paradigms of interpretive truth and cases in which, as philosophers say, a concept holds "by definition," as bachelorhood holds of unmarried men. Paradigms anchor interpretations, but no paradigm is secure from challenge by a new interpretation that accounts for other paradigms better and leaves that one isolated as a mistake. In our imaginary community, the paradigm of gender might have survived other transformations for a long time, just because it seemed so firmly fixed, until it became an unrecognized anachronism. Then one day women would object to men standing for them; they might call this the deepest possible discourtesy. Yesterday's paradigm would become today's chauvinism.

A DIGRESSION: JUSTICE

The distinctions and vocabulary so far introduced will all prove useful when we turn, in the next chapter, to law as an interpretive concept. It is worth pausing, however, to see how far our account of interpretive concepts holds of other important political and moral ideas, and in particular the idea of justice. The crude picture of how language works, the picture that makes us vulnerable to the semantic sting, fails for justice as it does for courtesy. We do not follow shared linguistic criteria for deciding what facts make a situation just or unjust. Our most intense disputes about justice— about income taxes, for example, or affirmative action programs—are about the right tests for justice, not about whether the facts satisfy some agreed test in some particular case. A libertarian thinks that income taxes are unjust because they take property from its owner without his consent. It does not matter to the libertarian whether or not the taxes contribute to the greatest happiness in the long run. A utilitarian, on the other hand, thinks that income taxes are just only if they do contribute to the greatest long-run happiness, and it does not matter to him whether or not they take property without the owner's consent. So if we applied to justice the picture of disagreement we rejected for courtesy, we would conclude that the libertarian and utilitarian can neither agree nor disagree about any issue of justice.

That would be a mistake, because justice is an institution we interpret.[20] Like courtesy, it has a history; we each join that history when we learn to take the interpretive attitude toward the demands, justifications, and excuses we find other people making in the name of justice. Very few of us self-consciously interpret this history the way I imagined the people in my story interpreting courtesy. But we each—some more reflectively than others—form a sense of justice that is an interpretation nonetheless, and some of us even revise our interpretation from time to time. Perhaps the institution of justice started as I imagined courtesy starting: in simple and straightforward rules about crime and punishment and debt. But the interpretive attitude flourished by the time the earliest political philosophy was written, and it has flourished since. The progressive reinterpretations and transformations have been much more complex than those I described for courtesy, but each has built on the rearrangement of practice and attitude achieved by the last.

Political philosophers can play the various roles I imagined for the philosopher of courtesy. They cannot develop semantic theories that provide rules for "justice" like the rules we contemplated for "book." They can, however, try to capture the plateau from which arguments about justice largely proceed, and try to describe this in some abstract proposition taken to define the "concept" of justice for their community, so that arguments over justice can be understood as arguments about the best conception of that concept. Our own philosophers of justice rarely attempt this, for it is difficult to find a statement of the concept at once sufficiently abstract to be uncontroversial among us and sufficiently concrete to be useful. Our controversies about justice are too rich, and too many different kinds of theories are now in the field. Suppose a philosopher proposes, for example, this statement of the concept: justice is different from other political and moral virtues because it is a matter of entitlement, a matter of what those who will be affected by the acts of individuals or institutions have a right to expect at their hands. This seems unhelpful, because the concept of entitlement is itself too close to justice to be illuminating, and somewhat too controversial to count as conceptual in the present sense, because some prominent theories of justice— the Marxist theory, if there is one,[21] and even utilitarianism—would nevertheless reject it. Perhaps no useful statement of the concept of justice is available. If so, this casts no doubt on the sense of disputes about justice, but testifies only to the imagination of people trying to be just.

In any case, we have something that is more important than a useful statement of the concept. We share a preinterpretive sense of the rough boundaries of the practice on which our imagination must be trained. We use this to distinguish conceptions of justice we reject, even deplore, from positions we would not count as conceptions of justice at all even if they were presented under that title. The libertarian ethic is, for many of us, an unattractive theory of justice. But the thesis that abstract art is unjust is not even unattractive; it is incomprehensible as a theory about justice because no competent preinterpretive account of the practice of justice embraces the criticism and evaluation of art.[22]

Philosophers, or perhaps sociologists, of justice can also do useful work in identifying the paradigms that play the role in arguments about justice that I said paradigms would play in arguments about courtesy. It is paradigmatic for us now that punishing innocent people is unjust, that slavery is unjust, that stealing from the poor for the rich is unjust. Most of us would reject out of hand any conception that seemed to require or permit punishing the innocent. It is a standing argument against utilitarianism, therefore, that it cannot provide a good account or justification of these central paradigms; utilitarians do not ignore that charge as irrelevant, but on the contrary use heroic ingenuity to try to refute it. Some theories of justice do contest much of what their contemporaries take as paradigmatic, however, and this explains not only why these theories—Nietzsche's, for example, or Marx's apparently contradictory thoughts about justice—have seemed not only radical but perhaps not really theories of justice at all. For the most part, however, philosophers of justice respect and use the paradigms of their time. Their main work consists neither in trying to state the concept of justice nor in redefining paradigms but in developing and defending what are plainly full-blooded conceptions of justice, controversial theories that go well beyond paradigms into politics. The libertarian philosopher opposes income taxes and the egalitarian philosopher calls for more redistribution because their conceptions of justice differ. There is nothing neutral about these conceptions. They are interpretive but they are committed, and their value to us springs from that commitment.

SKEPTICISM ABOUT INTERPRETATION
A Challenge

My exposition of interpretation has thus far been subjective in one sense of that troublesome word. I described how creative interpretation looks to interpreters, what someone must think in order to embrace one interpretation rather than another. But the interpretive attitude I described, the attitude I said interpreters take up, sounds more objective. They think the interpretations they adopt are better than, not merely different from, those they reject. Does this attitude make sense? When two people disagree about the correct interpretation of something—a poem or a play or a social practice like courtesy or justice—can one sensibly think he is right and others wrong? We must be careful to distinguish this question from a different one, about the complexity of interpretation. It sounds dogmatic, and is usually a mistake, to suppose that a complex work of art—*Hamlet,* for example—is "about" any one thing and nothing else, so that one production of that play would be uniquely right or accurate, and any other production that stressed another aspect or dimension just wrong. I mean to ask a question about challenge, not complexity. Can one interpretive view be objectively better than another when they are not merely different, bringing out different and complementary aspects of a complex work, but contradictory, when the content of one *includes* the claim that the other is wrong?

Most people think they can, that some interpretations

really are better than others. Someone just converted to a new reading of *Paradise Lost,* trembling with the excitement of discovery, thinks his new reading is *right,* that it is better than the one he has abandoned, that those yet uninitiated have missed something genuine and important, that they do not see the poem for what it really is. He thinks he has been driven by the truth, not that he has chosen one interpretation to wear for the day because he fancies it like a necktie. He thinks he has genuine, good reasons for accepting his new interpretation and that others, who cling to the older view he now thinks wrong, have genuine, good reasons to change their minds. Some literary critics, however, believe this is all deep confusion; they say it is a mistake to think one interpretive opinion can really be better than another.[23] We shall see, in Chapter 7, that many legal scholars say much the same thing about the decisions judges make in hard cases like our sample cases of Chapter 1: they say that there can be no right answer in hard cases but only different answers.

Much of what I have said about interpretation throughout this chapter might be thought to support this skeptical critique of the ordinary, right-wrong view. I offered this general and very abstract characterization of interpretation: it aims to make the object or practice being interpreted the best it can be. So an interpretation of *Hamlet* tries to make of the text the best play it can be, and an interpretation of courtesy tries to make of the various practices of courtesy the best social institution these practices can be. This characterization of interpretation seems hostile to any claim of uniqueness of meaning, for it insists that different people, with different tastes and values, will just for that reason "see" different meanings in what they interpret. It appears to support skepticism, because the idea that there can be a "right" answer to questions about aesthetic or moral or social value strikes many people as even stranger than that there can be a right answer to questions about the meanings of texts and practices. So my abstract description of the most general aim of interpretation might well reinforce, for many readers, the skeptical thesis that it is a philosophical mistake to suppose that interpretations can be right or wrong, true or false.

Internal and External Skepticism

In what remains of this chapter we measure the scope and force of this skeptical challenge, and we begin with a crucial distinction: between skepticism *within* the enterprise of interpretation, as a substantive position about the best interpretation of some practice or work of art, and skepticism *outside* and *about* that enterprise. Suppose someone says that *Hamlet* is best understood as a play exploring obliquity, doubling, and delay; he argues that the play has more artistic integrity, that it better unites lexical, rhetorical, and narrative themes, read with these ideas in mind. An "internal" skeptic might say, "You are wrong. *Hamlet* is too confused and jumbled to be about anything at all: it is an incoherent hotch-potch of a play." An "external" skeptic might say, "I agree with you; I too think this is the most illuminating reading of the play. Of course, that is only an opinion we share; we cannot sensibly suppose that *Hamlet*'s being about delay is an objective fact we have discovered locked up in the nature of reality, 'out there' in some transcendental metaphysical world where the meanings of plays subsist."

These are different forms of skepticism. The internal skeptic addresses the substance of the claims he challenges; he insists it is in every way a mistake to say that *Hamlet* is about delay and ambiguity, a mistake to suppose it is a better play read that way. Or indeed in any other particular way. Not because no view of what makes a play better can be "really" right, but because one view *is* right: the view that a successful interpretation must provide the kind of unity he believes no interpretation of *Hamlet* can provide. Internal skepticism, that is, relies on the soundness of a general interpretive attitude to call into question all possible interpretations of a particular object of interpretation. One can be skeptical in this way not just about a particular play but more generally about an enterprise. Suppose a citizen surveys the practices of courtesy his neighbors count as valuable and decides that this shared assumption is a shared mistake. He has convictions about what kinds of social institutions can be useful or valuable to a community; he concludes that the practices of courtesy, root and branch, serve no good purpose or, even worse, that they serve a malign one. So he condemns as perverse all the different interpretations of courtesy his colleagues construct and defend against one another: his internal skepticism is, with respect to courtesy, global. Once again he relies on, instead of scorning, the idea that some social practices are better than others; he relies on a general attitude about social value to condemn all the interpretations of courtesy offered by his fellows. He assumes his general attitudes are sound and their contrary ones wrong.

Global internal skepticism of this sort, if it were plausible for law and not just courtesy, would threaten our own enterprise. For we hope to develop a positive theoretical account of the grounds of law, a program of adjudication we can recommend to judges and use to criticize what they do. So we cannot ignore the possibility that some globally skeptical view about the value of legal institutions is, in the end, the most powerful and persuasive view; we cannot say that this possibility is irrelevant to legal theory. We shall return to this threat in Chapter 7. Our present interest is in the other, external form of skepticism.

External skepticism is a metaphysical theory, not an interpretive or moral position. The external skeptic does not challenge any particular moral or interpretive claim. He does not say that it is in any way a mistake to think that *Hamlet* is about delay or that courtesy is a matter of respect or that slavery is wrong. His theory is rather a second-level theory about the philosophical standing or classification of these claims. He insists they are not descriptions that can be proved or tested like physics: he denies that aesthetic or moral values can be part of what he calls (in one of the maddening metaphors that seem crucial to any statement of his view) the "fabric" of the universe. His skepticism is external because disengaged: it claims to leave the actual conduct of interpretation untouched by its conclusions. The external skeptic himself has opinions about *Hamlet* and slavery and can give reasons for preferring these opinions to those he rejects. He only insists that all these opinions are projected upon, not discovered in, "reality."

There is an ancient and flourishing philosophical debate about whether external skepticism, particularly external skepticism directed to morality, is a significant theory and, if it is, whether it is right.[24] I shall not enter that debate now, except to consider whether external skepticism, if it is sound, would in any way condemn the belief interpreters commonly have: that one interpretation of some text or social practice can be on balance better than others, that there can be a "right answer" to the question which is best even when it is controversial what the right answer is.[25] That depends on how these "objective" beliefs (as we might call them) should be understood. Suppose I say that slavery is wrong. I pause, and then I add a second group of statements: I say that slavery is "really" or "objectively" wrong, that this is not just a matter of opinion, that it would be true even if I (and everyone else) thought otherwise, that it gives the "right answer" to the question whether slavery is wrong, that the contrary answer is not just different but mistaken. What is the relation between my original opinion that slavery is wrong and these various "objective" judgments I added to it?

Here is one suggestion. The objective statements I added are meant to supply some special kind of evidence for my original opinion or some justification for my acting on it. They are meant to suggest that I can prove slavery is wrong the way I might prove some claim of physics, by arguments of fact or logic every rational person must accept: by showing that atmospheric moral quaverings confirm my opinion, for example, or that it matches a noumenal metaphysical fact. If this were the right way to understand my objective claims, then my claims would assert what external skepticism denies: that moral judgments are descriptions of some special metaphysical moral realm. But it is not the right way to understand them. No one who says slavery is "really" wrong thinks he has thereby given, or even suggested, an argument why it is. (How could quaverings or noumenal entities provide any argument for moral convictions?) The only kind of evidence I could have for my view that slavery is wrong, the only kind of justification I could have for acting on that view, is some substantive moral argument of a kind the "objective" claims do not even purport to supply.

The actual connection between my original judgment about slavery and my later "objective" comments is very different. We use the language of objectivity, not to give our ordinary moral or interpretive claims a bizarre metaphysical base, but to *repeat* them, perhaps in a more precise way, to emphasize or qualify their *content*. We use that language, for example, to distinguish genuine moral (or interpretive or aesthetic) claims from mere reports of taste. I do not believe (though some people do) that flavors of ice cream have genuine aesthetic value, so I would say only that I prefer rum raisin and would not add (though some of them would) that rum raisin is "really" or "objectively" the best flavor.[26] We also use the language of objectivity to distinguish between claims meant to hold only for persons with particular beliefs or connections or needs or interests (perhaps only for the speaker) and those meant to hold impersonally for everyone. Suppose I say I must dedicate my life to reducing the threat of nuclear war. It makes sense to ask whether I think this duty holds "objectively" for everyone or just for those who feel, as I do, a special compulsion in this issue. I combined these two uses of objective language in the conversation I just imagined about slavery. I said slavery was "really" wrong, and the rest, to make plain that my opinion was a moral judgment and that I thought slavery was wrong everywhere, not just in communities whose traditions condemned it. So if someone says I am mistaken in this judgment, and our disagreement is genuine, he must mean to express the opinion that slavery is *not* wrong everywhere, or perhaps that it is not wrong at all. That is a version of internal skepticism: it could be defended only by moral arguments of some kind, for example by appealing to a form of moral relativism that holds that true morality consists only in following the traditions of one's community.

So there is no important difference in philosophical category or standing between the statement that slavery is wrong and the statement that there is a right answer to the question of slavery, namely that it is wrong. I cannot intelligibly hold the first opinion as a moral opinion without also holding the second. Since external skepticism offers no reason to retract or modify the former, it offers no reason to retract or modify the latter either. They are both statements within rather than about the enterprise of morality. Unlike the global form of internal skepticism, therefore, genuine external skepticism cannot threaten any interpretive project. Even if we think we understand and accept that form of skepticism, it can provide no reason why we should not also think that slavery is wrong, that *Hamlet* is about ambiguity and that courtesy ignores rank, or, what comes to the same thing, that each of these positions is better (or is "really" better) than its rivals. If we were external skeptics, then in a calm philosophical moment, away from the moral or interpretive wars, we would take an externally skeptical view of the philosophical standing of *all* these opinions. We would classify them all as projections rather than discoveries. But we would not discriminate among them by supposing that only the latter were mistakes. I hasten to add that recognizing the crucial point I have been stressing—that the "objective" beliefs most of us have are moral, not metaphysical, beliefs, that they only repeat and qualify other moral beliefs—in no way weakens these beliefs or makes them claim something less or even different from what they might be thought to claim.

For we can assign them no sense, faithful to the role they actually play in our lives, that makes them not moral claims. If anything is made less important by that point, it is external skepticism, not our convictions.

Which Form of Skepticism?

How, then, should we understand the skeptic who makes such heavy weather of declaring that there cannot be right answers in morals or interpretation? He uses the metaphorical rhetoric of external skepticism; he says he is attacking the view that interpretive meanings are "out there" in the universe or that correct legal decisions are located in some "transcendental reality." He uses arguments familiar to external skeptics: he says that since people in different cultures have different opinions about beauty and justice, these virtues cannot be properties of the world independent of attitude. But he plainly thinks his attack has the *force* of internal skepticism: he insists that people interpreting poems or deciding hard cases at law should not talk or act as if one view could be right and others wrong. He cannot have it both ways.

He attacks our ordinary beliefs because he attributes to us absurd claims we do not make. *We* do not say (nor can we understand anyone who does say) that interpretation is like physics or that moral values are "out there" or can be proved. We only say, with different emphases, that *Hamlet* is about delay and that slavery is wrong. The practices of interpretation and morality give these claims all the meaning they need or could have. If he thinks they are mistakes—poor performances within these practices properly understood—he needs to match our reasons and arguments, our account of ourselves as participants, with contrary reasons and arguments of his own. We do better for this critic, therefore, by seeing how far we can recast his arguments as arguments of internal skepticism. Can we understand him to be accusing us of moral rather than metaphysical mistakes?

"Since people do not agree about the injustice of social rank," he might say, "and since people are likely to think rank unjust only if they are born into cultures of a certain sort, it is unfair to claim that everyone must despise and give up rank. The most we should say is that people who think it unjust should despise and reject it, or that people who live in communities of that opinion should do so." Or: "The fact that others, in different cultures, reject our moral views shows that we have these views only because of the moral upbringing we happen to have had, and realizing that casts doubt on those views."[27]

These are internally skeptical arguments because they assume some general and abstract moral position—that moral claims have genuine moral force only when they are drawn from the mores of a particular community, for example, or that moral beliefs are false unless they are likely to be accepted in any culture—as the basis for rejecting the more concrete moral claims in hand. Substantive moral arguments like these have actually been made, of course, and their latent appeal might explain why skepticism, disguised as external skepticism, has been so popular in interpretation and in law. They might not strike you as good arguments, once that disguise is abandoned, but that is, I suggest, because you find global internal skepticism about morality implausible.

The metamorphosis I describe is not costless, because the skeptic's arguments, recast as arguments of internal skepticism, can no longer be peremptory or a priori. He needs arguments that stand up as moral (or aesthetic or interpretive) arguments; or if not arguments, at least convictions of the appropriate kind. His skepticism can no longer be disengaged or neutral about ordinary moral (or aesthetic or interpretive) opinions. He cannot reserve his skepticism for some quiet philosophical moment, and press his own opinions about the morality of slavery, for example, or the connection between courtesy and respect, when he is off duty and only acting in the ordinary way. He has given up his distinction between ordinary and objective opinions; if he really believes, in the internally skeptical way, that no moral judgment is really better than any other, he cannot then add that in his opinion slavery is unjust.

Conclusions and Agenda

I end this long section with an apology and some advice. We have marched up a steep hill and then right down again. We know no more about interpretation, or about morality or courtesy or justice or law, than we did when we began to consider the skeptical challenge. For my argument has been entirely defensive. Skeptics declare deep error in the interpretive attitude as I described it; they say it is a mistake to suppose that one interpretation of a social practice, or of anything else, can be right or wrong or really better than another. If we construe that complaint on the model of external skepticism, then, for the reasons I gave, the complaint is confused. If we construe it more naturally as a piece of global internal skepticism, then all the argument waits to be made. We stand where we did, only put on more explicit notice of the possible threat of this latter, potentially very damaging, form of argument.

I marched up this hill and down again only because the skeptical challenge, sensed as the challenge of external skepticism, has a powerful hold on lawyers. They say, of any thesis about the best account of legal practice in some department of the law, "That's your opinion," which is true but to no point. Or they ask, "How do you know?" or "Where does that claim come from?" demanding not a case they can accept or oppose but a thundering knock-down metaphysical demonstration no one can resist who has the wit to understand. And when they see that no argument of that power is in prospect, they grumble that jurisprudence is subjective only. Then, finally, they return to their knitting—making, accepting, resisting, rejecting arguments in the normal way, consulting, revising, deploying convictions pertinent to deciding which of competing accounts of legal practice provides the best justification of that practice. My advice is straightforward: this preliminary dance of skepticism is silly and wasteful; it neither adds to nor subtracts from the business at hand. The only skepticism worth anything is skepticism of the internal kind, and this must be earned by arguments of the same contested character as the arguments it opposes, not claimed in advance by some pretense at hard-hitting empirical metaphysics.

We must continue our study of interpretation, and of law, in that spirit. I shall offer arguments about what makes one interpretation of a social practice better than another, and about what account of law provides the most satisfactory interpretation of that complex and crucial practice. These arguments will not—because they cannot—be demonstrations. They invite disagreement, and though it will not be wrong to reply, "But that's only your opinion," neither will it be helpful. You must then ask yourself whether, after reflection, it is your opinion as well. If it is, you will think that my arguments and conclusions are sound and that other, conflicting ones, are unsound and wrong. If it is not your opinion, then it falls to you to say why not, to match my arguments or naked convictions with your own. For the exercise in hand is one of discovery at least in this sense: discovering which view of the sovereign matters we discuss sorts best with the convictions we each, together or severally, have and retain about the best account of our common practices.

THREE

JURISPRUDENCE REVISITED

A NEW PICTURE

We have drawn the semantic sting and no longer need the caricature of legal practice offered in semantic theories. We can see more clearly now, and this is what we see. Law is an interpretive concept like courtesy in my imagined example. Judges normally recognize a duty to continue rather than discard the practice they have joined. So they develop, in response to their own convictions and instincts, working theories about the best interpretation of their responsibilities under that practice. When they disagree in what I called the theoretical way, their disagreements are interpretive. They disagree, in large measure or in fine detail, about the soundest interpretation of some pertinent aspect of judicial practice. So Elmer's fate will depend on the interpretive convictions of the particular panel of judges that decides his case. If a judge thinks it follows from the best interpretation of what judges characteristically do about statutes that he should never look to legislators' intentions, then he might well decide for Elmer. But if, on the contrary, he thinks that the best interpretation requires him to look to their intentions, then he will probably decide for Goneril and Regan. If Elmer's case comes before a judge who has not yet thought about this issue of interpretation, that judge will have to do so then, and he will find lawyers on both sides willing to help. Interpretations struggle side by side with litigants before the bar.

Each judge's interpretive theories are grounded in his own convictions about the "point"—the justifying purpose or goal or principle—of legal practice as a whole, and these convictions will inevitably be different, at least in detail, from those of other judges. Nevertheless, a variety of forces tempers these differences and conspires toward convergence. Every community has paradigms of law, propositions that in practice cannot be challenged without suggesting either corruption or ignorance. Any American or British judge who denied that the traffic code was part of the law would be replaced, and this fact discourages radical interpretations. The most powerful influences toward convergence, however, are internal to the character of interpretation. The practice of precedent, which no judge's interpretation can wholly ignore, presses toward agreement; each judge's theories of what judging really is will incorporate by reference, through whatever account and restructuring of precedent he settles on, aspects of other popular interpretations of the day. Judges think about law, moreover, within society, not apart from it; the general intellectual environment, as well as the common language that reflects and protects that environment, exercises practical constraints on idiosyncrasy and conceptual constraints on imagination. The inevitable conservatism of formal legal education, and of the process of selecting lawyers for judicial and administrative office, adds further centripetal pressure.

It would be a mistake to ignore these various unifying and socializing factors, but a more insidious and dangerous mistake to exaggerate their power. The dynamics of interpretation resist as well as promote convergence, and the centrifugal forces are particularly strong where the professional as well as the larger community is divided over justice. Different judges belong to different and rival political traditions, and the cutting edge of different judges' interpretations will be honed by different ideologies. Nor is this to be deplored. On the contrary, law gains in power when it is sensitive to the frictions and stresses of its intellectual sources. Law would founder if the various interpretive theories in play in court and classroom diverged too much in any one generation. Perhaps a shared sense of that danger provides yet another reason why they do not. But law would stagnate, and so founder in a different way, if it collapsed into the runic traditionalism I imagined as the final fate of courtesy.

We may take a longer view of our legal culture, noticing how it develops and how its general character changes over time. Certain interpretive solutions, including views about the nature and force of legislation and precedent, are very popular for a time, and their popularity, aided by normal intellectual inertia, encourages judges to take them as settled for all practical purposes. They are the paradigms and quasi-paradigms of their day. But at the same time other issues, perhaps equally fundamental, are matters of debate and controversy. Perhaps for decades no judge challenges— or even thinks of challenging—the doctrine that the intentions of particular legislators are irrelevant in fixing the meaning of a statute they have enacted. Everyone agrees that its meaning must be determined by the words of the statute alone, ignoring any indication that the legislators did not mean what the words say. But during this same period it might be controversial whether the words of a statute should be understood acontextually, as we might understand them knowing nothing about the situation the statute addresses or, on the contrary, contextually, as most people would understand them in that situation. Perhaps for decades no one doubts that courts may jail people who behave wickedly according to the community's popular morality, whether or not their acts have been declared criminal by the legislature. But there might be great disagreement during the same years whether the courts can properly enforce a wealth tax that was adopted after the wealth being taxed had been accumulated. This pattern of agreement and disagreement is temporary, however. Suddenly what seemed unchallengeable is challenged, a new or even radical interpretation of some important part of legal practice is developed in someone's chambers or study which then finds favor within a "progressive" minority. Paradigms are broken, and new paradigms emerge. These are the several elements of our new picture of adjudication in cross-section and over time. The old plain-fact picture of Chapter 1 told us not to take the opinions judges write in hard cases at face value; the new picture has the signal merit of allowing us once again to believe what our judges say.

CONCEPTS AND CONCEPTIONS OF LAW

Legal philosophers are in the same situation as philosophers of justice and the philosopher of courtesy we imagined. They cannot produce useful semantic theories of law. They cannot expose the common criteria or ground rules lawyers follow for pinning legal labels onto facts, for there are no such rules. General theories of law, like general theories of courtesy and justice, must be abstract because they aim to interpret the main point and structure of legal practice, not some particular part or department of it. But for all their abstraction, they are constructive interpretations: they try to show legal practice as a whole in its best light, to achieve equilibrium between legal practice as they find it and the best justification of that practice. So no firm line divides jurisprudence from adjudication or any other aspect of legal practice. Legal philosophers debate about the general part, the interpretive foundation any legal argument must have. We may turn that coin over. Any practical legal argument, no matter how detailed and limited, assumes the kind of abstract foundation jurisprudence offers, and when rival foundations compete, a legal argument assumes one and rejects others. So any judge's opinion is itself a piece of legal philosophy, even when the philosophy is hidden and the visible argument is dominated by citation and lists of facts. Jurisprudence is the general part of adjudication, silent prologue to any decision at law.

Law cannot flourish as an interpretive enterprise in any

community unless there is enough initial agreement about what practices are legal practices so that lawyers argue about the best interpretation of roughly the same data. That is a practical requirement of any interpretive enterprise: it would be pointless for two critics to argue over the best interpretation of a poem if one has in mind the text of "Sailing to Byzantium" and the other the text of "Mathilda Who Told Lies." I do not mean that all lawyers everywhere and always must agree on exactly which practices should count as practices of law, but only that the lawyers of any culture where the interpretive attitude succeeds must largely agree at any one time. We all enter the history of an interpretive practice at a particular point; the necessary preinterpretive agreement is in that way contingent and local.

In fact we have no difficulty identifying collectively the practices that count as legal practices in our own culture. We have legislatures and courts and administrative agencies and bodies, and the decisions these institutions make are reported in a canonical way. In the United States we have the Constitution as well. Each lawyer has joined the practice of law with that furniture in place and with a shared understanding that these institutions together form our legal system. It would be a mistake—another lingering infection from the semantic sting—to think that we identify these institutions through some shared and intellectually satisfying definition of what a legal system necessarily is and what institutions necessarily make it up.[1] Our culture presents us with legal institutions and with the idea that they form a system. The question which features they have, in virtue of which they combine as a distinctly legal system, is part of the interpretive problem. It is part of the controversial and uncertain process of assigning meaning to what we find, not a given of the preinterpretive structure.

We also have legal paradigms, proposition of law like the traffic code that we take to be true if any are; an interpretation that denies these will be for that reason deeply suspect. These paradigms give shape and profit to interpretive debates about law. They make possible a standard form of argument: seeking to test or embarrass an interpretation by confronting it with a paradigm it cannot explain. But paradigms are no more true "by definition" in law than they are in courtesy or justice. Someone who denies that the traffic code is law does not contradict himself, nor does he speak thoughts no one can understand.[2] We understand him only too well, and it is not inconceivable (though it is unlikely) that he will be able to defend his view through a radical reinterpretation of legal practice that is otherwise so appealing that it persuades us to abandon what was formerly a cardinal paradigm. We cannot be sure his views are really the nonsense we suppose except by hearing him out and discovering whether we share his conviction. If we remain convinced that his views are not only wrong but fundamentally wrong, that his radical interpretation has missed some main point any successful interpretation must recognize, it will be enough for us to say that his views are absurd. We do not need to add the more dramatic but mistaken charge encouraged by the semantic sting: that his error is verbal or conceptual. We will think him very wrong, but not wrong in some different way from other claims we reject but think less preposterous.

A legal philosopher, then, begins his work enjoying a fairly uncontroversial preinterpretive identification of the domain of law, and with tentative paradigms to support his argument and embarrass competitors in the familiar way. Now the question arises whether he and his competitors might also agree on what I called, in discussing courtesy and justice, a statement of the central concept of their institution that will allow them to see their arguments as having a certain structure, as arguments over rival conceptions of that concept. A conceptual statement of that sort would be useful in several ways. Just as we understood the practice of courtesy better at one stage in its career by finding general agreement about the abstract proposition that courtesy is a matter of respect, we might understand law better if we could find a similar abstract description of the point of law most legal theorists accept so that their arguments take place on the plateau it furnishes.

Neither jurisprudence nor my own arguments later in this book depend on finding an abstract description of that sort. Political philosophy thrives, as I said, in spite of our difficulties in finding any adequate statement of the concept of justice. Nevertheless I suggest the following as an abstract account that organizes further argument about law's character. Governments have goals: they aim to make the nations they govern prosperous or powerful or religious or eminent; they also aim to remain in power. They use the collective force they monopolize to these and other ends. Our discussions about law by and large assume, I suggest, that the most abstract and fundamental point of legal practice is to guide and constrain the power of government in the following way. Law insists that force not be used or withheld, no matter how useful that would be to ends in view, no matter how beneficial or noble these ends, except as licensed or required by individual rights and responsibilities flowing from past political decisions about when collective force is justified.

The law of a community on this account is the scheme of rights and responsibilities that meet that complex standard: they license coercion because they flow from past decisions of the right sort. They are therefore "legal" rights and responsibilities. This characterization of the concept of law sets out, in suitably airy form, what is sometimes called the "rule" of law. It is compatible with a great many competing claims about exactly which rights and responsibilities, beyond the paradigms of the day, do follow from past political decisions of the right sort and for that reason do license or require coercive enforcement. It therefore seems sufficiently abstract and uncontroversial to provide, at least provisionally, the structure we seek. No doubt there are exceptions to this claim, theories that challenge rather than elaborate the connection it assumes between law and the justification of coercion. But not as many as there might seem to be at first glance.[3]

Conceptions of law refine the initial, uncontroversial interpretation I just suggested provides our concept of law. Each conception furnishes connected answers to three questions posed by the concept. First, is the supposed link between law and coercion justified at all? Is there any point to requiring public force to be used only in ways conforming to rights and responsibilities that "flow from" past political decisions? Second, if there is such a point, what is it? Third, what reading of "flow from"—what notion of consistency with past decisions—best serves it? The answer a conception gives to this third question determines the concrete legal rights and responsibilities it recognizes.

In the next several chapters we shall study three rival conceptions of law, three abstract interpretations of our legal practice that I have deliberately constructed on this model as answers to this set of questions. These conceptions are novel in one way: they are not meant precisely to match the "schools" of jurisprudence I described in Chapter 1, and perhaps no legal philosopher would defend either of the first two exactly as I describe it. But each captures themes and ideas prominent in that literature, now organized as interpretive rather than semantic claims, and the argument among them is therefore more illuminating than the stale battles of the texts. I shall call these three conceptions "conventionalism," "legal pragmatism," and "law as integrity." I shall argue that the first of these, though it seems initially to reflect the ordinary citizen's understanding of law, is the weakest; that the second is more powerful and can be defeated only when our theater of argument expands to include political philosophy; and that the third is, all things considered, the best interpretation of what lawyers, law teachers, and judges actually do and much of what they say.

Conventionalism gives an affirmative answer to the first

question posed by our "conceptual" description of law. It accepts the idea of law and legal rights. It argues, in answer to the second question, that the point of law's constraint, our reason for requiring that force be used only in ways consistent with past political decisions, is exhausted by the predictability and procedural fairness this constraint supplies, though as we shall see conventionalists divide about the exact connection between law and these virtues. It proposes, in answer to the third question, a sharply restricted account of the form of consistency we should require with past decisions: a right or responsibility flows from past decisions only if it is explicit within them or can be made explicit through methods or techniques conventionally accepted by the legal profession as a whole. Political morality, according to conventionalism, requires no further respect for the past, so when the force of convention is spent judges must find some wholly forward-looking ground of decision.

Legal pragmatism is, from the point of view of my conceptual suggestion, a skeptical conception of law. It answers the first question I listed in the negative: it denies that a community secures any genuine benefit by requiring that judges' adjudicative decisions be checked by any supposed right of litigants to consistency with other political decisions made in the past. It offers a very different interpretation of our legal practice: that judges do and should make whatever decisions seem to them best for the community's future, not counting any form of consistency with the past as valuable for its own sake. So pragmatists, strictly speaking, reject the idea of law and legal right deployed in my account of the concept of law,[4] though as we shall see, they insist that reasons of strategy require judges sometimes to act "as if" people have some legal rights.

Like conventionalism, law as integrity accepts law and legal rights wholeheartedly. It answers the second question, however, in a very different way. It supposes that law's constraints benefit society not just by providing predictability or procedural fairness, or in some other instrumental way, but by securing a kind of equality among citizens that makes their community more genuine and improves its moral justification for exercising the political power it does. Integrity's response to the third question—its account of the character of consistency with past political decisions that law requires—is correspondingly different from the answer given by conventionalism. It argues that rights and responsibilities flow from past decisions and so count as legal, not just when they are explicit in these decisions but also when they follow from the principles of personal and political morality the explicit decisions presuppose by way of justification.

These are only skeletal descriptions of the three general conceptions of law we shall study. Their flesh and battle dress will be presented soon enough.

Law and Morals

The main test of my suggestion, that arguments of legal theory are best understood as arguments about how far and in what way past political decisions provide a necessary condition for the use of public coercion, lies ahead, when we elaborate and compare the three conceptions of law just described. We might now notice, however, how this suggestion helps us to reformulate some classical jurisprudential puzzles in a more illuminating way, to reveal substantive issues that the classical texts often obscure. If our community does indeed accept the abstract "conceptual" idea that legal rights are those flowing from past political decisions according to the best interpretation of what that means, then this helps to explain the complex relation between law and other social phenomena. How is a community's law different from its popular morality or traditional values? How is it different from what true justice requires of any state, no matter what its popular convictions or traditions? Our conceptual account provides this short answer to both these questions: it is different from each because its content may depend on the other.

I must explain that cryptic claim. Suppose we identify as the "popular morality" of a community the set of opinions about justice and other political and personal virtues that are held as matters of personal conviction by most of the members of that community, or perhaps of some moral elite within it. And suppose we identify as its "moral traditions" its popular morality over some sizable historical period including the present.[5] The distinction is then fairly straightforward between these ideas and the community's law. Its law belongs to the community not just passively, because its members hold certain views about what is right or wrong, but as a matter of active commitment, because its officials have taken decisions that commit the community to the rights and duties that make up law. But a particular conception of law may nevertheless make the question of what rights and duties do follow from past political decisions depend in some way on popular morality as well as on the explicit content of those decisions. Or it may deny that there is any such connection. The concept of law, understood as I have suggested, is itself neutral between—because more abstract than—these competing explanations of the connection between a community's reigning opinions and its legal commitments.

Law is also different from justice. Justice is a matter of the correct or best theory of moral and political rights, and anyone's conception of justice is his theory, imposed by his own personal convictions, of what these rights actually are. Law is a matter of which supposed rights supply a justification for using or withholding the collective force of the state because they are included in or implied by actual political decisions of the past. Once again, however, this statement of the difference is neutral among different theories about the role a person's convictions about justice should play in forming his convictions about law. The concept permits, as available conceptions, theories that insist that when the content of a political decision is in some way unclear, justice plays a part in deciding what legal rights in fact follow from that decision. The concept permits, that is, conceptions reminiscent of some of the theories I called natural law theories in Chapter 1, though under our new picture these are not semantic theories but general interpretations of legal practice. It also permits opposing conceptions that reject this suggested influence of justice over law and so remind us of legal positivism. And it also permits skeptical conceptions like legal pragmatism, which insist that law, conceived as a matter of rights over what forward-looking justice would otherwise demand, is empty.

So the assumption that the most general point of law, if it has one at all, is to establish a justifying connection between past political decisions and present coercion shows the old debate about law and morals in a new light. In jurisprudence texts that debate is pictured as a contest between two semantic theories: positivism, which insists that law and morals are made wholly distinct by semantic rules everyone accepts for using "law," and natural law, which insists, on the contrary, that they are united by these semantic rules. In fact the old debate makes sense only if it is understood as a contest between different political theories, a contest about how far that assumed point of law requires or permits citizens' and officials' views about justice to figure in their opinions about what legal rights have been created by past political decisions. The argument is not conceptual in our sense at all, but part of the interpretive debate among rival conceptions of law.

Anatomy of a Conception

The assumed connection between law and coercion is also a useful guide to the likely structure or anatomy of nonskeptical conceptions of law like conventionalism and law as integrity. Each such conception will deploy, as its organizing idea, some account of how the legal practices that define past political decisions contribute to the justification of collective coercive force. We know already which practices these are. Legislation—the practice of recognizing as law the explicit decisions of special bodies widely assumed to have that power—is a prominent part of our legal landscape, and no conception can ignore it. So every competent conception must include some answer to the question why, as a matter of political morality, past decisions of legislative institutions should have the justifying power the conception awards them. Precedent also has a prominent place in our practices: past decisions of courts count as sources of legal rights. So any competent conception must provide some answer to the question why a past judicial decision should in itself provide a reason for a similar use of state power by different officials later.

No conception need justify every feature of the political practices it offers to interpret: like any interpretation, it can condemn some of its data as a mistake, as inconsistent with the justification it offers for the rest, and perhaps propose that this mistake be abandoned in what I called, in Chapter 2, its postinterpretive stage. A conception of law might try to show, for example, that the explanation of legislation that provides the best justification of that institution requires, contrary to now-prevailing practice, that old and out-of-date statutes be treated as no longer law. Conceptions of law will be controversial just because they will differ in this way in their postinterpretive accounts of legal practice, in their opinions, that is, about the right way to expand or extend the practice in areas presently disputed or uncultivated. These controversial postinterpretive claims are the cutting edge of a conception of law, and that is why hard cases like our sample cases provide the best theater for displaying their power.

Here are some of the issues, controversial in our own practice, that a developed conception of law must take up in its postinterpretive stage. Given the general, foundational interpretation the conception offers of the main lines of legislation and precedent, what should be done when the text of a statute is unclear? Which is decisive: the "plain" or "literal" meaning of the words used to record the decision or the intentions or purposes of the officials whose decision it was? What is a "literal" meaning? What do "intention" and "purpose" here mean? What sense can we make of a collective purpose or intention? Does the content of a legislative or judicial decision go beyond the concrete intentions of its authors, to embrace issues that are analogous or in some way closely related? Can legislative or judicial decisions be made by implication, as it were, according to the internal logic of the more limited decisions these officials actually had in mind? Suppose legislators decided long ago that people who drive carriages carelessly must compensate those they run down. Did this decision already include the further decision that people who drive automobiles carelessly are liable in the same way?

Does this depend on which kind of official made the decision in question, and in what context? Perhaps a legislative decision should be understood more narrowly, so that a fresh piece of legislation is necessary to extend the rule to automobiles, but if a judge has established the rule about carriages it should extend to automobiles automatically, at least if every argument in favor of his initial decision applies to automobiles as well. Does the reason why legislative and judicial decisions provide valid licenses for state coercion carry over to different forms of communal decision? Should the rules or principles embraced in the community's conventional morality in the reductive sociological sense I described be counted as political decisions? If almost everyone thinks, as a matter of personal conviction, that murderers should not be allowed to inherit, does it follow that this too, along with decisions of the competent legislature and past judicial decisions, justifies the state's refusing Elmer his inheritance?

This is only the beginning of the long list of issues a satisfactory foundational interpretation of our own legal practice would consider. Each question raises hosts of others, and an interpretation of this kind is necessarily open-ended and incomplete. It must also be internally complex and cross-referenced. The different questions in this list, and the vast variety of further questions for which they stand surrogate, must be answered together, in one complex though incomplete theory, if the answers are to stand coherent or even make any sense at all. Each part will in some way depend on the rest because they will be knit together by some unifying vision of the connection between legal practice and political justification. So any general conception must also have external connections to other parts or departments of political morality and, through these, to more general ideological and even metaphysical convictions. I do not mean that any lawyer or philosopher who takes up a general conception of law will already have developed some explicit and articulate view about the point of law, or the large questions of personality, life, and community on which any such view must rest. I mean only that his conception of law, so far as he has developed it, will reveal some attitude toward these large topics whether or not he realizes this.

SKEPTICAL CONCEPTIONS AND WICKED LAW
Did the Nazis Have Law?

I said that legal pragmatism is a skeptical conception of law because it rejects the assumption that past decisions provide rights to future ones. Some legal philosophers, whose views closely resemble that conception, express them in the nihilistic claim that there is no law, that law is an illusion. We shall explore these claims further when we study legal pragmatism at greater length in Chapter 5. But we should first notice a different, more discriminating claim some legal philosophers have made: that in some nations or circumstances there is no law, in spite of the existence of familiar legal institutions like legislatures and courts, because the practices of these institutions are too wicked to deserve that title. We have little trouble making sense of that claim once we understand that theories of law are interpretive. For we understand it to argue that the legal practices so condemned yield to no interpretation that can have, in any acceptable political morality, any justifying power at all.

In the heyday of semantic theories, legal philosophers were more troubled by the suggestion that wicked places really had no law. Semantic rules were meant to capture the use of "law" generally and therefore to cover people's statements not only about their own law but about very different historical and foreign legal systems as well. It was a common argument against strong "natural law" theories, which claim that a scheme of political organization must satisfy certain minimal standards of justice in order to count as a legal system at all, that our linguistic practice does not deny the title of law to obviously immoral political systems. We say the Nazis had law, even though it was very bad law. This fact about our linguistic practice was widely thought to argue for positivism, with its axiom that the existence of law is independent of the value of that law, in preference to any "natural law" theory.

If useful theories of law are not semantic theories of this kind, however, but are instead interpretive of a particular stage of a historically developing practice, then the problem of immoral legal systems has a different character. Interpretive theories are by their nature addressed to a particular legal culture, generally the culture to which their authors belong. Unless these theories are deeply skeptical, they will treat that legal system as a flourishing example of law, one that calls for and rewards the interpretive attitude. The very detailed and concrete legal theories lawyers and judges construct for a particular jurisdiction, which extend into the detail of its adjudicative practice, are of course very much tied to that jurisdiction. The more abstract conceptions of law that philosophers build are not. It would be suspicious, even alarming, if conventionalism, for example, were said to be the most successful general interpretation of Rhode Island law but not of the law of Massachusetts or Britain in the same period. But there is no reason to expect even a very abstract conception to fit foreign legal systems developed in and reflecting political ideologies of a sharply different character. On the contrary. If a supportive conception of law offers to find in the general structure of a particular community's legal practice a political justification of coercion, then it should not be supportive, but in some way skeptical, about legal systems that lack features essential to that justification.

But it does not follow that if a lawyer finds the best interpretation of Anglo-American law in some feature the Nazi regime wholly lacked, he must then deny that the Nazis had law. His theory is not a semantic theory about all uses of the word "law" but an interpretive theory about the consequences of taking the interpretive attitude toward his own legal system. He may, with perfect linguistic propriety, insist that the Nazis did have law. We would know what he meant. His claim would be like the judgment I mentioned earlier, that very different stages of courtesy are yet stages of the same institution, or can be seen to be if we wish. He would mean that the Nazi system can be recognized as a strand in the rope, one historical realization of the general practices and institutions from which our own legal culture also developed. It is law, that is, in what we have been calling the "preinterpretive" sense.

So once the semantic sting is drawn, we need not worry so much about the right answer to the question whether immoral legal systems really count as law. Or rather we should worry about this in a different, more substantive way. For our language and idiom are rich enough to allow a great deal of discrimination and choice in the words we pick to say what we want to say, and our choice will therefore depend on the question we are trying to answer, our audience, and the context in which we speak. We need not deny that the Nazi system was an example of law, no matter which interpretation we favor of our own law, because there is an available sense in which it plainly was law. But we have no difficulty in understanding someone who does say that Nazi law was not really law, or was law in a degenerate sense, or was less than fully law. For he is not then using "law" in that sense; he is not making that sort of preinterpretive judgment but a skeptical interpretive judgment that Nazi law lacked features crucial to flourishing legal systems whose rules and procedures do justify coercion. His judgment is now a special kind of political judgment for which his language, if the context makes this clear, is entirely appropriate. We do not understand him fully, of course, unless we know which conception of flourishing legal systems he favors. But we catch his drift; we know the direction in which he will argue if he continues.

The Flexibility of Legal Language

Semantic theories like positivism crimp our language by denying us the opportunity to use "law" in this flexible way, depending on context or point. They insist that we must choose, once and for all, between a "wide" or preinterpretive and a "narrow" or interpretive sense.[6] But this buys linguistic tidiness at much too high a price. It is perfectly true that the lawyer who says that Nazi law was no law might have put the very same point in the different way favored by positivists. He might have said that the Nazis had law, but very bad law that lacked the features of a minimally decent system. But that would have told us less of what he thinks, revealed less of his overall jurisprudential position, because it would not have signaled his view about the consequences of lacking those features. On the other hand, on some occasions this curtailment might be an advantage. It might be unnecessary and even diversionary—productive of argument irrelevant to his present purpose—for him to reveal more. In that case the alternative "positivist" formulation of his point would be preferable, and there is no reason why we should artificially limit our language to make context-sensitive choices of this kind impossible.

Context sensitivity is even more important when the

question in play is sharper, more specialized, more practical than simply one of general classification or critique of a foreign and very different legal system. Suppose the question somehow arises how a judge in the foreign system we disapprove of—call him Judge Siegfried—should decide some hard case arising there. The focus has changed because this question requires, not merely a general comparison of the foreign system with our own, but an independent interpretation of that system in some detail. We must now put ourselves in Siegfried's shoes; if we despise the system in which he adjudicates, our interpretation for him might well be a fully skeptical one. We might decide that the interpretive attitude is wholly inappropriate there, that the practice, in the shape it has reached, can never provide any justification at all, even a weak one, for state coercion. Then we will think that in every case Siegfried should simply ignore legislation and precedent altogether, if he can get away with it, or otherwise do the best he can to limit injustice through whatever means are available to him. Once again we might, but need not, put that opinion in the dramatic language that denies there is any law in Siegfried's nation at all. Whichever language we choose, the important point is the point of political morality: that nothing in the mere fact that his nation has law in the preinterpretive sense provides any litigant with any right to win what he seeks in its courts.

Suppose, however, that on further reflection this is not exactly our view. For we find something in the history of the legal practices of Siegfried's community that we think justifies some claims of legal right by some litigants in some cases before him, even though we believe these practices as a whole to be so defective that no general supportive interpretation is possible. Suppose the case in question is an ordinary contract case that seems to involve no issue of racial or political discrimination or otherwise any piece of tyranny. We might think the plaintiff in this case has a right to win just because the statutes and precedents of his jurisdiction grant him that right, a right he would not have had otherwise. Our opinion in another case might be more guarded. Suppose the case does in some way involve discriminatory or otherwise unjust legislation. The defendant is a Jew, for example, and the plaintiff has appealed to some statute that denies Jews defenses available to Aryans in contract cases. We might still think the facts just cited justify a *weak* right in the plaintiff to win, even if we want to add that this weak right is overridden, all things considered, by a competing moral right in the defendant, so that Siegfried should do all in his power—even lie about the law if this would help—to dismiss the claim.

Now make the example more complex. Suppose that from the point of view of Siegfried's jurisdiction, these are hard cases. He and his fellow lawyers disagree about what, precisely, the pertinent rules of contract law are in the first case or just how to read the discriminatory statute in the second. Now we face a new difficulty. In ordinary cases in our own legal system, we reach opinions about hard cases by asking which decision flows from the best interpretation we can give of the legal process as a whole. In our new example, however, we cannot do this, because we believe that Siegfried's legal system is too wicked to be justified in any overall interpretation. In ordinary cases our belief that people have legal rights flows from and is part of the same interpretation we use to decide what rights they have. In the new example these two issues come apart: our reasons for supposing that people have legal rights are quite special—they depend on the idea that people should be protected in relying and planning on law even in wicked places—and they survive rather than depend on our interpretive judgments of the system as a whole. An analogy will be useful in showing how these issues can come apart. When someone makes a promise that is both ill-advised and vague, two distinct questions might be asked: whether he has any obligation to keep that promise and what its content is if he does. The second is an interpretive question, which we might try to answer by looking at the promise from the point of view of the parties to it while suspending judgment on the first issue altogether.

That would be a sensible approach to take in these circumstances to Siegfried's problem. We might ask which interpretation of the contract precedents or the discriminatory statute should be deemed best by someone who, unlike us, is in general sympathy with the system, who counts it as a flourishing example of law. We might assume that Siegfried has that attitude and then ask which interpretation of his country's legal practices would put them in what we believe would be their least bad light.

Now suppose, finally, that our practical problem requires us to decide not how Siegfried *should* decide his case, but instead how he probably *will* decide it. If we assume he will treat his problem as interpretive, as we would do if a similar problem arose in our own law, our question remains interpretative rather than descriptive in any simpler sense. But the premises of our interpretative question have shifted again. Now we put ourselves more fully in Siegfried's shoes and interpret from the point of view of the full set of his political and social convictions. Our problem can shift in many other ways as well. We can interest ourselves in the legal problems not of some contemporary system we consider immoral but of an ancient or primitive legal system whose morality does not concern us. Then we would find it easier to report our conclusions as straightforward and unqualified statements about their law. We can at least try to put ourselves fully in the position of Roman officials, for example, and then declare our opinion of what Roman law was, with no temptation to add that because Roman law supported slavery it was not fully law or not really law at all. We omit the qualification because nothing in the context of our study makes it pertinent.

The context shifts again when we find our own law immoral or unjustifiable, in whole or in pertinent part. Now one of the distinctions I mentioned grows in practical importance. Do our legal practices, though morally infirm, nevertheless generate some weak political or moral rights in those who have relied on them, so that they should be enforced except when some compelling overriding moral case can be made against this? Or are these practices so wicked that they should be seen as generating no rights at all, even weak ones? We might want to use the language of law to enforce that important distinction: to say in the former case that the judge may have to disregard the law and in the latter that there is no genuine law for him to disregard. But it is the distinction that is important, not the language we choose to enforce it, and other language is available to make the same distinction if we prefer.[7]

Here, then, is another example of a jurisprudential chestnut that owes its survival, in the form in which it has been debated in classes and treatises on legal philosophy, to a misunderstanding of what legal theory should be. Semantic theories of law take the various questions we have distinguished, all of which concern wicked or otherwise defective instances of what is law in the preinterpretive sense, to be the same question: the semantic question whether the linguistic rules we share for applying "law" include or exclude such legal systems. That is a fake question because we do not share any rules of the kind it assumes. It is also a dangerous question because it diverts us from the issues of political morality, about the role and power of imperfect law and of officials who have undertaken a duty to enforce it, which are our main interest. It disarms us by withdrawing the subtle and context-sensitive distinctions the rich language of law provides. The question of wicked legal systems is not a conceptual question at all in the sense we have developed as appropriate for interpretive enterprises. It is not one but many questions, and they all arise, for legal theory, at the level where conceptions compete.

GROUNDS AND FORCE OF LAW

I am defending this suggestion about how we might describe our concept of law: for us, legal argument takes place on a plateau of rough consensus that if law exists it provides a justification for the use of collective power against individual citizens or groups. General conceptions of law, like the three I named, begin in some broad thesis about whether and why past political decisions do provide such a justification, and this thesis then provides a unifying structure for the conception as a whole. I must now consider an apparently powerful objection. Our lawyers and citizens recognize a difference between the question what the law is and the question whether judges or any other official or citizen should enforce or obey the law. They regard these as separate questions, not only when they have in mind foreign, wicked legal systems in the various ways we just noticed, but even in considering how citizens and officials in our own communities should behave. The opinion that our judges should sometimes ignore the law and try to replace it with better law is far from a stranger to law school classrooms and even political debates. It is not regarded as absurd in the special way it would be if people thought the connection between law and coercion so uncontroversial as to be conceptual in our present sense. This might seem to provide an overwhelming argument for positivist semantic theories of law in spite of the trouble I have been trying to make for them. However misleading their theories may be in other respects, Austin and Hart at least noticed and tried to explain why people do not always treat the answer to a legal question as automatically an answer to the political question about what judges should do. They said that propositions of law are in essence factual and therefore make, in themselves, no claim at all about what any official or citizen should actually do. If we reject these theories because we treat jurisprudence as interpretation rather than linguistic analysis, we must offer an alternative explanation of this distinction, and my description of the concept of law, which ties law so closely to politics, might seem a poor start.

This objection calls for an important clarification. Our concept of law is furnished, on my suggestion, by rough agreement across the field of further controversy that law provides a justification *in principle* for official coercion. There is nothing absolute in that statement of the concept. It supposes only that in a flourishing legal system the fact of law provides a case for coercion that must stand unless some exceptional counterargument is available. If even that qualified claim cannot be made—if the fact of law provides no general case that can be overridden only by special circumstance—then only a skeptical conception of that legal system is appropriate. So much belongs, on the present hypothesis, to our concept of law: it leaves the connection between law and coercion at that abstract level. Any full theory of law, however, must be much more concrete. It must say much more about the kind of exceptional circumstance that might defeat law's case for coercion even in a flourishing system, more about when, if ever, officials may properly ignore the law, and more about what residuary obligations, if any, arise when they do.

A full political theory of law, then, includes at least two main parts: it speaks both to the *grounds* of law—circumstances in which particular propositions of law should be taken to be sound or true—and to the *force* of law—the relative power of any true proposition of law to justify coercion in different sorts of exceptional circumstance. These two parts must be mutually supportive. The attitude a full theory takes up on the question how far law is commanding, and when it may or should be set aside, must match the general justification it offers for law's coercive mandate, which in turn is drawn from its views about the controversial grounds of law. A general theory of law therefore proposes a solution to a complex set of simultaneous equations. When we compare two theories, we must take into account both parts of each in judging how far they differ in their overall practical consequences.

But this complexity poses a serious practical problem. All of us, but especially lawyers, develop attitudes toward law along with the rest of our general social knowledge, unselfconsciously and as we go along, before we examine these jurisprudentially, if we ever do. We then find it very difficult to achieve the distance from our own convictions necessary to examine these systematically as a whole. We can only inspect and reform our settled views the way sailors repair a boat at sea one plank at a time, in Otto Neurath's happy image. We must hold constant certain parts of our attitudes and convictions about law, as not under present study, in order to evaluate and refine the rest. We use the distinction between grounds and force to that end.

Academic tradition enforces a certain division of labor in thinking about law. Political philosophers consider problems about the force of law, and academic lawyers and specialists in jurisprudence study issues about its grounds. Philosophies of law are in consequence usually unbalanced theories of law: they are mainly about the grounds and almost silent about the force of law. They abstract from the problem of force, that is, in order to study the problem of grounds more carefully. This is possible only because there is sufficient rough agreement about force. We disagree about the exact force law has in certain special circumstances, when there are strong competing considerations of justice. We disagree, perhaps, about what the judges in Massachusetts who were asked to enforce the Fugitive Slave Law before the American Civil War should have done. But we share a general, unspecific opinion about the force of law when such special considerations of justice are not present, when people disagree about the justice or wisdom of legislation, for example, but no one really thinks the law wicked or its authors tyrants. Our different convictions about the force of law unite in such cases. We think the law should be obeyed and enforced, and there would be very little point to treating law as an interpretive concept if we did not. So we can isolate and concentrate on the grounds of law by assuming cases that are "normal" in that way. We can ask: given the (roughly agreed) force of law in normal circumstances, how, exactly, should it be decided when some rule or principle is part of our law? The conceptions of law we shall study are answers to that question.

Now we can reply to the objection that opened this discussion. Conceptions of law, which are theories about the grounds of law, commit us to no particular or concrete claims about how citizens should behave or judges should decide cases. It remains open to anyone to say that though the law is for Elmer or Mrs. McLoughlin or the snail darter, the circumstances of these cases are special in some way such that the judge should not enforce the law. When we are for some reason anxious to remind ourselves of this feature of our concept of law, we say that the law is one thing and what judges should do about it quite another; this accounts, I think, for the immediate appeal of the positivist's slogan. But it wildly overstates this point to insist, as the positivists did, that theories about the grounds of law cannot be political at all, that they must leave entirely open the question how judges should decide actual cases. For a theory about grounds, which in itself takes up no controversial position about the force of law, must nevertheless be political in a more general and diffuse way. It does not declare what a judge should do in any particular case; but unless it is a deeply skeptical conception it must be understood as saying what judges should do in principle, unless circumstances are special in the way just noticed. Otherwise we could not treat the theory as an interpretation of law, as a conception of our concept. It would be an orphan of scholasticism, a theory whose only use is to furnish memory tests for students who match slogans like "law is the command of the sovereign" to the philosopher whose motto that was. Jurisprudence has been too much like that for too long.

It is worth noticing, finally, how this process of abstraction, which permits legal philosophers to debate about the grounds of law, abstracting from its force, also permits political philosophers to argue in the other direction, about the force of law even though they differ among themselves to some degree about its grounds. Theories of civil disobedience, and more generally of the nature and scope of citizens' duties to obey the law, are complementary to classical theories of law, because theories of civil disobedience are mainly about force and hardly about grounds at all. They ask the complement of the question of jurisprudence: "Given the sort of thing that we all accept as grounds of law—the paradigms of the day—when are citizens morally free to disobey what counts as law on those grounds?" Of course this process of abstracting from one kind of disagreement to focus on another would be unsuccessful if the parties disagreed too much about the grounds of law, if one rejected everything the other took as paradigmatic. It would make no sense to debate how far law should be obeyed if one side thought that the enactments of Parliament were the only source of law and the other side gave that power to the Bible. But if many people in any community disagreed that far about grounds—if they shared no paradigms at all—civil disobedience would be the least of their problems.

FOUR

CONVENTIONALISM

ITS STRUCTURE

"The law is the law. It is not what the judges think it is, but what it really is. Their job is to apply it, not to change it to fit their own ethics or politics." This is the view of most laymen and the anthem of the legal conservative. Read word by word, it says almost nothing, certainly nothing controversial for us. Everyone in our sample cases agreed that the law is the law and must be enforced; they disagreed only about what the law in fact was. But the slogan, however carelessly drafted, means something more than banality; it stands for an attitude that is important and open to challenge. It is this: that collective force should be trained against individuals only when some past political decision has licensed this explicitly in such a way that competent lawyers and judges will all agree about what that decision was, no matter how much they disagree about morality and politics.

The first of the three conceptions of law I introduced in the last chapter, which I called conventionalism, shares the general ambition of the popular slogan, though the interpretation it builds is more subtle in two ways. First, conventionalism explains how the content of past political decisions can be made explicit and noncontestable. It makes law depend on distinct social conventions it designates as legal conventions; in particular on conventions about which institutions should have power to make law and how. Every complex political community, conventionalism insists, has such conventions. In America it is settled by convention that law is made by statutes enacted by Congress or the state legislatures in the manner prescribed by the Constitution, and in England that decisions by the House of Lords are binding on the lower courts. Conventionalism holds that legal practice, properly understood, is a matter of respecting and enforcing these conventions, of treating their upshot, and nothing else, as law. If Elmer has a right to the inheritance according to a convention of this sort—if he has a right to it according to social conventions about who has the power to legislate and how that power is to be exercised and how doubts created by the language are to be settled—then he has a legal right to it, but not otherwise.

Second, conventionalism corrects the popular layman's view that there is always law to enforce. Law by convention is never complete, because new issues constantly arise that have not been settled one way or the other by whatever institutions have conventional authority to decide them.[1] So conventionalists add this proviso to their account of legal practice. "Judges must decide such novel cases as best they can, but by hypothesis no party has any right to win flowing from past collective decisions—no party has a *legal* right to win—because the only rights of that character are those established by convention. So the decision a judge must make in hard cases is discretionary in this strong sense: it is left open by the correct understanding of past decisions. A judge must find some other kind of justification beyond law's warrant, beyond any requirement of consistency with decisions made in the past, to support what he then does. (This might lie in abstract justice, or in the general interest, or in some other forward-looking justification.) Of course convention may convert novel decisions into legal rights for the future. Our own conventions about precedent convert any decision the highest court makes about Elmer, for example, into law for future murdering heirs. In this way the system of rules sanctioned by convention grows steadily in our legal practice."

There are obvious resemblances between conventionalism and the positivist semantic theories I discussed in Chapter 1.[2] But there is this important difference. The semantic theories argue that the description just given is realized in and enforced by the very vocabulary of law, so that it would be a kind of self-contradiction for someone to claim that the law provides rights beyond those established through mechanisms sanctioned by convention. The conventionalist conception of law, on the contrary, is interpretive: it makes no linguistic or logical claim of that kind. Instead it takes up the double-aspect, Januslike posture of any interpretation. It argues that this way of describing legal practice shows that practice in its best light and therefore offers the most illuminating account of what lawyers and judges do. It insists that this is therefore the best guide to what they should do, that it points out the right direction for continuing and developing that practice. Conventionalism does not deny that many lawyers hold rival views about the best interpretation of the practice they share. It claims that these lawyers are wrong, lacking in insight and perception, that they misconceive their own behavior. But it does not deny that they mean what they say, does not suggest that they are talking nonsense.

Conventionalism makes two postinterpretive, directive claims. The first is positive: that judges must respect the established legal conventions of their community except in rare circumstances. It insists, in other words, that they must treat as law what convention stipulates is law. Since convention in Britain establishes that acts of Parliament are law, a British judge must enforce even acts of Parliament he considers unfair or unwise. This positive part of conventionalism most plainly corresponds to the popular slogan that judges should follow the law and not make new law in its place. The second claim, which is at least equally important, is negative. It declares that there is no law—no right flowing from past political decisions—apart from the law drawn from those decisions by techniques that are themselves matters of convention, and therefore that on some issues there is no law either way. There is no law on emotional damages, for instance, if it has never been decided by any statute or precedent or other procedure specified by convention either that people have a legal right to compensation for emotional damage or that they do not. It does not follow that judges faced with such an issue must throw up their hands and send the parties from court with no decision at all. This is the sort of case in which judges must exercise the discretionary power described a moment ago, to use extralegal standards to make what conventionalism declares to be new law. Then in future cases the convention of precedent will make this new law into old law.

ITS APPEAL

The heart of any positive conception of law, like conventionalism or law as integrity, is its answer to the question why past politics is decisive of present rights. For the distinctions a conception draws between legal rights and other forms of rights and between legal arguments and other forms of argument, signal the character and limits of the justification it believes political decisions provide for state coercion. Conventionalism provides one apparently attractive answer to that question. Past political decisions justify coercion because, and therefore only when, they give fair warning by making the occasions of coercion depend on plain facts available to all rather than on fresh judgments of political morality, which different judges might make differently. This is the ideal of protected expectations. The first of the two postinterpretive claims of conventionalism plainly serves that ideal. The first claim insists that once a crisp decision has been made by a body sanctioned by convention, and the content of that decision is fixed by conventions about how such decisions should be understood, judges must respect that decision, even if they think a different one would have been fairer or wiser.

It is not so obvious that the second, negative claim of conventionalism also serves the ideal of protected expectations. But a reasonable case can be made that it does. The negative claim insists that a judge may not appeal to the law's warrant for his decision when he cannot show that conventions force him to do what he does, because the ideal is corrupted by any suggestion that past political decisions can yield rights and duties other than those dictated by convention. Suppose it is clear that convention does not dictate an answer either way in *McLoughlin:* convention requires that precedents be followed, but only so far as a new case is like the precedents in relevant facts, and no past case has decided whether damages must be awarded for emotional injury away from the accident's scene. Suppose a judge then announces, in the style of law as integrity, that the precedents do establish a right to damages because that reading of the precedents makes them in retrospect morally sounder. That is dangerous from the point of view of the popular ideal. Once it is accepted that principles can be part of the law for reasons not reflecting convention but just because they are morally appealing, then a door is opened for the more threatening idea that some principles are part of the law because of their moral appeal, even though they contradict what convention has endorsed.

Conventionalism protects the authority of convention by insisting that conventional practices establish the end as well as the beginning of the past's power over the present. It insists that the past yields no rights tenable in court, except as these are made uncontroversial by what everyone knows and expects. If convention is silent there is no law, and the force of that negative claim is exactly that judges should not then pretend that their decisions flow in some other way from what has already been decided. We should protect convention in that way, according to conventionalism, even if we think judges should sometimes, in dramatic circumstances, flout convention. Suppose the conventions of American practice make past decisions of the Supreme Court part of the law. These conventions establish that the Court's decision in *Plessy v. Ferguson* should be followed in the future until the Constitution is amended. If a conventionalist thinks that the Court should have disregarded *Plessy* in *Brown* because racial segregation is especially immoral, he will insist that the Court should have made plain to the public the exceptional nature of its decision, that it should have admitted it was changing the law for nonlegal reasons. The conventionalist conception of law, which forbids the Court to claim any law beyond convention, would force it to do just that.

Conventionalism's negative claim might also be thought to serve the popular ideal in a different way, though this depends on adding a set of claims about how judges should decide hard cases when convention has run out. The conventionalist holds, as I just said, that there is no law in cases like *McLoughlin,* and that a judge must therefore exercise a discretion to make new law, which he then applies retrospectively to the parties to the case. There is ample room in that account of the situation for the further stipulation that the judge should decide in a way that engages his own political or moral convictions as little as possible and gives as much deference as possible to institutions conventionally authorized to make law. Once it is made clear that the judge makes new law in these circumstances, as conventionalism insists, then it seems plausible that he should choose the rule he believes the actual legislature then in power would choose, or, failing that, the rule he believes best represents the will of the people as a whole.

Of course that is not as good, from the point of view we are now considering, as finding an actual past decision made by an authorized body. The judge may be mistaken in his judgment of what the legislature would have chosen, and even if he is right, this hypothetical legislative decision has not been announced in advance, so the ideal of protected expectations has in that way been compromised. But by hypothesis this is as close to serving the ideal as the judge can come. Suppose, on the other hand, that he is guided by law as integrity, which does not limit law to what convention finds in past decisions but directs him also to regard as law what morality would suggest to be the best justification of these past decisions. This judge decides *McLoughlin* by employing his own moral convictions, which is just what the popular ideal abhors. Once he is satisfied that the law as he understands it is for Mrs. McLoughlin, he will feel justified in deciding in her favor, whatever the present legislature thinks and whether or not popular morality agrees.

LEGAL CONVENTIONS

Conventionalism is a conception—an interpretation—of legal practice and tradition; its fate depends on our ability to see in our practice conventions of the kind that it considers the exclusive grounds of law. If we cannot find the special legal conventions conventionalism requires, it is defeated in both its interpretive claims and its forward-looking, post-interpretive instructions. It will not fit our practice well enough to count as an eligible interpretation, and its normative program will be empty, because it instructs us to follow conventions that do not exist. So we must begin our inspection of this conception by asking how far our legal practice can be understood as exhibiting conventions of the required sort. Even if we do find such conventions, the appeal of the conception still depends on the political ideal of protected expectations. We must ask how attractive that ideal really is, how well the conception serves it, and whether it can be served as well or better through other conceptions of law.

I begin, however, with the more immediate question whether we have the conventions conventionalism needs. It does not claim that all lawyers and judges are already conventionalists. It concedes that some actual judicial decisions and practices are very different from those a conventionalist would make or approve: these it is prepared to count as mistakes. Nevertheless it insists that legal practice as a whole can be seen as organized around important legal conventions, and this claim requires showing that the behavior of judges generally, even those who are not conventionalists, converges sufficiently to allow us to find convention in that convergence.

At first sight this project looks promising. Almost everyone in Britain and the United States who has any acquaintance with law believes that Parliament and Congress and the various state legislatures make law and that past judicial decisions must be given credit in later ones. Indeed, all this seems self-evident, for these propositions are among the central legal paradigms of our day. Moreover, for most people the law these institutions make is the law that counts in their lives. All the legal rules vital to them—the rules fixing taxation, welfare payments, labor relations, credit arrangements, and rent—were born and live in particular acts of legislation, and litigation is increasingly a matter of judges finding pertinent sections in some statute or set of administrative regulations and deciding what these mean. No doubt many fewer laymen are aware of the parallel legal practice of precedent. But most of them have some vague understanding that past judicial decisions must be respected in the future, and anyone's practical experience with litigation will confirm this sense, for the opinions of judges are stuffed with references to earlier decisions of other judges. So the crucial interpretive assumption of conventionalism, that our legal practice can sensibly be seen as structured by central and pervasive legal conventions about legislation and precedent, seems to be reflected in ordinary experience. Now take a closer look.

Assume for the moment that in the United States the Constitution, the statutes enacted by Congress and the legislatures of the several states, and past judicial decisions are, by convention, all grounds of law. According to conventionalism, an American judge is therefore obliged, by the best interpretation of the practice to which he belongs, to enforce whatever these conventions declare to be law in particular cases, whether he approves of that law or not. But in order to do this he must decide in each case what these conventions declare the law to be; in order to do this he must decide what the content of each convention really is. He must decide, for example, whether it actually follows from the assumed convention of legislation that Elmer has a right to his inheritance because of the statute of wills, or from the putative convention of precedent that Mrs. McLoughlin had a right to compensation because of past judicial decisions.

But we have already noticed that judges and lawyers very often disagree about the correct answer to questions like these. They have different theories about how statutes and past decisions should be read. The New York judges who sat in Elmer's case, for example, all agreed that they must not disobey the decision of the legislature reported in the statute of wills. But they disagreed about what this requirement actually requires when the "literal" meaning of a statute suggests a result that strikes them as odd. Judicial disagreement of this kind presents an immediate and obvious problem for conventionalism. It shows that something more must be said about what a convention is, about how much and what kind of agreement is necessary in order that a particular proposition of law can be true in virtue of a particular legal convention.

When philosophers discuss conventions, they usually have in mind very precise and limited ones. The most important recent book on convention, for instance, discusses conventions about which party should call back when a telephone call is disconnected.[3] In the imaginary society of Chapter 2, courtesy began as a set of conventions like that. People obeyed flat rules about who takes off his hat in which circumstances. But when they began to take an interpretive attitude toward their conventional practices, the situation became much more complicated. For then they disagreed about what their conventions of courtesy "really" required. And then their moral and political convictions were engaged, not in contrast to the demands of convention, but just in deciding what these demands were, properly understood.

If the leading legal institutions like legislation and precedent are conventions, they are conventions of this different, more open kind. Lawyers agree on certain abstract formulations of these conventions—they agree that legislation and precedent are, in principle, sources of law. But they take the interpretive attitude toward these abstract propositions, and their opinions about Elmer's legal rights express an interpretation rather than a direct and uncontroversial application of the institution of legislation. Two lawyers are likely to differ about the best interpretation of the practices of legislation or precedent in a particular case because their general political and moral convictions differ.

So the distinguishing claim of conventionalism, that law is limited to what has been endorsed by legal conventions, might seem ambiguous. We can expose the ambiguity by introducing some technical distinctions. We define the "extension" of an abstract convention, like courtesy or legislation or precedent, as the set of judgments or decisions that people who are parties to the convention are thereby committed to accept. Now we distinguish between the "explicit" and the "implicit" extensions of a convention. The explicit extension is the set of propositions which (almost) everyone said to be a party to the convention actually accepts as part of its extension. The implicit extension is the set of propositions that follow from the best or soundest interpretation of the convention, whether or not these form part of the explicit extension. Suppose there is a convention in some legal community that judges must give both sides an equal opportunity to state their case. Everyone agrees that this means both sides must be heard, but it is disputed whether it also means that both sides must have equal time even though the arguments of one side are more complex or require more witnesses than the other. The explicit extension of the abstract convention then includes the proposition that both sides must be heard, but it does not include either the proposition that they must have equal time or the contrary proposition that the party with the more difficult case must have more time. Everyone thinks the implicit extension includes one or the other of these latter propositions, but they disagree which, because they disagree which solution best interprets the abstract goal—on which they agree—of equality of opportunity in court.

TWO KINDS OF CONVENTIONALISM

Now we can distinguish what might seem to be two forms or versions of conventionalism. The first, which we might call "strict" conventionalism, restricts the law of a community to the explicit extention of its legal conventions like legislation and precedent. The second, call it "soft" conventionalism, insists that the law of a community includes everything within the implicit extension of these conventions. (A group of judges who were all soft conventionalists would disagree about the exact content of the law because they would disagree about the content of this implicit extention.) It makes a great difference which of these two forms of conventionalism we are to consider. Strict conventionalism would be a very restrictive conception of law for us because the explicit extensions of our putative conventions of legislation and precedent contain very little that has much practical importance in actual litigation. If we tried to describe a theory of legislation sufficiently uncontroversial to command close to universal assent among our lawyers and judges, we would be limited to something like this: if the words of a statute admit of only one meaning, no matter in what context they are uttered, and if we have no reason to doubt that this is the meaning understood by all the legislators who voted for or against the statute or abstained, and the statute so understood achieves no results not intended by all those who voted for it and would be so understood by all the members of the public to whom it is addressed, and could not be thought by any sensible person to violate any of the substantive or procedural constraints of the Constitution, or otherwise offend any widely held view about fairness or efficiency in legislation, then the propositions contained in that statute, understood in that way, are part of the community's law.

That seems a comically weak claim. But Elmer's case and the snail darter case show that we could not report a much more robust explicit extension for the convention of legislation. We could not claim, as part of the explicit extension, that if the words of a statute are clear in themselves the law contains that clear meaning, for example. That proposition has much support among lawyers, and even more among laymen, but our sample cases show that it does not command anything like universal assent among judges in the United States. Nor does the contrary proposition, that the law does not contain the clear meaning if the legislators did not intend it and would have rejected it if it had been brought to their attention.

If conventionalism is strict conventionalism, then, its positive claim offers no help to judges faced with problematical lawsuits. For strict conventionalism gives only the negative advice that judges must not pretend to be deciding such cases on legal grounds. This explains the attraction soft conventionalism has had for a recent generation of legal philosophers.[4] The positive part of soft conventionalism instructs judges to decide according to their own interpretation of the concrete requirements of legislation and precedent, even though this may be controversial, and this advice is not irrelevant in hard cases. It would be easy to demonstrate, moreover, that all our judges, including those who decided our sample cases, have really been following that advice all along.

All those judges agreed on the abstract propositions that statutes make law and that precedent decisions must be allowed some influence over later decisions. They disagreed about the implicit extension of these supposed legal conventions. The majority in the snail darter case thought that the best interpretation of the convention about statutes required them to enforce the literal meaning of the Environmental Protection Act unless it could be proved that Congress intended otherwise. So they thought the implicit extension of the convention included the proposition that the TVA dam must be halted and the snail darter saved. The minority took a different view of the convention, and their conclusions about the implicit extension were correspondingly different. They thought it included the contrary proposition that the law did not protect the fish. Since the disagreement was only about the implicit extension of conventions they all recognized at a more abstract level, they could all be said to be soft conventionalists.

Strict conventionalism must claim a "gap" in the law, which calls for the exercise of extralegal judicial discretion to make new law, whenever a statute is vague or ambiguous or otherwise troublesome and there is no further convention settling how it must be read. Or when the dimensions of a string of precedents are uncertain and lawyers disagree about their force. A soft conventionalist need not concede any gap in such cases, however. He can argue plausibly that there is a correct, if controversial, way to interpret the abstract conventions of legislation and precedent so that they decide any case that might arise. He can say that according to the correct elaboration the snail darter is saved (or abandoned) by the law or that Mrs. McLoughlin is compensated (or denied compensation). He then claims these propositions for the implicit extension of legal conventions; that is, he claims them for law on his conception and so denies any gap in the law.

Indeed, a soft conventionalist would be able to deny that there were gaps even if lawyers disagreed about these abstract conventions, even if many lawyers denied that statutes make law or that precedents exert some influence over later decisions. With a little imagination the soft conventionalist could draft some even more abstract proposition everyone does accept, which he might then elaborate in such a way as to validate a proposition of law about snail darters. If there is a consensus that the Constitution is the fundamental law, for example, he might argue that this consensus provides an abstract convention whose implicit extension includes the proposition that statutes must be enforced because the best interpretation of the Constitution requires this, even though many lawyers deny it. He could then proceed as before to argue from that intermediate proposition to some concrete conclusion about snail darters.

Suppose there is not even consensus that the Constitution is fundamental law. The soft conventionalist could search for a more abstract consensus yet. Suppose, for example, that the suggestion I made in Chapter 3 is sound: that there is widespread if tacit agreement that the ultimate point of law is to license and justify state coercion of individuals and groups. The soft conventionalist could find in that exceedingly abstract consensus a convention that judges must follow whatever conception of law best justifies coercion, and he could then argue, via the route of declaring some conception best on that standard, that this abstract convention actually includes, within its implicit extension, the proposition that precedent cases must be followed when there is no difference in moral principle between the facts presented in the precedents and those in the present case. He then announces, only somewhat out of breath, that the law guarantees compensation to Mrs. McLoughlin, whatever anyone else might think. Other lawyers and judges who were equally soft conventionalists would disagree. They would have a different view about which more concrete conception provided the best justification of coercion, and so would have a different view of the implicit extension of the abstract convention in question.

I hope it is now apparent that soft conventionalism is not really a form of conventionalism at all in the spirit of the tripartite distinction among conceptions we are now using. My initial descriptions of conventionalism, in the last chapter and earlier in this one, did not fit it, as we can now see; they fit only strict conventionalism. It is, rather, a very abstract, underdeveloped form of law as integrity. It rejects the divorce between law and politics that a conventionalist theory with the motives I described tries to secure. A so-called soft-conventionalist judge is not barred by this spurious brand of conventionalism from engaging his own controversial moral and political convictions in his decision. On the contrary, it is precisely these convictions—about the best techniques for reading a statute, about the proper place of statutes in a constitutional structure, about the connection between a constitution and the idea of law, about the soundest conception of justice—that will determine for him which elaboration of abstract convention is best and therefore what the law requires.

Nothing in soft conventionalism guarantees, or even promotes, the ideal of protected expectations, that past decisions will be relied on to justify collective force only so far as their authority and their terms are made uncontroversial by widely accepted conventions. Nor does it protect that ideal in the further ways I described, by identifying as special those cases in which there is no explicit past decision to follow. For under soft conventionalism our sample cases are all cases governed by law, and soft conventionalist judges deciding these cases would have no reason to defer to their beliefs about what the present legislature would do or what the will of the people is. On the contrary, they would have the normal reason for disregarding any belief or information on that score: that the law is the law and must be followed, no matter how unpopular it might be in the present climate of political opinion.

If conventionalism is to provide a distinct and muscular conception of law, therefore, with even remote connections to the family of popular attitudes we took it to express, then it must be strict, not soft, conventionalism. We must accept that the positive part of conventionalism—that judges must respect the explicit extension of legal conventions—cannot offer any useful advice to judges in hard cases. These will inevitably be cases in which the explicit extension of the various legal conventions contains nothing decisive either way, and the judge therefore must exercise his discretion by employing extralegal standards. But it may now be said that, so far from being a depressing conclusion, this states precisely the practical importance of conventionalism for adjudication. On this account the positive part of that conception is the huge mass of the iceberg that lies beneath the surface of legal practice. This explains why cases do not come to court when the conditions of my comically weak description of the explicit extension of our legal conventions are met, which is most of the time. In hard cases, on the other hand, the negative part holds the stage. It tells judges that when statutes are disputed and precedents are of uncertain impact, they should set aside any idea that their decision can rest on rights already established through past political acts. They should face up to their fresh legislative responsibilities candidly.

In any case it is the strict version of conventionalism that we must test as a general interpretation of our legal practice. Strict conventionalism claims that judges are liberated from legislation and precedent in hard cases because the explicit extension of these legal conventions is not sufficiently dense to decide those cases. We must ask how well this interpretive claim fits our sample cases. But we should at least notice how the new emphasis on the negative part of conventionalism deflates the hypothesis I mentioned earlier, that the negative part supports the political ideal of protected expectations by marking off cases in which that ideal cannot be satisfied. As the positive part of conventionalism shrinks in practical importance in court, because there are so few occasions for judges to rely on law as conventionalism construes this, so this particular defense of the negative part becomes weaker, for the exceptions steadily eat up the rule. If all the cases that attract attention, because they are argued in important appellate courts before public scrutiny, are occasions on which judges are scrupulous in denying that they are serving the goal of protected expectations through their decisions, this can hardly do much to reinforce the public's faith in that ideal.

DOES CONVENTIONALISM FIT OUR PRACTICE?

Convention and Consistency

I come at last to the case against conventionalism. Strict conventionalism fails as an interpretation of our legal practice even when—especially when—we emphasize its negative part. It fails for the following paradoxical reason: our judges actually pay *more* attention to so-called conventional sources of law like statutes and precedents than conventionalism allows them to do. A self-consciously strict conventionalist judge would lose interest in legislation and precedent at just the point when it became clear that the explicit extension of these supposed conventions had run out. He would then acknowledge that there was no law, and he would have no further concern for consistency with the past; he would proceed to make new law by asking what law the present legislature would make or what the people want or what would be in the community's best interests for the future.

If the judges in Elmer's case had been strict conventionalists they would have decided that case in two stages. They would first have inspected judicial practice to see whether almost all other judges were agreed either that the words of a statute must be given their "literal" meaning, even when that was not what the legislators intended, or the opposite, that the words must not be given their literal meaning in these circumstances. The judges in that case would have answered that question quickly in the negative, for obviously other judges were not all agreed in either direction. Neither Earl nor Gray could have thought that his view was part of the explicit extension of the convention of legislation because each knew that many lawyers thought the other was right. So they would immediately have turned to the second, legislative stage: they would have tried to discover which decision was more sensible or just or democratic or would otherwise better serve the community. They would not have pressed on with the kind of arguments they actually did use, probing the statute, obsessed with the question whether one decision was more consistent with its text, or spirit, or the right relation between it and the rest of law.

These latter arguments, fixed in different ways on the question of how the statute should be read, make sense only on the assumption that the law judges have an *obligation* to enforce depends on the "correct" reading even when it is controversial what that is; this is exactly the assumption conventionalism denies. Nor is Elmer's case unusual in providing this kind of counterexample. In the snail darter case the justices of the Supreme Court argued about the proper way to read the Environmental Protection Act. They disagreed whether they were obligated by the correct theory of legislation to enforce the most literal or the most sensible reading of the statute in the absence of any reliable evidence about what Congress actually intended. The judges who decided *McLoughlin* worried about the most accurate description of the principles underlying the precedent cases cited to them, although they knew that nothing in the explicit extension of any convention settled what these principles were or what weight they should be given. In *Brown* the Supreme Court argued about which scheme of justice was presupposed by the structure of the Constitution, about the place of the equal protection clause in that scheme, about the true impact of that clause on the legal power of Kansas to legislate a school system, even though each justice knew that none of this was settled by convention.

I do not mean that a self-conscious conventionalist would ignore statutes and precedents altogether once it was controversial what force these should be given. He would not treat them as sources of law past that point, but his general responsibility when he believes that law has run out is to make the best new law he can for the future, and he might be con-

cerned with past legal doctrine for special reasons bearing on
that issue. If he believes he should make new law democratically, in the spirit of the present legislature or the present
climate of popular opinion, he might turn to past decisions
as evidence of what the legislature or public is likely to think
or want, for example. But he would then be treating the past
as evidence of present attitudes and convictions, not as important for its own sake, and he would lose interest in the
past as it aged and was therefore of less evidential value.

He would very probably find better evidence of present
attitudes in his own political experience or in the popular
press than in even fairly recent statutes enacted by a legislature most of whose members are now gone. Nor would his
evidentiary interest require him to examine past doctrine,
trying to chart its place in the law as a whole, in the ob-
sessive way judges do. If it is a nice and finely balanced
question whether the statute of wills is more consistent with
traditional principles of law if it is interpreted to forbid murderers to inherit, then wrestling with that question is hardly
a sensible way of deciding what most people would now
favor. If it is a matter of delicate legal analysis what the best
interpretation of the precedents cited in *McLoughlin* would
require in that case, then any answer provides very weak
evidence about which decision would be most popular or
most beneficial for the future.

It may now be said, however, that a self-conscious conventionalist would indeed ponder over past doctrine in the
way actual judges do, not for evidence of popular opinion
but more directly, because any lawmaker must take care to
make new law consistent with old. The search for consistency, on this account, can explain why judges are so concerned with the past, with the various statutes and
precedents lying in the neighborhood of the new law they
create in hard cases. There is a point in this suggestion, but
we cannot see it unless we are careful to distinguish between
two kinds of consistency a lawmaker might seek: consistency
in strategy and consistency in principle. Anyone who makes

law must worry about consistency in strategy. He must be careful that the new rules he lays down fit well enough with rules established by others or likely to be established in the future that the total set of rules will work together and make the situation better rather than pulling in opposite directions and making it worse.

A conventionalist judge exercising his discretion to make new law must pay particular attention to this danger because his power to change existing law is very limited. Suppose that before he looks to the legal record he thinks it would be best to decide for the defendant in *McLoughlin* because it would be cheaper for the community as a whole if prospective victims insure against emotional injury than if drivers insure against causing it. But when he discovers from his review of the precedents that mothers already have a legal right to compensation for emotional injury suffered on a direct view of the accident, and therefore that drivers must already insure against causing emotional damage in those circumstances, the question of insurance costs becomes more complex. He must now ask whether, given that drivers must insure anyway, it would be more or less expensive to force potential victims to insure against emotional injury in the very special circumstances of Mrs. McLoughlin's case, and he might well decide that splitting the risk in this particular way would be so inefficient as to offset the gains from assigning this part of the risk to the victims. We have, in this simple example, a paradigm case of a legislative judgment dominated by consistency in strategy.

But consistency in strategy would not require a judge to probe the past to discover the "best" interpretation of a statute or the Constitution when this is controversial or the "correct" account of a past judicial decision when lawyers disagree how it should be read. For a statute or a past decision poses problems of consistency in strategy only when it has assigned people legal rights that a judge forming a new rule is for some reason powerless to change, rights that would work badly with the new rights he wants to create. The conventionalist judge we just imagined, who worries whether deciding against Mrs. McLoughlin would be efficient in virtue of the precedents that mothers may recover for emotional injury sustained at the scene, has no need to look for any larger underlying principle "embedded" in these precedents or to defend one controversial view about the content of these principles. His interest in the precedents is exhausted, for this purpose at least, once he is satisfied that according to his conception of law they establish only that mothers at the scene have a right to recover, and this is clear immediately and with no reflection about larger underlying principles whose nature is a matter of dispute.

Consistency in principle is a different matter. It requires that the various standards governing the state's use of coercion against its citizens be consistent in the sense that they express a single and comprehensive vision of justice. A judge who aimed at consistency in principle would indeed worry, as the judges in our sample cases did, about the principles that should be understood to justify past statutes and precedents. If he were tempted to decide against Mrs. McLoughlin, he would indeed ask himself whether any principled distinction could be drawn between her case and the case of mothers who recover for emotional damage suffered at the scene. If he were inclined to decide against Elmer, he would worry whether this decision is consistent with the position statutes occupy in our general scheme of jurisprudence, as he understands this.

But conventionalism differs from law as integrity precisely because the former rejects consistency in principle as a source of legal rights. The latter accepts it: law as integrity supposes that people have legal rights—rights that follow from past decisions of political institutions and therefore license coercion—that go beyond the explicit extension of political practices conceived as conventions. Law as integrity supposes that people are entitled to a coherent and principled extension of past political decisions even when judges profoundly disagree about what this means. Conventionalism denies this: a conventionalist judge has no reason for acknowledging consistency in principle as a judicial virtue or for dissecting ambiguous statutes or inexact precedents to try to achieve it.

Of course, if conventionalism were just the semantic theory that the phrase "legal rights" should not be used to describe rights people have in virtue of consistency in principle, then a conventionalist judge could indeed take a lively interest in that form of consistency under a different description. He could say that when explicit convention runs out, people have a moral right to what law as integrity claims as their legal rights. Then he would decide difficult lawsuits exactly as his integrity-minded brethren do. But we are studying substantive interpretations of legal practice, not semantic theories, and our present interest in conventionalism lies in its negative claim that convention exhausts the intrinsic normative power of past decisions. Conventionalism is a theory about people's legal rights in the sense we identified as crucial for jurisprudence, not a proposal about how "legal" should be used. Anyone who thinks that consistency in principle, and not merely in strategy, must be at the heart of adjudication, has rejected conventionalism, whether he realizes he has or not.

Convention and Consensus

So the very feature of our own legal practice that seemed to make conventionalism a good interpretation of legal practice—the deep, constant concern judges and lawyers show about the "correct" reading of statutes and precedents in hard cases—is actually an embarrassment to that conception. It provides a near-fatal argument against conventionalism as even a decent interpretation of our practice. But I shall offer another line of argument against conventionalism, because exposing each flaw in that conception helps point our way to a more successful one. The argument just concluded studied legal reasoning in cross-section, the details of controversy case by case. I have not yet challenged the assumption with which conventionalism begins: that whatever consensus lawyers have achieved about legislation and precedent is properly seen as a matter of *convention*. Is it? That question asks us to change our focus and consider our legal practice not in cross-section but over some stretch of time.

Assume that almost every lawyer and judge in Britain accepts that if a statute is duly enacted by Parliament with royal assent, and there can be no real doubt about what the language of the statute means, then the law is what the statute plainly says it is. They all think this "goes without saying," and they count it among their paradigms of legal argument. This assumed consensus has two possible explanations, however. Perhaps lawyers and judges accept that proposition as true by convention, which means true just because everyone else accepts it, the way chess players all accept that a king can move only one square at a time. Or perhaps lawyers and judges all accept the proposition as obviously true though not true by convention: perhaps the consensus is a consensus of independent conviction, the way we all accept that it is wrong to torture babies or to convict people we know are innocent. The difference is this. If lawyers think a particular proposition about legislation is true by convention, they will not think they need any *substantive* reason for accepting it. So any substantive attack on the proposition will be out of order within the context of adjudication, just as an attack on the wisdom of the rules of chess is out of order within a game. But if the consensus is one of conviction, then dissent, however surprising, will not be out of order in the same way, because everyone will recognize that an attack on the substantive case for the proposition is an attack on the proposition itself. The consensus will last only so long as most lawyers accept the convictions that support it.

Which explanation provides the better description of how lawyers and judges treat propositions about legislation that "go without saying"? We are unlikely to find much evidence one way or the other just by reading judicial opinions at random, for judges are unlikely to explain why they believe what everyone believes. We must look to the pattern of judicial decisions over time. If we compare settled styles of legislative interpretation or doctrines of precedent in periods separated by, say, fifty years or more, we find considerable and sometimes dramatic change. Judicial attitudes in both Britain and America have changed sharply over the last two centuries about the issue common to Elmer's case and the snail darter case: how far and in what way legislative intention is relevant in reading statutes.[5] How shall we explain such a sea change in the dominant theory of legislation?

The facts are plain enough. Practice changed in response to arguments made in the context of adjudication, as arguments about what judges should do in particular cases, not in special miniconstitutional conventions. The successful arguments were drawn from more general movements in the political and social culture and so formed a part of intellectual as well as legal history. But they did have a distinct legal life. They appeared in law school classrooms and law review articles, then as lawyers' arguments in particular cases at law, then as judicial arguments in dissenting opinions explaining why the majority opinion, reflecting the orthodoxy of the time, was unsatisfactory, then as the opinions of the majority in a growing number of cases, and then as propositions no longer mentioned because they went without saying. All these arguments assumed, throughout their long careers, that the settled practices they challenged were orthodoxies of common conviction, not ground rules of convention. Such arguments would have been powerless, even silly, if everyone thought that the practices they challenged needed no support beyond convention or that these practices constituted the game of law in the way the rules of chess constitute that game.

Of course, the rules of games do change over time. But when these rules have become accepted as a matter of convention, then a crisp distinction has necessarily taken hold between arguments *about* and arguments *within* the rules. If a world chess congress were convened to reconsider the rules for future tournaments, arguments would be made in that congress that would clearly be out of order within a game of chess. And vice versa. Perhaps chess would be more exciting and interesting if the rules were changed to allow the king to move two spaces once a game. But no one who thought so would treat the suggestion as an argument that the king can now, as the rules stand, move two steps once a game. Lawyers, on the other hand, often call for changing even settled practice in midgame. Some of the earliest arguments that legislative intentions count were made to judges in the course of lawsuits. Important changes in the doctrine of precedent were also made in midgame: judges were persuaded or persuaded themselves that they were not in fact bound by court decisions their predecessors had taken as binding. Or—what comes to the same thing—judges changed their minds about what aspects or features of past decisions they were required to follow. Once again these changes, though dramatic over time, were changes within judicial practice, in response to shifting assumptions about the point of precedent and of judicial decision more generally. They were not the result of special agreements to have a new set of conventions.

This argument does not prove that absolutely nothing is settled among American or British lawyers as a matter of genuine convention. Perhaps no political argument could persuade American judges to reject the proposition that Congress must be elected in the manner prescribed by the Constitution, as amended from time to time in accordance with its own amending provisions. Perhaps all judges do accept the authority of the Constitution as a matter of convention rather than as the upshot of sound political theory. But we can safely draw two conclusions from our discussion. First, nothing *need* be settled as a matter of convention in order for a legal system not only to exist but to flourish. The interpretive attitude needs paradigms to function effectively,

but these need not be matters of convention. It will be sufficient if the level of agreement in conviction is high enough at
any given time to allow debate over fundamental practices
like legislation and precedent to proceed in the way I described in Chapter 2, contesting discrete paradigms one by
one, like the reconstruction of Neurath's boat one plank at a
time at sea. Second, so many features of our own constitutional practices are debated one at a time in just this way,
that it is implausible to claim conventionalism as a good interpretation of the process by which our legal culture shifts
and develops over time. Conventionalism fails here as it fails
in cross-section, in explaining how particular hard cases like
our samples are debated and decided. Our judges treat the
techniques they use for interpreting statutes and measuring
precedents—even those no one challenges—not simply as
tools handed down by the traditions of their ancient craft
but as principles they assume can be justified in some deeper
political theory, and when they come to doubt this, for whatever reason, they construct theories that seem to them better.

DOES CONVENTIONALISM JUSTIFY OUR PRACTICE?

A conception of law is a general, abstract interpretation of
legal practice as a whole. It offers to show that practice in its
best light, to deploy some argument why law on that conception provides an adequate justification for coercion. We
have so far been concerned wholly with one dimension on
which any general interpretation of that sort must be tested.
It must fit our practice, and we have discovered important
reasons for believing that conventionalism does not. What
about the other dimension? If, contrary to my argument,
conventionalism did fit our legal practices, would it provide
a sound or even decent justification of them? I described,
early in this chapter, an argument that it would. This
argument appealed to what I called the ideal of protected
expectation, that collective force should be used only in ac-

cordance with standards chosen and read through procedures the community as a whole knows will be used for that purpose, procedures so widely acknowledged that they are matters of general social or professional convention. We must now ask whether that ideal is sound, and how far it actually supports conventionalism.

Fairness and Surprise

We must clear away one possible source of confusion. It might be thought that the ideal of protected expectation is a distinctly democratic ideal, because it proposes that coercion be used only when authorized by procedures to which the people have consented.[6] This appeal to democracy, however, confuses two issues: Should the people have the final say, through democratically elected institutions, about how judges decide cases? Which theory about how judges should decide cases should the people choose or approve? In both the United States and Britain, and elsewhere in democratic countries, the people have residual power to alter whatever judicial practice is in place. They can elect legislators who have the power to impose their will on judges through one means or another.[7] We are asking now for answers to the second question. Can we find some reason why these legislators should choose a conventionalist system of adjudication?

Someone might say: "The conventionalist system is best because fairness requires that people be put on notice when their plans may be interrupted by the intervention of state power, depriving them of liberty or property or opportunity. Intervention of that kind is justified only when the occasions of intervention have been announced in advance so that anyone who is listening will hear and understand. Conventions must therefore be established and followed strictly, about the manner in which such instructions are to be given and their content fixed, so that it cannot be a matter of dispute what these instructions are. Of course, no matter how explicit these conventional procedures are or how scrupulously they are used, some cases will arise, as the sample cases showed, when the instructions will be seen to be unclear or incomplete. In such cases judges will cause some surprise no matter what decision they reach, so the idea of law, which counsels against surprise, is no longer pertinent. Then the judge must do his best for the community as a whole, frankly and honestly, not pretending to 'discover' some law beneath the surface of statutes or precedents that only he can see. For the pretense hides the fact that in this case the point of law has not been served but unavoidably disserved. If we pretend there can be law when it is not clear what the law is, we will lose sight of the intimate connection between law and fair warning, and our politics will be less just in the future. Only a system candidly committed to conventionalism, which admits no law beyond convention, can provide the protection we need."

This argument assumes that reducing surprise is a valuable and important goal of political morality. Is that true? Surprise occurs when people's predictions are defeated, but this is not in general unfair, even when the defeated predictions are reasonable, that is, well supported by the antecedent balance of probabilities. It is not unfair when my horse loses, even if I was confident, with good reason, that it would win. Surprise is, of course, unfair in one special circumstance: when a prediction has been specifically encouraged by those who deliberately defeat it. If conventionalism were so singlemindedly practiced in a particular jurisdiction and so often announced and confirmed by public institutions that people were thereby entitled to rely on that style of adjudication, of course it would be unfair for some judge suddenly to abandon it. But that is not true for us, as the argument up to now has established. We are considering arguments that try to justify conventionalism on political grounds, arguments that would hold, for example, for people deciding whether to institute conventionalism on a clean slate. The suggestion that conventionalism reduces surprise must assume, then, not that surprise is unfair but that it is undesirable for some other reason: that it is inefficient, for example, or imposes unnecessary risks, or frightens people, or is otherwise not in the general interest.

But conventionalism cannot be justified on the sole ground that surprise is inefficient or undesirable in these ways, because conventionalism does not protect against surprise as well as a simpler and more straightforward theory of adjudication would. We have already noticed the sense in which conventionalism is bilateral: it insists that if no decision of some case can be found within the explicit extension of a legal convention one way or the other, the judge is obliged to make new law as best he can. No convention decides either that Mrs. McLoughlin has a right to compensation for her emotional injury or that Mr. O'Brian has a right not to be made to pay it. So neither one has a right to a decision in his or her favor, and the judge must decide the case according to whichever rule he thinks best for the future, all things considered. But if he decides for Mrs. McLoughlin, then he has intervened in Mr. O'Brian's life even though the latter was not warned that this would happen.

The political argument for conventionalism I set out a moment ago supposes that this kind of situation is inevitable, that no theory of adjudication can prevent it. It defends conventionalism as protecting people from surprise as much as possible. But if we had that aim in mind exclusively, we would choose a different theory of adjudication, which we might call "unilateral conventionalism" or just "unilateralism." Roughly, unilateralism provides that the plaintiff must win if he or she has a right to win established in the explicit extension of some legal convention, but that otherwise the defendant must win.[8] It insists that the status quo be preserved in court unless some rule within the explicit extension of a legal convention requires otherwise. So unilateralism says Mr. O'Brian must not be made to pay damages for the emotional injury he caused Mrs. McLoughlin even though the judge thinks the opposite rule would be better for the future.[9]

In one department, criminal law, Anglo-American practice is very close to unilateralism.[10] We believe that no one should be found guilty of a crime unless the statute or other piece of legislation establishing that crime is so clear that he must have known his act was criminal, or would have known if he had made any serious attempt to discover whether it was. In the United States this principle has the status of a constitutional principle, and the Supreme Court has on many occasions overturned criminal convictions because the supposed crime was too vaguely defined to give the necessary notice.[11] But our legal practice is not unilateralist in this way over the broad reaches of the private law that we have mostly been discussing in this book—judges very often decide for the plaintiff, as they did in *McLoughlin,* when according to conventionalism the plaintiff had no legal right to win.

Our practice would be very different if it were generally unilateralist. Many fewer lawsuits would be started because a plaintiff would sue only if he had a clear right to win, in which case the prospective defendant would never defend but would pay instead. People might still sue when the facts were in dispute, because each party might hope to convince the judge or jury that his view of the facts was historically correct.[12] But no cases would be started in the hope of convincing a judge to "extend" an uncontroversial rule in a controversial way, and (what is even more important) no one would ever adjust his conduct in anticipation that a court might extend a rule if for some reason his affairs were brought before it. So unilateralism is not even a remotely eligible interpretation of our legal conduct and practice.

Strict conventionalism seems more eligible than unilateralism precisely because it is bilateral. It does not stipulate that the defendant has a right to win a lawsuit whenever and just because the plaintiff does not: it insists that neither side may have a right to win. But that very fact requires a conventionalist to find a more complex political justification than the one I just described. He must argue not merely that surprise is inefficient and undesirable but that in some circumstances surprise must nevertheless be accepted because of some other, then more important, principle or policy. He must show that the bilateral structure of conventionalism effectively distinguishes between different circumstances: those in which surprise should be avoided and those in which it must, for these competing reasons, be tolerated.

Convention and Coordination

Some legal philosophers offer an argument attempting exactly that. They try to explain why surprise is generally undesirable and also when it should nevertheless be accepted. I shall present this argument in what I think is its most persuasive form.[13] "The point of conventionalism is not just to protect litigants against surprise, but instead the more complex goal, which includes this one, of achieving the social benefits of coordinated private and commercial activity. People need rules in order to live and work together efficiently, and they need to be protected when they rely on those rules. But encouraging and rewarding reliance are not always of decisive importance; it is sometimes better to leave some matter unregulated by convention in order to allow the play of independent judgment both by judges and by the public in anticipation of what judges might do. This balance between reliance and flexibility is made possible by the bilateral framework of conventionalism. Convention establishes certain procedures so that when clear rules are adopted according to these procedures, people can rely on state intervention in their behalf; they can also rely on the state not to intervene at the behest of other citizens except as these rules stipulate and can plan and coordinate their affairs accordingly. But when these procedures have left gaps, people know they have no right to rely on anything, except that if their activities do provoke litigation judges will decide their fate by constructing what is, in the judges' opinion at least, the best rule for the future."

This account of the virtues of conventionalism falls in neatly with the difference I described earlier between agreement by convention and agreement in conviction, and also with recent philosophical explanations of what a convention is.[14] A convention exists when people follow certain rules or maxims for reasons that essentially include their expectation that others will follow the same rules or maxims, and they will follow rules for that reason when they believe that on balance having some settled rule is more important than having any particular rule. The convention that when a telephone call is disconnected the person who made the call will call back and the other party will wait follows that model exactly. So do the conventions that make up rules of the road. Our reason for driving on the right in America and on the left in Britain is just our expectation that this is what others will do, coupled with our further belief that it is more important that there be a common rule than that it be one rather than the other. In the rules-of-the-road case we have no reason to think that either rule is better. But even if we did have some such reason—even if we thought it slightly more natural for right-handed people, who form the majority, to drive on the right—our reasons for wanting everyone to drive on the same side would still be much stronger.

In the contrasting situation, when there is no convention but only agreement in conviction, everyone follows the same rule but principally because he thinks it independently the best rule to follow. We all think it wrong to inflict pain gratuitously, but our reason for obeying this principle is not that others do. It may be that if others did not follow the rule we think best we would have, in that fact, a reason not to follow it ourselves. Perhaps if no one else thought it wrong to kill or steal we would be ill-advised to act on our present scruples. But that would be a case of our having a competing or countervailing reason that conflicted with our main positive reason for not killing or stealing. In the present circumstances, when most people have the same beliefs about killing we do, that fact is not our dominant reason for acting as we think we should.

Our new argument for the political virtues of conventionalism uses these distinctions to show why the line this theory draws between cases decided by law and cases calling for judicial legislation strikes the right balance between predictability and flexibility. "It is very often the case that agreement in the rules of private law is more important than what rules these are, at least within broad limits. It is desirable to have conventional procedures like legislation and precedent so that people may rely on whatever decisions are actually reached through these procedures. It might be very important, for example, that it be settled, and settled decisively, whether and when careless drivers are liable for emotional injury to people other than their immediate victims. Insurers can then fix premiums intelligently, and people can make intelligent decisions about what kind and how much insurance to buy and what risks to run. That does not mean it makes no difference to social welfare which rules we settle upon. Rules of liability are not like rules of the road. It might be more or less efficient or more or less fair to assign liability to one party or the other, and this is why it is important that the legislature or the courts, whichever first have occasion to set the rule, make the right substantive decision. But once some set of rules has been established in this way, we might well think it more important that these rules be publicly regarded as settled, so that people can plan accordingly, than that they be the best rules that could have been found; this provides a reason why courts should leave the rule untouched even when they think the wrong choice was made in the first instance."

Now suppose a unilateralist were to object that since coordination is so important in this area, convention should be allowed to occupy the whole area in the way he recommends. We should take it as settled that drivers are liable only for such damage as has been explicitly stipulated in clear statutes, so that drivers and potential victims can insure and otherwise plan their affairs accordingly. The conventionalist now has a convincing defense of his bilateralism against this objection. "Since it matters to some extent (and perhaps a good deal) which rule is chosen, we do best to use convention only to protect decisions that some responsible political institution has actually taken on the merits and to not include under that umbrella decisions by default, that is decisions no one has actually made. If a decision has been taken about liability for emotional injury one way or the other, and there can be no controversy what decision that is, then everyone should have a right that that decision be enforced until it is publicly disavowed in the same way. But if no decision has been taken either way, then the court should be free to decide on the merits, making the best decision for the future, though of course taking into account strategic consistency."

Conventionalism and Pragmatism

The defense of conventionalism we have now constructed has two parts: first, that wise adjudication consists in finding the right balance between predictability and flexibility and, second, that the right balance is secured by judges always respecting past explicit decisions of political institutions but not enforcing decisions by default in the way unilateralism does. The second part seems more vulnerable than the first. Why does that rather rigid policy secure the right balance, rather than a more sophisticated policy that could be sensitive to the competing merits of predictability and flexibility case by case? The second general conception of law I introduced in the last chapter, legal pragmatism, holds that people are never entitled to anything but the judicial decision that is, all things considered, best for the community as a whole, without regard to any past political decision. They have no right, that is, that the collective power of the state be used for them or not be used against them just in virtue of what a legislature or another court has decided in the past.

We shall shortly see that pragmatism is less radical than this description makes it seem, for it recognizes reasons of strategy why statutes should generally be enforced in accordance with their plain and intended meaning and why past judicial decisions should normally be respected in present cases. Otherwise government would lose its power to control people's behavior, and this would obviously make the community as a whole worse off. But these are only reasons of strategy, and a pragmatist believes judges should always be ready to override such reasons when he thinks that changing rules laid down in the past would be in the general interest overall, notwithstanding some limited damage to the authority of political institutions.

A society frankly committed to legal pragmatism would be different from a self-consciously conventionalist society. Suppose Mrs. McLoughlin had been at the scene of the accident; according to conventionalism she would have a legal right to recover in virtue of past decisions. A pragmatist judge might possibly decide, in such a case, to overrule these past decisions. He must be sensitive to considerations of strategy, which will include a concern for the virtues of coordination. So even if he believed that from an economic point of view the best decision would be to deny any recovery for emotional injury, he would still ask whether the role of law in encouraging reliance and coordination would be much damaged if he ignored the precedents, and, if it would, whether this loss would be made up in the gains he foresees from the change. But he might conclude that the damage to law's role would be small and the economic gains great, and so decide to award no damages.

The practical difference between the two theories of adjudication is therefore this: in a conventionalist regime judges would not think themselves free to change rules adopted pursuant to the reigning legal conventions just because on balance a different rule would be more just or efficient. In a pragmatist regime no conventions of that sort would be recognized, and though judges would normally enforce decisions made by other political institutions in the past, they would recognize no general duty to do so. In a conventionalist society someone planning his affairs would be able to count on past decisions endorsed by convention. But in a pragmatist society he would have to predict whether the judges would be likely to consider his case as one in which the virtues of predictability were less important than the substance of the law, and whether, if they thought substance more important, they would think a decision for him better or worse for the community. Pragmatism makes it somewhat harder to predict what courts will do in what, from the point of view of conventionalism, are easy cases. But pragmatism has corresponding advantages. It leaves judges free to change rules when they think changing them would at least marginally outweigh whatever mischief would be caused by the change. It also encourages the community to anticipate such changes and so achieves a good part of the benefit of change without the waste of litigation, or the expensive, uncertain, and awkward process of legislation.

Which of these two different regimes—conventionalism or pragmatism—seems likely to produce the better balance between predictability and flexibility, and therefore the most efficient structure for coordinating citizens' actions in the long run? We have no reason to think one or the other would be best for all communities at all times. Too much will depend on details of economic development, patterns of commerce, technology, ideology, kinds and levels of social conflict, and the rest. Of course, these features of a society will themselves be influenced by its dominant style of adjudication. But this makes it all the more unreasonable to suppose that any a priori argument could show that one strategy will always be the right one. We have, just in this fact, an argument that if we had to choose one of the two strategies for the indefinite future we would do better to choose pragmatism, because it is so much more adaptive. If the economic and social structure of our community develops in such a way that in retrospect it seems a conven-

tionalist strategy would have been more suitable, then pragmatism will already have brought the reigning pattern of
adjudication very close to conventionalism. For both judges
and ordinary people will have come to see that the area that
should be dominated by predictability is very large, and citizens will make their plans assuming that judges take that
view and so will not often reverse settled legal practice. But
the reverse is not true. The conventionalist system lacks the
capacity to reach anything like the flexibility of pragmatism,
because any relaxation would inevitably involve the defeat
of publicly encouraged expectation.

I do not mean to endorse pragmatism. Its merits and
faults are the subject of the next chapter. I mean only to
provide the following answer to the argument from coordination as an argument for conventionalism. If we are
tempted to choose conventionalism on the ground that it
provides an acceptable strategy for reaching the most efficient balance between certainty and flexibility, then we
should choose pragmatism, which seems a far better strategy, instead. We can summarize. In the earlier part of this
chapter I argued that conventionalism fits our legal practices
badly. I asked whether that conception would justify these
practices, by providing an attractive picture of law's point, if
it fit well. We have now seen that it would not, that we have
no reason to strain to make it fit. The failure of conventionalism as an interpretation of our law is complete: it fails on
both dimensions of interpretation.

FIVE

PRAGMATISM AND PERSONIFICATION

A SKEPTICAL CONCEPTION

Many readers must have been shocked, and therefore some delighted, by my first description of legal pragmatism in Chapter 3. I must now replace it with a more complex, but I hope still arresting, account designed to bring out the main difference between pragmatism and law as integrity. The pragmatist takes a skeptical attitude toward the assumption we are assuming is embodied in the concept of law: he denies that past political decisions in themselves provide any justification for either using or withholding the state's coercive power. He finds the necessary justification for coercion in the justice or efficiency or some other contemporary virtue of the coercive decision itself, as and when it is made by judges, and he adds that consistency with any past legislative or judicial decision does not in principle contribute to the justice or virtue of any present one. If judges are guided by this advice, he believes, then unless they make great mistakes, the coercion they direct will make the community's future brighter, liberated from the dead hand of the past and the fetish of consistency for its own sake.

Of course judges will disagree about which rule, laid down in which circumstances, would in fact be best for the future without concern for the past. They will disagree in some cases because they disagree about the likely consequences of a particular rule, and in others because they have different visions of what a good community is like. Some will think that a good community never lays down coercive rules except to enforce moral duties, and therefore that Mr. O'Brian should be made to compensate Mrs. McLoughlin if, but only if, he has a moral duty to do so. Others will think that the value of a community depends on little beyond its prosperity, so Mr. O'Brian should be forced to compensate if a practice of requiring compensation in these circumstances would increase the wealth of the community as a whole. Pragmatism as a conception of law does not stipulate which of these various visions of good community are sound or attractive. It encourages judges to decide and act on their own views. It supposes that this practice will serve the community better—bring it closer to what really is a fair and just and happy society—than any alternative program that demands consistency with decisions already made by other judges or by the legislature.

A person has a legal right, according to our abstract, "conceptual" account of legal practice, if he has a right, flowing from past political decisions, to win a lawsuit. Conventionalism offers a positive, nonskeptical theory about what legal rights people have: they have as legal rights whatever rights legal conventions extract from past political decisions. Law as integrity is also a nonskeptical theory of legal rights: it holds that people have as legal rights whatever rights are sponsored by the principles that provide the best justification of legal practice as a whole. Pragmatism, on the contrary, denies that people ever have legal rights; it takes the bracing view that they are never entitled to what would otherwise be worse for the community just because some legislature said so or a long string of judges decided other people were.

Legal rights and duties are a familiar part of our legal scene; you might therefore be surprised that anyone would propose pragmatism as an eligible interpretation of our present practice. Pragmatists have an explanation, however, of why the language of rights and duties figures in legal discourse. They argue, on pragmatic grounds, that judges must sometimes act *as if* people had legal rights, because acting that way will serve society better in the long run. The argument for this as-if strategy is straightforward enough: civilization is impossible unless the decisions of some well-defined person or group are accepted by everyone as setting public standards that will be enforced if necessary through the police power. Only legislation can establish tax rates, structure markets, fix traffic codes and systems, stipulate permissible interest rates, or decide which Georgian squares should be protected from modernization. If judges were seen to pick and choose among legislation, enforcing only those statutes they approved, this would defeat the pragmatist's goal because it would make things not better but much worse. So pragmatism may be an eligible interpretation of our legal practice after all, if it turns out that our judges declare people to have legal rights only, or mainly, when a self-consciously pragmatist judge would pretend that they did. Pragmatism might be less radical in practice than it appears to be in theory.

It was made to seem very radical by the academic lawyers I mentioned in Chapter 1, who called themselves legal "realists." Some of them took great satisfaction in provocative statements of their position: there is no such thing as law, they said, or law is only the prediction of what the courts will do or only a matter of what the judge ate for breakfast. They sometimes put these dramatic claims in the form of semantic theories: some of them said that propositions of law are synonymous with predictions of what judges will do, or are only expressions of emotion and so not really propositions at all. Realism is now out of fashion, in large part as a consequence of those silly semantic claims. Obviously propositions of law are not disguised predictions or expressions of desire. So professors of jurisprudence teach their students that legal realism was an unnecessary exaggeration of facts about legal practice better described in a less heated way. But pragmatism is an interpretive conception of law, not a semantic theory. It is, as I shall try now to show, a more powerful and persuasive conception of law than conventionalism, and a stronger challenge to law as integrity.

DOES PRAGMATISM FIT?

As-If Rights

We should begin our test of pragmatism by pursuing the question raised a moment ago. Do judges and lawyers recognize legal rights mainly in circumstances that could be explained on pragmatist grounds? We must ask what strategy a self-conscious and sophisticated pragmatist judge would adopt in pretending that people had legal rights. He would try to find the right balance between the predictability necessary to protect the valuable institutions of legislation and precedent and the flexibility necessary for himself and other judges to improve the law through what they do in court. Any general strategy for achieving this would be tentative; a pragmatist judge would stand ready to revise his practice by enlarging or contracting the scope of what he counts as legal rights as experience improved the intricate calculations on which any such strategy would depend.

He would undoubtedly, for the reasons canvassed, include in his list of as-if legal rights the rights that clear legislation purports to create. But he would not necessarily decide to honor all rights provided in all statutes. He might well exclude old statutes like those forbidding contraception, however clear and precise these might be, if they are only the relics of long-abandoned policies, if they represent no contemporary political decision and therefore serve no useful role in coordinating social behavior now.[1] He would in general recognize as as-if rights those declared by other judges in past decisions, but again he would not include all such decisions. He would think judges should retain the power to overrule past judicial decisions, if they were especially ill-advised, even when they were clear enough to provide crisp guidance to litigants. So a sound as-if strategy would produce an attenuated doctrine of respect for statutes and precedents.

But a sophisticated pragmatist might nevertheless be tempted, for reasons he would believe fully respectable, to disguise these attenuations. He might think it best sometimes to pretend that he was enforcing an old and obsolete statute or a mischievous and silly precedent when he was really ignoring it. In that case he might offer his decision as a surprising "interpretation" of the statute or precedent when it is really nothing of the kind. A thoroughgoing pragmatist would regard the question whether and how far to disguise his actual decision in this way as just another strategic question. Is the community so anxious that its judges not behave as pragmatists that this "noble lie" will help him serve its true interests better in the long run? Or will the people discover the lie and then be less ready to accept and be guided by his rulings than if he had been more open from the start? Or will it be a worse society if it has been deceived, just for that reason alone, because it is never in people's true interests to lie to them, even if they never discover the lie? This need not be an all-or-nothing decision: a pragmatist might make his conception as openly pragmatic as he dares, disguising only those elements—his doctrine of obsolescence, perhaps—that the community is not quite ready to accept.

A Case Study: Prospective Rulemaking

So a self-conscious pragmatist might well decide cases in ways, and even in words, that are familiar to us. He will have other reasons, quite apart from any strategy of the noble lie, for falling in with certain familiar practices that he might be tempted, at first look, to discard. An imaginative pragmatist judge might be tempted, for example, to divorce the question of what rule he should lay down for the future from the question of how he should decide the case before him. Suppose he notes that Elmer is likely to use the inheritance in ways that will benefit the community more than any use Goneril and Regan are likely to make of it. He will invest it while he is in jail, and use it in socially beneficial ways when he is released, while they will spend it on imported luxuries. Why not achieve a forward-looking coup: preventing future murders by declaring that in the future murderers must not be allowed to inherit, but improving social prosperity by allowing Elmer himself to win. This subtle strategy would depend on other judges following the new rule when murderers appeared before them claiming inheritances, rather than themselves deciding whether the murderer would spend the money more usefully than the residuary legatees. But our judge might be able to guarantee this by making plain that he intends the new rule to govern all future cases, and that the exception for Elmer was made possible only by the fact that no judge had laid down a similar rule before Elmer committed his crime.

But if the pragmatist judge thinks the matter through, he will in the end reject this technique of "prospective-only" rulemaking, except in very special circumstances. For he will realize that if this technique became popular, people who might benefit from new, forward-looking rules would lose their incentive to bring to court novel cases in which these new rules might be announced for the future. People litigate such cases (which is both risky and expensive) only because they believe that if they succeed in persuading some judge that a new rule would be in the public interest, that new rule will be applied retrospectively in their own favor. If they are denied that prospect they will not litigate, and the community will lose the benefits the new rules would provide.

If, on the other hand, a pragmatist judge almost invariably applies his new rules retrospectively and encourages other judges to do the same, this will achieve a further, very great benefit for their community. We noticed this benefit in discovering why conventionalism does worse in coordinating social behavior than pragmatism. If people know that a new rule will be applied retrospectively they will behave in accordance with whatever rules they imagine courts would think in the general interest, and this will provide a great part of the advantage of such rules without the need actually to enact or adjudicate them. Suppose it has never been decided whether people who accept a check they have reason to believe is forged can nevertheless collect on it. The legislature has never had occasion to speak on this matter, and the issue has never come to court. But it is clear enough to anyone dealing in checks who thinks about the matter that it is in the public interest to deny collection in those circumstances. If someone who is offered an obviously forged check believes that if the issue is litigated a court will lay down a rule denying recovery for the future and apply that rule against him, he will not take the check in the first instance, and society will have the benefit of the better rule without actually paying the costs of litigation or incurring the disadvantages of bad commercial practice before the case is litigated.

The Old Hurdle

It suddenly appears that pragmatism, so far from fitting our legal practices worse than conventionalism does, fits them better. We tested conventionalism against two perspectives on our practice: in cross-section, as an account of what particular judges do about particular cases, and over time, as a story about how legal culture develops and changes as a whole. Conventionalism failed from the latter perspective. Its picture of law as a matter of conventions—as a game with holes between the rules—gives a most distorted account of how settled practices come to be questioned and changed. Pragmatism tells a more promising story. It points out that strategies for pursuing the general interest that seem obvious in one generation will come to be questioned in another, and so will be changed naturally, from within the judicial process, not outside it. Conventionalism also failed on the first perspective. It could not explain the most prominent feature of adjudication in hard cases like our samples: the constant and relentless concern judges show for explicating the "true" force of a statute or precedent decision when that force is problematical. Does the as-if strategy of pragmatism allow a better explanation? Or does it also stumble before this hurdle?

A pragmatist judge has no direct reason for worrying, as the judges in Elmer's case worried, about the intentions of the legislators who first adopted the New York statute of wills. He thinks the only good reason for enforcing statutes whose wisdom he doubts is to protect the legislature's ability to coordinate social behavior. He therefore sees no point in trying to enforce statutory instructions that are so unclear that any reliance on them would be speculative, so vague that they cannot aid coordination in any case. In particular he sees no point in trying to discover the intentions of legislators long dead, intentions that must anyway be obscure or controversial and unavailable to the general public. He thinks it plainly better to insist that when a statute is deeply unclear it cannot be the source of as-if legal rights at all, that the right rule is whichever rule is best for the future. So the pragmatist judge will behave like Earl in Elmer's case only if he has an indirect, noble-lie reason for pretending that legislative intentions are relevant. It is most unlikely that he will see any reason of that kind. For it hardly damages the contemporary legislature's ability to work its will if judges decline to speculate about how to read cloudy rules from the dead past or what the intentions of people very different from contemporary legislators would have been if they had thought about a problem they actually ignored.

A pragmatist judge will find room in his working theory of as-if legal rights for some doctrine of precedent. People can plan their affairs with more confidence if they have more guidance about when and how the state will intervene, and the community will therefore be better off if it can reasonably look to past judicial decisions to predict future ones. But once again this justification for respecting precedent does not hold when the scope of a past decision is unclear and controversial. So a pragmatist has no direct reason to strain to discover the "true" ground of that decision by attempting to read the minds of the judges who decided it or by any other process of divination. Nor does he feel compelled to decide later cases "by analogy" to earlier ones, at least when there is room for disagreement about whether a later case is really like or unlike them.

Imagine a pragmatist judge deciding *McLoughlin*. He sets aside the question whether there is any important difference of principle between the case of a mother who suffers emotional injury watching her child hit by a car and a mother who suffers the same sort of injury seeing her child bloody in a hospital. He insists that these two cases be divorced. There is direct precedent in the first case, and he knows that sound strategy might require him to follow that precedent. There is no direct precedent in the second, so he thinks himself free to decide as he thinks best, on a fresh slate, whether or not there is any difference in principle between the two cases. Linking the two cases does not promote planning, since the link is in any case controversial, and flexibility is improved by separating them. Once again, pragmatism can be defended as providing a good fit with what judges actually do and say in hard cases only if we assume that a pragmatist would have noble-lie reasons for constructing and deferring to the best account of the principle underlying past cases in these situations. Once again, this assumption is very implausible. The public will not be outraged if it is told that precedents will be confined to their facts. The general power of precedents to guide behavior will not be much jeopardized if judges refuse to follow them when the advice they give is garbled or murky.

So pragmatism can be rescued as a good explanation for our cross-section picture of adjudication only by procrustean machinery that seems wildly inappropriate. It can be rescued only if we do not take judicial opinions at face value at all; we must treat all the judges who worry about problematical statutes and precedents as practicing some unmotivated form of deception. They must be seen as inventing new rules for the future in accordance with their convictions about what is best for society as a whole, freed from any supposed rights flowing from consistency, but presenting these for unknown reasons in the false uniform of rules dug out of the past. Pragmatism requires epicycles to survive as an eligible interpretation of our own practice, and these epicycles can be tolerated only if pragmatism is so powerful along the second dimension of legal interpretation, so attractive as a political justification for state coercion, that it merits heroic life support. Does it?

LAW WITHOUT RIGHTS

Pragmatism is a skeptical conception of law because it rejects genuine, nonstrategic legal rights. It does not reject morality, or even moral and political rights. It says that judges should follow whichever method of deciding cases will produce what they believe to be the best community for the future, and though some pragmatic lawyers would think this means a richer or happier or more powerful community, others would choose a community with fewer incidents of injustice, with a better cultural tradition and what is called a higher quality of life. Pragmatism does not rule out any theory about what makes a community better. But it does not take legal rights seriously. It rejects what other conceptions of law accept: that people can have distinctly legal rights as trumps over what would otherwise be the best future properly understood. According to pragmatism what we call legal rights are only the servants of the best future: they are instruments we construct for that purpose and have no independent force or ground.

It is possible to miss this important point about pragmatism, however, and we should be careful not to fall into the trap. Lawyers who think that judges should take a pragmatic attitude toward legal rights sometimes say the community has actually decided that they should, at least tacitly. The community has decided, that is, to delegate to judges the power to decide lawsuits in whatever way they think is in the best interests of the community as a whole and to invent working as-if theories of legal rights, including theories of legislation and precedent, with that purpose in mind. This is a bold attempt to unite pragmatism and conventionalism. It takes pragmatism to be the content of a vast, overarching convention that judges should decide cases in the pragmatist way. Since conventionalism is at best no more powerful a conception of law than pragmatism, this marriage would hardly improve the case for the latter. But in any case the marriage is a fake.

It is not true that Americans or Britons, for instance, have tacitly agreed to delegate legislative power to judges in this way. The pragmatist may say: judges decide on pragmatic grounds all the time, and the people do not revolt or call for impeachment. That begs two questions. First, it assumes that pragmatism provides the best explanation of how judges actually decide cases. We have already seen that it leaves unexplained one prominent feature of judicial practice—the attitude judges take toward statutes and precedents in hard cases—except on the awkward hypothesis that this practice is designed to deceive the public, in which case the public has not consented to it. Second, it assumes that the community believes and accepts the pragmatist explanation of how judges decide cases, and that assumption seems just wrong. Surely there is no convention that judges may adjust their views about legal rights for purely strategic reasons. On the contrary, as we began this book by noticing, most people think that judges who act in this way are usurpers.

So if we want to support pragmatism on the second, political dimension, we must accept and then exploit its central feature, its skepticism about legal rights. The pragmatist thinks judges should always do the best they can for the future, in the circumstances, unchecked by any need to respect or secure consistency in principle with what other officials have done or will do. This idea explains the exciting rhetoric of the early "realist" movement I mentioned earlier: why they said there is no such thing as law, that law is only a matter of predicting what judges will do. These supposedly extreme propositions are much better understood as provocative statements of a political position than as semantic claims. I do not say this in any triumphant way. The fact that a true pragmatist rejects the idea of legal rights is not a decisive argument against that conception. For it is not self-evident that the idea of legal rights is attractive. Or even sane.

On the contrary, it is quite easy to make that idea seem foolish. The pragmatist will pay whatever attention to the past is required by good strategy. He accepts as-if legal rights in that spirit and for reasons of strategy will make mostly the same decisions a conventionalist would make when statutes are plain or precedents crisp and decisive. He will reject what a conventionalist accepts as law only in special cases, when a statute is old and out-of-date, for example, or when a line of precedent is widely regarded as unfair or inefficient, and it is difficult to see what of value is then lost. He rejects, it is true, the very idea of consistency in principle as important for its own sake. He denies that the decision in *McLoughlin* should turn on whether any distinction in principle can be found between the case of emotional injury suffered at the scene of an accident and the same kind of injury suffered later. But why should it? He knows that mothers who suffer such damage at the scene will continue to receive compensation unless and until the legislature decides otherwise. But if he believes this a matter for regret, if he believes the decisions that established that "right" were either unjust or inefficient or both, he sees no reason why he should extend the principle underlying these decisions any further than other judges already have.

He acknowledges that if he finds against Mrs. McLoughlin the law of emotional injury will then be incoherent in principle. But he counts that no disadvantage; he denies that this is, in itself, a matter of injustice. If he thinks recovery for emotional injury is unjust, he will have made the future less unjust in the only way that counts for him: fewer people will suffer the injustice of being made to compensate for this sort of injury, which is better than more people suffering that injustice. Of course he thinks it would be better still from the point of view of justice if no one was made to compensate for emotional injury. But he may not have the power to overrule the precedents; in any case, reasons of strategy argue against this. So he does the best he can to limit the damage done by the past, in efficiency or justice, by deciding against Mrs. McLoughlin; if we object, we seem to have succumbed to a fetishism of doctrinal elegance, slavery to coherence for its own sake.[2]

It is not a good objection to his argument that different pragmatist judges will make different decisions about how best to limit past damage in hard cases. Of course they will, but in hard cases judges must make controversial judgments of political morality whichever conception of law they hold. One party or the other will almost always be in a position to complain that the judge has made a mistake, that the "right" was his, not his opponent's. Pragmatism claims to risk error at least about the right issue. If judicial divisions and controversial judgments are in any case inevitable, the pragmatist asks, why should the controversy not be about what really matters, about which decision will produce the least inefficient practice or the fewest occasions of injustice in the future? How can that goal itself be unjust? How can consistency in principle be important for its own sake, particularly when it is uncertain and controversial what consistency really requires? These are the questions we must answer if we wish to sustain legal rights against the pragmatist challenge; they are in no way easy questions, nor is this a feeble challenge. If we cannot meet it—if we cannot sustain the importance of consistency in principle against the charge of fetishism—we must reconsider the popular disdain for pragmatism as an interpretation of our legal practice. For the rationality of our practice would then be in question, and a pragmatic interpretation, with all its epicycles, might be our only shield against a terrible indictment.

THE CLAIMS OF INTEGRITY

The great classics of political philosophy are utopian. They study social justice from the point of view of people committed in advance to no government or constitution, who are free to create the ideal state from first principles. So they imagine people living in a prepolitical state of "nature" writing social contracts on blank slates. But real people in ordinary politics act within a political structure as well as on it. Politics, for us, is evolutionary rather than axiomatic; we recognize, in working toward a perfectly just state, that we already belong to a different one.

Ordinary politics shares with utopian political theory certain political ideals, the ideals of a fair political structure, a just distribution of resources and opportunities, and an equitable process of enforcing the rules and regulations that establish these. I shall call these, for brevity, the virtues of fairness, justice, and procedural due process. (These names are somewhat arbitrary; different names are often used in political philosophy, and sometimes one of the virtues I distinguish is treated as a case of another. Procedural due process is often called a kind of fairness or a kind of justice, for example. I include due process as a separate virtue because I do not believe it collapses into either of the others as I describe these, but my arguments in this and the following chapters will pay much more attention to fairness and justice, and I shall mainly ignore procedural due process.)[3] Fairness in politics is a matter of finding political procedures—methods of electing officials and making their decisions responsive to the electorate—that distribute political power in the right way. That is now generally understood, in the United States and Britain at least, to mean procedures and practices that give all citizens more or less equal influence in the decisions that govern them. Justice, on the contrary, is concerned with the decisions that the standing political institutions, whether or not they have been chosen fairly, ought to make. If we accept justice as a political virtue we want our legislators and other officials to distribute material resources and protect civil liberties so as to secure a morally defensible outcome. Procedural due process is a matter of the right procedures for judging whether some citizen has violated laws laid down by the political procedures;[4] if we accept it as a virtue, we want courts and similar institutions to use procedures of evidence, discovery, and review that promise the right level of accuracy and otherwise treat people accused of violation as people in that position ought to be treated.

These quick distinctions are prologue to a crucial point.[5] Ordinary politics adds to these familiar ideals a further one that has no distinct place in utopian axiomatic theory. This is sometimes described in the catch phrase that we must treat like cases alike. It requires government to speak with one voice, to act in a principled and coherent manner toward all its citizens, to extend to everyone the substantive standards of justice or fairness it uses for some. If government relies on principles of majoritarian democracy to justify its decisions about who may vote, it must respect the same principles in designing voting districts.[6] If it appeals to the principle that people have a right to compensation from those who injure them carelessly, as its reason why manufacturers are liable for defective automobiles, it must give full effect to that principle in deciding whether accountants are liable for their mistakes as well.[7] If government says that a unanimous verdict is necessary for criminal conviction because special moral harm is suffered when someone is unjustly convicted of a crime, then it must take that special moral harm into account in considering, for example, the admissibility of confessions under various circumstances.[8]

This particular demand of political morality is not in fact well described in the catch phrase that we must treat like cases alike.[9] I give it a grander title: it is the virtue of political integrity. I choose that name to show its connection to a parallel ideal of personal morality. We want our neighbors to behave, in their day-to-day dealings with us, in the way we think right. But we know that people disagree to some extent about the right principles of behavior, so we distinguish that requirement from the different (and weaker) requirement that they act in important matters with integrity, that is, according to convictions that inform and shape their lives as a whole, rather than capriciously or whimsically. The practical importance of this latter requirement among people who know they disagree about justice is evident. Integrity becomes a political ideal when we make the same demand of the state or community taken to be a moral agent, when we insist that the state act on a single, coherent set of principles even when its citizens are divided about what the right principles of justice and fairness really are. We assume, in both the individual and the political cases, that we can recognize other people's acts as expressing a conception of fairness or justice or decency even when we do not endorse that conception ourselves. This ability is an important part of our more general ability to treat others with respect, and it is therefore a prerequisite of civilization.

I began this discussion of ordinary politics, and of its departments of political virtue, in the shadow of the pragmatist's challenge to the idea of legal rights. If we accept integrity as a distinct political virtue beside justice and fairness, then we have a general, nonstrategic argument for recognizing such rights. The integrity of a community's conception of fairness requires that the political principles necessary to justify the legislature's assumed authority be given full effect in deciding what a statute it has enacted means. The integrity of a community's conception of justice demands that the moral principles necessary to justify the substance of its legislature's decisions be recognized in the rest of the law. The integrity of its conception of procedural due process insists that trial procedures that are counted as striking the right balance between accuracy and efficiency in enforcing some part of the law be recognized throughout, taking into account differences in the kind and degree of moral harm an inaccurate verdict imposes. These several claims justify a commitment to consistency in principle valued for its own sake. They suggest what I shall argue: that integrity rather than some superstition of elegance is the life of law as we know it.

It will be useful to divide the claims of integrity into two more practical principles. The first is the principle of integrity in legislation, which asks those who create law by legislation to keep that law coherent in principle. The second is the principle of integrity in adjudication: it asks those responsible for deciding what the law is to see and enforce it as coherent in that way. The second principle explains how and why the past must be allowed some special power of its own in court, contrary to the pragmatist's claim that it must not. It explains why judges must conceive the body of law they administer as a whole rather than as a set of discrete decisions that they are free to make or amend one by one, with nothing but a strategic interest in the rest.

COMMUNITY PERSONIFIED

The adjudicative principle of integrity furnishes our third conception of law. We shall study law as integrity, and I shall commend it, in the chapters that follow. Many readers will be troubled, however, by one aspect of political integrity, which we might well take up in advance. Political integrity assumes a particularly deep personification of the community or state. It supposes that the community as a whole can be committed to principles of fairness or justice or procedural due process in some way analogous to the way particular people can be committed to convictions or ideals or projects, and this will strike many people as bad metaphysics.

We personify groups in ordinary conversation. We speak casually of the interests or goals of the working class, for example. But these expressions are often only convenient figures of speech, shorthand ways of talking about the average or representative members of a community. My account of political integrity takes the personification much more seriously, as if a political community really were some special kind of entity distinct from the actual people who are its citizens. Worse, it attributes moral agency and responsibility to this distinct entity. For when I speak of the community being faithful to its own principles I do not mean its conventional or popular morality, the beliefs and convictions of most citizens. I mean that the community has its own principles it can itself honor or dishonor, that it can act in good or bad faith, with integrity or hypocritically, just as people can. Can I really mean to personify the community in this vivid way? Do I really mean to attribute to the state or community principles that are not simply those of most of its members?

Two Arguments about Group Responsibility

Yes. But I must be clearer what kind of personification this is. I do not intend now to resurrect the metaphysical theory I said in Chapter 2 that we do not need. I do not suppose that the ultimate mental component of the universe is some spooky, all-embracing mind that is more real than flesh-and-blood people, nor that we should treat the state or community as a real person with a distinct interest or point of view or even welfare of its own, nor that we can ask the range of questions about a state's principles—for example whether it accepted them freely or was misled or misunderstands them—that we can ask about aspects of a real person's moral life. I mean only to endorse a complex, two-stage way of reasoning about the responsibilities of officials and citizens that finds a natural expression in the personification of community and cannot be reproduced by a reductive translation into claims about officials and citizens one by one.

Suppose an automobile manufacturer produces defective cars that cause terrible accidents in which hundreds of people are killed. Set aside the question of law, whether the corporation is guilty of a crime or legally responsible to compensate victims or their families. And the question of efficiency, whether imposing such liability would reduce accidents or contribute to a more efficient use of resources. We are interested now in the question of moral responsibility: What sense does it make to say that the corporation is morally responsible to compensate victims from the corporate treasury, with the consequence that its shareholders must bear the loss? We might proceed in the following way. We bring to bear on the various officers and employees and shareholders and others associated with the corporation our ordinary standards of personal responsibility. We ask of each person whether he did anything he should not have done such that he should be blamed for the deaths that followed, or whether he contributed to the accidents in such a way that, blameworthy or not, he should bear some portion of the damage or loss.

We might find someone to blame. Perhaps some employee neglected an inspection, perhaps some officer approved a design he should have known was faulty. Maybe the chief executive officer or some member of the board of directors had reason to doubt the standing procedures for reviewing design and failed to improve them. But we might not find anyone to blame. Perhaps no one acted in a way we can judge wrong by personal standards of conduct. We would then be unlikely to find any non-question-begging moral argument why a small shareholder should bear any part of the loss himself. A shareholder is no part of the causal chain leading to the accidents; he added no capital to the corporation's resources just by buying its stock on the exchange.

Someone might say: it is a principle of personal morality that if someone shares in the gains of another's action he must also share the responsibility for wrongs that other person does. This suggestion begs the question, however, for we still lack any reason to suppose that any wrong has been done. That is, our problem is not one of vicarious liability, of finding some reason why a shareholder should share some other person's or group's primary responsibility; it is rather that we can find no one else who is primarily responsible and in whose responsibility he might share.[10]

We might, however, have used a different method of argument. In that different method we frame our question in the first instance as a question about corporate responsibility. We suppose that the corporation must itself be treated as a moral agent, and then we proceed by applying facsimiles of our principles about individual fault and responsibility to *it*. We might say that anyone who has had full control over the manufacture of a defective product has a responsibility to compensate those injured by it. No individual employee or shareholder has had that control, but the corporation has. Then we ask, as a further and subsidiary question, how the various members and agents of the corporation should be seen to share in that fault or responsibility. But we approach that independent question using a different set of principles, among which might be found the principle just mentioned, that any member of the corporation who is entitled to share in its profits must share in its responsibilities as well. That principle would justify paying compensation from the corporate treasury, and thus from the account of shareholders, rather than, for example, deducting it from the wages of employees who actually played a causal part in the unfortunate story.

If we decided through the first of these two methods, which begins with moral assessment of each individual's record one by one, that each shareholder was indeed responsible for a share of the loss, then we might well report our conclusion in the language of personification. We might say that the corporation was liable, meaning only to summarize in a convenient way the responsibilities we ascribed to each of the shareholders. But this personification would be idle; it played no role in our argument and only decorated our conclusions. If, on the other hand, we reached the same conclusion through the second method, which begins in considering the responsibility of the institution as a whole, then the personification would have been not idle but working. For our conclusions about the group would then be in every way prior to any conclusions about individuals; we would have relied on principles of responsibility that draw their sense from a practice or way of thinking to which the personification is indispensable.

Indeed through the second method (but not the first) we might come to some decision about the responsibilities of the group or institution while still in doubt (or disagreeing among ourselves) about the consequent liabilities or responsibilities of the relevant individuals. The personification furnishes not only a necessary step on the way to judgments about particular people, but a plateau we can occupy to consider these judgments. None of this means that in the second method, when we begin with the group, we are interested in group responsibility for its own sake. There would be no point to developing or applying principles of group responsibility if we did not assume that these were connected to judgments about how real people must now act. But we can separate the two issues, reserving the question of individual responsibility as one to be taken up only after we have decided whether the group as a whole has met the standards appropriate for it. The personification is deep: it consists in taking the corporation seriously as a moral agent. But it is still a personification not a discovery, because we recognize that the community has no independent metaphysical existence, that it is itself a creature of the practices of thought and language in which it figures.

Personification at Work

The idea of political integrity personifies the community in the second way, as a working personification, because it assumes that the community can adopt and express and be faithful or unfaithful to principles of its own, distinct from those of any of its officials or citizens as individuals. Of course we must say what that means by describing how a community adopts or betrays a principle, and this will be part of constructing our conception of law as integrity. But we should take this chance to notice how the deep personification figures in ordinary ways of thought that are quite independent of law. Consider the phenomenon of communal electoral responsibility. At the height of the Watergate scandal bumper stickers appeared that read, "Don't blame me; I'm from Massachusetts." They did not say, "Don't blame me; I voted against Nixon," and the difference is important. People asked exoneration from a mistake made by a group to which they belonged—the nation—not in individual innocence but in membership of a different and more immediate community that had acted well, a state that had not voted for a dishonest president.

There are more important examples of group responsibility. Germans not alive when Nazis ruled their country feel shame and a sense of obligation toward Jews; white Americans who inherited nothing from slaveholders feel an indeterminate responsibility to blacks who never wore chains. Some of us are puzzled by this phenomenon, because it seems incompatible with another idea we cherish, which is that people must not be blamed for acts over which they had no control, nor held responsible for unfair gains when they have gained nothing themselves. So philosophers have struggled to reconcile these conflicting ideas, by finding ways in which all white Americans have profited from past discrimination against blacks, for example. These arguments ring hollow because they misunderstand the mode of responsibility in question. They suppose that collective responsibility can be assigned only through something like the first method we noticed in the accident example. In fact, the convictions these arguments try to explain are the product of the second approach, of a deep personification of political and social community, and that is why they do not challenge the Kantian thesis that no one is to blame for what he has not himself done. Of course it would be absurd to blame contemporary Germans for what the Nazis did; but, because this judgment lies at the end of a different and independent mode of argument, it is not absurd to suppose that contemporary Germans have special responsibilities because the Nazis were Germans too.

These are examples of collective responsibility for past wrongs. We find other and even more important examples of working personification in the logic of individual political rights against the state. We argue about whether everyone has a right that the state protect him from assaults by other citizens, or provide him a decent level of medical care, or guarantee his security from attack by foreign powers. We agree or disagree before we form any concrete opinions about which institutions or officials must act and what they must do in consequence of whatever rights we declare people have. When we say that individuals have a right to be protected against assault, we do not mean that this protection must be achieved through some particular scheme we already have in mind. But only that the community as a whole has a duty to provide adequate protection in some way. We can debate the scope of the community's duty and leave for separate consideration the different issue of which arrangement of official duties would best acquit the communal responsibility.[11]

My next and last example draws on our most abstract and widely shared convictions about political justice and fairness. We believe political officials have responsibilities we could not defend if we had to build these directly from the ordinary requirements of individual personal morality most of us accept for ourselves and others in nonpolitical life. We think they have a special and complex responsibility of impartiality among the members of the community and of partiality toward them in dealings with strangers. That is quite different from the responsibility each of us accepts as an individual. We each claim a personal point of view, ambitions and attachments of our own we are at liberty to pursue, free from the claims of others to equal attention, concern, and resource. We insist on an area of personal moral sovereignty within which each of us may prefer the interests of family and friends and devote himself to projects that are selfish, however grand. Any conception of justice in personal behavior, any theory about how the just person behaves toward others, will limit that area of personal sovereignty, but no conception acceptable to most of us will eliminate it entirely.

We allow officials acting in their official capacity no such area at all. They must, we say, treat all members of their community as equals, and the individual's normal latitude for self-preference is called corruption in their case. We cannot establish this special responsibility of officials merely by applying our ordinary convictions about individual responsibility to the circumstances of their case. Some officials have very great power. But so do many private individuals, and we do not believe that a citizen's sphere of personal freedom necessarily shrinks as his power and influence grow. (Thomas Nagel reminds us, in his article about the responsibility of political officials, that even giants have personal lives.)[12] We apply the strictest standards of impartiality even to officials whose power is relatively slight and substantially less than that of many private citizens; we have no sense that an official's duty of equal concern wanes as his power diminishes.

Someone may say that an official lies under a special responsibility of impartiality because he has accepted his office subject to that understanding, so these responsibilities are drawn from ordinary morality after all, from the morality of keeping promises. But this reverses the order of argument most of us would endorse: we share an understanding that our officials must treat all members of the community they govern as equals because we believe they should behave that way, not the other way around. We cannot explain the special responsibilities of political office, therefore, if we try to build these directly from ordinary principles of private morality. We need an idea that cannot be found there: that the community as a whole has obligations of impartiality toward its members, and that officials act as agents for the community in acquitting that responsibility. Here, as in the case of the corporation, we need to treat group responsibility as logically prior to the responsibilities of officials one by one.

These various examples of working personification of the community fit together as partners in a general system of thought. Once we accept that our officials act in the name of a community of which we are all members, bearing a responsibility we therefore share, then this reinforces and sustains the character of collective guilt, our sense that we must feel shame as well as outrage when they act unjustly. The practical principles of integrity I cited—integrity in legislation and in adjudication—take their places in this system of ideas. The adjudicative principle is our special interest because it provides a conception of law antagonistic to pragmatism. If that principle can be sustained, pragmatism must be rejected.

SIX

INTEGRITY

AGENDA

We have two principles of political integrity: a legislative
principle, which asks lawmakers to try to make the total set
of laws morally coherent, and an adjudicative principle,
which instructs that the law be seen as coherent in that way,
so far as possible. Our main concern is with the adjudicative
principle, but not yet. In this chapter I argue that the legislative principle is so much part of our political practice that no
competent interpretation of that practice can ignore it. We
measure that claim on the two dimensions now familiar. We
ask whether the assumption, that integrity is a distinct ideal
of politics, fits our politics, and then whether it honors our
politics. If the legislative principle of integrity is impressive
on both these dimensions, then the case for the adjudicative
principle, and for the conception of law it supports, will already be well begun.

DOES INTEGRITY FIT?

Integrity and Compromise

Integrity would not be needed as a distinct political virtue in
a utopian state. Coherence would be guaranteed because officials would always do what was perfectly just and fair. In
ordinary politics, however, we must treat integrity as an independent ideal if we accept it at all, because it can conflict
with these other ideals. It can require us to support legislation we believe would be inappropriate in the perfectly just

and fair society and to recognize rights we do not believe people would have there. We saw an example of this conflict in the last chapter. A judge deciding *McLoughlin* might think it unjust to require compensation for any emotional injury. But if he accepts integrity and knows that some victims of emotional injury have already been given a right to compensation, he will have a reason for deciding in favor of Mrs. McLoughlin nevertheless.

Conflicts among ideals are common in politics. Even if we rejected integrity and based our political activity only on fairness, justice, and procedural due process, we would find the first two virtues sometimes pulling in opposite directions. Some philosophers deny the possibility of any fundamental conflict between justice and fairness because they believe that one of these virtues in the end derives from the other. Some say that justice has no meaning apart from fairness, that in politics, as in roulette, whatever happens through fair procedures is just. That is the extreme of the idea called justice as fairness.[1] Others think that the only test of fairness in politics is the test of result, that no procedure is fair unless it is likely to produce political decisions that meet some independent test of justice. That is the opposite extreme, of fairness as justice.[2] Most political philosophers—and I think most people—take the intermediate view that fairness and justice are to some degree independent of one another, so that fair institutions sometimes produce unjust decisions and unfair institutions just ones.

If that is so, then in ordinary politics we must sometimes choose between the two virtues in deciding which political programs to support. We might think that majority rule is the fairest workable decision procedure in politics, but we know that the majority will sometimes, perhaps often, make unjust decisions about the rights of individuals.[3] Should we tamper with majority rule by giving special voting strength to one economic group, beyond what its numbers would justify, because we fear that straight majority rule would assign it less than its just share?[4] Should we accept constitutional constraints on democratic power to prevent the majority from limiting freedom of speech or other important liberties?[5] These difficult questions arise because fairness and justice sometimes conflict. If we believe that integrity is a third and independent ideal, at least when people disagree about one of the first two, then we may well think that fairness or justice must sometimes be sacrificed to integrity.

Internal Compromises

I shall try to show that our political practices accept integrity as a distinct virtue, and I begin with what I hope will strike you as a puzzle. Here are my background assumptions. We all believe in political fairness: we accept that each person or group in the community should have a roughly equal share of control over the decisions made by Parliament or Congress or the state legislature. We know that different people hold different views about moral issues that they all treat as of great importance. It would seem to follow from our convictions about fairness that legislation on these moral issues should be a matter not just of enforcing the will of the numerical majority, as if its view were unanimous, but of trades and compromises so that each body of opinion is represented, to a degree that matches its numbers, in the final result. We could achieve this compromise in a Solomonic way. Do the people of North Dakota disagree whether justice requires compensation for product defects that manufacturers could not reasonably have prevented? Then why should their legislature not impose this "strict" liability on manufacturers of automobiles but not on manufacturers of washing machines? Do the people of Alabama disagree about the morality of racial discrimination? Why should their legislature not forbid racial discrimination on buses but permit it in restaurants? Do the British divide on the morality of abortion? Why should Parliament not make abortion criminal for pregnant women who were born in even years but not for those born in odd ones? This Solomonic model treats a community's public order as a kind of commodity to be distributed in accordance with distributive justice, a cake to be divided fairly by assigning each group a proper slice.

Most of us, I think, would be dismayed by "checkerboard" laws that treat similar accidents or occasions of racial discrimination or abortion differently on arbitrary grounds.[6] Of course we do accept arbitrary distinctions about some matters: zoning, for example. We accept that shops or factories be forbidden in some zones and not others and that parking be prohibited on alternate sides of the same street on alternate days. But we reject a division between parties of opinion when matters of principle are at stake. We follow a different model: that each point of view must be allowed a voice in the process of deliberation but that the collective decision must nevertheless aim to settle on some coherent principle whose influence then extends to the natural limits of its authority.[7] If there must be compromise because people are divided about justice, then the compromise must be external, not internal; it must be compromise about which scheme of justice to adopt rather than a compromised scheme of justice.

But there lies the puzzle. Why should we turn our back on checkerboard solutions as we do? Why should we not embrace them as a general strategy for legislation whenever the community is divided over some issue of principle? Why is this strategy not fair and reasonable, reflecting political maturity and a finer sense of the political art than other communities have managed to achieve? What is the special defect we find in checkerboard solutions? It cannot be a failure in fairness (in our sense of a fair distribution of political power) because checkerboard laws are by hypothesis fairer than either of the two alternatives. Allowing each of two groups to choose some part of the law of abortion, in proportion to their numbers, is fairer (in our sense) than the winner-take-all scheme our instincts prefer, which denies many people any influence at all over an issue they think desperately important.

Can we defend these instincts on grounds of justice? Justice is a matter of outcomes: a political decision causes injustice, however fair the procedures that produced it, when it denies people some resource, liberty, or opportunity that the best theories of justice entitle them to have. Can we oppose the checkerboard strategy on the ground that it would produce more instances of injustice than it would prevent? We must be careful not to confuse two issues here. Of course any single checkerboard solution of an important issue will produce more instances of injustice than one of the alternatives and fewer than the other. The community can unite over that proposition while disagreeing about which alternative would be more and which less just. Someone who believes that abortion is murder will think that the checkerboard abortion statute produces more injustice than outright prohibition and less than outright license; someone who believes women have a right to abortion reverses these judgments. So both have a reason of justice for preferring some other solution to the checkerboard one. Our question is whether we collectively have a reason of justice for not agreeing, in *advance* of these particular disagreements, to the checkerboard strategy for resolving them. We have a reason of fairness, as we just noticed, for that checkerboard strategy, and if we have no reason of justice against it, our present practice needs a justification we have not yet secured.

We are looking for a reason of justice we all share for rejecting the checkerboard strategy in advance even if we would each prefer a checkerboard solution on some occasions to the one that will be imposed if the strategy is rejected. Shall we just say that a checkerboard solution is unjust by definition because it treats different people differently for no good reason, and justice requires treating like cases alike? This suggestion seems in the right neighborhood, for if checkerboard solutions do have a defect, it must lie in their distinctive feature, that they treat people differently when no principle can justify the distinction. But we cannot explain why this is always objectionable, so long as we remain on the plane of justice as I have defined it. For in the circumstances of ordinary politics the checkerboard strategy will prevent instances of injustice that would otherwise occur, and we cannot say that justice requires not eliminating any injustice unless we can eliminate all.

Suppose we can rescue only some prisoners of tyranny; justice hardly requires rescuing none even when only luck, not any principle, will decide whom we save and whom we leave to torture. Rejecting a checkerboard solution seems perverse in the same way when the alternative will be the general triumph of the principle we oppose. The internal compromise would have rescued some, chosen arbitrarily, from an injustice that others will be left to suffer, but the alternative would have been to rescue none. Someone may now say: nevertheless, though checkerboard solutions may be desirable for that reason on some occasions, we do better to reject their use out of hand in advance, because we have reason to think that in the long run more discrete injustice will be created than avoided through these solutions. But that would be a plausible prediction only for members of a constant and self-conscious majority of opinion, and if such a majority existed so would a self-conscious minority that would have the opposite opinion. So we have no hope of finding here a common reason for rejecting checkerboard solutions.

But perhaps we are looking in the wrong direction. Perhaps our common reason is not any prediction about the number of cases of injustice that the checkerboard strategy would produce or prevent, but our conviction that no one should actively engage in producing what he believes to be injustice. We might say: no checkerboard statute could be enacted unless a majority of the legislators voted for provisions they thought unjust. But this objection begs the main question. If each member of the legislature who votes for a checkerboard compromise does so not because he himself has no principles but because he wants to give the maximum possible effect to the principles he thinks right, then how has anyone behaved irresponsibly? Even if we were to accept that no legislator should vote for the compromise, this would not explain why we should reject the compromise as an *outcome*. For we can easily imagine a legislative structure that would produce compromise statutes mechanically, as a function of the different opinions about strict liability or racial discrimination or abortion among the various legislators, without any legislator being asked or required to vote for the compromise as a package. It might be understood in advance that the proportion of women who would be permitted an abortion would be fixed by the ratio of votes for permitting all abortions to total votes. If we still object, then our objection cannot be based on the principle that no individual should vote against his conscience.

So it seems we have no reason of justice for rejecting the checkerboard strategy in advance, and strong reasons of fairness for endorsing it. Yet our instincts condemn it. Indeed many of us, to different degrees in different situations, would reject the checkerboard solution not only in general and in advance, but even in particular cases if it were available as a possibility. We would prefer either of the alternative solutions to the checkerboard compromise. Even if I thought strict liability for accidents wrong in principle, I would prefer that manufacturers of both washing machines and automobiles be held to that standard than that only one of them be. I would rank the checkerboard solution not intermediate between the other two but third, below both, and so would many other people. In some cases this instinct might be explained as reflecting the unworkability or inefficiency of a particular checkerboard solution. But many of those we can imagine, like the abortion solution, are not particularly inefficient, and in any case our instinct suggests that these compromises are wrong, not merely impractical.

Not everyone would condemn every checkerboard solution. People who believe very strongly that abortion is always murder, for example, may indeed think that the checkerboard abortion statute is better than a wholly permissive law. They think that fewer murders are better than more no matter how incoherent the compromise that produces fewer. If they rank the checkerboard solution last in other circumstances, in the case of strict liability for manufacturers, for example, they nevertheless believe that internal compromise is wrong, though for reasons that yield when the substantive issue is very grave. So they share the instinct that needs explaining. This instinct is likely to be at work, moreover, in other, more complicated rankings they might make. Suppose you think abortion is murder and that it makes no difference whether the pregnancy is the result of rape. Would you not think a statute prohibiting abortion except in the case of rape distinctly better than a statute prohibiting abortion except to women born in one specified decade each century? At least if you had no reason to think either would in fact allow more abortions? You see the first of these statutes as a solution that gives effect to two recognizable principles of justice, ordered in a certain way, even though you reject one of the principles.[8] You cannot treat the second that way; it simply affirms for some people a principle it denies to others. So for many of us, our preferences in particular cases pose the same puzzle as our more comprehensive rejection of the checkerboard solution as a general strategy for resolving differences over principle. We cannot explain our hostility to internal compromise by appeal to principles of either fairness or justice as we have defined those virtues.

Astronomers postulated Neptune before they discovered it. They knew that only another planet, whose orbit lay beyond those already recognized, could explain the behavior of the nearer planets. Our instincts about internal compromise suggest another political ideal standing beside justice and fairness. Integrity is our Neptune. The most natural explanation of why we oppose checkerboard statutes appeals to that ideal: we say that a state that adopts these internal compromises is acting in an unprincipled way, even though no single official who voted for or enforces the compromise has done anything which, judging his individual actions by the

ordinary standards of personal morality, he ought not to
have done. The state lacks integrity because it must endorse
principles to justify part of what it has done that it must reject to justify the rest. That explanation distinguishes integrity from the perverse consistency of someone who refuses to
rescue some prisoners because he cannot save all. If he had
saved some, selected arbitrarily, he would not have violated
any principle he needs to justify other acts. But a state does
act that way when it accepts a Solomonic checkerboard solution; it is inconsistency in principle among the acts of the
state personified that integrity condemns.

Integrity and the Constitution

• Checkerboard statutes are the most dramatic violations of
the ideal of integrity, and they are not unknown to our political history. The United States Constitution contained at its
birth particularly hideous examples: the problem of slavery
was compromised by counting three-fifths of a state's slaves
in determining the state's representation in Congress and
forbidding Congress to limit the original states' power to
import slaves, but only before 1808.[9] Integrity is flouted not
only in specific compromises of that character, however, but
whenever a community enacts and enforces different laws
each of which is coherent in itself, but which cannot be defended together as expressing a coherent ranking of different
principles of justice or fairness or procedural due process. We
know that our own legal structure constantly violates integrity in this less dramatic way. We cannot bring all the various statutory and common-law rules our judges enforce
under a single coherent scheme of principle. (I discuss some
consequences of that fact in Chapter 11.) But we nevertheless accept integrity as a political ideal. It is part of our collective political morality that such compromises are wrong,
that the community as a whole and not just individual officials one by one must act in a principled way.

    In the United States this ideal is to some extent a matter

of constitutional law, for the equal protection clause of the Fourteenth Amendment is now understood to outlaw internal compromises over important matters of principle. The Supreme Court relies on the language of equal protection to strike down state legislation that recognizes fundamental rights for some and not others. The Constitution requires states to extend to all citizens certain rights—the right to free speech, for example—but leaves them free to recognize other, nonconstitutionally required rights if they wish. If a state accepts one of these nonconstitutionally required rights for one class of citizens, however, it must do so for all.[10] The Supreme Court's controversial 1973 abortion ruling, for example, allows states to prohibit abortions altogether in the last trimester of pregnancy.[11] But the Court would not allow a state to prohibit an abortion in the last trimester only to women born in even years.

This connection between integrity and the rhetoric of equal protection is revealing. We insist on integrity because we believe that internal compromises would deny what is often called "equality before the law" and sometimes "formal equality." It has become fashionable to say that this kind of equality is unimportant because it offers little protection against tyranny. This denigration assumes, however, that formal equality is only a matter of enforcing the rules, whatever they are, that have been laid down in legislation, in the spirit of conventionalism. The equal protection cases show how important formal equality becomes when it is understood to require integrity as well as bare logical consistency, when it demands fidelity not just to rules but to the theories of fairness and justice that these rules presuppose by way of justification.

We can find another lesson about the dimensions of integrity in the constitutional system of the United States, a lesson that will prove important later in this chapter. Integrity holds within political communities, not among them, so any opinion we have about the scope of the requirement of coherence makes assumptions about the size and character of these communities. The American Constitution provides a federal system: it recognizes states as distinct political communities and assigns them sovereignty over many issues of principle. So there is no violation of political integrity in the fact that the tort laws of some states differ from those of others even over matters of principle. Each sovereign speaks with a single voice, though not in harmony with other sovereigns. But in a federal system integrity makes demands on the higher-order decisions, taken at the constitutional level, about the division of power between the national and the more local levels. Some scholars and politicians opposed to the Supreme Court's 1973 abortion decision now argue that the Constitution should be understood to leave decisions about abortion to the various states, so that some could permit abortion on demand, others prohibit it in all circumstances, and others adopt intermediate regimes.[12] That suggestion is not itself a checkerboard solution: each state would retain a constitutional duty that its own abortion statute be coherent in principle, and the suggestion offers itself as recognizing independent sovereigns rather than speaking for all together. But a question of integrity remains: whether leaving the abortion issue to individual states to decide differently if they wish is coherent in principle with the rest of the American constitutional scheme, which makes other important rights national in scope and enforcement.

IS INTEGRITY ATTRACTIVE?

I shall offer no further argument for my claim that our political life recognizes integrity as a political virtue. The case is now strong enough for the weight of interest to shift to the other dimension of interpretation. Do we do well to interpret our politics that way? Is our political culture more attractive if seen as accepting that virtue? I have already described, in Chapter 5, an obvious challenge to integrity. A pragmatist anxious to reject integrity would attack the deep, working personification we use to define the ideal. We say that the state as a whole does wrong in accepting an internal compromise because "it" then compromises "its" principles. The pragmatist will insist that the state is not an entity that can have principles to compromise. Neither the state nor its government is a person; they are collections of people, and if none of these separate people has acted in any way inconsistently with his or her own principles, what sense can it make to say that the state they represent has done this?

The pragmatist who makes this argument tries to build political responsibility out of ordinary, nonpolitical principles of morality. He proceeds in the fashion of our first argument, in Chapter 5, about the responsibility of shareholders for defective automobiles, applying ordinary principles about the responsibility of one person for injury to another. He asks what each legislator might do, in the position he happens to occupy, to reduce the total number of incidents of injustice or unfairness according to his own views of what justice and fairness require. If we follow the pragmatist in this order of argument—if we begin with individual official responsibility—we will reach his conclusion because we will then lack any appropriate explanation of why a vote for a checkerboard solution is wrong, any explanation of why a particular official should regard the compromise as a worse outcome than the outcome he regards as more uniformly unjust. If, on the other hand, we insist on treating internally compromised statutes as the acts of a single distinct moral agent, then we can condemn them as unprincipled, and we then have a reason for arguing that no official should contribute to his state's unprincipled acts. In order to defend the legislative principle of integrity, therefore, we must defend the general style of argument that takes the community itself as a moral agent.

Our argument must be drawn from political virtue, not, so far as this is supposed to be different, from metaphysics. We must not say that integrity is a special virtue of politics because the state or community is a distinct entity, but that the community should be seen as a distinct moral agent because the social and intellectual practices that treat community in this way should be protected. Now we confront an obvious and deep difficulty. We have grown accustomed in political life to arguing about social and political institutions in a certain way: by attacking or defending them on grounds of justice or fairness. But we cannot hope to defend integrity in this normal way because we know that integrity will sometimes conflict with what fairness and justice recommend. We must expand the breadth of political argument if we are to claim political integrity as a distinct ideal on its own. But how? Here is one suggestion, though not the only possibility. French revolutionary rhetoric recognized a political ideal we have not yet considered. We should look for our defense of integrity in the neighborhood of fraternity[13] or, to use its more fashionable name, community.

I shall argue that a political society that accepts integrity as a political virtue thereby becomes a special form of community, special in a way that promotes its moral authority to assume and deploy a monopoly of coercive force. This is not the only argument for integrity, or the only consequence of recognizing it that citizens might value. Integrity provides protection against partiality or deceit or other forms of official corruption, for example. There is more room for favoritism or vindictiveness in a system that permits manufacturers of automobiles and of washing machines to be governed by different and contradictory principles of liability. Integrity also contributes to the efficiency of law in the way we noticed earlier. If people accept that they are governed not only by explicit rules laid down in past political decisions but by whatever other standards flow from the principles these decisions assume, then the set of recognized public standards can expand and contract organically, as people become more sophisticated in sensing and exploring what these principles require in new circumstances, without the need for detailed legislation or adjudication on each possible point of conflict. This process works less effectively, to be sure, when people disagree, as inevitably they sometimes will, about which principles are in fact assumed by the explicit rules and other standards of their community. But a community that accepts integrity has a vehicle for organic change, even if it is not always wholly effective, that it would not otherwise have at all.

These consequences of integrity are practical. Others are moral and expressive. We noticed in our initial, cursory discussion of integrity in the last chapter that many of our political attitudes, collected in our instinct of group responsibility, assume that we are in some sense the authors of the political decisions made by our governors, or at least that we have reason to think of ourselves that way. Kant and Rousseau based their conceptions of freedom on this ideal of self-legislation.[14] The ideal needs integrity, however, for a citizen cannot treat himself as the author of a collection of laws that are inconsistent in principle, nor can he see that collection as sponsored by any Rousseauian general will.

The ideal of self-government has a special aspect that integrity promotes directly, and noticing this will lead us into our main discussion of legitimacy and political obligation. Integrity expands and deepens the role individual citizens can play in developing the public standards of their community because it requires them to treat relations among themselves as characteristically, not just spasmodically, governed by these standards. If people understood formal legislation as only a matter of negotiated solutions to discrete problems, with no underlying commitment to any more fundamental public conception of justice, they would draw a sharp distinction between two kinds of encounters with fellow citizens: those that fall within and those that fall outside the scope of some past political decision. Integrity, in contrast, insists that each citizen must accept demands on him, and may make demands on others, that share and extend the moral dimension of any explicit political decisions. Integrity therefore fuses citizens' moral and political lives: it asks the good citizen, deciding how to treat his neighbor when their interests conflict, to interpret the common scheme of justice to which they are both committed just in virtue of citizen-ship.[15]

Integrity infuses political and private occasions each with the spirit of the other to the benefit of both. This continuity has practical as well as expressive value, because it facilitates the organic style of change I mentioned a moment ago as a practical advantage. But its expressive value is not exhausted, as its practical value might be, when citizens disagree about which scheme of justice is in fact embedded in the community's explicit political decisions. For the expressive value is confirmed when people in good faith try to treat one another in a way appropriate to common membership in a community governed by political integrity and to see each other as making this attempt, even when they disagree about exactly what integrity requires in particular circumstances. Political obligation is then not just a matter of obeying the discrete political decisions of the community one by one, as political philosophers usually represent it. It becomes a more protestant idea: fidelity to a scheme of principle each citizen has a responsibility to identify, ultimately for himself, as his community's scheme.

THE PUZZLE OF LEGITIMACY

We now turn to the direct connection between integrity and the moral authority of the law, and this bends our study back toward the main argument of the book. I said that the concept of law—the plateau where argument among conceptions is most useful—connects law with the justification of official coercion. A conception of law must explain how what it takes to be law provides a general justification for the exercise of coercive power by the state, a justification that holds except in special cases when some competing argument is specially powerful. Each conception's organizing center is the explanation it offers of this justifying force.

Every conception therefore faces the same threshold problem. How can *anything* provide even that general form of justification for coercion in ordinary politics? What can ever give anyone the kind of authorized power over another that politics supposes governors have over the governed? Why does the fact that a majority elects a particular regime, for example, give that regime legitimate power over those who voted against it?

This is the classical problem of the legitimacy of coercive power. It rides on the back of another classical problem: that of political obligation. Do citizens have genuine moral obligations just in virtue of law? Does the fact that a legislature has enacted some requirement in itself give citizens a moral as well as a practical reason to obey? Does that moral reason hold even for those citizens who disapprove of the legislation or think it wrong in principle? If citizens do not have moral obligations of that character, then the state's warrant for coercion is seriously, perhaps fatally, undermined. These two issues—whether the state is morally legitimate, in the sense that it is justified in using force against its citizens, and whether the state's decisions impose genuine obligations on them—are not identical. No state should enforce all of a citizen's obligations. But though obligation is not a sufficient condition for coercion, it is close to a necessary one. A state may have good grounds in some special circumstances for coercing those who have no duty to obey. But no general policy of upholding the law with steel could be justified if the law were not, in general, a source of genuine obligations.

A state is legitimate if its constitutional structure and practices are such that its citizens have a general obligation to obey political decisions that purport to impose duties on them. An argument for legitimacy need only provide reasons for that general situation. It need not show that a government, legitimate in that sense, therefore has moral authority to do anything it wants to its citizens, or that they are obligated to obey every decision it makes. I shall argue that a state that accepts integrity as a political ideal has a better case for legitimacy than one that does not. If that is so, it provides a strong reason of the sort we have just now been seeking, a reason why we would do well to see our political practices as grounded in that virtue. It provides, in particular, a strong argument for a conception of law that takes integrity to be fundamental, because any conception must explain why law is legitimate authority for coercion. Our claims for integrity are thus tied into our main project of finding an attractive conception of law.

Tacit Consent

Philosophers make several kinds of arguments for the legitimacy of modern democracies. One argument uses the idea of a social contract, but we must not confuse it with arguments that use that idea to establish the character or content of justice. John Rawls, for example, proposes an imaginary social contract as a device for selecting the best conception of justice in the circumstances of utopian political theory. He argues that under specified conditions of uncertainty everyone would choose certain principles of justice as in his interests, properly understood, and he says that these principles are therefore the right principles for us.[16] Whatever we may think of his suggestion, it has no direct connection to our present problem of legitimacy in the circumstances of ordinary politics where Rawls's principles of justice are very far from dominion. It would be very different, of course, if every citizen were a party to an actual, historical agreement to accept and obey political decisions taken in the way his community's political decisions are in fact taken. Then the historical fact of agreement would provide at least a good prima facie case for coercion even in ordinary politics. So some political philosophers have been tempted to say that we have in fact agreed to a social contract of that kind tacitly, by just not emigrating when we reach the age of consent. But no one can argue that very long with a straight face. Consent cannot be binding on people, in the way this argument requires, unless it is given more freely, and with more genuine alternate choice, than just by declining to build a life from nothing under a foreign flag. And even if the consent were genuine, the argument would fail as an argument for legitimacy, because a person leaves one sovereign only to join another; he has no choice to be free from sovereigns altogether.

The Duty to Be Just

Rawls argues that people in his original position would recognize a natural duty to support institutions that meet the tests of abstract justice and that they would extend this duty to the support of institutions not perfectly just, at least when the sporadic injustice lay in decisions reached by fair, majoritarian institutions.[17] Even those who reject Rawls's general method might accept the duty to support just or nearly just institutions. That duty, however, does not provide a good explanation of legitimacy, because it does not tie political obligation sufficiently tightly to the particular community to which those who have the obligation belong; it does not show why Britons have any special duty to support the institutions of Britain. We can construct a practical, contingent argument for the special duty. Britons have more opportunity to aid British institutions than those of other nations whose institutions they also think mainly just. But this practical argument fails to capture the intimacy of the special duty. It fails to show how legitimacy flows from and defines citizenship. This objection points away from justice, which is conceptually universalistic, and toward integrity, which is already more personal in its different demands on different communities, as the parent of legitimacy.

Fair Play

The most popular defense of legitimacy is the argument from fair play:[18] if someone has received benefits under a standing political organization, then he has an obligation to bear the burdens of that organization as well, including an obligation to accept its political decisions, whether or not he has solicited these benefits or has in any more active way consented to these burdens. This argument avoids the fantasy of the argument from consent and the universality and other defects of the argument from a natural duty of justice and might therefore seem a stronger rival to my suggestion that legitimacy is best grounded in integrity. But it is vulnerable to two counterarguments that have frequently been noticed. First, the fair play argument assumes that people can incur obligations simply by receiving what they do not seek and would reject if they had the chance. This seems unreasonable. Suppose a philosopher broadcasts a stunning and valuable lecture from a sound truck. Do all those who hear it—even all those who enjoy and profit by it—owe him a lecture fee?[19]

Second, the fair play argument is ambiguous in a crucial respect. In what sense does it suppose that people benefit from political organization? The most natural answer is this: someone benefits from a political organization if his overall situation—his "welfare" in the way economists use that phrase—is superior under that organization to what it would otherwise be. But everything then turns on the benchmark to be used, on what "otherwise" means, and when we try to specify the benchmark we reach a dead end. The principle is plainly too strong—it justifies nothing—if it requires showing that each citizen is better off under the standing political system than he would be under any other system that might have developed in its place. For that can never be shown for all the citizens the principle is meant to embrace. And it is plainly too weak—it is too easy to satisfy and therefore justifies too much—if it requires showing only that each citizen is better off under the standing organization than he would be with no social or political organization at all, that is, under a Hobbesian state of nature.

We can deflect this second objection if we reject the

"natural" interpretation I described of the crucial idea of benefit. Suppose we understand the argument in a different way: it assumes not that each citizen's welfare, judged in some politically neutral way, has been improved *by* a particular social or political organization, but that each has received the benefits *of* that organization. That is, that he has actually received what is due him according to the standards of justice and fairness on which it is constructed. The principle of fair play, understood that way, states at least a condition necessary to legitimacy. If a community does not aim to treat someone as an equal, even according to its own lights, then its claim to his political obligation is fatally compromised. But it remains unclear how the negative fact that society has not discriminated against someone in this way, according to its own standards, could supply any positive reason why he should accept its laws as obligations. Indeed, the first objection I described becomes more powerful yet if we make this response to the second. For now the argument from fair play must be understood as claiming, not that someone incurs an obligation when his welfare is improved in a way he did not seek, but that he incurs an obligation by being treated in a way that might not even improve his welfare over any appropriate benchmark. For there is nothing in the fact that some individual has been treated fairly by his community according to its own standards that guarantees him any further, more material advantage.

OBLIGATIONS OF COMMUNITY

Circumstances and Conditions

Is it true that no one can be morally affected by being given what he does not ask for or choose to have? We will think so if we consider only cases of benefits thrust upon us by strangers like philosophers in sound trucks. Our convictions are quite different, however, when we have in mind obligations that are often called obligations of role but that I shall call, generically, associative or communal obligations. I mean the special responsibilities social practice attaches to membership in some biological or social group, like the responsibilities of family or friends or neighbors. Most people think that they have associative obligations just by belonging to groups defined by social practice, which is not necessarily a matter of choice or consent, but that they can lose these obligations if other members of the group do not extend them the benefits of belonging to the group. These common assumptions about associative responsibilities suggest that political obligation might be counted among them, in which case the two objections to the argument from fair play would no longer be pertinent. On the whole, however, philosophers have ignored this possibility, I believe for two reasons. First, communal obligations are widely thought to depend upon emotional bonds that presuppose that each member of the group has personal acquaintance of all others, which of course cannot be true in large political communities. Second, the idea of special communal responsibilities holding within a large, anonymous community smacks of nationalism, or even racism, both of which have been sources of very great suffering and injustice.

We should therefore reflect on the character of familiar associative obligations to see how far these apparent objections actually hold. Associative obligations are complex, and much less studied by philosophers than the kinds of personal obligations we incur through discrete promises and other deliberate acts. But they are an important part of the moral landscape: for most people, responsibilities to family and lovers and friends and union or office colleagues are the most important, the most consequential obligations of all. The history of social practice defines the communal groups to which we belong and the obligations that attach to these. It defines what a family or a neighborhood or a professional colleague is, and what one member of these groups or holder of these titles owes to another. But social practice defines groups and obligations not by the fiat of ritual, not through the explicit extension of conventions, but in the more complex way brought in with the interpretive attitude. The concepts we use to describe these groups and to claim or reject these obligations are interpretive concepts; people can sensibly argue in the interpretive way about what friendship really is and about what children really owe their parents in old age. The raw data of how friends typically treat one another are no more conclusive of an argument about the obligations of friendship than raw data were conclusive for arguments about courtesy in the community I imagined or for arguments about law for us.

Suppose we tried to compose, not just an interpretation of a single associative practice, like family or friendship or neighborhood, but a more abstract interpretation of the yet more general practice of associative obligation itself. I cannot carry that project very far here or develop any deep and thorough study of that abstract practice. But even a quick survey shows that we cannot account for the general practice if we accept the principle many philosophers have found so appealing, that no one can have special obligations to particular people except by choosing to accept these. The connection we recognize between communal obligation and choice is much more complex and more a matter of degree that varies from one form of communal association to another. Even associations we consider mainly consensual, like friendship, are not formed in one act of deliberate contractual commitment, the way one joins a club, but instead develop through a series of choices and events that are never seen, one by one, as carrying a commitment of that kind.

We have friends to whom we owe obligations in virtue of a shared history, but it would be perverse to describe this as a history of *assuming* obligations. On the contrary, it is a history of events and acts that *attract* obligations, and we are rarely even aware that we are entering upon any special status as the story unfolds. People become self-conscious about the obligations of friendship in the normal case only when some situation requires them to honor these obligations, or when they have grown weary of or embarrassed by the friendship, and then it is too late to reject them without betrayal. Other forms of association that carry special responsibilities—of academic colleagueship, for example—are even less a matter of free choice: someone can become my colleague even though I voted against his appointment. And the obligations some members of a family owe to others, which many people count among the strongest fraternal obligations of all, are matters of the least choice.[20]

We must therefore account for associative obligations, if we accept these at all, in the different way I suggested a moment ago in describing how most people think of them. We have a duty to honor our responsibilities under social practices that define groups and attach special responsibilities to membership, but this natural duty holds only when certain other conditions are met or sustained. Reciprocity is prominent among these other conditions. I have special responsibilities to my brother in virtue of our brotherhood, but these are sensitive to the degree to which he accepts such responsibilities toward me; my responsibilities to those who claim that we are friends or lovers or neighbors or colleagues or countrymen are equally contingent on reciprocity. But we must be careful here: if associative concepts are interpretive—if it can be an open question among friends what friendship requires—then the reciprocity we demand cannot be a matter of each doing for the other what the latter thinks friendship concretely requires. Then friendship would be possible only between people who shared a detailed conception of friendship and would become automatically more contractual and deliberative than it is, more a matter of people checking in advance to see whether their conceptions matched well enough to allow them to be friends.[21]

The reciprocity we require for associative obligations must be more abstract, more a question of accepting a kind of responsibility we need the companion ideas of integrity and interpretation to explain. Friends have a responsibility to treat one another as friends, and that means, put subjectively, that each must act out of a conception of friendship he is ready to recognize as vulnerable to an interpretive test, as open to the objection that this is not a plausible account of what friendship means in our culture. Friends or family or neighbors need not agree in detail about the responsibilities attached to these forms of organization. Associative obligations can be sustained among people who share a general and diffuse sense of members' special rights and responsibilities from or toward one another, a sense of what sort and level of sacrifice one may be expected to make for another. I may think friendship, properly understood, requires that I break promises to others to help a friend in need, and I will not refuse to do this for a friend just because he does not share this conviction and would not do it for me. But I will count him a friend and feel this obligation only if I believe he has roughly the same concern for me as I thereby show for him, that he would make important sacrifices for me of some other sort.

Nevertheless, the members of a group must by and large hold certain attitudes about the responsibilities they owe one another if these responsibilities are to count as genuine fraternal obligations. First, they must regard the group's obligations as *special,* holding distinctly within the group, rather than as general duties its members owe equally to persons outside it. Second, they must accept that these responsibilities are *personal:* that they run directly from each member to each other member, not just to the group as a whole in some collective sense. My brother or my colleague may think he has responsibilities to the reputation of the family or the university he best acquits by concentrating on his own career and thus denying me help when I need it or company when I want it. He may be right about the best use of his time overall from the standpoint of the general good of these particular communities. But his conduct does not form the necessary basis for my continuing to recognize fraternal obligations toward him.

Third, members must see these responsibilities as flowing from a more general responsibility each has of *concern* for the well-being of others in the group; they must treat discrete obligations that arise only under special circumstances, like the obligation to help a friend who is in great financial need, as derivative from and expressing a more general responsibility active throughout the association in different ways. A commercial partnership or joint enterprise, conceived as a fraternal association, is in that way different from even a long-standing contractual relationship. The former has a life of its own: each partner is concerned not just to keep explicit agreements hammered out at arm's length but to approach each issue that arises in their joint commercial life in a manner reflecting special concern for his partner as partner. Different forms of association presuppose different kinds of general concern each member is assumed to have for others. The level of concern is different—I need not act toward my partner as if I thought his welfare as important as my son's—and also its range: my concern for my union "brother" is general across the economic and productive life we share but does not extend to his success in social life, as my concern for my biological brother does. (Of course my union colleague may be my friend as well, in which case my overall responsibilities to him will be aggregative and complex.) But within the form or mode of life constituted by a communal practice, the concern must be general and must provide the foundation for the more discrete responsibilities.

Fourth, members must suppose that the group's practices show not only concern but an *equal* concern for all members. Fraternal associations are in that sense conceptually egalitarian. They may be structured, even hierarchical, in the way a family is, but the structure and hierarchy must reflect the group's assumption that its roles and rules are equally in the interests of all, that no one's life is more important than

anyone else's. Armies may be fraternal organizations if that
condition is met. But caste systems that count some members
as inherently less worthy than others are not fraternal and
yield no communal responsibilities.

We must be careful to distinguish, then, between a "bare"
community, a community that meets the genetic or geographical or other historical conditions identified by social
practice as capable of constituting a fraternal community,
and a "true" community, a bare community whose practices
of group responsibility meet the four conditions just identified. The responsibilities a true community deploys are special and individualized and display a pervasive mutual
concern that fits a plausible conception of equal concern.
These are not psychological conditions. Though a group
will rarely meet or long sustain them unless its members by
and large actually feel some emotional bond with one another, the conditions do not themselves demand this. The
concern they require is an interpretive property of the
group's practices of asserting and acknowledging responsibilities—these must be practices that people with the right
level of concern would adopt—not a psychological property
of some fixed number of the actual members. So, contrary to
the assumption that seemed to argue against assimilating
political to associative obligations, associative communities
can be larger and more anonymous than they could be if it
were a necessary condition that each member love all others,
or even that they know them or know who they are.

Nor does anything in the four conditions contradict our
initial premise that obligations of fraternity need not be fully
voluntary. If the conditions are met, people in the bare community have the obligations of a true community whether or
not they want them, though of course the conditions will not
be met unless most members recognize and honor these obligations. It is therefore essential to insist that true communities must be bare communities as well. People cannot be
made involuntary "honorary" members of a community to

which they do not even "barely" belong just because other members are disposed to treat them as such. I would not become a citizen of Fiji if people there decided for some reason to treat me as one of them. Nor am I the friend of a stranger sitting next to me on a plane just because he decides he is a friend of mine.

Conflicts with Justice

An important reservation must be made to the argument so far. Even genuine communities that meet the several conditions just described may be unjust or promote injustice and so produce the conflict we have already noticed in different ways, between the integrity and justice of an institution. Genuine communal obligations may be unjust in two ways. First, they may be unjust to the members of the group: the conception of equal concern they reflect, though sincere, may be defective. It may be a firm tradition of family organization in some community, for example, that equal concern for daughters and sons requires parents to exercise a kind of dominion over one relaxed for the other.[22] Second, they may be unjust to people who are not members of the group. Social practice may define a racial or religious group as associative, and that group may require its members to discriminate against nonmembers socially or in employment or generally. If the consequences for strangers to the group are grave, as they will be if the discriminating group is large or powerful within a larger community, this will be unjust.[23] In many cases, requiring that sort of discrimination will conflict, not just with duties of abstract justice the group's members owe everyone else, but also with associative obligations they have because they belong to larger or different associative communities. For if those who do not belong to my race or religion are my neighbors or colleagues or (now I anticipate the argument to follow) my fellow citizens, the question arises whether I do not have responsibilities to them, flowing from those associations, that I ignore in deferring to the responsibilities claimed by my racial or religious group.

We must not forget, in puzzling about these various conflicts, that associative responsibilities are subject to interpretation, and that justice will play its normal interpretive role in deciding for any person what his associative responsibilities, properly understood, really are. If the bare facts of social practice are indecisive, my belief that it is unjust for parents to exercise absolute dominion over their children will influence my convictions about whether the institution of family really has that feature, just as a citizen's beliefs about the justice of social rank influences his beliefs about courtesy in the imaginary community of Chapter 2. Even if the practice of dominion is settled and unquestioned, the interpretive attitude may isolate it as a mistake because it is condemned by principles necessary to justify the rest of the institution. There is no guarantee, however, that the interpretive attitude will always justify reading some apparently unjust feature of an associative institution out of it. We may have to concede that unjust dominion lies at the heart of some culture's practices of family, or that indefensible discrimination is at the heart of its practices of racial or religious cohesion. Then we will be aware of another possibility we have also noticed before, in other contexts. The best interpretation may be a deeply skeptical one: that no competent account of the institution can fail to show it as thoroughly and pervasively unjust, and that it should therefore be abandoned. Someone who reaches that conclusion will deny that the practice can impose genuine obligations at all. He thinks the obligations it purports to impose are wholly canceled by competing moral principle.

So our account of associative obligation now has the following rather complex structure. It combines matters of social practice and matters of critical interpretation in the following way. The question of communal obligation does not arise except for groups defined by practice as carrying such obligations: associative communities must be bare communities first. But not every group established by social practice counts as associative: a bare community must meet the four conditions of a true community before the responsibilities it declares become genuine. Interpretation is needed at this stage, because the question whether the practice meets the conditions of genuine community depends on how the practice is properly understood, and that is an interpretive question. Since interpretation is in part a matter of justice, this stage may show that apparently unjust responsibilities are not really part of the practice after all, because they are condemned by principles needed to justify other responsibilities the practice imposes. But we cannot count on this: the best interpretation available may show that its unjust features are compatible with the rest of its structure. Then, though the obligations it imposes are prima facie genuine, the question arises whether the injustice is so severe and deep that these obligations are canceled. That is one possibility, and practices of racial unity and discrimination seem likely examples. But sometimes the injustice will not be that great; dilemmas are then posed because the unjust obligations the practice creates are not entirely erased.

I can illustrate this complex structure by expanding an example already used. Does a daughter have an obligation to defer to her father's wishes in cultures that give parents power to choose spouses for daughters but not sons? We ask first whether the four conditions are met that transform the bare institution of family, in the form this has taken there, into a true community, and that raises a nest of interpretive questions in which our convictions about justice will figure. Does the culture genuinely accept that women are as important as men? Does it see the special parental power over daughters as genuinely in the daughters' interest? If not, if the discriminatory treatment of daughters is grounded in some more general assumption that they are less worthy than sons, the association is not genuine, and not distinctly associative responsibilities, of any character, arise from it. If the culture does accept the equality of the sexes, on the other

hand, the discrimination against daughters may be so inconsistent with the rest of the institution of family that it
may be seen as a mistake within it and so not a real requirement even if the institution is accepted. Then the conflict
disappears for that reason.

But suppose the culture accepts the equality of sexes but
in good faith thinks that equality of concern requires pater-
nalistic protection for women in all aspects of family life,
and that parental control over a daughter's marriage is consistent with the rest of the institution of family. If that institution is otherwise seriously unjust—if it forces family
members to commit crimes in the interest of the family, for
example—we will think it cannot be justified in any way
that recommends continuing it. Our attitude is fully skeptical, and again we deny any genuine associative responsibilities and so deny any conflict. Suppose, on the other hand,
that the institution's paternalism is the only feature we are
disposed to regard as unjust. Now the conflict is genuine.
The other responsibilities of family membership thrive as
genuine responsibilities. So does the responsibility of a
daughter to defer to parental choice in marriage, but this
may be overridden by appeal to freedom or some other
ground of rights. The difference is important: a daughter
who marries against her father's wishes, in this version of the
story, has something to regret. She owes him at least an ac-
counting, and perhaps an apology, and should in other ways
strive to continue her standing as a member of the community she otherwise has a duty to honor.

I have paid such great attention to the structure of associative obligation, and to the character and occasions of its
conflict with other responsibilities and rights, because my
aim is to show how political obligation can be seen as associative, and this can be plausible only if the general structure
of associative obligations allows us to account for the conditions we feel must be met before political obligation arises,
and the circumstances we believe must either defeat it or
show it in conflict with other kinds of obligations. The dis-

cussion just concluded echoes our first discussion, in Chapter 3, about the kinds of conflict citizens and judges might discover between the law of their community and more abstract justice. We used, there, much the same structure and many of the same distinctions to disentangle the moral and legal issues posed by law in wicked places. That echo supports our present hypothesis that political obligation—including an obligation to obey the law—is a form of associative obligation. Our study of conflict within associative obligation is important, too, in responding to an objection to that hypothesis I noticed briefly earlier. The objection complains that treating political obligation as associative supports the more unattractive aspects of nationalism, including its strident approval of war for national self-interest. We can now reply that the best interpretation of our own political practices disavows that feature, which is anyway no longer explicitly endorsed even by bare practice. When and where it is endorsed any conflict between militant nationalism and standards of justice must be resolved in favor of the latter. Neither of these claims threatens the more wholesome ideals of national community and the special responsibilities these support, which we are about to consider.

FRATERNITY AND POLITICAL COMMUNITY

We are at last able to consider our hypothesis directly: that the best defense of political legitimacy—the right of a political community to treat its members as having obligations in virtue of collective community decisions—is to be found not in the hard terrain of contracts or duties of justice or obligations of fair play that might hold among strangers, where philosophers have hoped to find it, but in the more fertile ground of fraternity, community, and their attendant obligations. Political association, like family and friendship and other forms of association more local and intimate, is in itself pregnant of obligation. It is no objection to that claim that most people do not choose their political communities but are born into them or brought there in childhood. If we arrange familiar fraternal communities along a spectrum ranging from full choice to no choice in membership, political communities fall somewhere in the center. Political obligations are less involuntary than many obligations of family, because political communities do allow people to emigrate, and though the practical value of this choice is often very small the choice itself is important, as we know when we contemplate tyrannies that deny it. So people who are members of bare political communities have political obligations, provided the other conditions necessary to obligations of fraternity, appropriately defined for a political community, are met.

We must therefore ask what account of these conditions is appropriate for a political community, but first we should pause to consider the following complaint about this "solution" of the problem of legitimacy. "It does not solve the problem but evades it by denying there is any problem at all." There is some justice in this complaint, but not enough to be damaging here. The new approach, it is true, relocates the problem of legitimacy and so hopes to change the character of the argument. It asks those who challenge the very possibility of political legitimacy to broaden their attack and either deny all associative obligations or show why political obligation cannot be associative. It asks those who defend legitimacy to test their claims on a new and expanded field of argument. It invites political philosophers of either disposition to consider what a bare political community must be like before it can claim to be a true community where communal obligations flourish.

We have no difficulty finding in political practice the conditions of bare community. People disagree about the boundaries of political communities, particularly in colonial circumstances or when standing divisions among nations ignore important historical or ethnic or religious identities. But these can be treated as problems of interpretation, and anyway they do not arise in the countries of our present main concern. Practice defines the boundaries of Great Britain[24] and of the several states of the United States well enough for these to be eligible as bare political communities. We have noticed this already: we noticed that our most widespread political convictions suppose the officials of these communities to have special responsibilities within and toward their distinct communities.[25] We also have no difficulty in describing the main obligations associated with political communities. The central obligation is that of general fidelity to law, the obligation political philosophy has found so problematic. So our main interest lies in the four conditions we identified. What form would these take in a political community? What must politics be like for a bare political society to become a true fraternal mode of association?

Three Models of Community

We are able to imagine political society as associative only because our ordinary political attitudes seem to satisfy the first of our four conditions. We suppose that we have special interests in and obligations toward other members of our own nation. Americans address their political appeals, their demands, visions, and ideals, in the first instance to other Americans; Britons to other Britons; and so forth. We treat community as prior to justice and fairness in the sense that questions of justice and fairness are regarded as questions of what would be fair or just within a particular political group. In that way we treat political communities as true associative communities. What further assumptions about the obligations and responsibilities that flow from citizenship could justify that attitude by satisfying its other conditions? This is not a question of descriptive sociology, though that discipline may have a part to play in answering it. We are not concerned, that is, with the empirical question of which attitudes or institutions or traditions are needed to create and protect political stability, but with the interpretive question of what character of mutual concern and responsibility our political practices must express in order to justify the assumption of true community we seem to make.

A community's political practices might aim to express one of three general models of political association. Each model describes the attitudes members of a political community would self-consciously take toward one another if they held the view of community the model expresses. The first supposes that members of a community treat their association as only a de facto accident of history and geography, among other things, and so as not a true associative community at all. People who think of their community this way will not necessarily treat others only as means to their own personal ends. That is one possibility: imagine two strangers from nations that despise each other's morals and religion are washed up on a desert island after a naval battle between the two countries. The strangers are thrown together initially by circumstance and nothing more. Each may need the other and may refrain from killing him for that reason. They may work out some division of labor, and each may hold to the agreement so long as he thinks it is to his advantage to do so, but not beyond that point or for any other reason. But there are other possibilities for de facto association. People might regard their political community as merely de facto, not because they are selfish but because they are driven by a passion for justice in the world as a whole and see no distinction between their community and others. A political official who takes that view will think of his constituents as people he is in a position to help because he has special means—those of his office—for helping them that are not, regrettably, available for helping other groups. He will think his responsibilities to his own community special in no other way, and therefore not greater in principle. So when he can improve justice overall by subordinating the interests of his own constituents, he will think it right to do so.

I call the second model of community the "rulebook"

model. It supposes that members of a political community accept a general commitment to obey rules established in a certain way that is special to that community. Imagine self-interested but wholly honest people who are competitors in a game with fixed rules or who are parties to a limited and transient commercial arrangement. They obey the rules they have accepted or negotiated as a matter of obligation and not merely strategy, but they assume that the content of these rules exhausts their obligation. They have no sense that the rules were negotiated out of common commitment to underlying principles that are themselves a source of further obligation; on the contrary, they take these rules to represent a compromise between antagonistic interests or points of view. If the rules are the product of special negotiation, as in the contract case, each side has tried to give up as little in return for as much as possible, and it would therefore be unfair and not merely mistaken for either to claim that their agreement embraces anything not explicitly agreed.

The conventionalist's conception of law we considered in Chapter 4 is a natural mate to this rulebook model of community. Conventionalism suits people each trying to advance his or her own conception of justice and fairness in the right relation through negotiation and compromise, subject only to the single overriding stipulation that once a compromise has been reached in the appropriate way, the rules that form its content will be respected until they are changed by a fresh compromise. A conventionalist philosophy coupled to a rulebook model of community would accept the internal compromises of our checkerboard statutes, as compromises reached through negotiation that ought to be respected as much as any other bargain. The first two models of community—community as a matter of circumstance and as a matter of rules—agree in rejecting the only basis we might have for opposing checkerboard compromises, which is the idea of integrity, that the community must respect principles necessary to justify one part of the law in other parts as well.

The third model of community is the model of principle. It agrees with the rulebook model that political community requires a shared understanding, but it takes a more generous and comprehensive view of what that understanding is. It insists that people are members of a genuine political community only when they accept that their fates are linked in the following strong way: they accept that they are governed by common principles, not just by rules hammered out in political compromise. Politics has a different character for such people. It is a theater of debate about which principles the community should adopt as a system, which view it should take of justice, fairness, and due process, not the different story, appropriate to the other models, in which each person tries to plant the flag of his convictions over as large a domain of power or rules as possible. Members of a society of principle accept that their political rights and duties are not exhausted by the particular decisions their political institutions have reached, but depend, more generally, on the scheme of principles those decisions presuppose and endorse. So each member accepts that others have rights and that he has duties flowing from that scheme, even though these have never been formally identified or declared. Nor does he suppose that these further rights and duties are conditional on his wholehearted approval of that scheme; these obligations arise from the historical fact that his community has adopted that scheme, which is then special to it, not the assumption that he would have chosen it were the choice entirely his. In short, each accepts political integrity as a distinct political ideal and treats the general acceptance of that ideal, even among people who otherwise disagree about political morality, as constitutive of political community.

Now our stage is properly set (or rather managed) for the crucial question. Each of these three models of community describes a general attitude that members of a political community take toward one another. Would political practices expressing one or another of these attitudes satisfy the conditions of true associative community we identified? We need not pause long over the de facto model of circumstance. It violates even the first condition: it adds nothing, by way of any special attitudes of concern, to the circumstances that define a bare political community. It admits community among people who have no interest in one another except as means to their own selfish ends. Even when this form of community holds among selfless people who act only to secure justice and fairness in the world as they understand these virtues, they have no special concern for justice and fairness toward fellow members of their own community. (Indeed, since their only concern is abstract justice, which is universalistic in its character, they can have no basis for special concern.)

The rulebook model of community might seem more promising. For its members do show a special concern for one another beyond each person's general concern that justice be done according to his lights, a special concern that each other person receive the full benefit of whatever political decisions have in fact been taken under the standing political arrangements. That concern has the necessary individualized character to satisfy the second condition: it runs separately from each person directly to everyone else. But it cannot satisfy the third, for the concern it displays is too shallow and attenuated to count as pervasive, indeed to count as genuine concern at all. People in a rulebook community are free to act in politics almost as selfishly as people in a community of circumstances can. Each one can use the standing political machinery to advance his own interests or ideals. True, once that machinery has generated a discrete decision in the form of a rule of law or a judicial decision, they will accept a special obligation to secure the enforcement of that decision for everyone whom it happens to benefit. But that commitment is too formal, too disconnected from the actual circumstances it will promote, to count as expressing much by way of genuine concern, and that is why it rings hollow as an expression of fraternity. It takes hold too late in the political process; it permits someone to act at the crucial legislative stage with no sense of responsibility or concern for those whom he pretends, once every possible advantage has been secured at their expense, to count as brothers. The familiar version of the argument from fair play—these are the rules under which you have benefited and you must play by them—is particularly appropriate to a rulebook community, which takes politics, as I said, to be a kind of game. But that is the version of the argument most vulnerable to all the objections we began by noticing.

The model of principle satisfies all our conditions, at least as well as any model could in a morally pluralistic society. It makes the responsibilities of citizenship special: each citizen respects the principles of fairness and justice instinct in the standing political arrangement of his particular community, which may be different from those of other communities, whether or not he thinks these the best principles from a utopian standpoint. It makes these responsibilities fully personal: it commands that no one be left out, that we are all in politics together for better or worse, that no one may be sacrificed, like wounded left on the battlefield, to the crusade for justice overall. The concern it expresses is not shallow, like the crocodile concern of the rulebook model, but genuine and pervasive. It takes hold immediately politics begins and is sustained through legislation to adjudication and enforcement. Everyone's political acts express on every occasion, in arguing about what the rules should be as well as how they should be enforced, a deep and constant commitment commanding sacrifice, not just by losers but also by the powerful who would gain by the kind of logrolling and checkerboard solutions integrity forbids. Its rationale tends toward equality in the way our fourth condition requires: its command of integrity assumes that each person is as worthy as any other, that each must be treated with equal concern according to some coherent conception of what that means. An association of principle is not automatically a just community; its conception of equal concern may be defective or it may violate rights of its citizens or citizens of other nations in the way we just saw any true associative community might. But the model of principle satisfies the conditions of true community better than any other model of community that it is possible for people who disagree about justice and fairness to adopt.

Here, then, is our case for integrity, our reason for striving to see, so far as we can, both its legislative and adjudicative principles vivid in our political life. A community of principle accepts integrity. It condemns checkerboard statutes and less dramatic violations of that ideal as violating the associative character of its deep organization. Internally compromised statutes cannot be seen as flowing from any single coherent scheme of principle; on the contrary, they serve the incompatible aim of a rulebook community, which is to compromise convictions along lines of power. They contradict rather than confirm the commitment necessary to make a large and diverse political society a genuine rather than a bare community: the promise that law will be chosen, changed, developed, and interpreted in an overall principled way. A community of principle, faithful to that promise, can claim the authority of a genuine associative community and can therefore claim moral legitimacy—that its collective decisions are matters of obligation and not bare power—in the name of fraternity. These claims may be defeated, for even genuine associative obligations may conflict with, and must sometimes yield to, demands of justice. But any other form of community, whose officials rejected that commitment, would from the outset forfeit any claim to legitimacy under a fraternal ideal.

The models of community used in this argument are ideal in several ways. We cannot suppose that most people in our own political societies self-consciously accept the attitudes of any of them. I constructed them so that we could decide which attitudes we should try to interpret our political practices to express, which is a different matter, and the exercise warrants the following conclusion. If we can understand our practices as appropriate to the model of principle, we can support the legitimacy of our institutions, and the political obligations they assume, as a matter of fraternity, and we should therefore strive to improve our institutions in that direction. It bears repeating that nothing in this argument suggests that the citizens of a nation state, or even a smaller political community, either do or should feel for one another any emotion that can usefully be called love. Some theories of ideal community hold out that possibility: they yearn for each citizen to embrace all others in emotions as profound, and with an equivalent merger of personality, as those of lovers or the most intimate friends or the members of an intensely devoted family.[26] Of course we could not interpret the politics of any political community as expressing that level of mutual concern, nor is this ideal attractive. The general surrender of personality and autonomy it contemplates would leave people too little room for leading their own lives rather than being led along them; it would destroy the very emotions it celebrates. Our lives are rich because they are complex in the layers and character of the communities we inhabit. If we felt nothing more for lovers or friends or colleagues than the most intense concern we could possibly feel for all fellow citizens, this would mean the extinction not the universality of love.

Summary

It is time to collect the strands of a long argument. This chapter claims that any successful constructive interpretation of our political practices as a whole recognizes integrity as a distinct political ideal that sometimes calls for compromise with other ideals. Since this is an interpretive claim, it must be measured along two dimensions. Integrity as a political ideal fits and explains features of our constitutional structure and practice that are otherwise puzzling. So its standing as part of an overall successful interpretation of these practices hinges on whether interpreting them in this way helps show them in a better light. We noticed various reasons, both practical and expressive, a community might have for accepting integrity as a political virtue. I emphasized one of these by constructing and contrasting three models of community. I argued that a community of principle, which takes integrity to be central to politics, provides a better defense of political legitimacy than the other models. It assimilates political obligations to the general class of associative obligations and supports them in that way. This defense is possible in such a community because a general commitment to integrity expresses a concern by each for all that is sufficiently special, personal, pervasive, and egalitarian to ground communal obligations according to standards for communal obligation we elsewhere accept.

Neither this argument nor the others we noticed more briefly provides any conclusive argument for integrity on first principles of political morality. I began by conceding that integrity would have no distinct role to play in a community that was understood by all its members to be perfectly just and fair. I am defending an interpretation of our own political culture, not an abstract and timeless political morality; I claim only that the case for integrity is powerful on the second, political dimension of interpretation, which reinforces its strong claims on the first dimension of fit.

UNTIDY ENDNOTES

In the next several chapters we shall study a narrower and more focused claim: that integrity is the key to the best constructive interpretation of our distinct legal practices and particularly of the way our judges decide hard cases at law. I shall argue that law as integrity provides a better interpretation of legal practice than the other two conceptions we have considered. I must first add some further points to our general account of integrity, however, points that could not conveniently have been noticed in the main argument. I can do this most efficiently, I am afraid, by collecting observations in the untidy form of a list under two general headings.

Legislation and Adjudication

I do not claim, as part of my interpretive thesis, that our political practices enforce integrity perfectly. I conceded that it would not be possible to bring all the discrete rules and other standards enacted by our legislatures and still in force under any single, coherent scheme of principle. Our commitment to integrity means, however, that we must report this fact as a defect, not as the desirable result of a fair division of political power between different bodies of opinion, and that we must strive to remedy whatever inconsistencies in principle we are forced to confront. Even this weaker claim requires further qualification, or at least clarification.

I distinguished two branches or forms of integrity by listing two principles: integrity in legislation and integrity in adjudication. The first restricts what our legislators and other lawmakers may properly do in expanding or changing our public standards. The second requires our judges, so far as this is possible, to treat our present system of public standards as expressing and respecting a coherent set of principles, and, to that end, to interpret these standards to find implicit standards between and beneath the explicit ones. Integrity, for us, is a virtue beside justice and fairness and due process, but that does not mean that in either of the two forms just distinguished integrity is necessarily or always sovereign over the other virtues. The legislature should be guided by the legislative principle of integrity, and that explains why it must not enact checkerboard statutes just out of a concern for fairness. But checkerboard statutes are a flagrant and easily avoidable violation of integrity; it does not follow that the legislature must never, in any circumstances, make law more inconsistent in principle than it already is. Suppose the legislature is persuaded that the standing scheme of accident law, which allows people compensation for defective products only when the manufacturer is negligent, is unjust, and therefore it proposes to enact a scheme of strict liability for defective automobiles. Integrity would require it to enact strict liability for all other products as well. But preparing an adequate general statute for all products might take a great deal of legislative time that is needed for other matters. Or the manufacturers of some products might form a powerful lobby, making it politically impossible to pass a general statute yet. In that case the legislature, faced with a hard choice, might well be justified in enacting the automobile defect compensation statute alone, leaving other products to another day or other days. Integrity condemns the result, but justice recommends it over no change at all, and on balance half the loaf might be better than none. The legislature would abandon its general commitment to integrity, and so forfeit the argument for legitimacy we canvassed, if it made that choice in every case or even characteristically. But that does not mean it should never choose justice over integrity.

Nor is the adjudicative principle of integrity absolutely sovereign over what judges must do at the end of the day. That principle is decisive over what a judge recognizes as law. It is sovereign, that is, over the grounds of law, because it admits no other view of what "flows from" past political decisions. But we saw in Chapter 3 that any theory about the grounds of law abstracts from detailed issues about the force of law. A judge who accepts integrity will think that the law it defines sets out genuine rights litigants have to a decision before him. They are entitled, in principle, to have their acts and affairs judged in accordance with the best view of what the legal standards of the community required or permitted at the time they acted, and integrity demands that these standards be seen as coherent, as the state speaking with a single voice. But though this requirement honors the political virtue of procedural due process, which would at least prima facie be violated if people were judged against standards other than the legal standards of the day, other and more powerful aspects of political morality might outweigh this requirement in particular and unusual circumstances. Perhaps the law of the United States, properly interpreted in deference to integrity, did include the Fugitive Slave Act enacted by Congress before the Civil War.[27] If a judge's own sense of justice condemned that act as deeply immoral because it required citizens to help send escaped slaves back to their masters, he would have to consider whether he should actually enforce it on the demand of a slave owner, or whether he should lie and say that this was not the law after all, or whether he should resign. The principle of integrity in adjudication, therefore, does not necessarily have the last word about how the coercive power of the state should be used. But it does have the first word, and normally there is nothing to add to what it says.

Integrity and Consistency

Is integrity only consistency (deciding like cases alike) under a prouder name? That depends on what we mean by consistency or like cases. If a political institution is consistent only when it repeats its own past decisions most closely or precisely in point, then integrity is not consistency; it is something both more and less. Integrity demands that the public standards of the community be both made and seen, so far as this is possible, to express a single, coherent scheme of justice and fairness in the right relation. An institution that accepts that ideal will sometimes, for that reason, depart from a narrow line of past decisions in search of fidelity to principles conceived as more fundamental to the scheme as a whole.

The plainest examples come from adjudication, and I choose one that illustrates only a partial victory for integrity so far. For some time British judges declared that although members of other professions were liable for damage caused by their carelessness, barristers were immune from such liability. Consistency, narrowly understood, would have required continuing that exception, but integrity condemns the special treatment of barristers unless it can be justified in principle, which seems unlikely. The House of Lords has now curtailed the exemption: to that extent it has preferred integrity to narrow consistency.[28] Integrity will not be satisfied, however, until the exemption is entirely erased.

That observation might help to quiet a suspicion encouraged by the discussion so far. Integrity might seem too conservative a basis for a conception of law, particularly in contrast to pragmatism, its most powerful rival. The judge who defers to integrity in deciding in favor of Mrs. McLoughlin, in spite of his opinion that it would be better to allow emotional damages to no one, seems timid beside his pragmatist brother who sees no obstacles to making the law better bit by bit. But once we grasp the difference between integrity and narrow consistency, this contrast becomes more complex. Integrity is a more dynamic and radical standard than it first seemed, because it encourages a judge to be wide-ranging and imaginative in his search for coherence with fundamental principle. In some cases, as in *McLoughlin* on the premises just assumed, the judge who takes integrity as his model will indeed seem more cautious than the pragmatist. But in other cases his decisions will seem more radical.

Consider, for example, the Supreme Court's decision in *Brown.* A pragmatist justice of a general utilitarian cast of mind would have asked himself whether a decision for the plaintiff schoolchildren, based on the illegality of all official segregation in schools, was really best for the future, all things considered. He might well have decided that it was, but he would have had to consider strong practical arguments to the contrary. It was perfectly sensible to think that such a dramatic change in the social structure of a large part of the country, ordered by a court that is not responsible to any electorate, would produce a backlash that would damage rather than advance racial equality and make education more difficult for everyone for a generation. It was also sensible to think that the Court's order would never be fully obeyed, and that its failure would impair the power of the Court to protect minorities and enforce constitutional rights in the future.

Even if a pragmatist decided in the end that the decision the Court actually reached was the best, all things considered, he might well have paused before extending that decision in the dramatic way the Supreme Court did in subsequent years. The practical arguments against busing black children to white schools, and vice versa, were and remain very powerful, as the menace and hatred in several northern cities continue to make plain. A conception of law built on the interpretive principle of integrity provides much less room for practical arguments of that sort in establishing substantive constitutional rights.[29] It is therefore more demanding and much more radical in circumstances like those of *Brown*, when the plaintiff succeeds in showing that an important part of what has been thought to be law is inconsistent with more fundamental principles necessary to justify law as a whole.

Integrity is also narrower than consistency in a way we have already noticed, though it is sufficiently important to notice again. Integrity is about principle and does not require any simple form of consistency in policy.[30] The legislative principle of integrity demands that the legislature strive to protect for everyone what it takes to be their moral and political rights, so that public standards express a coherent scheme of justice and fairness. But the legislature makes many decisions that favor a particular group, not on the ground that the best conception of justice declares that that group has a right to that benefit, but only because benefiting that group happens to work for the general interest. If the legislature provides subsidies for farmers who grow wheat, for example, in order to ensure an adequate crop, or pays corn farmers not to plant because there is too much corn, it does not recognize any right of the farmers to these payments. A blind form of consistency would require the legislature to offer subsidies or payments for not planting to all farmers, or at least to all farmers whose crops were essential or who produced crops now in oversupply. But there might be sound reasons of policy—perhaps of a very different sort—why the legislature should not generalize these policies in that way. Integrity is not violated just by accepting these reasons and refusing to make the policy of subsidy more general.

We shall notice in Chapter 8 an argument that might seem to threaten this distinction because it shows that integrity has force even in these decisions of policy. A government that accepts what I shall there call the abstract egalitarian principle, that it must treat its citizens as equals, needs a conception of equal concern, and integrity demands that the government settle on a single conception that it will not disavow in any decision, including those of policy. Many politicians, for example, think that treating people as equals means counting the welfare of each in some overall utilitarian calculation; an institution that used that conception of equal concern to justify some laws could not use a contradictory conception—that equal concern requires material equality among citizens, for instance—to justify other laws. But in ordinary politics legislators must take a long view of these requirements. They would be paralyzed if they undertook to ensure that each decision, one by one, left each citizen with exactly what the most sensitive utilitarian calculation, for example, would assign him. A working political theory must be more relaxed: it requires only that government pursue general strategies that promote the overall good as defined roughly and statistically to match what equal concern requires according to the conception in play. So a government committed to the utilitarian conception aims at legislative strategies that, as a whole and in the long run, improve average welfare better than alternate strategies would; a government committed to material equality adopts programs that make sections and classes more equal in material wealth as groups, and so forth. Decisions in pursuit of these strategies, judged one by one, are matters of policy, not principle; they must be tested by asking whether they advance the overall goal, not whether they give each citizen what he is entitled to have as an individual. Subsidies to one set of farmers may be justified on that test, even though subsidies to a different set, as part of a different overall strategy, would also have improved the general welfare, perhaps just as much.

Most working political theories also recognize, however, distinct individual rights as trumps over these decisions of policy, rights that government *is* required to respect case by case, decision by decision. These may be grand political rights, like the right of each citizen to have his vote counted as equal to any other citizen's, or not to be denied freedom of speech or conscience, even when violating these rights would contribute to the general welfare. Or rights drawn more directly from personal morality, like the right to be compensated for injuries caused by another's carelessness. Integrity fixes its gaze on these matters of principle: government must speak with one voice about what these rights are and so not deny them to anyone at any time. Integrity's effect on decisions of policy is more diffuse. It requires, as I said, that government pursue some coherent conception of what treating people as equals means, but this is mainly a question of general strategies and rough statistical tests. It does not otherwise require narrow consistency within policies: it does not require that particular programs treat everyone the same way.[31] Integrity's concern with rights and principle does, however, sometimes disqualify inconsistency of a certain special kind. An American legislature could not decide that no Catholic farmer should receive subsidies even if, incredibly, there were sound reasons of policy for this discrimination.

The distinction between policy and principle and the direct connection between integrity and principle are important outside legislation as well. Consider prosecutor's discretion and other policy decisions in the criminal process. Consistency might be thought to argue that if some people who commit a particular crime have been and will be punished, all such people should be, and that punishments should be uniform, given an equal level of culpability. Integrity is more discriminating. If a prosecutor's reason for not prosecuting one person lies in policy—if the prosecution would be too expensive, for example, or would for some reason not contribute effectively to deterrence—integrity offers no reason why someone else should not be prosecuted when these reasons of policy are absent or reversed. But if the reasons that argue against prosecution in one case are reasons of principle—that the criminal statute did not give adequate notice, for example—then integrity demands that these reasons be respected for everyone else. Obviously integrity would also condemn prosecutors' decisions that discriminate, even for reasons of ostensible policy, on grounds that violate rights otherwise recognized, as if our prosecutors saved expense by prosecuting only blacks for a kind of crime that was particularly prevalent in mainly black communities.[32]

SEVEN

INTEGRITY IN LAW

A LARGE VIEW

In this chapter we construct the third conception of law I introduced in Chapter 3. Law as integrity denies that statements of law are either the backward-looking factual reports of conventionalism or the forward-looking instrumental programs of legal pragmatism. It insists that legal claims are interpretive judgments and therefore combine backward- and forward-looking elements; they interpret contemporary legal practice seen as an unfolding political narrative. So law as integrity rejects as unhelpful the ancient question whether judges find or invent law; we understand legal reasoning, it suggests, only by seeing the sense in which they do both and neither.

Integrity and Interpretation

The adjudicative principle of integrity instructs judges to identify legal rights and duties, so far as possible, on the assumption that they were all created by a single author—the community personified—expressing a coherent conception of justice and fairness. We form our third conception of law, our third view of what rights and duties flow from past political decisions, by restating this instruction as a thesis about the grounds of law. According to law as integrity, propositions of law are true if they figure in or follow from the principles of justice, fairness, and procedural due process that provide the best constructive interpretation of the community's legal practice. Deciding whether the law grants Mrs.

McLoughlin compensation for her injury, for example, means deciding whether legal practice is seen in a better light if we assume the community has accepted the principle that people in her position are entitled to compensation.

Law as integrity is therefore more relentlessly interpretive than either conventionalism or pragmatism. These latter theories offer themselves *as* interpretations. They are conceptions of law that claim to show our legal practices in the best light these can bear, and they recommend, in their postinterpretive conclusions, distinct styles or programs for adjudication. But the programs they recommend are not themselves programs *of* interpretation: they do not ask judges deciding hard cases to carry out any further, essentially interpretive study of legal doctrine. Conventionalism requires judges to study law reports and parliamentary records to discover what decisions have been made by institutions conventionally recognized to have legislative power. No doubt interpretive issues will arise in that process: for example, it may be necessary to interpret a text to decide what statutes our legal conventions construct from it. But once a judge has accepted conventionalism as his guide, he has no further occasion for interpreting the legal record as a whole in deciding particular cases. Pragmatism requires judges to think instrumentally about the best rules for the future. That exercise may require interpretation of something beyond legal material: a utilitarian pragmatist may need to worry about the best way to understand the idea of community welfare, for example. But once again, a judge who accepts pragmatism is then done with interpreting legal practice as a whole.

Law as integrity is different: it is both the product of and the inspiration for comprehensive interpretation of legal practice. The program it holds out to judges deciding hard cases is essentially, not just contingently, interpretive; law as integrity asks them to continue interpreting the same material that it claims to have successfully interpreted itself. It offers itself as continuous with—the initial part of—the more detailed interpretations it recommends. We must therefore now return to the general study of interpretation we began in Chapter 2. We must continue the account given there of what interpretation is and when it is done well, but in more detail and directed more to the special interpretive challenge put to judges and others who must say what the law is.

Integrity and History

History matters in law as integrity: very much but only in a certain way. Integrity does not require consistency in principle over all historical stages of a community's law; it does not require that judges try to understand the law they enforce as continuous in principle with the abandoned law of a previous century or even a previous generation. It commands a horizontal rather than vertical consistency of principle across the range of the legal standards the community now enforces. It insists that the law—the rights and duties that flow from past collective decisions and for that reason license or require coercion—contains not only the narrow explicit content of these decisions but also, more broadly, the scheme of principles necessary to justify them. History matters because that scheme of principle must justify the standing as well as the content of these past decisions. Our justification for treating the Endangered Species Act as law, unless and until it is repealed, crucially includes the fact that Congress enacted it, and any justification we supply for treating that fact as crucial must itself accommodate the way we treat other events in our political past.

Law as integrity, then, begins in the present and pursues the past only so far as and in the way its contemporary focus dictates. It does not aim to recapture, even for present law, the ideals or practical purposes of the politicians who first created it. It aims rather to justify what they did (sometimes including, as we shall see, what they said) in an overall story worth telling now, a story with a complex claim: that present practice can be organized by and justified in principles sufficiently attractive to provide an honorable future. Law as integrity deplores the mechanism of the older "law is law" view as well as the cynicism of the newer "realism." It sees both views as rooted in the same false dichotomy of finding and inventing law. When a judge declares that a particular principle is instinct in law, he reports not a simple-minded claim about the motives of past statesmen, a claim a wise cynic can easily refute, but an interpretive proposal: that the principle both fits and justifies some complex part of legal practice, that it provides an attractive way to see, in the structure of that practice, the consistency of principle integrity requires. Law's optimism is in that way conceptual; claims of law are endemically constructive, just in virtue of the kind of claims they are. This optimism may be misplaced: legal practice may in the end yield to nothing but a deeply skeptical interpretation. But that is not inevitable just because a community's history is one of great change and conflict. An imaginative interpretation can be constructed on morally complicated, even ambiguous terrain.

THE CHAIN OF LAW

The Chain Novel

I argued in Chapter 2 that creative interpretation takes its formal structure from the idea of intention, not (at least not necessarily) because it aims to discover the purposes of any particular historical person or group but because it aims to impose purpose over the text or data or tradition being interpreted. Since all creative interpretation shares this feature, and therefore has a normative aspect or component, we profit from comparing law with other forms or occasions of interpretation. We can usefully compare the judge deciding what the law is on some issue not only with the citizens of courtesy deciding what that tradition requires, but with the literary critic teasing out the various dimensions of value in a complex play or poem.

Judges, however, are authors as well as critics. A judge deciding *McLoughlin* or *Brown* adds to the tradition he interprets; future judges confront a new tradition that includes what he has done. Of course literary criticism contributes to the traditions of art in which authors work; the character and importance of that contribution are themselves issues in critical theory. But the contribution of judges is more direct, and the distinction between author and interpreter more a matter of different aspects of the same process. We can find an even more fruitful comparison between literature and law, therefore, by constructing an artificial genre of literature that we might call the chain novel.

In this enterprise a group of novelists writes a novel *seriatim;* each novelist in the chain interprets the chapters he has been given in order to write a new chapter, which is then added to what the next novelist receives, and so on. Each has the job of writing his chapter so as to make the novel being constructed the best it can be, and the complexity of this task models the complexity of deciding a hard case under law as integrity. The imaginary literary enterprise is fantastic but not unrecognizable. Some novels have actually been written in this way, though mainly for a debunking purpose, and certain parlor games for rainy weekends in English country houses have something of the same structure. Television soap operas span decades with the same characters and some minimal continuity of personality and plot, though they are written by different teams of authors even in different weeks. In our example, however, the novelists are expected to take their responsibilities of continuity more seriously; they aim jointly to create, so far as they can, a single unified novel that is the best it can be.[1]

Each novelist aims to make a single novel of the material he has been given, what he adds to it, and (so far as he can control this) what his successors will want or be able to add. He must try to make this the best novel it can be construed as the work of a single author rather than, as is the fact, the product of many different hands. That calls for an overall judgment on his part, or a series of overall judgments as he writes and rewrites. He must take up some view about the novel in progress, some working theory about its characters, plot, genre, theme, and point, in order to decide what counts as continuing it and not as beginning anew. If he is a good critic, his view of these matters will be complicated and multifaceted, because the value of a decent novel cannot be captured from a single perspective. He will aim to find layers and currents of meaning rather than a single, exhaustive theme. We can, however, in our now familiar way give some structure to any interpretation he adopts, by distinguishing two dimensions on which it must be tested. The first is what we have been calling the dimension of fit. He cannot adopt any interpretation, however complex, if he believes that no single author who set out to write a novel with the various readings of character, plot, theme, and point that interpretation describes could have written substantially the text he has been given. That does not mean his interpretation must fit every bit of the text. It is not disqualified simply because he claims that some lines or tropes are accidental, or even that some events of plot are mistakes because they work against the literary ambitions the interpretation states. But the interpretation he takes up must nevertheless flow throughout the text; it must have general explanatory power, and it is flawed if it leaves unexplained some major structural aspect of the text, a subplot treated as having great dramatic importance or a dominant and repeated metaphor. If no interpretation can be found that is not flawed in that way, then the chain novelist will not be able fully to meet his assignment; he will have to settle for an interpretation that captures most of the text, conceding that it is not wholly successful. Perhaps even that partial success is unavailable; perhaps every interpretation he considers is inconsistent with the bulk of the material supplied to him. In that case he must abandon the enterprise, for the consequence of taking the interpretive attitude toward the text in question is then a piece of internal skepticism: that nothing can count as continuing the novel rather than beginning anew.

He may find, not that no single interpretation fits the bulk of the text, but that more than one does. The second dimension of interpretation then requires him to judge which of these eligible readings makes the work in progress best, all things considered. At this point his more substantive aesthetic judgments, about the importance or insight or realism or beauty of different ideas the novel might be taken to express, come into play. But the formal and structural considerations that dominate on the first dimension figure on the second as well, for even when neither of two interpretations is disqualified out of hand as explaining too little, one may show the text in a better light because it fits more of the text or provides a more interesting integration of style and content. So the distinction between the two dimensions is less crucial or profound than it might seem. It is a useful analytical device that helps us give structure to any interpreter's working theory or style. He will form a sense of when an interpretation fits so poorly that it is unnecessary to consider its substantive appeal, because he knows that this cannot outweigh its embarrassments of fit in deciding whether it makes the novel better, everything taken into account, than its rivals. This sense will define the first dimension for him. But he need not reduce his intuitive sense to any precise formula; he would rarely need to decide whether some interpretation barely survives or barely fails, because a bare survivor, no matter how ambitious or interesting it claimed the text to be, would almost certainly fail in the overall comparison with other interpretations whose fit was evident.

We can now appreciate the range of different kinds of judgments that are blended in this overall comparison. Judgments about textual coherence and integrity, reflecting different formal literary values, are interwoven with more substantive aesthetic judgments that themselves assume different literary aims. Yet these various kinds of judgments, of each general kind, remain distinct enough to check one another in an overall assessment, and it is that possibility of contest, particularly between textual and substantive judgments, that distinguishes a chain novelist's assignment from more independent creative writing. Nor can we draw any flat distinction between the stage at which a chain novelist interprets the text he has been given and the stage at which he adds his own chapter, guided by the interpretation he has settled on. When he begins to write he might discover in what he has written a different, perhaps radically different, interpretation. Or he might find it impossible to write in the tone or theme he first took up, and that will lead him to reconsider other interpretations he first rejected. In either case he returns to the text to reconsider the lines it makes eligible.

Scrooge

We can expand this abstract description of the chain novelist's judgment through an example. Suppose you are a novelist well down the chain. Suppose Dickens never wrote *A Christmas Carol,* and the text you are furnished, though written by several people, happens to be the first part of that short novel. You consider these two interpretations of the central character: Scrooge is inherently and irredeemably evil, an embodiment of the untarnished wickedness of human nature freed from the disguises of convention he rejects; or Scrooge is inherently good but progressively corrupted by the false values and perverse demands of high capitalist society. Obviously it will make an enormous difference to the way you continue the story which of these interpretations you adopt. If you have been given almost all of *A Christmas Carol* with only the very end to be written— Scrooge has already had his dreams, repented, and sent his turkey—it is too late for you to make him irredeemably wicked, assuming you think, as most interpreters would, that the text will not bear that interpretation without too much strain. I do not mean that no interpreter could possibly think Scrooge inherently evil after his supposed redemption.

Someone might take that putative redemption to be a final act of hypocrisy, though only at the cost of taking much else in the text not at face value. This would be a poor interpretation, not because no one could think it a good one, but because it is in fact, on all the criteria so far described, a poor one.[2]

But now suppose you have been given only the first few sections of *A Christmas Carol*. You find that neither of the two interpretations you are considering is decisively ruled out by anything in the text so far; perhaps one would better explain some minor incidents of plot that must be left unconnected on the other, but each interpretation can be seen generally to flow through the abbreviated text as a whole. A competent novelist who set out to write a novel along either of the lines suggested could well have written what you find on the pages. In that case you have a further decision to make. Your assignment is to make of the text the best it can be, and you will therefore choose the interpretation you believe makes the work more significant or otherwise better. That decision will probably (though not inevitably) depend on whether you think that real people somewhat like Scrooge are born bad or are corrupted by capitalism. But it will depend on much else as well, because your aesthetic convictions are not so simple as to make only this aspect of a novel relevant to its overall success. Suppose you think that one interpretation integrates not only plot but image and setting as well; the social interpretation accounts, for example, for the sharp contrast between the individualistic fittings and partitions of Scrooge's countinghouse and the communitarian formlessness of Bob Cratchit's household. Now your aesthetic judgment—about which reading makes the continuing novel better as a novel—is itself more complex because it must identify and trade off different dimensions of value in a novel. Suppose you believe that the original sin reading is much the more accurate depiction of human nature, but that the sociorealist reading provides a deeper and more interesting formal structure for the novel. You must then ask yourself which interpretation makes the work of art better on the whole. You may never have reflected on that sort of question before—perhaps the tradition of criticism in which you have been trained takes it for granted that one or the other of these dimensions is the more important—but that is no reason why you may not do so now. Once you make up your mind you will believe that the correct interpretation of Scrooge's character is the interpretation that makes the novel better on the whole, so judged.

This contrived example is complex enough to provoke the following apparently important question. Is your judgment about the best way to interpret and continue the sections you have been given of *A Christmas Carol* a free or a constrained judgment? Are you free to give effect to your own assumptions and attitudes about what novels should be like? Or are you bound to ignore these because you are enslaved by a text you cannot alter? The answer is plain enough: neither of these two crude descriptions—of total creative freedom or mechanical textual constraint—captures your situation, because each must in some way be qualified by the other. You will sense creative freedom when you compare your task with some relatively more mechanical one, like direct translation of a text into a foreign language. But you will sense constraint when you compare it with some relatively less guided one, like beginning a new novel of your own.

It is important not only to notice this contrast between elements of artistic freedom and textual constraint but also not to misunderstand its character. It is *not* a contrast between those aspects of interpretation that are dependent on and those that are independent of the interpreter's aesthetic convictions. And it is not a contrast between those aspects that may be and those that cannot be controversial. For the constraints that you sense as limits to your freedom to read *A Christmas Carol* so as to make Scrooge irredeemably evil are as much matters of judgment and conviction, about which different chain novelists might disagree, as the convictions and attitudes you call on in deciding whether the novel would have been better if he had been irredeemably evil. If the latter convictions are "subjective" (I use the language of external skepticism, reluctantly, because some readers will find it helpful here) then so are the former. Both major types of convictions any interpreter has—about which readings fit the text better or worse and about which of two readings makes the novel substantively better—are internal to his overall scheme of beliefs and attitudes; neither type is independent of that scheme in some way that the other is not.

That observation invites the following objection. "If an interpreter must in the end rely on what seems right to him, as much in deciding whether some interpretation fits as in deciding whether it makes the novel more attractive, then he is actually subject to no genuine constraint at all, because no one's judgment can be constrained except by external, hard facts that everyone must agree about." The objection is misconceived because it rests on a piece of dogmatism. It is a familiar part of our cognitive experience that some of our beliefs and convictions operate as checks in deciding how far we can or should accept or give effect to others, and the check is effective even when the constraining beliefs and attitudes are controversial. If one scientist accepts stricter standards for research procedure than another, he will believe less of what he would like to believe. If one politician has scruples that another politician in good faith rejects, the first will be constrained when the second is not. There is no harm, once again, in using the language of subjectivity the external skeptic favors. We might say that in these examples the constraint is "internal" or "subjective." It is nevertheless phenomenologically genuine, and that is what is important here. We are trying to see what interpretation is like from the point of view of the interpreter, and from that point of view the constraint he feels is as genuine as if it were uncontroversial, as if everyone else felt it as powerfully as he does. Suppose someone then insists that from an "objective" point of view there is no real constraint at all, that the constraint is *merely* subjective. If we treat this further charge as the external skeptic's regular complaint, then it is pointless and misleading in the way we noticed in Chapter 2. It gives a chain novelist no reason to doubt or abandon the conclusions he reaches, about which interpretations fit the text well enough to count, for example, or so poorly that they must be rejected if other interpretations, otherwise less attractive, are available.

The skeptical objection can be made more interesting, however, if we weaken it in the following way. It now insists that a felt constraint may sometimes be illusory not for the external skeptic's dogmatic reason, that a genuine constraint must be uncontroversial and independent of other beliefs and attitudes, but because it may not be sufficiently disjoint, within the system of the interpreter's more substantive artistic convictions, ever actually to check or impede these, even from his point of view.[3] That is a lively possibility, and we must be on guard against it when we criticize our own or other people's interpretive arguments. I made certain assumptions about the structure of your aesthetic opinions when I imagined your likely overall judgment about *A Christmas Carol*. I assumed that the different types of discrete judgments you combine in your overall opinion are sufficiently independent of one another, within the system of your ideas, to allow some to constrain others. You reject reading Scrooge's supposed redemption as hypocritical for "formal" reasons about coherence and integration of plot and diction and figure. A decent novel (you think) would not make a hypocritical redemption the upshot of so dramatic and shattering an event as Scrooge's horrifying night. These formal convictions are independent of your more substantive opinions about the competing value of different literary aims: even if you think a novel of original sin would be more exciting, that does not transform your formal conviction into one more amenable to the original sin interpretation. But suppose I am wrong in these assumptions about your mental life. Suppose we discover in the process of argument that your formal convictions are actually soldered to and driven by more substantive ones. Whenever you prefer a reading of some text on substantive grounds, your formal convictions automatically adjust to endorse it as a decent reading of that text. You might, of course, only be pretending that this is so, in which case you are acting in bad faith. But the adjustment may be unconscious, in which case you think you are constrained but, in the sense that matters, you actually are not. Whether any interpreter's convictions actually check one another, as they must if he is genuinely interpreting at all, depends on the complexity and structure of his pertinent opinions as a whole.

Our chain-novel example has so far been distorted by the unrealistic assumption that the text you were furnished miraculously had the unity of something written by a single author. Even if each of the previous novelists in the chain took his responsibilities very seriously indeed, the text you were given would show the marks of its history, and you would have to tailor your style of interpretation to that circumstance. You might not find any interpretation that flows through the text, that fits everything the material you have been given treats as important. You must lower your sights (as conscientious writers who join the team of an interminable soap opera might do) by trying to construct an interpretation that fits the bulk of what you take to be artistically most fundamental in the text. More than one interpretation may survive this more relaxed test. To choose among these, you must turn to your background aesthetic convictions, including those you will regard as formal. Possibly no interpretation will survive even the relaxed test. That is the skeptical possibility I mentioned earlier: you will then end by abandoning the project, rejecting your assignment as impossible. But you cannot know in advance that you will reach that skeptical result. You must try first. The chain-novel fantasy will be useful in the later argument in various ways, but that is the most important lesson it teaches. The wise-sounding judgment that no one interpretation could be best must be earned and defended like any other interpretive claim.

A Misleading Objection

A chain novelist, then, has many difficult decisions to make, and different chain novelists can be expected to make these differently. But his decisions do not include, nor are they properly summarized as, the decision whether and how far he should depart from the novel-in-progress he has been furnished. For he has nothing he *can* depart from or cleave to until he has constructed a novel-in-process from the text, and the various decisions we have canvassed are all decisions he must make just to do this. Suppose you have decided that a sociorealist interpretation of the opening sections of *A Christmas Carol* makes that text, on balance, the best novel-so-far it can be, and so you continue the novel as an exploration of the uniformly degrading master-servant relation under capitalism rather than as a study of original sin. Now suppose someone accuses you of rewriting the "real" novel to produce a different one that you like better. If he means that the "real" novel can be discovered in some way other than by a process of interpretation of the sort you conducted, then he has misunderstood not only the chain-novel enterprise but the nature of literature and criticism. Of course, he may mean only that he disagrees with the particular interpretive and aesthetic convictions on which you relied. In that case your disagreement is not that he thinks you should respect the text, while you think you are free to ignore it. Your disagreement is more interesting: you disagree about what respecting this text means.

LAW: THE QUESTION OF EMOTIONAL DAMAGES

Law as integrity asks a judge deciding a common-law case like *McLoughlin* to think of himself as an author in the chain of common law. He knows that other judges have decided cases that, although not exactly like his case, deal with related problems; he must think of their decisions as part of a long story he must interpret and then continue, according to his own judgment of how to make the developing story as good as it can be. (Of course the best story for him means best from the standpoint of political morality, not aesthetics.) We can make a rough distinction once again between two main dimensions of this interpretive judgment. The judge's decision—his postinterpretive conclusions—must be drawn from an interpretation that both fits and justifies what has gone before, so far as that is possible. But in law as in literature the interplay between fit and justification is complex. Just as interpretation within a chain novel is for each interpreter a delicate balance among different types of literary and artistic attitudes, so in law it is a delicate balance among political convictions of different sorts; in law as in literature these must be sufficiently related yet disjoint to allow an overall judgment that trades off an interpretation's success on one type of standard against its failure on another. I must try to exhibit that complex structure of legal interpretation, and I shall use for that purpose an imaginary judge of superhuman intellectual power and patience who accepts law as integrity.

Call him Hercules.[4] In this and the next several chapters we follow his career by noticing the types of judgments he must make and tensions he must resolve in deciding a variety of cases. But I offer this caution in advance. We must not suppose that his answers to the various questions he encounters *define* law as integrity as a general conception of law. They are the answers I now think best. But law as integrity consists in an approach, in questions rather than answers, and other lawyers and judges who accept it would give different answers from his to the questions it asks. You might think other answers would be better. (So might I, after further thought.) You might, for example, reject Hercules' views about how far people's legal rights depend on the reasons past judges offered for their decisions enforcing these rights, or you might not share his respect for what I shall call "local priority" in common-law decisions. If you reject these discrete views because you think them poor constructive interpretations of legal practice, however, you have not rejected law as integrity but rather have joined its enterprise.

Six Interpretations

Hercules must decide *McLoughlin*. Both sides in that case cited precedents; each argued that a decision in its favor would count as going on as before, as continuing the story begun by the judges who decided those precedent cases. Hercules must form his own view about that issue. Just as a chain novelist must find, if he can, some coherent view of character and theme such that a hypothetical single author with that view could have written at least the bulk of the novel so far, Hercules must find, if he can, some coherent theory about legal rights to compensation for emotional injury such that a single political official with that theory could have reached most of the results the precedents report.

He is a careful judge, a judge of method. He begins by setting out various candidates for the best interpretation of the precedent cases even before he reads them. Suppose he makes the following short list: (1) No one has a moral right to compensation except for physical injury. (2) People have a moral right to compensation for emotional injury suffered at the scene of an accident against anyone whose carelessness caused the accident but have no right to compensation for emotional injury suffered later. (3) People should recover compensation for emotional injury when a practice of requiring compensation in their circumstances would diminish the overall costs of accidents or otherwise make the community richer in the long run. (4) People have a moral right to compensation for any injury, emotional or physical, that is the direct consequence of careless conduct, no matter how unlikely or unforeseeable it is that that conduct would result in that injury. (5) People have a moral right to compensation for emotional or physical injury that is the consequence of careless conduct, but only if that injury was reasonably foreseeable by the person who acted carelessly. (6) People have a moral right to compensation for reasonably foreseeable injury but not in circumstances when recognizing such a right would impose massive and destructive financial burdens on people who have been careless out of proportion to their moral fault.

These are all relatively concrete statements about rights and, allowing for a complexity in (3) we explore just below, they contradict one another. No more than one can figure in a single interpretation of the emotional injury cases. (I postpone the more complex case in which Hercules constructs an interpretation from competitive rather than contradictory principles, that is, from principles that can live together in an overall moral or political theory though they sometimes pull in different directions.)[5] Even so, this is only a partial list of the contradictory interpretations someone might wish to consider; Hercules chooses it as his initial short list because he knows that the principles captured in these interpretations have actually been discussed in the legal literature. It will obviously make a great difference which of these principles he believes provides the best interpretation of the precedents and so the nerve of his postinterpretive judgment. If he settles on (1) or (2), he must decide for Mr. O'Brian; if on (4), for Mrs. McLoughlin. Each of the others requires further thought, but the line of reasoning each suggests is different. (3) invites an economic calculation. Would it reduce the cost of accidents to extend liability to emotional injury away from the scene? Or is there some reason to think that the most efficient line is drawn just between emotional injuries at and those away from the scene? (5) requires a judgment about foreseeability of injury, which seems to be very different, and (6) a judgment both about foreseeability and the cumulative risk of financial responsibility if certain injuries away from the scene are included.

Hercules begins testing each interpretation on his short list by asking whether a single political official could have given the verdicts of the precedent cases if that official were consciously and coherently enforcing the principles that form the interpretation. He will therefore dismiss interpretation (1) at once. No one who believed that people never have rights to compensation for emotional injury could have reached the results of those past decisions cited in *McLoughlin* that allowed compensation. Hercules will also dismiss interpretation (2), though for a different reason. Unlike (1), (2) fits the past decisions; someone who accepted (2) as a standard would have reached these decisions, because they all allowed recovery for emotional injury at the scene and none allowed recovery for injury away from it. But (2) fails as an interpretation of the required kind because it does not state a principle of justice at all. It draws a line that it leaves arbitrary and unconnected to any more general moral or political consideration.

What about (3)? It might fit the past decisions, but only in the following way. Hercules might discover through economic analysis that someone who accepted the economic theory expressed by (3) and who wished to reduce the community's accident costs would have made just those decisions. But it is far from obvious that (3) states any principle of justice or fairness. Remember the distinction between principles and policies we discussed toward the end of the last chapter. (3) supposes that it is desirable to reduce accident costs overall. Why? Two explanations are possible. The first insists that people have a right to compensation whenever a rule awarding compensation would produce more wealth for the community overall than a rule denying it. This has the form, at least, of a principle because it describes a general right everyone is supposed to have. I shall not ask Hercules to consider (3) understood in that way now, because he will study it very carefully in Chapter 8. The second, quite different, explanation suggests that it is sometimes or even always in the community's general interest to promote overall wealth in this way, but it does not suppose that anyone has any right that social wealth always be increased. It therefore sets out a policy that government might or might not decide to pursue in particular circumstances. It does not state a principle of justice, and so it cannot figure in an interpretation of the sort Hercules now seeks.[6]

Law as integrity asks judges to assume, so far as this is possible, that the law is structured by a coherent set of principles about justice and fairness and procedural due process, and it asks them to enforce these in the fresh cases that come before them, so that each person's situation is fair and just according to the same standards. That style of adjudication respects the ambition integrity assumes, the ambition to be a community of principle. But as we saw at the end of Chapter 6, integrity does not recommend what would be perverse, that we should all be governed by the same goals and strategies of policy on every occasion. It does not insist that a legislature that enacts one set of rules about compensation today, in order to make the community richer on the whole, is in any way committed to serve that same goal of policy tomorrow. For it might then have other goals to seek, not necessarily in place of wealth but beside it, and integrity does not frown on this diversity. Our account of interpretation, and our consequent elimination of interpretation (3) read as a naked appeal to policy, reflects a discrimination already latent in the ideal of integrity itself.

We reach the same conclusion in the context of *McLoughlin* through a different route, by further reflection on what we have learned about interpretation. An interpretation aims to show what is interpreted in the best light possible, and an interpretation of any part of our law must therefore attend not only to the substance of the decisions made by earlier officials but also to how—by which officials in which circumstances—these decisions were made. A legislature does not need reasons of principle to justify the rules it enacts about driving, including rules about compensation for accidents,

even though these rules will create rights and duties for the
future that will then be enforced by coercive threat. A legislature may justify its decision to create new rights for the future by showing how these will contribute, as a matter of
sound policy, to the overall good of the community as a
whole. There are limits to this kind of justification, as we noticed in Chapter 6. The general good may not be used to
justify the death penalty for careless driving. But the legislature need not show that citizens already have a moral right
to compensation for injury under particular circumstances
in order to justify a statute awarding damages in those circumstances.

Law as integrity assumes, however, that judges are in a
very different position from legislators. It does not fit the
character of a community of principle that a judge should
have authority to hold people liable in damages for acting in
a way he concedes they had no legal duty not to act. So
when judges construct rules of liability not recognized before, they are not free in the way I just said legislators are.
Judges must make their common-law decisions on grounds
of principle, not policy: they must deploy arguments why the
parties actually had the "novel" legal rights and duties they
enforce at the time the parties acted or at some other pertinent time in the past.[7] A legal pragmatist would reject that
claim. But Hercules rejects pragmatism. He follows law as
integrity and therefore wants an interpretation of what
judges did in the earlier emotional damage cases that shows
them acting in the way he approves, not in the way he thinks
judges must decline to act. It does not follow that he must
dismiss interpretation (3) read in the first way I described, as
supposing that past judges acted to protect a general legal
right to compensation when this would make the community richer. For if people actually have such a right, others
have a corresponding duty, and judges do not act unjustly in
ordering the police to enforce it. The argument disqualifies
interpretation (3) only when this is read to deny any such
general duty and to rest on grounds of policy alone.

Expanding the Range

Interpretations (4), (5), and (6) do, however, seem to pass these initial tests. The principles of each fit the past emotional injury decisions, at least on first glance, if only because none of these precedents presented facts that would discriminate among them. Hercules must now ask, as the next stage of his investigation, whether any one of the three must be ruled out because it is incompatible with the bulk of legal practice more generally. He must test each interpretation against other past judicial decisions, beyond those involving emotional injury, that might be thought to engage them. Suppose he discovers, for example, that past decisions provide compensation for physical injury caused by careless driving only if the injury was reasonably foreseeable. That would rule out interpretation (4) unless he can find some principled distinction between physical and emotional injury that explains why the conditions for compensation should be more restrictive for the former than the latter, which seems extremely unlikely.

Law as integrity, then, requires a judge to test his interpretation of any part of the great network of political structures and decisions of his community by asking whether it could form part of a coherent theory justifying the network as a whole. No actual judge could compose anything approaching a full interpretation of all of his community's law at once. That is why we are imagining a Herculean judge of superhuman talents and endless time. But an actual judge can imitate Hercules in a limited way. He can allow the scope of his interpretation to fan out from the cases immediately in point to cases in the same general area or department of law, and then still farther, so far as this seems promising. In practice even this limited process will be largely unconscious: an experienced judge will have a sufficient sense of the terrain surrounding his immediate problem to know instinctively which interpretation of a small set of cases would survive if the range it must fit were expanded.

But sometimes the expansion will be deliberate and controversial. Lawyers celebrate dozens of decisions of that character, including several on which the modern law of negligence was built.[8] Scholarship offers other important examples.[9]

Suppose a modest expansion of Hercules' range of inquiry does show that plaintiffs are denied compensation if their physical injury was not reasonably foreseeable at the time the careless defendant acted, thus ruling out interpretation (4). But this does not eliminate either (5) or (6). He must expand his survey further. He must look also to cases involving economic rather than physical or emotional injury, where damages are potentially very great: for example, he must look to cases in which professional advisers like surveyors or accountants are sued for losses others suffer through their negligence. Interpretation (5) suggests that such liability might be unlimited in amount, no matter how ruinous in total, provided that the damage is foreseeable, and (6) suggests, on the contrary, that liability is limited just because of the frightening sums it might otherwise reach. If one interpretation is uniformly contradicted by cases of that sort and finds no support in any other area of doctrine Hercules might later inspect, and the other is confirmed by the expansion, he will regard the former as ineligible, and the latter alone will have survived. But suppose he finds, when he expands his study in this way, a mixed pattern. Past decisions permit extended liability for members of some professions but not for those of others, and this mixed pattern holds for other areas of doctrine that Hercules, in the exercise of his imaginative skill, finds pertinent.

The contradiction he has discovered, though genuine, is not in itself so deep or pervasive as to justify a skeptical interpretation of legal practice as a whole, for the problem of unlimited damages, while important, is not so fundamental that contradiction within it destroys the integrity of the larger system. So Hercules turns to the second main dimension, but here, as in the chain-novel example, questions of fit surface again, because an interpretation is *pro tanto* more satisfactory if it shows less damage to integrity than its rival. He will therefore consider whether interpretation (5) fits the expanded legal record better than (6). But this cannot be a merely mechanical decision; he cannot simply count the number of past decisions that must be conceded to be "mistakes" on each interpretation. For these numbers may reflect only accidents like the number of cases that happen to have come to court and not been settled before verdict. He must take into account not only the numbers of decisions counting for each interpretation, but whether the decisions expressing one principle seem more important or fundamental or wide-ranging than the decisions expressing the other. Suppose interpretation (6) fits only those past judicial decisions involving charges of negligence against one particular profession—say, lawyers—and interpretation (5) justifies all other cases, involving all other professions, and also fits other kinds of economic damage cases as well. Interpretation (5) then fits the legal record better on the whole, even if the number of cases involving lawyers is for some reason numerically greater, unless the argument shifts again, as it well might, when the field of study expands even more.

Now suppose a different possibility: that though liability has in many and varied cases actually been limited to an amount less than interpretation (5) would allow, the opinions attached to these cases made no mention of the principle of interpretation (6), which has in fact never before been recognized in official judicial rhetoric. Does that show that interpretation (5) fits the legal record much better, or that interpretation (6) is ineligible after all? Judges in fact divide about this issue of fit. Some would not seriously consider interpretation (6) if no past judicial opinion or legislative statement had ever explicitly mentioned its principle. Others reject this constraint and accept that the best interpretation of some line of cases may lie in a principle that has never been recognized explicitly but that nevertheless offers a brilliant account of the actual decisions, showing them in a bet-

ter light than ever before.[10] Hercules will confront this issue
as a special question of political morality. The political history of the community is *pro tanto* a better history, he thinks,
if it shows judges making plain to their public, through their
opinions, the path that later judges guided by integrity will
follow and if it shows judges making decisions that give voice
as well as effect to convictions about morality that are widespread through the community. Judicial opinions formally
announced in law reports, moreover, are themselves acts of
the community personified that, particularly if recent, must
be taken into the embrace of integrity.[11] These are among
his reasons for somewhat preferring an interpretation that is
not too novel, not too far divorced from what past judges
and other officials said as well as did. But he must set these
reasons against his more substantive political convictions
about the relative moral value of the two interpretations,
and if he believes that interpretation (6) is much superior
from that perspective, he will think he makes the legal record
better overall by selecting it even at the cost of the more procedural values. Fitting what judges did is more important
than fitting what they said.

Now suppose an even more unpatterned record. Hercules
finds that unlimited liability has been enforced against a
number of professions but has not been enforced against a
roughly equal number of others, that no principle can explain the distinction, that judicial rhetoric is as split as the
actual decisions, and that this split extends into other kinds
of actions for economic damage. He might expand his field
of survey still further, and the picture might change if he
does. But let us suppose he is satisfied that it will not. He will
then decide that the question of fit can play no more useful
role in his deliberations even on the second dimension. He
must now emphasize the more plainly substantive aspects of
that dimension: he must decide which interpretation shows
the legal record to be the best it can be from the standpoint
of substantive political morality. He will compose and com-

pare two stories. The first supposes that the community personified has adopted and is enforcing the principle of foreseeability as its test of moral responsibility for damage caused by negligence, that the various decisions it has reached are intended to give effect to that principle, though it has often lapsed and reached decisions that foreseeability would condemn. The second supposes, instead, that the community has adopted and is enforcing the principle of foreseeability limited by some overall ceiling on liability, though it has often lapsed from that principle. Which story shows the community in a better light, all things considered, from the standpoint of political morality?

Hercules' answer will depend on his convictions about the two constituent virtues of political morality we have considered: justice and fairness.[12] It will depend, that is, not only on his beliefs about which of these principles is superior as a matter of abstract justice but also about which should be followed, as a matter of political fairness, in a community whose members have the moral convictions his fellow citizens have. In some cases the two kinds of judgment—the judgment of justice and that of fairness—will come together. If Hercules and the public at large share the view that people are entitled to be compensated fully whenever they are injured by others' carelessness, without regard to how harsh this requirement might turn out to be, then he will think that interpretation (5) is plainly the better of the two in play. But the two judgments will sometimes pull in different directions. He may think that interpretation (6) is better on grounds of abstract justice, but know that this is a radical view not shared by any substantial portion of the public and unknown in the political and moral rhetoric of the times. He might then decide that the story in which the state insists on the view he thinks right, but against the wishes of the people as a whole, is a poorer story, on balance. He would be preferring fairness to justice in these circumstances, and that preference would reflect a higher-order level of his own political convictions, namely his convictions about how a decent government committed to both fairness and justice should adjudicate between the two in this sort of case.

Judges will have different ideas of fairness, about the role each citizen's opinion should ideally play in the state's decision about which principles of justice to enforce through its central police power. They will have different higher-level opinions about the best resolution of conflicts between these two political ideals. No judge is likely to hold the simplistic theory that fairness is automatically to be preferred to justice or vice versa. Most judges will think that the balance between the opinions of the community and the demands of abstract justice must be struck differently in different kinds of cases. Perhaps in ordinary commercial or private law cases, like *McLoughlin,* an interpretation supported in popular morality will be deemed superior to one that is not, provided it is not thought very much inferior as a matter of abstract justice. But many judges will think the interpretive force of popular morality very much weaker in constitutional cases like *Brown,* because they will think the point of the Constitution is in part to protect individuals from what the majority thinks right.[13]

Local Priority

I must call special attention to a feature of Hercules' practice that has not yet clearly emerged. His judgments of fit expand out from the immediate case before him in a series of concentric circles. He asks which interpretations on his initial list fit past emotional injury cases, then which ones fit cases of accidental damage to the person more generally, then which fit damage to economic interests, and so on into areas each further and further from the original *McLoughlin* issue. This procedure gives a kind of local priority to what we might call "departments" of law. If Hercules finds that neither of two principles is flatly contradicted by the accidental damage cases of his jurisdiction, he expands his study into, say, contract cases to see which of these principles, if either, fits contract decisions better. But in Hercules' view, if one principle does *not* fit accident law at all—if it is contradicted by almost every decision in the area that might have confirmed it—this counts dramatically against it as an eligible interpretation of that body of law, even if it fits other areas of the law superbly. He will not treat this doctrine of local priority as absolute, however; he will be ready to override it, as we shall soon see, in some circumstances.

The compartmentalization of law into separate departments is a prominent feature of legal practice. Law schools divide courses and their libraries divide treatises to distinguish emotional from economic or physical injury, intentional from unintentional torts, tort from crime, contract from other parts of common law, private from public law, and constitutional law from other parts of public law. Legal and judicial arguments respect these traditional divisions. Judicial opinions normally begin by assigning the case in hand to some department of law, and the precedents and statutes considered are usually drawn exclusively from that department. Often the initial classification is both controversial and crucial.

Compartmentalization suits both conventionalism and pragmatism, though for different reasons. Departments of law are based on tradition, which seems to support conventionalism, and they provide a strategy a pragmatist can manipulate in telling his noble lies: he can explain that his new doctrine need not be consistent in principle with past decisions because the latter, properly understood, belong to a different department. Law as integrity has a more complex attitude toward departments of law. Its general spirit condemns them, because the adjudicative principle of integrity asks judges to make the law coherent as a whole, so far as they can, and this might be better done by ignoring academic boundaries and reforming some departments of law radically to make them more consistent in principle with others.[14] But law as integrity is interpretive, and compartmentalization is a feature of legal practice no competent interpretation can ignore.

Hercules responds to these competing impulses by seeking a constructive interpretation of compartmentalization. He tries to find an explanation of the practice of dividing law into departments that shows that practice in its best light. The boundaries between departments usually match popular opinion; many people think that intentional harm is more blameworthy than careless harm, that the state needs a very different kind of justification to declare someone guilty of a crime than it needs to require him to pay compensation for damage he has caused, that promises and other forms of explicit agreement or consent are a special kind of reason for state coercion, and so forth. Dividing departments of law to match that sort of opinion promotes predictability and guards against sudden official reinterpretations that uproot large areas of law, and it does this in a way that promotes a deeper aim of law as integrity. If legal compartments make sense to people at large, they encourage the protestant attitude integrity favors, because they allow ordinary people as well as hard-pressed judges to interpret law within practical boundaries that seem natural and intuitive.

Hercules accepts that account of the point of compartmentalization, and he shapes his doctrine of local priority accordingly. He allows the doctrine most force when the boundaries between traditional departments of law track widely held moral principles distinguishing types of fault or responsibility, and the substance of each department reflects those moral principles. The distinction between criminal and civil law meets that test. Suppose Hercules thinks, contrary to most people's opinion, that being made to pay compensation is just as bad as being made to pay a fine, and therefore that the distinction between criminal and civil law is unsound in principle. He will nevertheless defer to local priority. He will not claim that criminal and civil law should be treated as one department; he will not argue that a criminal defendant's guilt need only be established as probable rather than beyond a reasonable doubt because the probable standard fits the combined department as well as any other.

But Hercules will not be so ready to defer to local priority when his test is not met, when traditional boundaries between departments have become mechanical and arbitrary, either because popular morality has shifted or because the substance of the departments no longer reflects popular opinion.[15] Compartments of law do sometimes grow arbitrary and isolated from popular conviction in that way, particularly when the central rules of the departments were developed in different periods. Suppose the legal tradition of a community has for many decades separated nuisance law, which concerns the discomfort of interference that activities on one person's land cause to neighbors, from negligence law, which concerns the physical or economic or emotional injuries someone's carelessness inflicts on others. Suppose that the judges who decided the crucial nuisance cases disdained any economic test for nuisance; they said that an activity counts as a nuisance, and must therefore be stopped, when it is not a "natural" or traditional use of the land, so that someone who starts a factory on land traditionally used for farming is guilty of nuisance even though the factory is an economically more efficient use. But suppose that in recent years judges have begun to make economic cost crucial for negligence. They say that someone's failure to take precautions against injuring others is negligent, so that he is liable for the resulting injury if the precaution was "reasonable" in the circumstances, and that the economic cost of the precaution counts in deciding whether it was in fact reasonable.

The distinction between negligence and nuisance law no longer meets Hercules' test, if it ever did. It makes some sense to distinguish nuisance from negligence if we assume that nuisance is intentional while negligence is unintentional; then the distinction tracks the popular principle that it is worse to injure someone knowingly than unknowingly. But the developments in negligence law I just described are not consistent with that view of the distinction, because failing to guard against an accident is not necessarily unintentional in the required sense. So Hercules would be ready to ignore the traditional boundary between these two departments of law. If he thought that the "natural use" test was silly, and the economic cost test much more just, he would argue that the negligence and nuisance precedents should be seen as one body of law, and that the economic cost test is a superior interpretation of that unified body. His argument would probably be made easier by other legal events that already had occurred. The intellectual climate that produced the later negligence decisions would have begun to erode the assumption of the earlier nuisance cases, that novel enterprises that annoy people are necessarily legal wrongs. Perhaps the legislature would have adopted special statutes rearranging liability for some new forms of inconvenience, like airport noise, that the "natural" theory has decided or would decide in what seems the wrong way, for example. Or perhaps judges would have decided airport cases by straining the historical meaning of "natural" to reach decisions that seemed sensible given developing technology. Hercules would cite these changes as supporting his interpretive argument consolidating nuisance and negligence. If he persuades the profession to his view, nuisance and negligence will no longer be distinct departments of law but joint tenants of a new province which will shortly attract a new name attached to new law school courses and new treatises. This process is in fact under way in Anglo-American law, as is, though less securely, a new unification of private law that blurs even the long-established and once much firmer boundary between contract and tort.

A PROVISIONAL SUMMARY

In the next three chapters we continue constructing Hercules' working theory of law as integrity by exploring in more detail issues raised in three departments of adjudication: common-law cases, cases turning on statutes, and cases of constitutional dimension. But first we will take stock, though this means some repetition, and then consider certain objections to the argument so far. Judges who accept the interpretive ideal of integrity decide hard cases by trying to find, in some coherent set of principles about people's rights and duties, the best constructive interpretation of the political structure and legal doctrine of their community. They try to make that complex structure and record the best these can be. It is analytically useful to distinguish different dimensions or aspects of any working theory. It will include convictions about both fit and justification. Convictions about fit will provide a rough threshold requirement that an interpretation of some part of the law must meet if it is to be eligible at all. Any plausible working theory would disqualify an interpretation of our own law that denied legislative competence or supremacy outright or that claimed a general principle of private law requiring the rich to share their wealth with the poor. That threshold will eliminate interpretations that some judges would otherwise prefer, so the brute facts of legal history will in this way limit the role any judge's personal convictions of justice can play in his decisions. Different judges will set this threshold differently. But anyone who accepts law as integrity must accept that the actual political history of his community will sometimes check his other political convictions in his overall interpretive judgment. If he does not—if his threshold of fit is wholly derivative from and adjustable to his convictions of justice, so that the latter automatically provide an eligible interpretation—then he cannot claim in good faith to be interpreting his legal practice at all. Like the chain novelist whose judgments of fit automatically adjusted to his substantive literary opinions, he is acting from bad faith or self-deception.

Hard cases arise, for any judge, when his threshold test does not discriminate between two or more interpretations of some statute or line of cases. Then he must choose between eligible interpretations by asking which shows the community's structure of institutions and decisions—its public standards as a whole—in a better light from the standpoint of political morality. His own moral and political convictions are now directly engaged. But the political judgment he must make is itself complex and will sometimes set one department of his political morality against another: his decision will reflect not only his opinions about justice and fairness but his higher-order convictions about how these ideals should be compromised when they compete. Questions of fit arise at this stage of interpretation as well, because even when an interpretation survives the threshold requirement, any infelicities of fit will count against it, in the ways we noticed, in the general balance of political virtues. Different judges will disagree about each of these issues and will accordingly take different views of what the law of their community, properly understood, really is.

Any judge will develop, in the course of his training and experience, a fairly individualized working conception of law on which he will rely, perhaps unthinkingly, in making these various judgments and decisions, and the judgments will then be, for him, a matter of feel or instinct rather than analysis. Even so, we as critics can impose structure on his working theory by teasing out its rules of thumb about fit— about the relative importance of consistency with past rhetoric and popular opinion, for example—and its more substantive opinions or leanings about justice and fairness. Most judges will be like other people in their community, and fairness and justice will therefore not often compete for them. But judges whose political opinions are more eccentric or radical will find that the two ideals conflict in particular cases, and they will have to decide which resolution of that conflict would show the community's record in the best light. Their working conceptions will accordingly include higher-order principles that have proved necessary to that further decision. A particular judge may think or assume, for example, that political decisions should mainly respect majority opinion, and yet believe that this requirement relaxes and even disappears when serious constitutional rights are in question.

We should now recall two general observations we made in constructing the chain-novel model, because they apply here as well. First, the different aspects or dimensions of a judge's working approach—the dimensions of fit and substance, and of different aspects of substance—are in the last analysis all responsive to his political judgment. His convictions about fit, as these appear either in his working threshold requirement or analytically later in competition with substance, are political not mechanical. They express his commitment to integrity: he believes that an interpretation that falls below his threshold of fit shows the record of the community in an irredeemably bad light, because proposing that interpretation suggests that the community has characteristically dishonored its own principles. When an interpretation meets the threshold, remaining defects of fit may be compensated, in his overall judgment, if the principles of that interpretation are particularly attractive, because then he sets off the community's infrequent lapses in respecting these principles against its virtue in generally observing them. The constraint fit imposes on substance, in any working theory, is therefore the constraint of one type of political conviction on another in the overall judgment which interpretation makes a political record the best it can be overall, everything taken into account. Second, the mode of this constraint is the mode we identified in the chain novel. It is not the constraint of external hard fact or of interpersonal consensus. But rather the structural constraint of different kinds of principle within a system of principle, and it is none the less genuine for that.

No mortal judge can or should try to articulate his instinctive working theory so far, or make that theory so concrete and detailed, that no further thought will be necessary case by case. He must treat any general principles or rules of thumb he has followed in the past as provisional and stand ready to abandon these in favor of more sophisticated and searching analysis when the occasion demands. These will be moments of special difficulty for any judge, calling for fresh political judgments that may be hard to make. It would be absurd to suppose that he will always have at hand the necessary background convictions of political morality for such occasions. Very hard cases will force him to develop his conception of law and his political morality together in a mutually supporting way. But it is nevertheless possible for any judge to confront fresh and challenging issues as a matter of principle, and this is what law as integrity demands of him. He must accept that in finally choosing one interpretation over another of a much contested line of precedents, perhaps after demanding thought and shifting conviction, he is developing his working conception of law in one rather than another direction. This must seem to him the right direction as a matter of political principle, not just appealing for the moment because it recommends an attractive decision in the immediate case. There is, in this counsel, much room for deception, including self-deception. But on most occasions it will be possible for judges to recognize when they have submitted an issue to the discipline it describes. And also to recognize when some other judge has not.

SOME FAMILIAR OBJECTIONS
Hercules Is Playing Politics

Hercules has completed his labors in *McLoughlin*. He declares that the best interpretation of the emotional damage cases, all things considered, is (5): the law allows compensation for all emotional injury directly caused by careless driving and foreseeable by a reasonably thoughtful motorist. But he concedes that in reaching that conclusion he has relied on his own opinion that this principle is better—fairer and more just—than any other that is eligible on what he takes to be the right criteria of fit. He also concedes that this opinion is controversial: it is not shared by all of his fellow judges, some of whom therefore think that some other interpretation, for example (6), is superior. What complaints are his arguments likely to attract? The first in the list I propose to consider accuses Hercules of ignoring the actual law of emotional injury and substituting his own views about what the law should be.

How shall we understand this objection? We might take it in two very different ways. It might mean that Hercules was wrong to seek to justify his interpretation by appealing to justice and fairness because it does not even survive the proper threshold test of fit. We cannot assume, without reviewing the cases Hercules consulted, that this argument is mistaken. Perhaps this time Hercules nodded; perhaps if he had expanded the range of his study of precedents further he would have discovered that only one interpretation did survive, and this discovery would then have settled the law, for him, without engaging his opinions about the justice of requiring compensation for accidents. But it is hardly plausible that even the strictest threshold test of fit will always permit only one interpretation, so the objection, understood this way, would not be a general objection to Hercules' methods of adjudication but only a complaint that he had misapplied his own methods in the particular case at hand.

We should therefore consider the second, more interesting reading of the objection: this claims that a judge must never rely on his personal convictions about fairness or justice the way Hercules did in this instance. Suppose the critic says, "The correct interpretation of a line of past decisions can always be discovered by morally neutral means, because the correct interpretation is just a matter of discovering what principles the judges who made these decisions intended to lay down, and that is just a matter of historical fact." Hercules will point out that this critic needs a political reason for his dictum that interpretations must match the intentions of past judges. That is an extreme form of the position we have already considered, that an interpretation is better if it fits what past judges said as well as did, and even that weaker claim depends on the special arguments of political morality I described. The critic supposes that these special reasons are not only strong but commanding; that they are so powerful that a judge always does wrong even to consider an interpretation that does not meet the standard they set, no matter how well that interpretation ties together, explains, and justifies past decisions.

So Hercules' critic, if his argument is to have any power, is not relying on politically neutral interpretive convictions after all. He, too, has engaged his own background convictions of political morality. He thinks the political values that support his interpretive style are of such fundamental importance as to eliminate any competing commands of justice altogether. That may be a plausible position, but it is hardly uncontroversial and is in no sense neutral. His difference with Hercules is not, as he first suggested, about whether political morality is relevant in deciding what the law is, but about which principles of morality are sound and therefore decisive of that issue. So the first, crude objection, that Hercules has substituted his own political convictions for the politically neutral correct interpretation of the past law, is an album of confusions.

Hercules Is a Fraud

The second objection is more sophisticated. Now the critic says, "It is absurd to suppose that there is any single correct interpretation of the emotional injury cases. Since we have discovered two interpretations of these cases, neither of which can be preferred to the other on 'neutral' grounds of fit, no judge would be forced by the adjudicative principle of integrity to accept either. Hercules has chosen one on frankly political grounds; his choice reflects only his own political morality. He has no choice in the circumstances but to legislate in that way. Nevertheless it is fraudulent for him to claim that he has discovered, through his political choice, what the *law* is. He is only offering his own opinion about what it should be."

This objection will seem powerful to many readers, and we must take care not to weaken it by making it seem to claim more than it does. It does not try to reinstate the idea of conventionalism, that when convention runs out a judge is free to improve the law according to the right legislative standards; still less the idea of pragmatism that he is always free to do this, checked only by considerations of strategy. It acknowledges that judges must choose between interpretations that survive the test of fit. It insists only that there can be no best interpretation when more than one survives that test. It is an objection, as I have framed it, from within the general idea of law as integrity; it tries to protect that idea from corruption by fraud.

Is the objection sound? Why is it fraudulent, or even confusing, for Hercules to offer his judgment as a judgment of law? Once again, two somewhat different answers—two ways of elaborating the objection—are available, and we cannot do credit to the objection unless we distinguish them and consider each. The first elaboration is this: "Hercules' claim is fraudulent because it suggests that there can be a right answer to the question whether interpretation (5) or (6) is fairer or more just; since political morality is subjective there cannot be a single right answer to that question, but only answers." This is the challenge of moral skepticism I discussed at length in Chapter 2. I cannot escape saying something more about it now, but I will use a new critic, with a section of his own, to do so. The second elaboration does not rely on skepticism: "Hercules is a fraud even if morality is objective and even if he is right that the principle of foreseeability he settled on is objectively fairer and more just. He is a fraud because he pretends he has discovered what the law is, but he has only discovered what it should be." That is the form of the objection I shall consider here.

We ask of a conception of law that it provide an account

of the grounds of law—the circumstances under which claims about what the law is should be accepted as true or sound—that shows why law licenses coercion. Law as integrity replies that the grounds of law lie in integrity, in the best constructive interpretation of past legal decisions, and that law is therefore sensitive to justice in the way Hercules recognizes. So there is no way Hercules *can* report his conclusion about Mrs. McLoughlin's case except to say that the law, as he understands it, is in her favor. If he said what the critic recommends, that she has no legal right to win but has a moral right that he proposes to honor, he would be *misstating* his view of the matter. He would think that a true account of some situations—if he found the law too immoral to enforce, for example—but not of this one. A critic might disagree with Hercules at many levels. He might reject law as integrity in favor of conventionalism or pragmatism or some other conception of law. Or he might accept it but reach different conclusions from Hercules because he holds different ideas about the necessary requirements of fit, or different convictions about fairness or justice or the relation between them. But he can regard Hercules' use of "law" as fraudulent (or grammatically wrong) only if he suffers from the semantic sting, only if he assumes that claims of law are somehow out of order when they are not drawn directly from some set of factual criteria for law every competent lawyer accepts.

One aspect of the present objection, however, might be thought immune from my arguments against the rest. Even if we agree that Hercules' conclusions about Mrs. McLoughlin are properly presented as conclusions of law, it might seem extravagant to claim that these conclusions in any way follow from integrity understood as a distinct political ideal. Would it not be more accurate to say that integrity is at work in Hercules' calculations just up to the point at which he has rejected all interpretations that fail the threshold test of fit, but that integrity plays no part in selecting among those that survive that test? Should we not say that his conception of law is really two conceptions: law as integrity supplemented, when integrity gives out, by some version of natural law theory? This is not a very important objection; it only suggests a different way of reporting the conclusions it no longer challenges. Nevertheless the observation that prompts it is too crude. For it is a mistake to think that the idea of integrity is irrelevant to Hercules' decision once that decision is no longer a matter of his convictions about fit but draws on his sense of fairness or justice as well.

The spirit of integrity, which we located in fraternity, would be outraged if Hercules were to make his decision in any way other than by choosing the interpretation that he believes best from the standpoint of political morality as a whole. We accept integrity as a political ideal because we want to treat our political community as one of principle, and the citizens of a community of principle aim not simply at common principles, as if uniformity were all they wanted, but the best common principles politics can find. Integrity is distinct from justice and fairness, but it is bound to them in that way: integrity makes no sense except among people who want fairness and justice as well. So Hercules' final choice of the interpretation he believes sounder on the whole—fairer and more just in the right relation—flows from his initial commitment to integrity. He makes that choice at the moment and in the way integrity both permits and requires, and it is therefore deeply misleading to say that he has abandoned the ideal at just that point.

Hercules Is Arrogant and Anyway a Myth

I shall deal much more briefly with two less important critics who nevertheless must be heard. I have been describing Hercules' methods in what some will call a subjective way, by describing the questions he must answer and judgments he must make for himself. Other judges would answer these differently, and you might agree with one of them rather than Hercules. We shall consider in a moment whether any of this means that neither Hercules nor any other judge or critic can be "really" right about what the law is. But Hercules' opinion will be controversial no matter how we answer that philosophical question, and his new critic seizes just on the fact of controversiality, untainted by any appeal to either external or internal skepticism. "Whether or not there are right answers to the interpretive questions on which Hercules' judgment depends, it is unfair that the answer of one judge (or a bare majority of judges on a panel) be accepted as final when he has no way to *prove,* against those who disagree, that his opinion is better."

We must return, for an answer, to our more general case for law as integrity. We want our officials to treat us as tied together in an association of principle, and we want this for reasons that do not depend on any identity of conviction among these officials, either about fit or about the more substantive principles an interpretation engages. Our reasons endure when judges disagree, at least in detail, about the best interpretation of the community's political order, because each judge still confirms and reinforces the principled character of our association by striving, in spite of the disagreement, to reach his own opinion instead of turning to the usually simpler task of fresh legislation. But even if this were not so, the present objection could not count as an objection to law as integrity distinctly, for it would apply in its full force to pragmatism or to conventionalism, which becomes pragmatism in any case hard enough to come before an appellate court. How can it be fairer for judges to enforce their own views about the best future, unconstrained by any requirement of coherence with the past, than the more complex but no less controversial judgments that law as integrity requires?

Another minor critic appears. His complaint is from a different quarter. "Hercules," he says, "is a myth. No real judge has his powers, and it is absurd to hold him out as a model for others to follow. Real judges decide hard cases much more instinctively. They do not construct and test various rival interpretations against a complex matrix of intersecting political and moral principles. Their craft trains them to see structure in facts and doctrine at once; that is what thinking as a lawyer really is. If they decided to imitate Hercules, trying in each case to secure some general theory of law as a whole, they would be paralyzed while their docket choked." This critic misunderstands our exercise. Hercules is useful to us just because he is more reflective and self-conscious than any real judge need be or, given the press of work, could be. No doubt real judges decide most cases in a much less methodical way. But Hercules shows us the hidden structure of their judgments and so lays these open to study and criticism. We must be careful to distinguish, moreover, two senses in which he might be said to have more powers than any actual judge could. He works so much more quickly (and has so much more time available) that he can explore avenues and ideas they cannot; he can pursue, not just one or two evident lines in expanding the range of cases he studies but all the lines there are. That is the sense in which he can aim at more than they: he can aim at a comprehensive theory, while theirs must be partial. But he has no vision into transcendental mysteries opaque to them. His judgments of fit and political morality are made on the same material and have the same character as theirs. He does what they would do if they had a career to devote to a single decision; they need, not a different conception of law from his, but skills of craft husbandry and efficiency he has never had to cultivate.

Now this critic trims his sails. "In any case Hercules has too much theory for easy cases. Good judges just know that the plain meaning of a plain statute, or a crisp rule always applied and never doubted in precedent, is law, and that is all there is to it. It would be preposterous, not just time-consuming, to subject these undoubted truths to interpretive tests on each occasion. So law as integrity, with its elaborate and top-heavy structure, is at best a conception for hard cases alone. Something much more like conventionalism is a better interpretation of what judges do in the easy ones." The distinction between easy and hard cases at law is neither so clear nor so important as this critic assumes, as we shall see in Chapter 9, but Hercules does not need that point now. Law as integrity explains and justifies easy cases as well as hard ones; it also shows why they are easy. It is obvious that the speed limit in California is 55 because it is obvious that any competent interpretation of California traffic law must yield that conclusion. So easy cases are, for law as integrity, only special cases of hard ones, and the critic's complaint is then only what Hercules himself would be happy to concede: that we need not ask questions when we already know the answer.

SKEPTICISM IN LAW

The Challenge of Internal Skepticism

No aspect of law as integrity has been so misunderstood as its refusal to accept the popular view that there are no uniquely right answers in hard cases at law. Here is a representative statement of the view Hercules rejects. "Hard cases are hard because different sets of principles fit past decisions well enough to count as eligible interpretations of them. Lawyers and judges will disagree about which of two is fairer or more just, all things considered, but neither side can be 'really' right because there are no objective standards of fairness and justice a neutral observer could use to decide between them. So law as integrity ends in the result that there is really no law at all in hard cases like *McLoughlin*. Hercules is a fraud because he pretends that his own subjective opinions are in some sense really better than those of others who disagree. It would be more honest of him to admit that he has no ground for his decision beyond his subjective preferences."

In Chapter 2 we distinguished what I there called external and internal skepticism. Even if external skepticism is sound as a philosophical position, it offers no threat to our case for law as integrity or to Hercules' methods of adjudication under it. I have been careful, as I just said, to describe law as integrity in a manner that is impeccable from the external skeptic's point of view. I described the questions which, according to that conception of law, judges should put to themselves and answer from their own convictions. External skepticism does not deny that these questions make sense; the external skeptic will have his own answers to them, which he will prefer to those of others, and he can play Hercules as well as any of his philosophical opponents can. He only objects to what he believes is a bad description of the process—that it seeks to discover interpretive or moral truths "out there" or "locked into the fabric of the universe." But these metaphors are treacherous representations of what someone means who says, for example, that the principles of interpretation (5) are really better than those of interpretation (6); that claim is a clarification of his interpretive opinion, not a philosophical classification of it. So Hercules might agree never to use the nearly redundant words "objective" or "really" to decorate his judgments, which have the same meaning for him without these words, and external skeptics would then have no further complaint or argument against his way of deciding *McLoughlin*.

I admitted, however, that internal skepticism offers a much more powerful challenge to our project, and I shall use a new critic to develop and assess that suggestion. What forms might his internal skepticism take? There are several possibilities. He might agree, for example, that interpretations (5) and (6) both pass the appropriate threshold test of fit, but he might deny that either is superior to the other in political morality because both are morally wrong or irrelevant in some fundamental way. But that argument seems implausible. Perhaps he rejects the very idea of liability in negligence altogether; he thinks that no one does wrong except maliciously. This would not justify local skepticism about interpretations (5) and (6), however; it endorses (6) as superior to (5), however dubious in itself. So we must imagine him thinking that it is wholly inappropriate to ask whether people have a duty to compensate for their negligence; it is the wrong kind of question, like asking which hand courtesy insists be used to remove one's hat. Even this would not justify skepticism about what decision Hercules should make, however. If morality has nothing to do with negligence, then the state can have no warrant for intervening to coerce compensation, and once again this argues in favor of interpretation (6) as at least preferable to (5), because the former allows the state to trespass somewhat less often where it has no business.

So our skeptical critic is unlikely to persuade us through this kind of argument. He might argue for internal skepticism in a different way, however, by trying to show that legal practice is too deeply contradictory to yield to any coherent interpretation at all. Hercules knows that the law is far from perfectly consistent in principle overall. He knows that legislative supremacy gives force to some statutes that are inconsistent in principle with others, and that the compartmentalization of the common law, together with local priority, allows inconsistency even there. But he assumes that these contradictions are not so pervasive and intractable within departments of law that his task is impossible. He assumes, that is, that some set of reasonably plausible principles can be found, for each general department of law he must enforce, that fit it well enough to count as an eligible interpretation of it. This is the assumption the critic now challenges. He insists that the law of accidents, for example, is so shot through with contradiction that no interpretation can fit more than an arbitrary and limited part of it.

This is a much stronger skeptical challenge because it attacks the feasibility of integrity at its root. It forces us to take up an aspect of the requirement of fit that I postponed, the pivotal distinction between competition and contradiction in principle. Suppose Hercules finds, as in the worst-case variation just mentioned, that both interpretation (5) and interpretation (6) fit a substantial part of the relevant precedents and neither fits the bulk of these. He responds by expanding his range and seeking a more general interpretation of the law of accidents that isolates and limits this contradiction. He proposes this account: "Our law as a whole recognizes two principles as pertinent to the loss people should be permitted to suffer through accidents. The first is a principle of collective sympathy. It holds that the state should try to protect people from being ruined by accidents even when the accident is their own fault. This principle is most apparent in regulative safety programs of different sorts, in workmen's compensation statutes and in state-subsidized schemes of insurance for risks to property and person not adequately covered in the private insurance market. The second is a principle apportioning the costs of an accident among the private actors in the drama that produced it. It holds that accidental loss should be borne by the person at fault, not the innocent victim. This principle is most evidently at work in negligence law, including legislative amendments or supplements to the common law of negligence.

"These are independent principles and it would be a serious misunderstanding of the logic of principle to consider them contradictory. There is no incoherence in recognizing both as principles; on the contrary, any moral vision would be defective if it wholly disowned either impulse. But in some cases they will conflict, and coherence does then require some nonarbitrary scheme of priority or weighting or accommodation between the two, a scheme that reflects their respective sources in a deeper level of political morality. An accident in which the negligent actor would be ruined if he were liable for all the damage he caused is an example of such conflict. The first principle urges the state to protect him from catastrophic loss because his liability would then be as much an accident for him, although his fault, as an industrial accident that was the fault of its victim. The second principle declares, however, that if either of the two actors in the drama is to suffer, it must be the actor at fault. It urges the state to compel him to compensate each of his victims in full. It might be a desirable accommodation of the two principles for the state to require the defendant to compensate some victims, or some victims to some extent, and then make up the balance of loss to other victims from the public treasury. But in the absence of any statute providing this, or any common-law tradition of state compensation that might be tapped, this is not an interpretive possibility. I am limited by the record I find to deciding that one of the two principles must yield in these circumstances. If the first prevails, it is decisive for the defendant that the loss would be much greater for him if full liability were imposed than for any potential plaintiff if it were not. If the second prevails, the fact of the defendant's fault is decisive against him in spite of the magnitude of his potential overall loss.

"It must be conceded [we are still assuming the worst case] that the state has thus far not spoken with one voice about such cases. Some judicial decisions have allowed the second principle to prevail over the first, which is the solution claimed by interpretation (5), and some have allowed the first to prevail over the second, in the way recommended by (6). My interpretive situation is therefore as follows. The constraints of fit require me to find a place in any general interpretation of our legal practice for both of the more abstract principles of sympathy and responsibility. No general interpretation that denied either one would be plausible; integrity could not be served if either were wholly disavowed. But integrity demands some resolution of their competing impact on accident cases when unlimited liability would be disastrous, a choice that our practice has not made but that must flow, as a postinterpretive judgment, from my analysis. Integrity demands this because it demands that I continue the overall story, in which the two principles have a definite place, in the best way, all things considered. In my view this is done best by ranking the second principle prior to the first, at least in automobile accident cases when liability insurance is available privately on sensible terms. I settle on this choice because I believe that though the impulse behind each of the two principles is attractive, the second is more powerful in these circumstances. This requires me to declare a certain number of past judicial decisions mistakes and to overrule these if my jurisdiction permits. But the number of decisions I must count as mistakes is neither so great nor of such fundamental importance, viewed from the perspective of legal practice as a whole, that disregarding them leaves me no solid foundation for the more general interpretation I have just described."

Critical Legal Studies

The internal skeptic need not accept this argument, but he must confront it. Hercules assumed that the two abstract principles he identified could live together comfortably in the same general interpretation of our legal practice, even though they sometimes conflict. The skeptic might challenge this and argue that the principles are more deeply antagonistic than Hercules realizes, that they are drawn from two incompatible visions of human action or responsibility and so cannot stand together in any coherent scheme of government. On that view the conflict between them is not an occasional practical problem but a symptom of deep doctrinal schizophrenia. Some law teachers, mainly though not entirely American, appear now to be making that deeply critical claim about the legal practices of their community.[16] They see only philosophical contradiction where Hercules hopes to show system.

"Critical legal studies," which is their name for their movement, is so far defined mainly by subscription: its acolytes assemble in conferences whose purposes include deciding what the movement is.[17] They do share important attitudes about legal education; they hope to "demystify" law for law students by reminding them of what American jurisprudence has emphasized more quietly for many decades, which is that political conviction plays an important role in adjudication and that the shape of the law at any time reflects ideology and power as well as what is wrongly called "logic." They also aim to make law students more sensitive to other disciplines, particularly French linguistics and Hegelian metaphysics. Their political attitudes place them, as a group, on the left of the American political spectrum (they have been particularly active in various aspects of law school politics), and much of their writing opposes what they take to be conservative developments in legal theory. In particular they oppose the other main academic movement in recent American legal education, sometimes called the economic approach to law, which we study in Chapter 8.

In all this, save in its self-conscious leftist posture and its particular choice of other disciplines to celebrate, critical legal studies resembles the older movement of American legal realism, and it is too early to decide whether it is more than an anachronistic attempt to make that dated movement reflower. Much of its rhetoric, like that of legal realism, is borrowed from external skepticism: its members are fond of short denunciations of "objectivism" or "natural law metaphysics" or of the idea of values "out there" in the universe. At its best and most promising, however, it escapes the limits of legal realism by reaching for the global and threatening form of internal skepticism I just described. It argues that our legal culture, far from having any shape amenable to a uniform and coherent justification of principle, can only be grasped through the infertile metric of contradiction. It would reject, as I said an internal skeptic might, Hercules' latest account of independent, though sometimes conflicting, principles respecting individual loss in accidents. Critical legal studies would tell a very different story: of two deeply antagonistic ideologies at war within the law, one drawn, perhaps, from communitarian impulses of altruism and mutual concern and the other from the contradictory ideas of egoism, self-sufficiency, and judgmental moralism.

Unfortunately, much of the literature of critical legal

studies announces rather than defends these claims, as if they were self-evident. This may reflect a serious misunderstanding of the kind of argument necessary to establish a skeptical position: the argument must be interpretive rather than historical. Critical legal historians describe law genetically by tracing different pieces of legal doctrine back to the interests and ideologies that originally placed each in the law or molded or retained it. They take as their targets other historians who offer causal theories claiming to explain the historical development of law as the unfolding of some general functionalist design; they have no difficulty in defending, against these causal accounts, a less structured approach to causal explanation in law, an approach more permissive to contingency and accident.[18] Their work is useful to Hercules, and he would neglect it at his peril, because it reminds him that nothing in the way his law was produced guarantees his success in finding a coherent interpretation of it. But neither does history guarantee his failure, because his ambitions are interpretive in the sense appropriate to the philosophical foundations of law as integrity. He tries to impose order over doctrine, not to discover order in the forces that created it. He struggles toward a set of principles he can offer to integrity, a scheme for transforming the varied links in the chain of law into a vision of government now speaking with one voice, even if this is very different from the voices of leaders past. He might fail—we have been charting the ways he might fail—but his failure is not ensured by anything even the most careful and sensitive history teaches.

There is a second, more philosophical strain in the literature of critical legal studies, however, which is more directly in point because its claims are more easily understood as interpretive. It aims to show, not merely that different ideologies produced different parts of the law, but that any competent contemporary justification of these different parts would necessarily display fundamental contradictions of principle, that Hercules must fail in imposing a coherent structure on law's empire as a whole. This skeptical interpretive claim is powerful and germane, however, only if it begins where Hercules begins: it must claim to have looked for a less skeptical interpretation and failed. Nothing is easier or more pointless than demonstrating that a flawed and contradictory account fits as well as a smoother and more attractive one. The internal skeptic must show that the flawed and contradictory account is the only one available.

Liberalism and Contradiction

Is there a quick route to that ambitious negative claim? Critical legal studies purports to find one in what it takes to be the philosophical faults of liberal political theory. This argument has two steps. It claims, first, that the constitutional structure and main doctrinal lines of modern Western democracies can be justified only as an elaboration of a fundamentally liberal view of personality and community. It insists that the distinction between adjudication and legislation, which is prominent in that structure, reflects a liberal conception of freedom; it points to those features of the private law of contract, tort, and property, for example, that enforce liberal ideals of individual responsibility. It argues, second, that liberalism, as a philosophical system combining metaphysical and ethical ideas, is profoundly self-contradictory and that the contradictions of liberalism therefore ensure the chaos and contradiction of any available interpretation of our law, the doom of Hercules' project. This is an exciting argument, and anyone drawn to liberalism will find its first step compelling. Arguments for its second step, however, about the incoherence of liberalism, have so far been spectacular and even embarrassing failures. They begin and end in a defective account of what liberalism is, an account supported by no plausible reading of the philosophers they count as liberals.[19]

They seem wholly to ignore, moreover, the distinction we have just found crucial to any internally skeptical argument, the distinction between competition and contradiction in principles. This failure is also remarkable in the more detailed and doctrinal exercises of critical legal studies, including some meant to be directly critical of law as integrity. I quote and discuss a recent example at some length in a note because it treats just the area of law we have been using as our leading illustration in this chapter.[20] Critical legal studies should be rescued from these mistakes because its general skeptical ambitions, understood in the mode of internal skepticism, are important. We have much to learn from the critical exercise it proposes, from its failures as well as its successes. This assumes, however, that its aims are those of law as integrity, that it works to discover whether, and how far, judges have avenues open for improving law while respecting the virtues of fraternity integrity serves. These are indeed the aims of at least some members of the movement.[21] But others may have a different and converse goal. They may want to show law in its worst rather than its best light, to show avenues closed that are in fact open, to move toward a new mystification in service of undisclosed political goals.

EIGHT

THE COMMON LAW

THE ECONOMIC INTERPRETATION

In the last chapter we used Hercules to explore a single issue in the law of accidents. In this chapter we let him rest for more labors later; we study accident law as a whole in a more abstract and academic fashion, trying to find a deeper, more general, and philosophical justification for the "reasonable foresight" principle he settled on. A large interpretive claim has recently excited lawyers in the United States and been noticed in Britain, called the "economic" theory of the law of unintended damage. This offers a general interpretation of the decisions our judges have made about accidents and nuisance and other unintended injury.[1] It finds the key to these decisions in the "economic" principle that people should always act in whatever way will be financially least expensive for their community as a whole. Suppose I can avoid injuring you by fitting my car with a safety device. If I do not, and I injure you, then under this principle I must compensate you for your losses if the safety device would have cost me less than the "discounted" cost of the accident, that is, the cost discounted by the chance that it might not occur even without the device. But I need not compensate you if the cost of installing the device would have been higher than the discounted cost of the accident.[2]

Community Wealth and the Coase Theorem

The economic theory suggests that the best interpretation of accident cases is furnished by the economic principle. We must therefore study that principle by asking what decisions, about who should bear what costs of accidents, a statesman would make who accepted it as sovereign. He would need, first, a definition of community wealth in order to decide which decisions cost the community least. The economic theory offers a rather special (and in many ways counterintuitive) definition for this purpose: the wealth of a community is the value of all its goods and services, and the value of something is the maximum amount in money or money's worth that anyone is willing and able to pay for it. If there is a market price for something, its value is taken to be that market price; if there is no proper market, its value is what people would be willing and able to pay if there were. It follows that market transactions improve community wealth. It also follows that when market transactions are impossible, wealth is improved if people "simulate" markets by behaving as if they had the rights and duties they would have if negotiation were possible and were used.[3]

Now we can ask how a statesman who accepted the economic principle and this definition of community wealth would design rules of law fixing liability for accidents. Consider a type of accident that used to occupy the courts. A train speeding along tracks adjacent to a farm throws off sparks that ignite and destroy crops planted near the tracks. Must the farmer bear this loss? Or must the train company compensate him? Which rule would an informed lawmaker, anxious to improve total community wealth, lay down? Imagine that the economic facts are as follows (call this Case 1). If the train company slows the train to the speed at which it will not throw off sparks, the company's profits will be $1,000 less. If the train runs at the speed that is otherwise most profitable to the company, the farmer will lose crops that would earn him a profit of $1,100. In these circumstances the community is richer on the whole (according to the stipulated definition of community wealth) if the train slows. Now suppose (Case 2) that the economic facts are reversed. If the train slows, the company will lose profits of $1,100, and if it does not, the farmer will lose profits of only $1,000. Now the community is richer on the whole if the train speeds and the crops are burned. So it appears that someone anxious to improve community wealth would lay down different rules of liability for the two cases. He would make the train company liable for the damage in the first case so that the train would slow down, and would require the farmer to bear the loss in the second so that it would not slow down.

But under a certain further assumption about the economic facts it would, surprisingly, make no difference to community wealth which rule the lawmaker chose in either case.[4] This is the assumption that (in the language of economists) transaction costs between the train company and the farmer are zero, meaning that it would cost neither party anything to negotiate a private agreement changing the results of whatever rule the legislator lays down. If transaction costs are zero, and the train company is liable for the damage in Case 2, then the train will still speed and will produce all the wealth for the community it would have if it were not liable. It will still speed because the train company will offer the farmer some sum between $1,000 and $1,100 not to plant crops near the tracks (or not to sue for loss if he does), and the farmer will accept some such offer. They strike that bargain because it benefits them both: the train company saves the difference between what it offers and the $1,100 it would lose if it slowed the train, and the farmer gains the difference between that sum and the $1,000 he would make from planting the corn. Similarly, in Case 1, if the legislator leaves the loss on the farmer instead of making the train company liable, the crops will still be planted and the community will be just as rich as if he took the opposite decision. For now the farmer will offer the train company some sum between $1,000 and $1,100 to slow the train, and the company will accept some such offer because it will gain the difference between the offer and the $1,000 it forfeits by slowing the train.

So under the zero-transaction-cost assumption it makes no difference to overall community wealth which rule the law-maker chooses. Of course it makes a considerable difference to the train company and the farmer which rule he chooses. If he makes the train company liable in either case, the company will be poorer and the farmer richer than if he does not. But that in itself is a matter of indifference to the wealth test. That test is concerned with the community's total wealth, which is not affected by transfers from one group to another unless for some special reason these increase or re-duce the total. You may well wonder, however, about the practical importance of the point that it makes no difference to community wealth which rule is chosen if transaction costs are zero, because they never are. Even if the farmer has read law books in his leisure time and so has no need to hire a lawyer to negotiate for him, he could be reading seed cata-logues instead of pondering whether to offer $1,050 or $1,075. If transaction costs are sufficiently high, they will prevent a bargain being made that would improve commu-nity wealth. Suppose the legislature ordered trains to com-pensate farmers in circumstances like Case 2, and it would cost the parties together more than $100 to negotiate an agreement under which the farmer would not plant crops near the tracks. That agreement would then not be made— the transaction costs would more than wipe out at least one party's anticipated gain—so the train would not speed and the community would be poorer overall in consequence.

But the theoretical exercise of imagining that transaction costs are zero is nevertheless important, according to the eco-nomic interpretation, because it identifies the crucial role these costs play and yields the following practical advice about how a legislator who accepts the economic principle should decide, assuming he must choose between a flat rule making trains liable for all crops burned by their sparks and a flat rule denying all such liability. He should choose whichever rule he thinks will come closer to producing the overall pattern of economic activity—trains slowing or crops not being planted—that the various train companies and farmers would arrange through contract if transaction costs were zero. But he should also take into account the likely transaction costs to facilitate bargains in those discrete and special situations where the economic facts are contrary to his overall prediction.[5] If he thinks, for example, that it would be cheaper for the train company to initiate and conduct negotiation when the facts fall out as in Case 2 than for the farmer to do this when they fall out as in Case 1, then this argues for imposing liability generally on train companies rather than letting the loss fall on farmers. In this way a lawmaker maximizes community wealth by trying to gauge what actual negotiation would have produced if it were possible.

COMPLEXITIES

The Reasonable Man

A lawmaker need not always choose between flat general rules of that character. A more sophisticated economic analysis might show that some more complex rule, more sensitive to the balance of economic facts in particular cases, would produce more wealth for the community. Suppose that if the Vulcan Express runs at its highest possible speed over its particular route it will destroy $1,100 in crops planted near its tracks; if it runs at the lower speed necessary to avoid all sparks, the train company will lose $1,000. But if it runs at the intermediate speed of (say) 70 miles an hour, the train company will lose $500 in income, and the fewer sparks will destroy only $400 in grain. Community wealth is greater in this case than in either of the former cases, and so a legislator would do better, by the wealth test, to choose a rule making that train liable for that damage only if it exceeds 70 miles an hour. But there might be a still better speed for him to choose. And even if he had all the facts necessary to choose the optimal speed for the Vulcan Express over its route, that might be very much the wrong speed to choose for the Thor Flyer, which runs through very different terrain.

Perhaps a Herculean legislator with an adequate timetable could set the optimal speed for each train separately. But any rules even he designs that way will soon be obsolete. For the optimal speed will depend on technology, which changes, on the enormously complex economics of passenger and freight transportation, and on the price of grain, among other fluctuating data. Besides, the problem of trains traveling next to crops likely to be burned by their sparks is only one example of the kind of conflict we are now considering. There are countless other kinds of circumstances in which one person, pursuing an otherwise lawful activity, may cause unintended damage to someone else. A musician plays rock music when his neighbor is trying to study algebra. A poet thunders his Maserati along country lanes where people walk. A builder digs out foundations on his own site and accidentally cuts an underground power line running to someone else's factory some distance away. A statesman who wants the law that governs these different forms of unintended damage to increase overall community wealth needs a general rule of the following kind. Anyone whose activity causes unintended damage to anyone else's person or goods will be liable for that damage if his activity was, under the circumstances, unreasonable, and an activity is unreasonable if the marginal cost to the actor of avoiding the activity is less than the cost of the damage the activity threatens to cause others.

This general and abstract rule forces people in the position of the train companies to calculate for themselves the balance of social cost in deciding, for example, how fast to drive each of their trains and to recalculate that balance from time to time as technology and various components of supply and demand change. But there is a certain danger latent in this rule. Our legislator does not want people to spend too much time or money trying to calculate the full economic consequences of some activity, because that in itself will reduce community wealth. He therefore stipulates that the calculation of relative costs must reflect facts and opinions that a "reasonable" person, devoting a "reasonable" amount of time and expense to the calculation, would know or have. Once again, the test of reasonableness would be whether the community would be richer overall if people devoted that much time and expense in those circumstances. Community wealth is maximized by encouraging activities that, in the ordinary run and on the basis of readily available information, improve community wealth, not by forcing people to examine the full economic consequences of each individual act in every circumstance.

So an effective "reasonableness" test would exempt some people from liability even though they caused damage far in excess of what it would have cost them to avoid the activity that caused the damage. Suppose a train company has calculated, using information readily available to it, that the cost of slowing down would be greater than the value of the wheat and other crops it is likely to destroy. But one farmer has stored his private collection of Renaissance paintings near the tracks, under deep straw, which burns. It would have been cheaper for the community, as things turned out, if this particular train had driven very slowly. But if the company were liable for such damage, it would have to make statistical estimates about the amount of loss fluke accidents might cause to unknown and valuable property not usually found on farms. This would be more expensive and less accurate than the sum of the investigations each farmer would make, about the relative costs of storing his own valuable and unusual property elsewhere or buying more insurance, if the risk of such loss fell on him.[6]

Contributory Negligence

Now consider another possibility. Perhaps it would improve community wealth to make trains liable for only some of the damage caused by their sparks, even if it was unreasonable for them to drive at the speed they did. Suppose a train drives at 150 miles per hour, which is unreasonable because it endangers crops that are worth more than the marginal profits gained by driving at that speed; the sparks do in fact burn the crops, but as it turns out, only because the farmer has spilled lighter fluid in the area. Our legislator might consider three rules for situations of that sort. He might say, first, that since the train's activity was concededly unreasonable, it should be liable for all the damage that resulted from that activity, even the damage that would not have been caused had the farmer not also behaved carelessly. Or he might say, second, that since the farmer's carelessness was an essential part of the causal chain, he should bear the entire loss, because he was, in the phrase that has been developed to make this point, "contributorily negligent." Or he might decide that since the train company and the farmer both acted unreasonably, the company must compensate the farmer for part but not all of his loss. In that case he would have chosen what is sometimes called the doctrine of "comparative" negligence, which assigns loss to all the parties behaving unreasonably in a particular situation in accordance with how unreasonably each behaved, or how far the unreasonable behavior of each contributed to the accident, or some combination of both. It is an interesting and complex question of economics which of these various rules about compensation, when more than one party behaves unreasonably, would actually contribute most to community wealth.

The Question of Fit

The champions of the economic theory try to show (in much greater detail and with much more subtlety, noticing qualifications and difficulties I have ignored) what my argument has now begun to suggest. For the various rules and devices I have described—those a legislator who is concerned only to maximize the total wealth of the community would consider in designing a law of accidents—are by and large the rules Anglo-American judges constructed and debated in the formative periods of the modern law of negligence, and these rules still make up the main doctrines of accident law in most jurisdictions. If it is true that a legislator dedicated to the economic principle would have laid down the familiar standards of our own legal practice, like the "reasonable man" rule, and the rules about proximate causation, foreseeability, contributory negligence, comparative negligence, and scope of damages, then the economic interpretation has passed an important test. It meets a reasonable threshold requirement of fit. Almost no one would claim a perfect fit, for these rules vary, at least in detail, from jurisdiction to jurisdiction. Many prominent academic lawyers do claim a very substantial fit, and that claim is hotly disputed. Critics of the economic interpretation argue that on a more careful look, the rules courts have developed about negligence and the rest do not maximize community wealth, that a legislator self-consciously dedicated to maximizing community wealth would have chosen different rules.[7] The argument has brought economic theory, and the appearance, at least, of proficiency in formal economic analysis, into the pages of law reviews and even into some judicial opinions.[8]

Assume, for the sake of our general project, that the economic interpretation fits accident law well enough to count as a successful interpretation on that score. This does not mean that past judges actually had wealth maximization in mind. Whether the contributory negligence rule, for example, maximizes community wealth depends on the most subtle mathematical analyses, which very few of these judges could even have understood. But an interpretation need not be consistent with past judicial attitudes or opinions, with how past judges saw what they were doing, in order to count as an eligible interpretation of what they in fact did. Some lawyers do think, as we noticed in Chapter 7, that an interpretation is ineligible unless it is consistent with past judicial rhetoric and opinion as well as actual decisions. But it seems more reasonable to regard that kind of fit as one desideratum that might be outweighed by others in deciding whether an interpretation fits well enough. So we cannot reject the economic interpretation on the sole ground that it would have amazed the judges whose decisions it proposes to interpret.

THE QUESTION OF JUSTICE
Academic and Practical Theory

A successful interpretation must not only fit but also justify the practice it interprets. The judicial decisions we have been describing force some people to compensate others for losses suffered because their otherwise lawful activities conflicted, and since these decisions are made after the event, they are justified only if it is reasonable to suppose that people held in damages should have acted in some other way or should have accepted responsibility for the damage they caused. So the decisions can be justified only by deploying some general scheme of moral responsibility the members of a community might properly be deemed to have, about not injuring others or about taking financial responsibility for their acts. Can we find a plausible scheme of responsibility, a plausible account of how people should behave, that would suggest making liability turn on the market simulation test?

We need yet another distinction: between what we might call the academic and the practical elaboration of a moral theory. People self-consciously settling on a scheme of personal responsibility for accidents, guided by an abstract moral theory, would not try to define very concrete rules capturing exactly what the abstract theory would require in every imaginable circumstance if it were elaborated by an academic moral philosopher able to take account of every nuance of fact. If they did, they would produce too many rules to understand and master. They would have two options which they could combine. They could settle on rules

using words, like "reasonable under the circumstances," that
call for more specific calculation on particular occasions, or
they could construct crude rules, clear in themselves, that
ignore subtleties. We are looking for a moral theory, then,
whose practical rather than academic elaboration would require market-simulating rules of law. Nevertheless, when we
come to inspect any such theory, to see whether it is sound *as*
a moral theory, we must study its academic elaboration, because then we are concerned, not with the practical adjust-
ments required to make that theory manageable and
efficient in politics and daily life, but with the very different
question whether we can accept that theory in the first place.
If we cannot accept its academic elaboration because some
part of this strikes us as morally wrong, the theory is not rescued because its practical elaboration would be different.
For it is the academic elaboration that reveals the true nature or character of a moral theory. We shall see the importance of this distinction at once when we consider the most
natural, because simplest, defense of market-simulating rules
on moral grounds.

Do We Have a Duty to Maximize Wealth?

This defense lies in a two-step argument. (1) People have a
moral duty to advance the good of the community as a
whole in whatever they do and a corresponding moral right
that others always act in that way. (2) The good of the community as a whole lies in its overall wealth according to the
definition I described earlier; a community is always better
when it is richer in that sense. The second step of this argument is absurd, as we learn by considering the academic
elaboration of the claim that a richer society is necessarily a
better society.[9] Suppose a poor, sick man needs medicine and
is therefore willing to sell a favored book, his sole source of
pleasure, for the $5 the medicine costs. His neighbor is will-
ing to pay $10 to have the book, if necessary, because he is
the famous (and rich) grandson of the author, and if he au-

tographs the book he can sell it for $11. The community is made richer, according to the economic definition of community wealth, if the police just take the book from the poor sick man and give it to his rich neighbor, leaving the poor man with neither book nor medicine. The community is richer because the book is worth $11 in the rich man's hands and only $5 to the poor man. The community's aggregate wealth is increased if the book is taken from the poor man, even beyond what it would gain if the two struck a bargain, because a forced transfer saves the transaction costs of that negotiation.

This solution would not be part of the *practical* elaboration of the thesis that people always have a duty to do whatever will make the community richer. A statesman anxious to provide rules of law reflecting that duty would avoid any rule permitting forced transfers even in circumstances like these. I assumed that we know the poor man would sell the book for $5 and the rich man would pay $10. But the best means of discovering how much people value things is to require them actually to conclude transactions. Otherwise we have no good means of testing whether they actually would do what they say they would. No doubt it costs the community more to allow the neighbors to haggle over the exact price of the book than it does to take the book from the poor man without wasting the time a bargain would take. But we gain more in accuracy over the long run by insisting that people do bargain, in order to make sure that wealth is actually increased by a transfer. So a statesman who thought people always have a duty to maximize community wealth would insist that the law refuse to allow forced transfers when negotiation is possible. Nevertheless our simple argument against the wealth-maximizing duty stands, because the argument is meant to show, not that the duty would produce horrifying results in practice, but that what it recommends, if this were feasible, is deeply wrong in principle. Even if we were *certain* that the rich man would pay more than the poor man would charge, so that social wealth would indeed be increased by just taking the book from the poor man and giving it to his rich neighbor, we would not think the situation in any way more just or the community in any way better after a transfer made in that way. So increasing social wealth does not in itself make the community better.

THE UTILITARIAN DUTY

A Utilitarian Argument

If there is a good moral argument for the wealth-maximizing, market-simulating approach to personal liability, therefore, it must be more complicated than the simple one we have now rejected. We should next consider whether an argument might be found in the popular moral theory of utilitarianism, which holds that political decisions should aim to improve average happiness (or average welfare on some other conception) in the community as a whole. The utilitarian argument we inspect recognizes the point I first emphasized, that any successful interpretation of accident and other unintended injury decisions at law must begin in some theory of individual responsibility for acts and risk.[10] This argument has three steps. (1) Everyone has a general moral duty always to act, in each decision he makes including decisions about the use of his own property, as if the interests of all others were just as important as his own interests and those of people close to him like family and friends. (2) People act in that way when they make decisions that improve average happiness in the community as a whole, trading off losses in some people's happiness against gains to others. (3) The best practical elaboration of the duty that flows from these two first steps, the duty to maximize average happiness, takes the form of market-simulating rules of personal liability, that is, rules that require people to act as if they had made bargains in costless negotiations like those I imagined between train companies and farmers. People should simulate markets and make the community richer in that way, not because a richer community is necessarily happier on average but because it generally is, and because no other practical code of responsibility could be expected to do better for average happiness. The utilitarian argument concedes that people have no ultimate or fundamental duty to maximize community wealth; it proposes that the best practical realization of the duty they do have, the duty to maximize happiness, is achieved by their acting as if they did have a duty to maximize wealth.

We must study this argument in stages, beginning with its third step. This declares that if citizens accept and follow market-simulating, and therefore wealth-maximizing, rules in deciding what risks to run of injuring others and when to take financial responsibility for the injuries they do cause, this practice will improve the average happiness of citizens in the long run. That is not a claim about the immediate consequences of particular acts considered one by one. Some market-simulating decisions, in and of themselves, will probably decrease overall happiness. But according to this view, general happiness is increased in the long run if everyone follows such rules in the cases we are considering. History provides no useful evidence for this supposition. It does not confirm that the best way to make a community happier on average is to make it richer on the whole with no direct constraints of distribution; that thesis remains an article of faith more popular among the rich than the poor. No doubt people on average have better lives, at least according to conventional views of what makes a life better, in prosperous nations than in very poor ones. But the present question is different. Do we have any reason to think that average happiness is generally improved in prosperous nations by still more prosperity, measured by the sums its citizens are collectively willing and able to pay for the goods they make and trade? Or that happiness could not be improved even more if citizens accepted other standards of personal responsibility, standards that sometimes ignored prosperity for other values? I think not; these claims may be true, but we have no persuasive evidence that they are.

We might, however, want to assume that they are true just for the sake of the utilitarian argument we are considering. We must then move back to the second step in that argument and ask whether its thesis is correct that treating people with equal concern means acting so as to improve average happiness. Critics of utilitarianism invent stories— sometimes very fanciful stories—that seem to cast doubt on that thesis. Suppose racial bigots are so numerous and so sadistic that torturing an innocent black man would improve the overall level of happiness in the community as a whole. Would this justify the torture? Utilitarian philosophers have a standard reply to these horrifying examples of what utilitarianism might require.[11] They say that good moral reasoning proceeds on two levels. On the first, or theoretical, level we should aim to discover those rules or principles of morality which, as maxims of conduct, are likely to provide the greatest average happiness within the community over the long run. On the second, or practical, level we should apply the maxims so chosen in concrete cases. We should decide what to do on particular occasions, not by asking which particular decision seems likely to produce more happiness considered on its own, but by asking what the standards we chose at the first level would require us to do. Obviously, we should choose, at the first level of theory, rules that condemn torture and racial prejudice. This explains and justifies our "intuition" that it would be wrong to pander to sadism or prejudice even in special circumstances when we thought a direct utilitarian calculation, applied only to the immediate facts, would require this.

But this standard defense of utilitarianism evades the hard question. Once again it mistakes a powerful criticism of its academic elaboration for an erroneous claim about its practical elaboration, about the moral intuitions it would encourage statesmen and philosophers to cultivate in ordinary people. It is not so difficult to imagine changes in the economic or social or psychological climate that would make our familiar intuitions not the best for a utilitarian to instill. Sadistic bigots *might* become so numerous among us, their capacity for delight so profound, and their tastes so ineradicable that even at the first level—when we are considering what rules would increase happiness in the very long run— we would be forced to make exceptions to our general rules and to permit the torture of blacks alone. It is not a good answer that luckily there is no genuine possibility of that situation arising. For once again the point of horrifying stories is not to provide a practical warning—that if we are seduced by utilitarianism we may well find ourselves advocating torture—but to expose defects in the academic elaboration of the theory by calling attention to moral convictions that remain powerful even in hypothetical form. If we believe that it would be unjust to torture blacks even in the (extremely improbable) circumstances when that would increase average happiness, if we think that that practice would not treat people as equals, then we reject the second step of our utilitarian argument.

Two Strategies

But let us once again, for the sake of the argument, assume that the second step is sound, that treating people with equal concern does mean maximizing average happiness. We now move back to the first step. Now we ask whether, even if we concede the last two steps, it is reasonable to suppose that everyone has a moral duty always to act in market-simulating ways when actual negotiation is for some reason not feasible. It is time to notice an intuitive connection between wealth maximization and equality that might make that idea seem reasonable. The legal doctrines of negligence and nuisance I described strike a moral chord. It seems plausible that when accidents are likely, people ought to look out for each other's interests in the same way and to the same degree that they look after their own. We might try to explain that conviction in two ways. We might assume, first, that people always have that egalitarian responsibility, that they must always, in everything they do, consider the interests of all others to be as important as their own or those of their family and friends. Then the egalitarian responsibility that accident law enforces is only a special instance of a pervasive moral responsibility. Or we might try to show, second, that though people do not have that burdensome responsibility generally, they do in the circumstances of negligence or nuisance cases, for a reason we must then disclose.

The present utilitarian argument, we now see, takes up the first of these strategies. It supposes that we must always, in everything we do, treat the interests of others as equally important to our own. It offers a debatable account of what that means in practice, but we are accepting that account, for the sake of the argument, by conceding the argument's second and third steps. We are now studying the first step, which assumes that we each have a pervasive moral responsibility always to show equal concern for others. Most of us do not accept that pervasive responsibility. We think we are normally free, morally as well as legally, to prefer our own interests and projects, and those of a small number of other people to whom we feel special associative responsibilities and ties, in the day-to-day decisions we make using our own property. We accept that sometimes we must *not* favor ourselves and those close to us in that way, and in particular we accept that we must not do so in the circumstances of nuisance and negligence, but must instead count an injury to a stranger as equal in importance to an injury to ourselves. But we feel that these circumstances are for some reason special. We use, that is, the second strategy to explain them.

We think the circumstances of negligence and nuisance are special, moreover, in a particular way that makes our moral responsibilities parasitic on, and thus sensitive to, our legal responsibilities. I shall have to explain this connection in more detail and more apt language later in this chapter, when we consider a nonutilitarian account of accident and nuisance law I shall argue is superior. But the connection can be described informally in this way. Our legal practice recognizes what are often called prima facie legal rights in property, but which I shall call abstract rights. I have an abstract legal right to run my trains along the road bed I own, as you have to plant corn on your field next to it. I have an abstract right to use my apartment as I wish and therefore to play my trumpet, as you have to use yours as you wish and therefore to be free to study algebra in peace. We call these rights prima facie or abstract because we know that they can conflict: my exercise of my right may invade or restrict yours, in which case the question arises which of us has an actual or concrete right to do what he wishes. It is in these circumstances—the domain of negligence and nuisance and other forms of unintended damage law—that we believe the egalitarian responsibility arises. I must decide on my concrete rights—may I speed my train or blow my trumpet here and now?—in some way that respects your interests as much as my own, not because I must always act in that way, but because I must do so when our abstract rights compete. I have no such responsibility when they do not compete. I make most of the important decisions of my life on the premise that I am morally free to pay somewhat more attention to my life than to the lives of others, though of course that does not mean I am free to ignore others entirely.

That is a fair statement of ordinary moral attitudes, which someone who takes up the utilitarian argument we are testing must confront. He might say these attitudes are wrong because they display an indefensible selfishness. He might insist that, however radical this might seem, we must always, in everything we do, test our conduct by asking whether it treats everyone's interests as equally important to our own. But that is a very implausible claim, at least when joined to the market simulation theory of what it would require in practice. Almost any decision we make can be thought of as the subject of some hypothetical negotiation, so we should constantly have to consider whether others would pay more for our not doing something than we would or could pay for the privilege of doing it, and if they would, we should have to forbear (though of course without actually being paid to do so). I know, for example, that many conscientious professors of law feel a responsibility to read whatever is published in legal philosophy and therefore wish that much less were written. It seems reasonable to think that if such a negotiation were possible and costless, the academic community as a whole would pay me more to not publish this book than I could pay for the right to publish it, because I could not earn enough from royalties to meet their bid even if I wanted to do so. If I had a moral responsibility not to publish just for that reason, my life, in this respect and then in countless others, would collapse into only those activities I could and would want to outbid others for the privilege of performing. Personal autonomy would almost disappear in a society whose members accepted the market-simulating duty, because the duty would never sleep.

The utilitarian market simulator might want, therefore, to consider a different tack. He might want to fall back on the distinction I described between two levels of utilitarian argument; he might hope to show that overall happiness is best served in the long run if people do not accept his strict requirement always to consider other people's interests as equal in importance to their own but instead act in the more relaxed way they presently do. No such argument has ever been produced, and we must wait until one is to evaluate his chances of success. Any attempt, however, is likely to seem ad hoc. For the two-level argument must show not just that more utility would be produced by relaxing the strict requirement in practice, but that most utility is produced by relaxing that requirement in a particular way: by insisting on it when, and only when, abstract legal rights in property conflict. Perhaps this can be shown, but it is hardly evident, and the danger is lively that someone who attempts it will in fact be arguing backward, from the fact that our moral practices do make these discriminations to the unwarranted conclusion that they must promote utility better in the long run than other feasible schemes of responsibility.

THE EGALITARIAN INTERPRETATION
Private and Public Responsibility

We should therefore look for a different scheme of responsibility that also recommends market-simulating behavior when abstract legal rights conflict but does not suppose any personal duty always to act in whatever way would make the community happier on the whole. So far we have been assuming that because market-simulating behavior minimizes financial losses among those affected by some conduct and therefore improves the wealth of the community as a whole, it must be required, when it is, for that reason. We should explore another possibility: that though market-simulating behavior normally does improve the wealth of the community, it is required for some different reason. Our argument has already suggested the general character of another reason. Someone who abstains from some act on the ground that it would cost his neighbor more than it would benefit him takes his neighbor's welfare into account on equal terms with his own; a duty to act in that way might be thought to rest on some egalitarian basis.

The utilitarian argument I constructed just now exploited that idea in one way. It supposed that we each have a general duty always to treat the interests of others as equal in importance to our own, and it derived from that general duty a further duty always to act to make the community richer on the whole. We found the derivation doubtful but accepted it *arguendo* to consider the general duty, which we then found implausible. Can we exploit the egalitarian basis of accident law more successfully if we reject the general duty and take up the second strategy I distinguished, which matches ordinary moral intuitions better? Can we show that a duty to take others' interests as of equal importance holds only sometimes, including occasions when abstract legal rights conflict?

Most of us believe, as I said, that we have no general duty to treat all other members of our community with equal care and concern in everything we do. But we believe our government, the community personified, *does* have this duty, and we might hope to find in this pervasive public responsibility some explanation of why we as individuals sometimes have that duty as well. Government makes decisions touching the production, distribution, and ownership of property and the uses people are entitled to make of property they own. These decisions together constitute a scheme of property, and the government's responsibility to treat people as equals in all its decisions governs the property scheme it creates and enforces. That raises the following problem about the permissive attitude we take as individuals, the attitude that allows us to favor ourselves and those close to us in the use we make of the property the scheme assigns to us. Why should government not countermand that permissive attitude by adopting rules of law that forbid it? Why should it not, in the exercise of its egalitarian responsibilities, adopt exactly the demanding principle I said we reject, that we should never use our property except in ways that recognize rather than flout the equal concern for all that guided the government in designing its scheme?

We must think harder about the scope and character of that public duty. Government, we say, has an abstract responsibility to treat each citizen's fate as equally important.[12] Rival conceptions or theories of equality are rival answers to the question of what system of property would meet that standard. We must begin by noticing how these conceptions of equality differ from one another, limiting our attention to those that figure in contemporary political argument.

Conceptions of Equality

Libertarian conceptions of equality suppose that people have "natural" rights over whatever property they have acquired in certain canonical ways and that government treats people as equals when it protects their possession and enjoyment of that property. Welfare-based conceptions, on the other hand, deny any natural right in property and insist instead that government must produce, distribute, and regulate property to achieve results defined by some specified function of the happiness or welfare of individuals. Utilitarianism, in the form just discussed, is one welfare-based conception of equality: it holds that government treats people as equals in its scheme of property when its rules secure roughly the greatest possible average welfare, counting the happiness or success of each person in the same way. Equality of welfare is a different theory of this same class: it requires government to design and distribute property so as to make the welfare of all citizens roughly equal, so far as possible.

A third group of theories demands that government aim at outcomes defined in the vocabulary not of welfare but of goods, opportunities, and other resources. One such theory—material equality—requires government to make the material wealth of all citizens as nearly equal as possible throughout their lives. Another, which I shall call equality of resources, requires it to make an equal share of resources available for each to consume or invest as he wishes. Equality of resources, unlike material equality, assumes that people's wealth should differ as they make different choices about investment and consumption. It supposes that if people begin with the same wealth and other resources, then equality is preserved through market transactions among them, even though some grow richer than others and some happier through these transactions. Equality of resources recognizes, however, that differences in talent are differences in resources, and for that reason it seeks in some way to compensate the less talented beyond what the market awards them.[13]

Now we must make a new distinction among these familiar conceptions of equality. Some are competitive with the private ambitions people might pursue in the use of their property, in the following way. Imagine that government has succeeded in designing the best available property scheme on each of these conceptions and then leaves each citizen free to use or exchange property assigned to him under that scheme in whatever way he wishes, free from any responsibility to show equal regard for the interests of all. In the case of some, but not all, of the conceptions we listed, the result is likely to undermine the form of equality the scheme originally secured. This is inevitably true of both equality of welfare and material equality. Some citizens will achieve more welfare or add more to their wealth through their decisions and trades than others, so initial equality in either welfare or wealth will be corrupted. It is likely though not inevitable that the utilitarian conception of equality would also be undermined. A government of marvelous skill and knowledge might design a scheme such that the choices people actually make, free to favor themselves, will in fact maximize average utility. But when tastes and attachments change, their choices will no longer have that result, and changes in the scheme, through further redistribution or different regulatory rules, will become necessary to restore the utilitarian results initially achieved. In that sense these three theories—welfare equality, material equality, and utilitarianism—all make private choice competitive with public responsibility, so their supporters have difficulty in answering the question I posed, why government should not enforce some general legal principle requiring people to avoid private decisions that will disturb the existing distribution of welfare or wealth. They can solve this problem only by showing what seems implausible, that the form of equality they favor can be achieved more constantly and securely without such a principle than with it.[14]

The remaining two conceptions on our list—libertarianism and equality of resources—are not competitive with private ambition but on the contrary perfectly compatible with it. If people have natural rights in property, and government accurately identifies these rights and protects their exercise, then the choices people make in using their property will employ rather than threaten what government has achieved. So, too, with equality of overall resources. If government succeeds in securing for each citizen a genuinely equal share of resources to use as he wishes in making his life successful according to his lights, then once again his choices will give effect to rather than corrupt what government has done. Though these two theories are very different from each other, neither condemns the permissive attitude we began by finding problematic in a community politically committed to equality of concern. On the contrary, they take equality to consist in establishing the appropriate conditions for that attitude, and so they cannot be threatened or corrupted, once successful in establishing these conditions, by people acting in the way the attitude permits.

We reach this preliminary conclusion. Our familiar convictions, which require government to treat people as equals in the scheme of property it designs but do not require people to treat others as equals in using whatever the scheme assigns them, assume a division of public and private responsibility. They suppose we have a duty in politics that does not carry over as any general duty of private life. We need a conception of public duty that makes this division of responsibility coherent, which explains why the duty sovereign in one realm is much less demanding in the other. This argues, if we take the division of responsibility to be important and fundamental, for a compatible rather than a competitive conception of equality as defining public responsibility, because compatible conceptions explain the division naturally and systematically, while competitive theories can explain it at best only artificially and improbably.[15]

That is an important conclusion generally for any broad

interpretation of our political and moral practices, but it has special importance in this chapter. It recommends the second strategy for explaining why we have a duty to treat others with equal concern in nuisance and negligence situations, the strategy which accepts that we have no general duty to treat others that way in all situations and tries to explain why we do have that duty when abstract legal rights conflict. The division between public and private responsibility in property draws a crucial distinction between the responsibilities individual citizens have on two kinds of occasions: first, when they decide how to use what the public scheme of property has clearly assigned them and, second, when they must decide *what* it has assigned them, either because its explicit rules are unclear or incomplete or because the abstract rights it deploys conflict in some way. On the first kind of occasion a citizen can suppose himself entitled to act for himself or others he chooses, as a member of a community of principle whose scheme secures, according to the latest public settlement, what it deems are the conditions for a permissive, self-interested attitude. But on the second kind of occasion he cannot allow himself that freedom, because the question is then what that scheme, properly understood, should be taken to be, which means asking how those conditions should be more particularly defined. Each citizen must answer that interpretive question for himself, by refining and applying the compatible conception of equality he believes supplies the best interpretation of the main structure of the settled scheme.

On these latter occasions, that is, his attitudes must be egalitarian rather than permissive. That is the foundation we need for an improved egalitarian justification of the market-simulating approach to certain hard cases at law. It allows us to state that justification in this preliminary and rough way. Market-simulating rules provide at least part of the best practical elaboration of the best compatible conception of equality. So these rules should guide citizens when they are properly engaged, not just in employing, but in elaborating their community's public scheme of property, as they are when its abstract rights conflict. I will expand and defend these claims in the remainder of this chapter, but we should notice that the argument even thus far provides another example of how law as integrity encourages a reciprocal interplay between law and morals in ordinary practical life, even when no lawsuit is in prospect and each citizen is judge for and of himself.

EQUALITY AND COMPARATIVE COST

The Exercise

The two compatible conceptions of equality I mentioned differ in fundamental ways. The practical elaboration of equality of resources, for example, requires compensating for unequal inheritance of wealth and health and talent through redistribution, but the libertarian conception rejects redistribution as theft in principle. It would make some difference, and in some cases a considerable difference, which of these conceptions a citizen brought to occasions when abstract legal rights conflict, which of them he used to decide whose right is concrete and whose must yield. Since my main purpose is to show the connection between a conception of equality and accident law, I shall not argue but only assume that equality of resources is superior to the libertarian conception: it fits our legal and moral practices no worse and is better in abstract moral theory.[16]

Nor shall I try to improve on the crude statement of equality of resources I gave a moment ago; I rely on arguments elsewhere to give it more shape and, I hope, appeal.[17] We need only the crude account to continue our construction of the egalitarian justification of market-simulating judicial decisions. I shall try to show that if someone does accept equality of resources as furnishing a better overall interpretation of his community's property scheme than other conceptions of equality, then he should adopt a view of his private responsibilities that produces market-simulating choices on most occasions when abstract legal rights compete. My argument is not deductive. It does not show that once anyone accepts the root idea of equality of resources he will automatically and inevitably be driven to the conclusions I report. I argue only that he will be required to make a series of choices refining that conception for the cases we are considering and that plausible choices would then direct him to market simulation in most ordinary cases. My argument will not recommend the economic principle in all cases in which partisans of the economic interpretation would think it appropriate, however, because the egalitarian justification condemns rather than approves much of what they claim.

The Main Line

Suppose you and I have roughly equal wealth, and neither is handicapped or otherwise has special needs or requirements. We discover that the activities we independently plan, each in the enjoyment of general rights secured by property assignments, conflict. I want to learn some trumpet piece one evening, and you want to work at algebra in the next apartment. Or I want to drive my car very fast on a road you would like to walk on in safety. Or I want my trains to run next to a field on which you want to plant grain. My projects intersect yours, and I have to decide, before I proceed, how far I should adjust my plans to take account of your interests and how far I should assume responsibility for any injury I might cause you. It seems intuitively correct that this is at least in part a matter of the relative costs to each of us of the decisions I might make. If it would cost me only a little to forgo my plans, but would cost you a great deal if I do not, then this seems a good reason for my holding back or for compensating you if I do go ahead.

The theory of private responsibility we are testing explains why relative cost figures in these moral decisions. According to that theory we must act as if the concrete rights we cannot both exercise had not yet been distributed between us, and we must distribute these ourselves as best we can, in the way equality of resources commends. If we had time and occasion and good will enough to work out some compromise—if we agreed on hours for my trumpet-playing, for example—then equality might be protected in that way. If compromise is not possible in the circumstances, however, we must each act so as to minimize the inequality of the distribution we achieve, and that means so that the loser loses less. This principle of comparative harm cries out for elaboration, however. How shall we measure the relative costs of seizing or forgoing some opportunity? Our root assumption, that we are carrying forward a scheme of equality of resources rather than of utilitarian equality or some other welfarist conception, rules out some measures. We must not measure comparative cost in terms of happiness or satisfaction or some other dimension of welfare. So we must calculate who would lose less in these circumstances by comparing financial costs, not because money is more important than anything else but because it is the most abstract and therefore the best standard to use in deciding which of us will lose more in resources by each of the decisions we might make.

This poses a problem when the losses in question are not obviously or immediately financial. Perhaps neither of us has income at stake when I want to practice and you want to study. How should I decide whether the principle of comparative cost gives me a right to play my trumpet? I should ask not whether I will have more pleasure from learning my piece than you will have from mastering your proof, but whether the damage to my overall plans will be larger than the damage to yours. Since we both have roughly equal funds at our disposal, it seems sensible to measure the potential damage in the way the market simulation test suggests: by asking whether you would pay more for me to stop playing the music, if you had to, than I would pay for the opportunity to play it. This may sound callous, reducing the joys of art and scholarship to money, but it is a perfectly plausible way of attempting roughly to measure what we want to discover: the relative importance of the two activities to each of us in our overall schemes of what we want to do with our lives. It is a better test for this purpose than any comparison of the pleasure or enjoyment each of us would gain or lose, or of the relative importance of the activities from the standpoint of the ethically best life.

Suppose, however, that what I want to do will affect not only you but many other people as well. If my train speeds and sends out sparks, this will increase the price that people generally must pay for bread; if the train slows and the grain is saved, this will increase the price of transporting the people and goods the train carries. Because this is a commercial case, however, the impact on others is adequately represented in the comparison between what my train company and your farm stand to lose under each decision. But the trumpet and algebra case is different. The effects of my decision on others, if these should count at all, would have to be figured separately. Perhaps playing my trumpet is more important to me, measured by what I would spend for the privilege if necessary, than my silence is to you or any other single neighbor, but less important than my silence is to all the neighbors collectively, as a group. Which comparison should be decisive for the principle of comparative harm? This is a difficult question, and both answers have some initial plausibility. But the second answer seems better. If equality of resources can be assumed already to hold not only between us, but throughout the community of those whom my practicing will affect, then I must measure the cost of some opportunity I might take for myself by measuring its importance for others generally; the true cost to others of my playing the trumpet is what they, together, would be willing to spend to make me stop.

Qualifications

We now have the main outlines of a partial theory of personal responsibility. We will not apply this theory—at least not in so simple a form—on every occasion when uses of private property conflict in ways not governed by explicit past political decisions. When should we reject it? I assumed, in considering the conflict between my trumpet and your algebra, that the explicit distribution of property between us was equal, judged from the viewpoint of equality of resources. That does not necessarily mean (although I did in fact assume this) that neither of us is richer than the other. For you might be richer than me for reasons perfectly consistent with resource equality between us. I might have spent more than you in the past or chosen a job that paid me less. Nevertheless I might know something about you that made the assumption of resource equality between us implausible: I might know that you are severely handicapped, for example, and had received no social resources by way of compensation. In that case the principle of comparative financial harm, which makes concrete rights turn on the question which of us would pay more for the opportunity, might not be appropriate because it might not secure the distribution between us that resource equality recommends in these circumstances.[18] But when my action will affect, not some particular known person or group about whom I can discover information of that character, but unknown people about whom I cannot, I should presume that comparative cost provides the right test. Even if I believe that resources have been distributed unequally, I normally have no reason to presume anything about the direction of the inequality with respect to the particular people my act will affect.

I also assumed, implicitly, that it was proper to regard my all-or-nothing decision whether to take up some opportunity, in the absence of a realistic opportunity for negotiation, as an isolated issue. If we really are neighbors, this assumption would be a mistake: I should treat a particular decision as part of a continuing series of linked decisions each of us makes. I might care less about playing my trumpet on each occasion than you care about silence, less about burning my leaves than you care about avoiding smoke, and so forth; but if I simply defer to you every time, the balance will grow progressively lopsided. If I forgo an opportunity in one case, because the relative loss to you would be greater, this should be entered to my credit in a moral ledger against the next decision I (or you) have to make. A moral ledger will normally be possible, however, only between people, like neighbors, who do have a continuing and self-conscious relationship. There is no sensible or tolerable way of keeping that sort of ledger for the decisions each of us makes that affect others generally, or a stranger only once. We must rely on the hypothesis that if everyone treats such decisions as isolated cases, this will work out roughly fairly for everyone in the long run.

We are moving toward this conclusion. I should follow the principle of comparative financial harm when I know that my taking up some concrete right will conflict with the exercise of abstract rights of others with whom I have no special continuing relationship and about whom I have no special information of the relevant sort. My ignorance may make the principle much harder to apply. For how shall I then decide whether those who are likely to be affected would indeed pay more, either individually or collectively, for the opportunity than I would? In a commercial context, as in the train and farmer example, my rough knowledge of the market may supply enough information. If I run a train company and know that the farmers along the railroad route will together suffer more than a particular sum in the market value of lost grain, I may assume that they would pay that sum for the opportunity to be free of that loss. In noncommercial contexts, as in the noise pollution examples, I may need to fall back on the idea of the "reasonable" or "representative" person in the affected neighborhood, on my general knowledge of how much most people dislike or would be frustrated by the injury I will inflict on them. But we do have sufficient general knowledge of that sort to make the principle of comparative financial harm workable enough in most such cases.

Even so, we must qualify that principle in another and much more important way. For in some circumstances it would obviously be unfair to measure the importance of some loss or damage by asking only whether the victim would and could pay more to avoid that loss than others collectively would pay to do what threatens to produce it. We must, to see why, notice something more about the general scheme of equality of resources. I said it presumes that equality is preserved and protected through market transactions but that this is subject to qualifications. I have already said that the assumption must be qualified to take account of differences in talent. It must also be qualified to take account of individual rights. Under equality of resources, people have rights that protect fundamental interests, including those that rational people would insure against damage if insurance were available to everyone on equal and economically efficient terms. They also have rights securing each person's independence from other people's prejudices and dislikes which, if these were allowed to influence market transactions, would defeat rather than advance the goal of making distribution sensitive to the true costs of people's choices. I have discussed these two kinds of rights at length elsewhere,[19] but even this brief description shows why recognizing these rights would displace the market-simulating model in certain dramatic cases. Suppose, for example, that my child's life depends on a noisy ambulance that annoys a large number of people who would collectively pay more not to be annoyed than all the funds I have. Or suppose I am black, and my neighbors would together pay more for me not to burn leaves in my yard than I could or would pay to burn them, simply because they hate the sight of me. These are not, of course, the only kinds of occasions when the comparative financial harm test would seem an unjust method of adjudicating concrete rights; I cite them only to show that the test would have to be qualified in a variety of ways beyond those so far considered.

The Practical Elaboration

If we pursue these exceptions and qualifications, our theory of personal responsibility will grow more complex. But nothing we have discovered suggests that it would justify less of the body of accident law our judges have developed than the utilitarian argument would. Even if the academic elaboration of equality of resources must be sensitive, as we saw, to information touching the justice of the standing distribution of wealth between an actor and someone he knows his activities will damage or put at risk, the practical elaboration would be much less sensitive, case by case, to information of that sort, and it would therefore be likely to include the various doctrines about reasonableness, contributory negligence, and the other baggage of the law of tort that we met earlier. A legislator enforcing the resource equality model of personal responsibility would have good reason, for example, not to encourage people to speculate about whether those they are likely to injure have more or less wealth than equality of resources would justify. He would think that justice overall would be better protected by leaving redistribution to legislative schemes less capricious in their impact. He would have other reasons for that conclusion as well: it seems unjust that compensation to a victim should depend on the relative wealth of the actor, if for no other reason than the difficulty that would pose to someone anxious to insure against injury on sensible terms. So a legislator would do better to allow people to base their decisions about risk and liability on general information about the tastes and preferences of "average" people than to require them to search for the special information that a full academic elaboration of resource equality would make pertinent in particular cases. But even though that practical elaboration would use "objective" standards, it would also be alert to special circumstances in which the principle of comparative financial harm would be likely to ignore rights or otherwise prove unjust. It would insist that liability for certain kinds of damage—threats to life, for example, and injury flowing from racial prejudice—not be subject to the straightforward financial tests of that principle.

PRIVATE PEOPLE AND PUBLIC BODIES

We have good reasons, then, drawn from the ambitions of law as integrity, for preferring the egalitarian to the utilitarian justification of accident law. It is much more successful on the substantive dimensions of interpretation. An interpretation of accident law must deploy a scheme of personal responsibility, and the utilitarian argument, we discovered, could not provide a plausible one. The egalitarian argument does; it supplies a scheme of responsibility that is attractive in itself and also recognizes the dynamic interaction among law, public virtue, and private responsibility that is one of the most appealing features of a community of principle.

The egalitarian argument has another feature important to our argument as a whole: it limits the range of market simulation, not only in the various ways we have already noticed but institutionally as well. The utilitarian argument provides an ideal that, once accepted, must be sovereign over legislation as well as adjudication. If a community is more just whenever it is happier, and legal rules governing liability for accidents or nuisances contribute most to overall happiness when they make the community richer on the whole by mimicking hypothetical markets, then whenever Parliament is asked to regulate the speed at which trains may drive when their sparks risk destroying crops, or whenever the New York city government must decide when musical instruments may be played in apartment buildings or crowded neighborhoods, it should aim to create exactly the legal rights that market transactions, were these feasible, would have established. The egalitarian argument does not have that consequence, because the legislature, unlike private citizens, has both obligations and opportunities to improve the distribution its law has so far created; it has responsibilities they do not have, and means and strategies not open to them.

Our case for the egalitarian interpretation began, in fact, in exactly that distinction. We assumed that government has a general, pervasive duty that private citizens, as individuals, do not. Government must constantly survey and alter its rules of property, radically if necessary, to bring them closer to the ideal of treating people as equals under the best conception. Market simulation, which assumes the adequacy of the scheme already in place, would be a grotesquely circular and feeble weapon for that purpose. So our explanation, beginning in a division of responsibility, denies that the economic principle furnishes an exclusive test for legislation touching either the main structures of the economic system or more detailed regulations of it.

We must end this study of equality and property by returning once more to the distinction between policy and principle, because it adds another dimension to the contrast between public and private responsibility we have been exploring. Our main argument supposes that private citizens must treat occasions of conflict between abstract legal rights as raising issues of principle about the concrete rights each party finally has. But it does not follow that the legislature must treat every decision it makes in regulating and distributing property, or even its statutes about nuisance and negligence, as matters of principle rather than policy. We insist that government design its system of property to treat people as equals under an appropriate conception; that is the foundation of our argument for the egalitarian interpretation of these branches of the law. But as we saw in Chapter 6, government must treat that requirement mainly in the fashion of policy, as commending a general collective goal that respects equality of concern overall and statistically, rather than as supposing that each individual statute or regulation, judged on its own, must award each citizen something he is entitled to have. Every legislative decision about property must respect certain individual political rights, of course. (We shall have to consider, in Chapter 10, how far these political rights are made legal rights under the best interpretation of the United States Constitution.) But a legislature may otherwise pursue the collective general interest through a variety of different measures and techniques, each of which achieves a somewhat different distribution person by person. No citizen has a right that one rather another of these programs be selected just because it will benefit him more. The choice is a matter of policy rather than principle.

A legislator has no general need to make policy choices that produce the allocations of rights and opportunities that would have been negotiated by the parties specially affected. A legislator may think, for example, that the best solution to the problem of speeding trains and burned crops must be sensitive to national transportation and agricultural policies, or even to national defense and the balance of payments or foreign exchange. He may treat his decisions about noise pollution as an aspect of more general policies about land use and city planning, or even about support for music or the arts. His decisions need not be all-or-nothing in the way practical circumstances force all-or-nothing decisions on citizens acting for themselves. Legislation provides the opportunity to develop a complex scheme of regulation that depends for its efficacy on overall strategy. It may regulate train speed differently in different parts of the country, in response to a thousand complex variations in transportation and agricultural use and need, for example, or it may divide cities into zones where noise is treated in different ways, so long as the divisions are not arbitrary and do not mask illegitimate discriminations that would violate individual rights.

Once the legislature has made its choice, however, then individuals do have legal rights to what they have been assigned, and under law as integrity these rights extend not only to the explicit assignments but to the principled extension of these into cases not expressly decided. In this chapter we have been studying the proper ground of that principled extension in certain cases. I can now restate my thesis in the following way. When private citizens encounter conflicts between their general abstract common-law rights in property (as distinct from their rights under particular regulative statutes embodying discrete policies like those I just imagined) they must adjudicate these conflicts by repairing to the basic principle the overall scheme is meant to respect, which is the principle that it must treat them as equals. They must ask which conception of equal concern the scheme as a whole is best interpreted as expressing, and assume the extension of concrete rights that, of the choices available to them in the circumstances, best serves that conception. I have been supposing, in order to illustrate the character and complexity of that interpretive problem, that resource equality provides the right conception for that purpose, and I claim that the main lines of American and British nuisance and negligence law match a plausible solution of the interpretive problem on that assumption. That process is not appropriate, however, when conflicts arise under particular regulative statutes with distinct policies, because the rights people have under such a statute depend too much on those special policies to authorize any direct repair to a conception of equality. Citizens' responsibilities then depend on a different set of issues, and these form our next topic.

NINE

STATUTES

LEGISLATIVE INTENTION

One day the snail darter case comes to Hercules' court. He must decide whether the Endangered Species Act gives the secretary of the interior power to halt a vast, almost finished federal power project to save a small and ecologically uninteresting fish, so he must first decide how to read statutes whose meaning is uncertain. My argument is complex, and I shall tell you at once how it ends. Hercules will use much the same techniques of interpretation to read statutes that he uses to decide common-law cases, the techniques we studied in the last two chapters. He will treat Congress as an author earlier than himself in the chain of law, though an author with special powers and responsibilities different from his own, and he will see his own role as fundamentally the creative one of a partner continuing to develop, in what he believes is the best way, the statutory scheme Congress began. He will ask himself which reading of the act—permitting or not permitting the secretary to halt projects almost completed—shows the political history including and surrounding that statute in the better light. His view of how the statute should be read will in part depend on what certain congressmen said when debating it. But it will also depend on the best answer to political questions: how far Congress should defer to public opinion in matters of this sort, for example, and whether it would be absurd as a matter of policy to protect a minor species at so great an expense of funds.[1] He must rely on his own judgment in answering these questions, of course, not because he thinks his opinions are automatically right, but because no one can properly answer any question except by relying at the deepest level on what he himself believes.

Before I develop that general description of how judges should interpret statutes under law as integrity, however, I must first consider an important objection to it, and the argument this objection provokes will occupy us for many pages. "Hercules' method ignores the important principle, firmly rooted in our legal practice, that statutes should be read, not according to what judges believe would make them best, but according to what the legislators who actually adopted them intended. Suppose Hercules decides, after taking into account everything his interpretive method commends, that the act is a better piece of legislation if it is understood not to give the secretary the power to halt almost completed and very expensive projects. The congressmen who enacted it may have intended to give the secretary exactly that power. In those circumstances our legal practice, supported by democratic principles, insists that Hercules defer to their intention, not to his own different view."

It is true that in American legal practice, judges constantly refer to the various statements congressmen and other legislators make, in committee reports or formal debates, about the purpose of an act. Judges say these statements, taken together, form the "legislative history" of the act, which they must respect. We may, however, take two rather different views of this practice of deferring to legislative history. One is Hercules' view. He treats the various statements that make up the legislative history as political acts that his interpretation of the statute must fit and explain, just as it must fit and explain the text of the statute itself. The other is the view presupposed by the objection I just described. It treats these statements not as events important in themselves, but as evidence of the mental states of the particular legislators who made them, presumed to be representative of the mental states of the majority of legislators whose votes created the statute.

I shall call this the "speaker's meaning" view because it assumes that legislation is an occasion or instance of communication and that judges look to legislative history when a statute is not clear on its face to discover what state of mind the legislators tried to communicate through their votes. It supposes, in short, that proper interpretation of a statute must be what I called in Chapter 2 conversational rather than constructive interpretation. The ruling model of this theory is the familiar model of ordinary speech. When a friend says something, we may ask, "What did he mean by that?" and think that our answer to that question describes something about his state of mind when he spoke, some idea he meant to communicate to us in speaking as he did. Wittgenstein and other philosophers warn us against a crude misunderstanding of this picture. Having a thought and choosing words to represent that thought are not two separate activities. Nor are people free to mean anything they like by the words they use, so the question, "What did he mean by those words?" is not purely the question of what he had in mind when he spoke. But the picture serves well enough as a rough description of how we conceive the problem of understanding someone who has spoken ambiguously, and the speaker's meaning theory proposes that we use the same picture for ambiguous or unclear legislation.

If someone accepts the speaker's meaning view, his theory about how to read statutes will have a particular structure. He will present his conclusions as statements about the intention of the statute itself. Is it the purpose or intention of the Endangered Species Act to give the secretary a certain power? But he regards the intention of the statute as a theoretical construction, a compendious statement of the discrete intentions of particular actual people, because only these can actually have conversational intentions of the sort he has in mind. So his theory of statutes must answer the following set of questions. Which historical people count as the legislators? How are their intentions to be discovered? When these intentions differ somewhat from one to another, how are they to be combined in the overall, composite institutional intention? His answers must, moreover, establish a fixed moment when the statute was spoken, when it acquired all the meaning it ever has.

Hercules' view requires no such structure. He understands the idea of a statute's purpose or intention, not as some combination of the purposes or intentions of particular legislators, but as the upshot of integrity, of taking the interpretive attitude toward the political events that include the statute's enactment. He takes note of the statements the legislators made in the process of enacting it, but he treats them as political events important in themselves, not as evidence of any mental state behind them. So he has no need for precise views about which legislators' mental states are in question, or what mental states these are, or how he should combine them into some super-mental state of the statute or institution itself. Nor does he suppose any canonical moment of speech toward which his historical research bends; the history he interprets begins before a statute is enacted and continues to the moment when he must decide what it now declares.

Hercules' methods provide a better interpretation of actual judicial practice than the speaker's meaning theory. The defects of the latter can be cured only by transforming it, in stages, into Hercules' method. The three crucial questions I just mentioned, which must be answered in order to put the speaker's meaning theory into practice, cannot be answered just by probing the root model of communication, just by exploring the internal connections between intention and legislation conceived as a form of speech. They must be answered in political theory, by taking up particular views about controversial issues of political morality. So the speaker's meaning theory cannot make good its presumed claims of political neutrality, its ambition to separate a judge's personal convictions from the way he reads a statute. The most plausible answers to the crucial questions, moreover, push us steadily away from the speaker's meaning theory, as it is commonly understood, toward a different view, one that aims to enforce the most abstract and general political convictions from which legislators act rather than the hopes or expectations or more detailed political opinions they have in mind when voting. This different idea, however, is only a poorly stated and unstable form of Hercules' own method, into which it therefore collapses.

SPEAKER'S MEANING

Hermes

I shall argue these large claims in considerable detail, not only because the speaker's meaning theory of legislation is so popular but because the argument that exposes its defects provides distinctions we shall need when we consider Hercules' own method more directly. I now suppose a new judge, Hermes, who is almost as clever as Hercules and just as patient, who also accepts law as integrity but accepts the speaker's meaning theory of legislation as well. He thinks legislation is communication, that he must apply statutes by discovering the communicative will of the legislators, what they were trying to say when they voted for the Endangered Species Act, for example. Since Hermes is self-conscious in everything he does, he will pause to reflect over each of the choices he must make in order to put the speaker's meaning theory into practice.

He is aware from the start of one difficulty in that theory. It is hard enough to discover the intentions of friends and colleagues and adversaries and lovers. How can he hope to discover the intentions of strangers in the past, who may all be dead? How can he be sure there were any helpful intentions to be discovered? The New York statesmen who adopted the statute of wills probably never foresaw the murdering heir; perhaps many senators and congressmen never contemplated the problem of small fish and almost finished dams. But Hermes starts by taking a practical attitude toward these evidential difficulties. He accepts that he must take more pains to discover the mental attitudes that lie behind legislation than the mental states of people he meets in pubs, that he must sometimes settle for judgments of speculative probability, not practical certainty, and that in some cases he must admit that he has no useful evidence of any pertinent state of mind one way or the other and then be prepared to decide that particular case some other way. I shall not press this evidential difficulty. It is the least of Hermes' problems.

Who Are the Authors of a Statute?

Before he looks for evidence of thoughts past, he must decide whose thoughts these were. Whose mental states count in fixing the intention behind the Endangered Species Act? Every member of the Congress that enacted it, including those who voted against? Are the thoughts of some—for example, those who spoke, or spoke most often, in the debates—more important than the thoughts of others? What about the executive officials and assistants who prepared the initial drafts? What about the president who signed the bill and made it law? Should his intentions not count more than any single senator's? What about private citizens who wrote letters to their congressmen or promised or threatened to vote for or against them, or to make or withhold campaign contributions, depending upon how they voted? What about the various lobbies and action groups who played their now-normal role? Any realistic view of the legislative process includes the influence of these groups; if they contributed to making the statute law, does Hermes have any good reason for not counting their intentions in determining what law they made?

There is a further complication. A statute owes its existence not only to the decision people made to enact it but also to the decision of other people later not to amend or repeal it. Of course "decision" may be too strong to describe the negative attitudes that allow most statutes to survive, sometimes long after they serve much use. They survive by inattention and default rather than by any conscious and collective decision. But even inattention may reflect some common understanding about the point and detailed consequences of a statute that is different from the understanding held by the legislators who enacted it in the first place; in the more dramatic cases, when people have campaigned for amendment or repeal, the decision to let it stand may be more active and explicit. Should Hermes ever consider the intentions of the various legislators who might have repealed the statute over the course of years and decades but did not?

These are not academic questions. Hermes must answer them before he can put the speaker's meaning theory to practical use. He cannot find answers by asking how those whose intentions count would answer them. For he is trying to discover whose intentions count. He has no option but to confront these questions in the following spirit. He has opinions about the influence that the attitudes, beliefs, and ambitions of particular groups of officials and citizens ought to have in the process of legislation. He will see that one set of choices he might make about whose intention should count in calculating legislative intention would, if generally accepted by judges, bring that process closer to his ideal, and that another set would push it farther away. Since the speaker's meaning theory does not in itself decide whose intention counts, it would be perverse for Hermes to choose any answers in the second set over those in the first.[2]

So his judgments about whose thoughts count will be sensitive to his views on the old question whether representative legislators should be guided by their own opinions and convictions, answerable only to their own conscience, and on the newer question whether lobbying, logrolling, and political action committees are a corruption of the democratic process or valuable devices for making that process more efficient and effective. His judgments will also be sensitive to his convictions about the relative importance of fairness, as he conceives it, and certainty in legislation. He might be led to prefer a more restrained account of whose intention counts—eliminating, for example, both contemporary lobbyists and later legislators who might have repealed the statute but did not—not because he believes a legislative process fairer that ignores public pressure or is insensitive to change, but because a wider account would make the idea of a legislative intention too vague or formless to be of any practical use in making ambiguous legislation clearer.

How Do They Combine?

Suppose Hermes decides in the end that only the intentions of actual congressmen who voted for the statute when it was adopted should count and that the intentions of all of them should count equally. Now suppose he finds that the pertinent intentions differed even among this selected group. One set of congressmen intended that the secretary have power to halt any project whatsoever, another that he have power to halt a project if that decision was not plainly unreasonable, and a third that he have no power over any project begun before he designated a species threatened by that project. The speaker's meaning theory requires Hermes to combine these various opinions into some composite group intention. Should he use a "majority intention" approach, so that the institutional intention is that of whichever group, if any, would have been large enough to pass the statute if that group alone has voted for it?[3] Or a "plurality" intention scheme, so that the opinion of the largest of the three groups would count as the opinion of the legislature even if the other two groups, taken together, were much larger? Or some "representative intention" approach, which supposes a mythical average or representative legislator whose opinion comes closest to those of most legislators, though identical to none of them? If the last, how is this mythical average legislator to be constructed? There are many other possible ways of combining individual intentions into a group or institutional intention. How should Hermes settle on one?

He must rely, once again, on his own political judgment. Suppose he thinks that as a matter of sound principles of democratic theory no change should be made in the status quo of people's legal rights unless a majority of legislators intended that change. That opinion would incline him toward the majority intention theory. But suppose he thinks, on the contrary, that people's legal rights should be as close as possible to those deemed appropriate by a majority of legislators. This would attract him to the representative intention view, at least as against the majority intention view, because he would then prefer people to be in the position contemplated by the representative intention, even though it was in detail the intention of less than a majority, than that they remain in the status quo no one intended.

What Mental State? Hopes and Expectations

Assume, however, that the problem of combining intentions solves itself in this way. Hermes knows somehow that each member of the majority voting for the Endangered Species Act had exactly the same opinions, so that if he discovers the intentions of one—Senator Smith, say—he has discovered the intentions of all. Assume also that Smith has never expressed her opinions in any formal way, in committee report or legislative debate, for example, but that Hermes has some other way of discovering what her opinions were. Now he must confront the most difficult issue. Smith's mental life is complex; which of her beliefs, attitudes, or other mental states constitutes her "intention"? We explored the question of intention in Chapter 2; I said that in some contexts intentions are not limited to conscious mental states. The speaker's meaning theory, however, ties intention to the picture of legislators intending to communicate something in particular and so does aim at discovering what a legislator might be thought to have actually had in mind as he spoke through his vote.

But in one respect the ordinary legislator—the backbencher—is not in the position of an ordinary speaker at all. People who talk to one another in the ordinary way can choose their words, and so choose words they expect to have the effect they want. They expect to be understood the way they hope to be understood. But some people are not in charge of their own words: a hostage telephoning at gunpoint may very much hope not to be understood the way he expects to be. Or someone who signs a group letter he cannot rewrite for the group, or the author of that letter who drafts it to attract the most signatures possible. Legislators are very often in that position. A congressman who voted for the Endangered Species Act may have regretted that it contained no explicit clause stating that the secretary could not interrupt expensive projects once started, although he did not have the power or time to have such a clause inserted. In that case he might well expect that the act would be interpreted to realize his worst fears, but he would hope that it would not be. He is therefore not like someone choosing to communicate some thought or idea or wish. He occupies a position intermediate between speaker and hearer. He must decide what thought the words on the paper before him are likely to be taken to express and then decide whether he wishes that message to be sent to the public and its officials, including judges, given the only realistic alternative of sending no message at all. That change of role is important, for he treats the document, not himself or any other person, as the author of the message he agrees to send.

Hermes thinks he must decide whether a congressman's pertinent intention is a matter of the latter's hopes or his expectations when these come apart. Suppose Smith realized that the Endangered Species Act, as drafted, might be construed to give the secretary power to halt almost completed projects, hoped that it would not, but expected that it would be. (She did not suggest an amendment, let us assume, because she did not know how many others shared her hopes, or because she feared other amendments if she did, or because she did not think the issue worth the delay.) Hermes might be tempted for a moment by the idea that in these circumstances Smith's intention should be taken to be her hopes rather than her expectations. After all, he might think, legislation should express the will of a majority of the legislators, and will is more a matter of hope than of prediction. But he knows that congressmen's hopes very often do them no credit. Smith may have voted for the Endangered Species Act because she feared the opposition of the conservationist lobby at the next election, or because she knew her constituents wanted her to vote that way. If these were her reasons, she may have hoped the act would be construed as narrowly as possible because she thought it foolish or because the act was bad news for corporations controlled by her friends. So Hermes might be inclined to the apparently opposite view, that Smith's intentions should be taken to be a matter of how she expects the statute to be understood. After all, if she votes for a statute that she expects to have particular consequences, then she has consented to these consequences, even though she might regret them, as part of an overall inclusive compromise she prefers to what she believes would be the alternative. So a theory of legislative intention constructed on predictions seems to guarantee that a majority of legislators will have consented to the statute as enforced. But Hermes' enthusiasm for the expectation solution will be short lived, because just as a legislator's hopes may reflect selfish ambitions that have no place in any acceptable theory of legislative interpretation, so his expectations may be based on predictions that have no place in any such theory either. Smith may expect the Endangered Species Act to be construed narrowly only because she thinks, rightly or wrongly, that the first case applying the act will come before anticonservationist judges. In any case the expectation solution would be paradoxical if generally accepted. If it is understood that judges will enforce an unclear statute in whatever way most congressmen as a matter of psychological fact predict it will be enforced, then a judge must decide what Smith predicted he would do, which means what she predicted he would think she had predicted he would do, and so forth indefinitely. That sets a puzzle for games theory, not a practical technique for understanding statutes. Legislators can usefully predict how judges will interpret their statutes only if they think judges are using some method of statutory interpretation that is independent of legislators' predictions.[4]

Now Hermes is in some difficulty. He began by accepting that he should defer to legislative intention, by discovering, combining, and enforcing the mental states of particular people in the past. But he cannot identify these mental states as consisting either in the hopes or in the expectations of these people when hopes and expectations come apart. Nor even (as he will now see) when they come together, because the various arguments that led him to reject either the hopes or the expectations technique alone hold just as firmly against the two in combination. Smith might hope that the statute would be construed narrowly, because this would benefit her corporate friends and contributors, and predict that it would be because she believes anticonservationist judges will decide the first cases. It seems wrong to count her opinions as decisive even when they combine her hopes and predictions in that way. Hermes will shortly find an escape from this apparent dilemma in a new idea: that the speaker's meaning theory of statutory interpretation requires taking Smith's intentions to lie in her *convictions,* that is, her beliefs about what justice or sound policy would require, which may, of course, be different from either her hopes or her expectations. When Hermes follows this lead he will develop a rather different method for reading statutes from those he has so far considered.

Counterfactual Mental States

I want to assume that he has not yet had this idea, however, and is still wrestling with hopes and expectations. So far he has made the quite unreasonable assumption that Smith actually had some pertinent hope or had actually made some prediction when she cast her vote. He realizes this may not be so, that she may not have thought about unfinished dams at all, any more than the legislators who voted for the statute of wills thought about murderers like Elmer. How shall Hermes calculate her intention then? Many lawyers say that in these circumstances judges should ask a *counterfactual* question of this form: what would Smith have intended if she had thought of the problem? The best answer to a counterfactual question may be that there is no answer. If Smith never thought about the snail darter, then it may be neither true nor false that she would have wanted the snail darter saved if she had thought about it.[5] But counterfactual questions do have good answers sometimes. We can easily imagine evidence that if she had thought of the problem she would have wanted the fish saved or, on the contrary, the dam finished and opened. Or evidence that she would have expected the courts to protect the fish or, on the contrary, expected them to allow the dam to open. But since Hermes has already decided that Smith's intention is not a matter of her actual hopes or expectations, he will not think it can be a matter of her hypothetical, counterfactual hopes or expectations either. He might be tempted to construe the pertinent counterfactual question, therefore, as this one: if an amendment had been introduced, specifying that the secretary did not have power to halt the TVA dam once that dam had been almost completed, would Smith have voted for or against that amendment? It was, after all, a regrettable accident that no one thought of the problem and introduced such an amendment, and it seems sensible to ask what would have happened had that accident not occurred.

But Smith might have voted for or against any such amendment for any number of reasons: because she was anxious to delay a congressional recess, for example, or did not wish to antagonize its sponsor whose help she needed on other matters, or because she was being blackmailed by someone who happened to be a TVA official. It seems odd to let the application of the statute depend on her counterfactual vote for any of these reasons. There is a more basic difficulty: how she would have voted would undoubtedly depend on when and in what circumstances the amendment was introduced and also on how it was worded. She might have voted for it if it had been introduced early in the legislative process, but not at the end, because then she would not have wished to delay passage of the bill as a whole. Or she may have voted for it in spite of her reservations if it had been introduced as part of a package of amendments containing others she wanted very much. Hermes must therefore design some more precise counterfactual question: he must say more than simply that it was an accident that no amendment was introduced; he must state which amendment he assumes would have been introduced but for that accident. That question has no reasonable answer. It would be arbitrary to assume, for example, that if the problem had been noticed a clarifying amendment would have been introduced on its own just before the final vote. Should he say, then, that Smith's intention included a particular view about the snail darter only if she would have voted for an amendment to that effect no matter when or under what circumstances it was offered? That is too strict: no provision could pass that test. Indeed, it would seem too strong even to say that the New York legislators would have approved an amendment disabling murderers from inheriting no matter when and in what circumstances that amendment had been introduced.

The second contingency I mentioned—about the wording of the hypothetical amendment—is even more troublesome. I supposed that Smith was asked to vote on an amendment specifically exempting the TVA project from the secretary's control. But it is extremely unlikely that any amendment that specific would have been proposed. It is more likely that an amendment would have exempted any project authorized before the species in question had been designated as threatened, or any project whose construction had actually begun before that time, or any project which had been substantially completed. Or that an amendment would have provided that in the case of projects already authorized (or perhaps already begun) the secretary must exercise his power "reasonably," having regard for the importance of the species and of the project, the state of completion, the amount already spent on the project, and so forth. There could have been countless other amendments that, if adopted, might be thought to justify an exception for the TVA project. Smith would have voted for some of these amendments had they been proposed and had she been present to vote, and against others. Once again Hermes would need to choose a particular form of amendment as canonical in order to decide whether she would have voted for or against the TVA if a suitable amendment had been proposed; once again, any choice would be arbitrary.

CONVICTIONS

A Fresh Start

Now return to the new idea Hermes was on the verge of having before I made him think about counterfactual intentions. He would not look to Smith's hopes or expectations or to what she would have done in circumstances that did not arise but to the political convictions out of which she voted for the act, or would have if she had been voting on principle. Smith, we may assume, had a variety of beliefs and attitudes about justice and fairness and about which policies of conservation would be most effective in making the community better on the whole. I do not mean that she had a complete political, moral, and economic theory. Her convictions of justice, fairness, and wise policy might have been ill formed, incomplete, and more a matter of unreflective intuition or instinct than considered philosophical conclusions. But she had convictions of this sort nevertheless, and that is perfectly consistent with her having the other motives I imagined earlier: a wish to advance her own political or financial career or the political fortunes of her party or the prosperity of her friends who control large corporations. It is also consistent with her acting on these other motives in place of her convictions from time to time or even more often.

Hermes' new proposal takes Smith's "intention" in voting for the Endangered Species Act to consist in those of her convictions that would justify her vote, if any would. Now, when he discovers that she did not think about the snail darter, he has no need to speculate counterfactually about what she would have hoped or expected or how she would have voted. He can ask an entirely noncounterfactual question: what position about the secretary's power to halt an unfinished dam follows most naturally from her political convictions, so far as he has been able to discover these? Even if she had never heard of the snail darter, she may nevertheless have had convictions that bear on the problem: she may have believed, for example, that conservation of species is a matter of capital importance, that it would be a national disgrace to allow even one species to perish if it could be saved. In that case Hermes would be justified in concluding that her actual convictions, so far revealed, would be better served by protecting the fish rather than the dam. So the convictions approach altogether avoids the often mysterious and always arbitrary counterfactual devices so popular in textbooks on statutory interpretation. Hermes will prefer the convictions reading to the others he considered on more general grounds as well, because the convictions reading is much better suited to the aims of a community of principle. Members of such a community expect their legislators to act on principle and with integrity, and that goal is promoted if legislation is enforced in the light, not of personal ambitions prominent among legislators, but of convictions dominant in the legislature as a whole.

When Hermes for these various reasons takes up the convictions reading, he has moved very far from the original picture of legislation as communication. Smith's votes should be evidence of her convictions, but they are not statements of them in the way a speaker's sentences are statements of the thought he uses them to express.

Conflicting and Dominant Convictions

Hermes' new idea, however, is the seat of new problems. Smith's political convictions, however rough and incomplete, are not just a shopping list of random beliefs and attitudes. She has a variety of opinions about what is fair or unfair, just or unjust, wise or silly, in or against the national or collective interest, but she sees these as having a hierarchical structure: she treats some as more basic and fundamental than others, and some as depending on others, or supporting them, or both. Unless she is a Herculean moralist, these various opinions will not be perfectly coherent. Or—more to the present point—they will not seem perfectly coherent to anyone who undertakes, as Hermes must, to lay over them the single, coherent justifying structure integrity demands. Her opinions about conservation policy might seem to him to be in deep conflict with her views about how far it is just and reasonable for government to impose national aesthetic standards, as expressed in her statements or votes on housing or zoning law. Or with her convictions, reflected in statements or votes about local government or tax policy, about how far the economic interests of a discrete locality should be sacrificed to the tastes of a national majority, most of whom will not suffer comparable financial loss. Or with her views about political fairness, about how far government is

permitted to lead rather than follow national opinion in fixing on some conception of what the public interest is, as suggested by her opinions and votes about national subsidies for
the arts, for instance.

None of these potential conflicts worried Hermes when he
considered treating Smith's various opinions as either hopes
or expectations or when he puzzled about how she would
have voted had the snail darter question been raised. His
initial reasons for thinking it important whether she would
have voted for a particular amendment had it been introduced would not have been undermined if that counterfactual vote had been inconsistent with other votes. But
Hermes' new convictions approach is different. He now believes that statutes should be read to promote the aims of a
community of principle, that is, that they should be read to
express a coherent scheme of conviction dominant within
the legislature that enacted them. He is assuming that
Smith's views are representative of those of her colleagues; if
he suspects that some of her concrete opinions are in conflict
with, and are condemned by, her more general and fundamental political convictions, he must ask which reading of
the statute would best serve all her convictions taken together, as a structured system of ideas, made coherent so far
as this is possible.

That is an important conclusion, for as we shall shortly
see, it will lead Hermes steadily toward Hercules' interpretive methods for reading a statute, the methods Hermes
began by rejecting. We should pause, however, to notice a
logical mistake that might tempt someone to deny its importance: I mean the mistake of thinking that Smith's various
convictions can never really be in conflict with each other. I
start by describing a crude form of this mistake, which no
one would be tempted to make. Suppose Smith believes, as
we just imagined, that the conservation of species is a matter
of such importance that the nation must make great sacrifice
to achieve this goal. She has thought about the snail darter,
and she believes that the TVA dam should be completed

and opened. She has obviously made some mistake of fact: she may not have realized, for example, that the dam would wipe out that fish's only beds. Once we know she has made a factual mistake of that character, we think it right to say that her concrete conviction, that the dam should be opened, is in conflict with her more abstract one, that species should be saved at all but the greatest cost. Now consider this absurd objection to that conclusion. "Smith's opinions are not in conflict, because her first conviction does not condemn all acts that actually threaten species but only acts she *thinks* threaten species. So though she has made some mistake about the impact of the dam on the snail darter, she is not guilty of any contradiction, and Hermes serves her convictions only by allowing the dam to be opened." The absurdity lies in the view this objection takes of the content of a conviction. We can say that Smith *knows* she is opposed only to acts she thinks threaten species; we mean that these are the only acts she *realizes* her convictions condemn. But it is wrong to report her conviction itself—the meaning it has for her—as the conviction that only acts she believes threaten species are wrong. Nothing counts as someone's conviction unless he recognizes that what actually follows from it depends on what is in fact true, not on what he thinks is true.

The contrast between knowledge and conviction is crucial here. Compare the following two arguments. (1) Oedipus killed the man he met at the crossroads. The man he met at the crossroads was his father. So Oedipus killed his father. (2) Oedipus knew he was killing the man he met at the crossroads. The man he met at the crossroads was his father. So Oedipus knew he was killing his father. The first argument is valid, but the second is not, because we cannot substitute different descriptions, even though they refer to the same thing, in propositions describing what someone thought or knew rather than what he did. (Philosophers call contexts of thought or knowledge "opaque" rather than "transparent" contexts.)[6] The following argument is invalid for the same reason: since Smith believes that projects that threaten species should be halted, and this project threatens a species, Smith believes that this project should be halted. But statements *of* convictions, as made by people whose convictions they are, are transparent to substitution, and so it is not wrong or misleading, but on the contrary exactly right, to say that Smith "is committed" to halting the dam, or that it "follows" from her convictions that the dam must be stopped.

So we easily dismiss the objection I called absurd because it rests on a mistake about the logic of statements of conviction. We must, however, guard against the same objection, resting on the same mistake, in a different setting where it might initially seem more plausible. Suppose Smith has a more moderate set of convictions. She thinks it important that species be preserved, but not overwhelmingly important, and that therefore the secretary should not have the power to protect unimportant species when this would plainly be "unreasonable," given the effect on public finance and other public goals. She also thinks the TVA project should be halted to save the snail darter. She has not, we assume, made any "factual" mistake, but her judgment that it would not be unreasonable to halt the dam in these circumstances may be inconsistent with other opinions Hermes can sensibly attribute to her. She may have voted on other occasions in ways that assume a very different judgment about the relative importance of conservation and public expenditure. She may have voted against much less expensive conservation measures and for cuts in important public expenditures that would save much less money than would be wasted by halting the dam. Hermes will then think that her specific opinion about the snail darter is inconsistent with her convictions more generally, that once again she has made a mistake in applying these general convictions to this particular case, though her mistake is now of a different character.

Once again the objection might be made that her opinions are not in conflict because although she believes projects should not be stopped when it would be unreasonable to do so, she does not think it would be unreasonable to halt the TVA dam. But this is no better an objection here than it was a moment ago. It takes the wrong view of the content of Smith's abstract conviction. She does not think that the secretary should have no power to make decisions *she* regards as unreasonable—that would be an extraordinary opinion—but that he should not have power to make decisions that are *in fact* unreasonable. No other reading of her conviction makes sense of it as a conviction, and it makes no difference to this point that the conviction is expressed in "judgmental" language about reasonableness rather than in "factual" language about the actual consequences of the new dam. Hermes must still ask whether this specific conviction about the snail darter is consistent with her more abstract convictions about reasonableness in general, and if not, which of these convictions he must enforce.

Toward Hercules

If he treats this as an interpretive problem, trying to find the assignment of opinions about the relative importance of species and other goals that makes sense of her political behavior as a whole, he will probably decide that her opinion about the snail darter is, within the larger set of her more general opinions, a mistake. He will then think he respects her convictions as a whole better by ignoring her concrete opinion about the snail darter and allowing the dam to open. What reason could he have for the contrary decision, that her convictions are respected better by deferring to that concrete opinion? (Remember that she has never expressed that concrete opinion in any official way; Hermes just knows she has it the way he knows she has the other, more general convictions he believes inconsistent with it.) Someone might say: when judges and legislators disagree on *any* matter, the principle of legislative supremacy argues that the legislators' opinion must govern. Smith and Hermes do disagree about something, namely whether her opinion about snail darters is consistent with her more general opinions about reasonable government. She does not think them inconsistent. So if he ignores her specific opinion about the snail darter, he replaces her opinion about consistency with his own, and that is exactly what judges should not do.

But this objection repeats the fallacy we have now noticed several times. A judge must ultimately rely on his own opinions in developing and applying a theory about how to read a statute. He cannot, without circularity, remit any part of that task to the legislature whose enactments he will use his theory to understand. Hermes has reached the point in his argument when he must decide under which circumstances a legislator's various convictions should be understood to conflict and, when they do, which convictions he should prefer. He cannot remit that question to the legislators whose convictions these are. For his question is whether their opinions conflict, not whether they think they do, and this is a question he must answer for himself. He knows, of course, that his opinion about which of Smith's convictions are inconsistent is itself controversial, that different judges would make that decision differently. But that is inevitable and no more to be avoided here than in deciding the other issues we already noticed, about who counts, for example, as a legislator. His own political convictions, which these various questions engage, are the only ones he has.

So Hermes has no option but to study Smith's convictions in a more general and interpretive way—noticing how she votes and what she says on other occasions about matters that seem far removed from the conservation of species—in order to see which decision in the snail darter case best respects her convictions as a set or system. He may end by disregarding what he knows to be her specific opinion about the snail darter. Of course the evidence he needs for this interpretive project will be furnished mainly by her votes and statements, her legislative record or history over the course of her career or, if her opinions seem to have changed, her recent career. He will ask what system of convictions provides overall the best justification for what she has done in office. Now notice how this affects his decision about an earlier problem he faced: the problem of combining the "intentions" of discrete legislators one by one into an overall or institutional intention of the legislature itself.

We "solved" that problem for him by an impossible assumption: that the problem does not arise because all the legislators who voted for the act had exactly the same "intentions." If we continued to use that assumption to solve the combinatorial problem, it would have to be revised to take account of Hermes' new conclusions. We would now have to assume not just that each legislator had the same concrete opinions about the snail darter, but that each had the same more general system of political and moral convictions, exhibited in similar votes on the whole range of legislative issues, which is absurd. So the combinatorial problem seems to be alive again, and Hermes might, for a brief second, consider the following new answer to it. He must study each legislator's political record separately, to discover what view about the secretary's power to halt the dam would follow from that legislator's general system of convictions once conflicts had been identified and resolved. Then he must choose some method of consolidating these separate views into the overall view of the legislature itself. He suddenly realizes, however, that he has an alternative strategy he might use, which offers a more direct and much more manageable route to the same goal. He can train his interpretive imagination, not on the legislative record of different legislators one by one, but on the record of the legislature itself, asking what coherent system of political convictions would best justify what *it* has done.

It seemed a metaphysical mistake to take the "intention" of the legislature itself as primary so long as Hermes was in the grip of some mental-state version of the speaker's meaning theory of legislative intent. So long as we think legislative intention is a matter of what someone has in mind and means to communicate by a vote, we must take as primary the mental states of particular people because institutions do not have minds, and then we must worry about how to consolidate individual intentions into a collective, fictitious group intention. But Hermes abandoned the search for mental states when he decided that a legislator's pertinent intention is a matter of his overall convictions, organized by constructive interpretation, not his particular hopes or expectations or discrete concrete opinions. Constructive interpretation can be directed to the record of institutions and practices as well as individuals, and Hermes has no reason not to attribute convictions directly to the legislature itself.

So Hermes has two strategies to compare. He can build a legislative "intention" in two steps, by interpreting the record of individual legislators to discover the convictions that would justify what each has done, and then by combining these individual convictions into an overall institutional conviction. Or in one step, by interpreting the record of the legislature itself to discover the convictions that would justify what it has done. He will choose the second of these strategies, for the following reason. If he chooses the first, he needs a formula for combining individual convictions into a group intention, and that formula must respect his reasons for looking to a legislator's general structure of convictions rather than to a legislator's hopes or expectations or concrete opinions most directly in point. His reasons are reasons of integrity; he looks to general convictions because legislation in a community of principle should be understood so far as possible to express a coherent scheme of principle. So the formula he needs for the first strategy is this: he should combine individual convictions in whatever manner will provide the most plausible set of convictions to attribute to the legislature as a whole acting as the servant of a community of principle. But that means that the first (implausible and unmanageable) strategy would fail unless it somehow reached the same result the second reaches directly. The combinatorial problem that seemed so daunting has now become a false problem; Hermes needs no combinatorial function of individual legislators' convictions because from the start he interprets the record of the institution not their records one by one. The doctrine celebrated in judicial rhetoric—that statutes must be enforced looking to the intentions behind them—now shows its true colors. It is only the principle of adjudicative integrity we embraced in Chapter 6, cast as a motto for judges reading statutes. We may leave Hermes. His new method needs careful elaboration, but not by him, because he has become Hercules' twin.

HERCULES' METHOD

The method I said Hercules uses to read statutes seemed, at first glance, to pay too little attention to the actual opinions and wishes of those who made them law. So we considered the more orthodox version of legislative intention I called the speaker's meaning theory. But this led us in stages back to Hercules' idea that statutes must be read in whatever way follows from the best interpretation of the legislative process as a whole. We must see what this means in practice. We have some idea, because we know how Hercules interprets common-law precedents. But statutes are different from precedent judicial decisions, and we must study how Hercules proceeds when a statute rather than a set of law reports has been placed before him. What would he do about the snail darter case?

I assume he has his own opinions about all the issues at stake in the snail darter controversy. He has views about conservation in general, about public power, about the wisest way to develop the Appalachian area, about the conservation of species—in sum, about whether it would be best, all things considered, to halt the TVA dam. Suppose he wants the dam halted, not because he cares about the snail darter or even about conservation of species, but on aesthetic grounds because he prefers to leave the water courses the dam would disturb as they are. (Some of those who pressed the secretary to declare the snail darter a threatened species no doubt had that motive.) Would his method permit him to say that, since the community would in fact be best served by halting the dam, the act should be read as allowing the secretary that power? Does that decision not make of the act (at least in his opinion) the best piece of statesmanship it can be?

It does not. For Hercules is not trying to reach what he believes is the best substantive result, but to find the best justification he can of a past legislative event. He tries to show a piece of social history—the story of a democratically elected legislature enacting a particular text in particular circumstances—in the best light overall, and this means his account must justify the story as a whole, not just its ending. His interpretation must be sensitive, that is, not only to his convictions about justice and wise conservation policy, though these will play a part, but also to his convictions about the ideals of political integrity and fairness and procedural due process as these apply specifically to legislation in a democracy.

Textual Integrity

Integrity and fairness will constrain justice and wisdom, for Hercules, in a variety of ways. Integrity requires him to construct, for each statute he is asked to enforce, some justification that fits and flows through that statute and is, if possible, consistent with other legislation in force.[7] This means he must ask himself which combination of which principles and policies, with which assignments of relative importance when these compete, provides the best case for what the plain words of the statute plainly require. Since Hercules is now justifying a statute rather than a set of common-law precedents, the particular constraint we identified in Chapter 7 no longer holds: he must consider justifications of policy as well as of principle, and in some cases it might be problematic which form of justification would be more appropriate. (A law subsidizing contraception might be justified either out of respect for presumed rights that are violated when contraceptives are unavailable, which is a matter of principle, or out of concern that the population not grow too rapidly, which is a matter of policy, or both.) But the justification of policy we just imagined Hercules giving, that the point of the statute is to protect rural areas from unsightly or disturbing development, does not fit the text at all. For it is absurd to suggest that a statesman anxious to secure that policy would choose the fortuitous, even irrational, method of forbidding only and all projects that jeopardized species, whether or not they were otherwise disturbing or helpful to the rural environment.

Any competent justification of the Endangered Species Act, then, must appeal to a policy of protecting endangered species. No interpretation that disavowed that policy or ranked it of little importance could even begin to justify the provisions of the act, let alone its name.[8] Suppose Hercules accepts this, and yet he thinks that no reasonable policy of species conservation would require halting an almost completed dam in this particular case. He will have no difficulty describing a competing policy that would justify that qualification: the policy that public funds not be wasted. But the question remains whether he can attribute enough weight to that competing policy, within the dimensions of the statute's text, to include that qualification in its overall justification; that in turn will depend on how much weight he must assign to the main policy of species preservation in order to justify the remainder of the statute. (That interdependence of policy and weight explains much of the argument in the Supreme Court in the snail darter case.) If the text makes other exemptions or qualifications to the secretary's power, even if these have nothing to do with his power to halt projects under way, that will suggest a lower level of importance for the main policy and so will improve the case for the qualification about waste. If, on the contrary, the statute underscores the importance of the main policy by expressly accepting sacrifices in other important policies or even principles in order to promote the main policy—for example, if some other section of the act declares that the secretary need not consider impact on unemployment in making his protection orders—then this would argue that no qualifying policy sufficient to exempt the TVA project can find a place in the overall interpretation.

Fairness

We shall return to the constraints of integrity. But now we turn for a moment to fairness. Suppose Hercules is devoted to the preservation of species: he thinks the loss of even one an immeasurable evil. He thinks it much better to halt the dam than to lose the snail darter; indeed he would prefer that huge dams already in existence be dismantled if that would help save the fish. Suppose he is satisfied that nothing in the text of the Endangered Species Act contradicts his view about the importance of conserving species. The secretary's power is not explicitly qualified in any way that suggests anything less than a commanding concern with conservation. It does not follow that Hercules will think that the best interpretation of the statute, the interpretation that makes the story of government the best it can be, is one that saves the snail darter. He knows that his own views—he is blunt with himself—are eccentric. Almost no one else shares them. So he must ask himself whether it is better for legislators to reach the right result even when their constituents think it very much the wrong one.

He knows, of course, that the voters can throw a legislator out of office at the end of his term if the voters disagree with what he has done. But that is no argument: a wrong is not justified by an opportunity for revenge. Nor does the fate of the snail darter, however important Hercules believes this to be, involve any question of principle, of rights particular citizens might be thought to have against others or the community as a whole. It is a question of what state of affairs is best for everyone: Hercules believes that everyone's life is diminished when a species becomes extinct, but he does not believe that allowing a species to disappear unjustly favors some people at the expense of others. So the conservation of species is a paradigm of a kind of decision that should be governed by the will of the people, the kind of decision that even legislators who accept the Burkean model of legislative responsibility should not impose on their constituents when the latter are united in the opposite opinion. If Hercules agrees, he will conclude that a legislative story that supposes Congress to have indulged in unjustified paternalism would be worse than a story in which it respected the people's choice, even though Hercules thinks this the wrong choice.

So in these circumstances Hercules' convictions about fairness place important obstacles between his own preferences, even those that are consistent with the language of the statute, and his judgment which interpretation is best, all things considered. Since his judgment in this situation is sensitive to general public opinion, it is also sensitive, for several different reasons, to the expressed concrete convictions of the various legislators who spoke in the debates, drafted committee reports, and so forth. These statements are ordinarily good evidence of public opinion across the community as a whole. Politicians are very often typical, at least in their convictions, of the people who elect them; more to the point, they are typically skillful at judging the convictions of their constituents and choosing their public statements to reflect these. If the debates over the Endangered Species Act expressed some widespread and uncontradicted conviction about the relative importance of the conservation of a minor species, this would be strong evidence of a general public sentiment in the same direction.

LEGISLATIVE HISTORY

Hercules respects textual integrity, as I said, so he will not think that he makes a statute the best it can be merely by projecting his own convictions onto it; he respects political fairness, so he will not wholly ignore the public's opinion as this is revealed and expressed in legislative statements. The argument from fairness takes us some distance toward explaining why Hercules will pay considerable attention to the concrete convictions legislators express. We turn back to integrity to consider a different, and even more powerful, reason for that practice, though it discriminates among such expressions.

American legal practice now treats some statements of legislative purpose as especially important in deciding how a statute should be read. These include statements made on the floor by the senators or congressmen who are the sponsors of a bill or its managers through the congressional process, and also statements contained in the formal reports of the special congressional committees through which the bill passes. American courts pay a great deal of attention to these specially privileged statements, and American legislators take great trouble to ensure that statements they approve are among them. Legislative history dominated the Supreme Court's discussion of the snail darter case, as we saw in Chapter 1, though the justices disagreed about which parts of that history were particularly important.

Why are some congressional statements, those regarded as central parts of the legislative history, more important than others? If we look only to fairness, we would think them more important because they are especially good evidence of public opinion. Statements sponsors make on the floor or in committee reports are usually carefully considered. Other legislators listen to or read them with more than ordinary care. But the importance most judges attach to legislative history cannot be fully explained in this way. For a sponsor's speech to an almost empty chamber is part of the core of leg-

islative history, though her remarks in a nationally televised
speech, which are better evidence of what the public is in-
vited to think about a statute, are not part of legislative history at all. The main explanation lies elsewhere. Hercules
will see, for reasons I shall try to describe, that official statements of purpose, made in the canonical form established by
the practice of legislative history, should be treated as themselves acts of the state personified. They are themselves political decisions, so the chief command of integrity, that the
state act in a principled way, embraces them as well as the
more discrete decisions captured in statutes. Hercules aims
to make the legislative story as a whole as good as it can be;
he would make the story worse if his interpretation showed
the state saying one thing while doing another.

Promises and Purposes

It would be absurd, of course, to count every statement any
legislator makes about the purpose of a statute as itself the
act of the state; if two senators argue about what the state is,
or should be, doing in enacting the bill, they are debating
about the state's act, not themselves acting for it. But a formal committee report, or the unchallenged statement of a
bill's manager, is different; these can be seen as part of what
the legislative process has actually produced, something to
which the community as a whole is thereby committed.[9]
They can be seen that way, that is, if practice designates
them as special, which American practice does. In order to
understand this practice and apply it when its force is disputed, as in the snail darter case, Hercules must interpret it:
he must find some account of the practice that fits and justifies it. Can any case be made in political morality for counting certain formal declarations of point and intention as the
acts of the state itself? We should begin by framing the most
evident argument against doing so. The legislative process
already has means available for making such statements
part of the state's formal decision when this would be desir-

able: they can be written into the text of the statute itself. British lawyers have that argument for British practice, which insists that statements made in Parliament must not be used as guides to statutory interpretation. It is an important argument, not because it is decisive against the different American practice, but because it shows that the latter is justified only if it establishes some special role for legislative history, some status intermediate between the informal observations of legislators, made tactically in the heat of debate, and the formal text of the statute itself.

It is not difficult to identify an intermediate status, for we have one available, well suited for the purpose, in personal morality. We distinguish between a person's promises and other commitments and the explanations or interpretations he himself offers of them, his account of how these fit into and flow from his more general beliefs and purposes; we treat both as having moral significance, but we count the explanations as more tentative, more open to revision and change. Suppose I give my nephew $100, and I explain that I admire his choice of a military career and wish to help him in it. He may then expect that I will help him in that career in other ways; he will be surprised when I later say that I now think his career unsavory and will oppose it in whatever way I can, by refusing to introduce him to my martial friends, for example. Or suppose I start up a new factory and promise the community that I will install and maintain any "reasonable" device to ensure that my factory does not increase pollution. I am asked in a television interview whether I think a particular device is reasonable, and I say that I do. But later I decide not to install that device: I say that further information has convinced me, contrary to my previous opinion, that it is not reasonable because almost as much protection can be provided by different and much less expensive measures. In each case my earlier explanatory statement is part of my moral record, something for which I must take responsibility because I made the statement knowing others would probably rely on it and encouraging them to do so. The story would have been better, from the moral point of view, if I had already come to my later opinions and expressed them at the outset. I owe my nephew and the community an apology. But the situation is nevertheless different from what it would have been if I had explicitly promised to help my nephew's career in the way he later asked, or had promised to install the particular device I originally thought was reasonable. Then I would not have been so free to change my mind.

We can explain the difference in this way. A promise has mainly a performative character and therefore a life of its own.[10] It expresses but does not report purposes or beliefs or convictions. It may be insincere, because the promisor has no genuine intention to keep it, but it is not inaccurate even in the way self-understanding can be. A statement of intention, on the other hand, is mainly a report rather than a performance, and it can be either insincere or inaccurate in much the way other self-reports are. If an interpretive statement of intention had the same performative force as a promise, it could not be used as it is used, to place a promise in a context of actual beliefs and purposes and so help other people to assess the promisor and predict what else he is likely to do. Collapsing the statement into the promise would squeeze out the report and only enlarge the performative act. It would then raise a new question, of what more general purposes and beliefs supported the enlarged promise, and this could not be answered, because any further statement would collapse in the same way into the black hole of the promise itself.

Purposes and Principle

We can be guided by this aspect of personal morality in constructing a political role for legislative history. A community of principle does not see legislation the way a rulebook community does, as negotiated compromises that carry no more or deeper meaning than the text of the statute declares;

it treats legislation as flowing from the community's present commitment to a background scheme of political morality. The practice of legislative history, of formal declarations of general institutional purpose and convictions made on behalf of the state itself, expresses and confirms that attitude. The practice also protects one of the practical advantages of a community of principle: it encourages citizens to rely on a particular account of the public scheme when they develop and enforce it themselves. But these advantages depend on just the kind of moral distance between the explicit decisions of the statute and the explanatory system of legislative history that we find in personal morality. They depend on treating the various official statements that make up the explanatory system as having mainly a reporting rather than a performative function. Legislative history offers a contemporary interpretation of the statute it surrounds, an interpretation that may later be revised by courts or the legislature itself, even though any important revision would, in retrospect, make the legislative history a matter of regret.

A community of principle is best served by a complex structure of legislation like that, a structure that includes a distinction between performative legislative acts and interpretive explanations of these acts. So Hercules has reasons both for counting the formal statements that make up legislative history as acts of the state and for not treating them as part of the statute itself. He must take them into account in deciding which story of the legislative event is overall the best story, but he must do this in the right way. He acknowledges that legislation is seen in a better light, all else being equal, when the state has not misled the public; for that reason he will prefer an interpretation that matches the formal statements of legislative purpose, particularly when citizens might well have made crucial decisions relying on these statements. If the legislative debates surrounding the statute of wills had been studded with uncontradicted statements that wills must be read in an acontextual way—giving their

words the meanings people would assign them if they knew
nothing special about the context of their use—then the
public would have received the statute, and wills might well
have been drafted, under that assumption. Hercules would
then count that fact as a strong, though not necessarily decisive, argument in favor of that construction. But as we shall
see, it is an argument whose force grows weaker with the
passage of time.

The legislative history surrounding the Endangered Species Act was much more complex. We reviewed it in Chapter
1 and noticed that the justices of the Supreme Court disagreed about whether the legislative history should include
the fact that Congress tried to make plain in various decisions taken after the act was passed that the TVA dam was
not to be threatened. Hercules has no reason to doubt that
these later decisions of Congress should be taken into account. They are part of the public record, later political decisions about the relative importance, in the community's
overall scheme of purposes, of the different interests at stake.
The contrary view, that these decisions must not be counted,
assumes the temporal constraint we are about to consider,
that a statute's meaning is fixed in some initial act of creation. It is not difficult, then, to see how Hercules will decide
the snail darter case if he shares the substantive opinion that
seemed dominant on the Court, that the wiser course would
be to sacrifice the fish to the dam. He thinks reading the statute to save the dam would make it better from the point of
view of sound policy. He has no reason of textual integrity
arguing against that reading, nor any reason of fairness, because nothing suggests that the public would be outraged or
offended by that decision. Nothing in the legislative history
of the bill itself, properly understood and taken as the record
of public decision, argues the other way, and the later legislative decisions of the same character argue strongly for the
reading he himself thinks best. He joins the justices who dis-
sented in the case.

STATUTES OVER TIME

The speaker's meaning theory begins in the idea I said was the root of its troubles: that legislation is an act of communication to be understood on the simple model of speaker and audience, so that the commanding question in legislative interpretation is what a particular speaker or group "meant" in some canonical act of utterance. Hence the catalogue of mysteries I began by reviewing. Who is the speaker? When did he speak? What mental state supplied his meaning? These mysteries are spawned by a single domineering assumption: that their solutions must converge on a particular moment of history, the moment at which the statute's meaning is fixed once and for all, the moment at which the true statute is born. That assumption has a sequel: that as time passes and the statute must be applied in changed circumstances, judges are faced with a choice between enforcing the original statute with the meaning it has always had or amending it covertly to bring it up to date. That is the dilemma old statutes are often supposed to present: judges must choose, it is said, between the dead but legitimate hand of the past and the distinctly illicit charm of progress.

Hercules' method challenges that aspect of the speaker's meaning theory along with all the rest. It rejects the assumption of a canonical moment at which a statute is born and has all and only the meaning it will ever have. Hercules interprets not just the statute's text but its life, the process that begins before it becomes law and extends far beyond that moment. He aims to make the best he can of this continuing story, and his interpretation therefore changes as the story develops. He does not identify particular people as the exclusive "framers" of a statute and then attend only to their hopes or expectations or concrete convictions or statements or reactions. Each of the political considerations he brings to bear on his overall question, how to make the statute's story the best it can be, identifies a variety of people and groups and institutions whose statements or convictions might be relevant in different ways.

Consider the argument from fairness that made him pay attention to concrete legislative convictions so far as he could discover these, even when they disagreed with his own. That argument does not require Hercules to identify particular legislators as crucial, or to fix on the opinions of any decisive number of legislators as if convictions were counted like votes. Fairness tells Hercules to look to whichever expression of political views seems relevant to deciding whether a particular statute, constructed according to an interpretation he is considering, would be fair, given the character and spread of public opinion. In this context the televised address of an important politician might be *more* important than the fine print of a committee report.

Now consider how passing time affects this argument from fairness. The speaker's meaning theory stares at convictions present and expressed when a statute was passed and ignores later changes. Only "original" intentions can be pertinent to discovering a statute's meaning at its birth; an appeal to changed opinion must be an anachronism, a logically absurd excuse for judicial amendment. Hercules' attitude is very different. Suppose the Endangered Species Act had been enacted in a climate of public opinion very different from what he encounters when he must decide the snail darter case. He asks which interpretation provides the best account of a political history that now includes not only the act but the failure to repeal or amend it later, and he will therefore look not to public opinion at the beginning, when conservation was in flower, but now, when it must be decided whether the secretary can waste large public funds to save a minor species. The argument from fairness will have a very different impact than it would have if the case had come before him much earlier.

The argument from textual integrity will also be sensitive to time because it will take account of other decisions that Congress and the courts have made in the meantime; if shifts in public opinion or economic or ecological circumstance have been great, those intervening political decisions will have been made in a very different spirit, so an interpretation embracing them and the act will likely be different from an interpretation required to fit the act alone. The argument from legislative history will again be sensitive to time, but in a different way. That argument is the converse of the argument from fairness: it ignores private convictions; it fixes on formal public statements that quality as declarations of the community itself. These declarations are nevertheless not part of the statute; they are reports of public purpose and conviction, and so they are naturally vulnerable to reassessment.

People have less reason to rely on these statements as the statute ages because they will have been supplemented and perhaps replaced, as formal interpretations of public commitment, by a variety of other interpretive explanations attached to later statutes on related issues. These later statements provide a more contemporary account of how the community's officials understand its standing commitments of principle and operating strategies of policy.[11] So Hercules will pay less and less attention to the original legislative history, and here again his method stands in contrast to the speaker's meaning theory, which looks only to statements contemporary with a statute's enactment. Hercules interprets history in motion, because the story he must make as good as it can be is the whole story through his decision and beyond. He does not amend out-of-date statutes to suit new times, as the metaphysics of speaker's meaning would suggest. He recognizes what the old statutes have since become.

WHEN IS THE LANGUAGE CLEAR?

I must now pay a debt that has been steadily growing larger. I have been asking how Hercules should read a statute when its language it not clear, that is, when it does not, as we might say, enforce itself. But how does he decide whether it is clear, in which case he has nothing more to do, or unclear, in which case he must deploy the complex and politically sophisticated apparatus I just sketched? That now seems a very important distinction. How should it be drawn?

It need not be drawn at all. The distinction I relied on is just an expository device that need be given no place in Hercules' final developed theory. Notice the different ways or senses in which the text of a statute might be said to be unclear. It might contain an ambiguous word whose meaning is not decisively resolved by the context. It might declare, for example, that it shall be a crime to be found within fifty yards of a bank after dark, with nothing to indicate whether the bank in question is a building where money is stored or a place by the side of a river. It might contain a vague word that in practice cannot remain vague: it might declare, for example, that old people are exempt from income tax. It might use an abstract word, like "reasonable" or "fair," such that people can be expected to disagree whether some decision or act meets the standard the abstract word is used to state. These are familiar types or occasions of linguistic unclarity. None of them fits the two cases we have taken as our leading examples of problems in the application of statutes. In both Elmer's case and the snail darter case judges disagreed about how a statute should be read, and law students and scholars continue to disagree. But we cannot locate the unclarity of the text in the ambiguity or vagueness or abstraction of any particular word or phrase in the statutes that provoked these cases.

Is the statute of wills unclear on the question whether murderers may inherit? If we find it so, this can only be because we ourselves have some reason to think that murderers should not inherit. No language in the New York statute of wills specifically declares that blue-eyed people may inherit, yet no one thinks the statute is unclear on the question whether they can. Why is it different with murderers—or rather why was it different when Elmer's case was decided?

If we followed the speaker's meaning theory we would be tempted to say: because we have reason to think that those who adopted the statute did not intend murderers to inherit. But we can make sense of that claim only counterfactually, and then we see that it is too strong. Does it become unclear whether Nazis may inherit if we think the original authors of the statute would not have wanted Nazis to inherit if they had anticipated them? It is only because *we* think the case for excluding murderers from a general statute of wills is a strong one, sanctioned by principles elsewhere respected in the law, that we find the statute unclear on that issue.

This is just as plainly true of the Endangered Species Act. Our doubts whether that statute gave the secretary power to halt projects well begun cannot be located in the ambiguity or vagueness or abstraction of some phrase or word. No one would claim that it is unclear whether the act applies to dams at all, although dams are not explicitly mentioned. Once again we think the statute unclear about projects already begun because it strikes many people as silly that so much money should be wasted to save an unappealing and scientifically unimportant species. But we must be careful not to generalize this point in the wrong way: Hercules will not regard a statute as unclear whenever its acontextual meaning proposes a decision many people think wrong. That is also much too strong a test: many people think the whole Endangered Species Act wrong—tragically silly—through and through. But no one would say that it is therefore unclear whether that act has any force at all, whether the secretary has power to bar any project at all in any circumstance.

The description "unclear" is the *result* rather than the *occasion* of Hercules' method of interpreting statutory texts. We will not call a statute unclear unless we think there are decent arguments for each of two competing interpretations of it.[12] This explains why no one—even if he thinks the Endangered Species Act silly—is tempted to say that it is unclear whether that act gives the secretary any power ever to halt any project. No decent interpretation of the act could suggest it commands nothing, in spite of its language and in spite of the debates and committee reports, the presidential statements and congressional announcements that launched it. I do not mean that no one will say a statute is unclear unless he has already decided that the acontextual interpretation is the wrong one. He will concede that it is unclear if he thinks the interpretive question is complex or debatable even if in the end he thinks the acontextual interpretation best. Nevertheless, the distinction between clear and unclear statutes, so understood, need have no place in any formal statement of Hercules' theory of legislation. In particular, it would not serve as I have used it in the discussion until this section, to suggest a theoretical switching point, such that interpretation would continue one way if the switch were thrown and another way if it were not.

Nor does Hercules need a preanalytic or switchpoint distinction between clear and unclear statutes when the putative unclarity is indeed located in a particular word or phrase. A statute limiting aggregate deposits in banks is not unclear for us, but it might have been in a Keynesian community of pirate bands. Hercules will find a statute troublesome because of the ambiguity or vagueness or abstraction of some word only when there is at least some doubt whether the statute would be a better performance of the legislative function read one way rather than another. When there is no doubt, the statute is clear, not because Hercules has some distinction, outside his general method, for distinguishing clear from unclear uses of a word, but because the method he always uses is then so easy to apply. It applies itself.

We have, in this discussion, another example of a problem frequently encountered in this book, which we might now call the easy-case problem. We have been attending mainly to hard cases, when lawyers disagree whether some crucial proposition of law is true or false. But questions of law are sometimes very easy for lawyers and even for nonlawyers. It "goes without saying" that the speed limit in Connecticut is

55 miles an hour and that people in Britain have a legal duty to pay for food they order in a restaurant. At least this goes without saying except in very unusual circumstances. A critic might therefore be tempted to say that the complex account we have developed of judicial reasoning under law as integrity is a method for hard cases only. He might add that it would be absurd to apply the method to easy cases— no judge needs to consider questions of fit and political morality to decide whether someone must pay his telephone bill—and then declare that in addition to his theory of hard cases, Hercules needs a theory about when cases are hard, so he can know when his complex method for hard cases is appropriate and when not. The critic will then announce a serious problem: it can be a hard question whether the case at hand is a hard case or an easy case, and Hercules cannot decide by using his technique for hard cases without begging the question.[13]

This is a pseudoproblem. Hercules does not need one method for hard cases and another for easy ones. His method is equally at work in easy cases, but since the answers to the questions it puts are then obvious, or at least seem to be so, we are not aware that any theory is at work at all.[14] We think the question whether someone may legally drive faster than the stipulated speed limit is an easy one because we assume at once that no account of the legal record that denied that paradigm would be competent. But someone whose convictions about justice and fairness were very different from ours might not find that question so easy; even if he ended by agreeing with our answer, he would insist that we were wrong to be so confident. This explains why questions considered easy during one period become hard before they again become easy questions—with the opposite answers.

TEN

THE CONSTITUTION

IS CONSTITUTIONAL LAW BUILT ON A MISTAKE?

We began with a depressing report of the state of the popular argument about how judges should decide cases. In the United States the argument is most heated and most confused when the judges in question belong to the Supreme Court and the cases in point are constitutional events testing whether Congress or some state or the president has the legal power to do something it or he has tried to do. The Constitution creates only limited powers in these institutions and declares important disabilities in each. It denies the Senate power to originate a money bill, and it denies the commander in chief power to quarter soldiers in private houses in peacetime. Other constraints are notoriously abstract. The Fifth Amendment insists that Congress not take "life, liberty or property" without "due process of law," the Eighth outlaws "cruel and unusual" punishments, and the Fourteenth, which dominated our sample case *Brown*, requires that no state deny any person "the equal protection of the law."

It does not follow as a matter of iron logic that the Supreme Court should have the power to decide when these limits have been transgressed. For the Constitution might have been interpreted as laying down directions to Congress, the president, and state officials that these officers had a legal as well as a moral duty to follow, but making them their own judges. The Constitution would then have played a very different and much weaker role in American politics: it would have served as a background for political arguments among different institutions about the limits of their constitutional jurisdiction rather than as a source of the authority of one of these institutions, the courts, to fix those limits for the rest. In 1803 the Supreme Court seized an opportunity to reject that weaker role.[1] Chief Justice John Marshall said that the Court's power and duty to enforce the Constitution followed from that document's own declaration that the Constitution was the supreme *law* of the land.

Marshall has often been accused, in the long debates that continue yet, of begging all the important questions. That charge is easy to sustain under the plain-fact picture of law we considered and rejected early in this book, the picture that insists on a firm analytical distinction between legal questions about what the law is and political questions about whether courts should enforce the law. If this distinction were sound, then of course we could not drag any conclusion about what any court should do from the proposition that American law includes the Constitution, which is only a statement about what the law is. Law as integrity, on the contrary, supports Marshall's argument. He was right to think that the most plausible interpretation of the developing legal practices of the young country, as well as of its colonial and British roots, supposed that an important part of the point of law was to supply standards for the decision of courts. History has vindicated the substantive dimension of that interpretation. The United States is a more just society than it would have been had its constitutional rights been left to the conscience of majoritarian institutions.[2] In any event Marshall decided that the courts in general and the Supreme Court in the last analysis have the power to decide for the government as a whole what the Constitution means and to declare acts of the other departments of government invalid if they exceed the powers provided for them by the Constitution, properly understood. His decision was accepted, at least in that abstract form, and subsequent constitutional practice has coagulated firmly around it. No interpretation would fit that practice if it denied the powers

Marshall declared. Even those who think he made a mistake concede that almost two centuries of practice have put his position beyond challenge as a proposition of law, and the constitutional wars are now fought on the terrain it defines.

The capital question now is not what power the Court has but how its vast power should be exercised. Should it undertake to enforce the whole Constitution, including those provisions that require almost pure political judgment to interpret? Should it decide, for example, whether the details of some state's own constitutional structure provide the "republican form of government" the federal Constitution demands, or should it leave that to the judgment of Congress or the state itself? What strategy should the Court use in interpreting and applying the constitutional provisions it does have authority to enforce? Should it defer in some degree to the judgment of Congress or a state legislature about whether some form of punishment, like death, is "cruel and unusual" within the meaning of the Eighth Amendment or whether some scheme of racial division in education does or does not provide children the "equal protection" of the Fourteenth? Should it accept the judgment of these institutions unless it thinks them plainly wrong, or should it replace them whenever it would have preferred a different decision? In either case, what test should it use to decide which decisions are plainly wrong, or wrong on balance?

LIBERALS AND CONSERVATIVES

Popular imagination sorts justices into camps according to the answers they are thought to give to questions like these. It deems some justices "liberal" and others "conservative" and on the whole seems to prefer the latter. The ground of this distinction, however, is famously elusive, and one familiar reading has contributed to the lamentable character of the public debate. People say that conservative justices obey the Constitution while liberal ones try to reform it according to their personal convictions. We know the fallacy in that description. It ignores the interpretive character of law. Justices who are called liberal and those who are called conservative agree about which words make up the Constitution as a matter of preinterpretive text. They disagree about what the Constitution is as a matter of postinterpretive law, about what standards it deploys for testing official acts. Each kind of justice tries to enforce the Constitution as law, according to his interpretive judgment of what it is, and each kind thinks the other is subverting the true Constitution. So it is useless as well as unfair to classify justices according to the degree of their fidelity to their oath.

Nor is it clear that the popular distinction between conservative and liberal justices is a useful distinction at all. Justices who were thought liberal when appointed were later thought conservative—Felix Frankfurter is the most cited example—and justices who seem conservative in one way because they make decisions that please people of conservative political opinions seem liberal, even radical, in another because they disregard constitutional precedent to do this.[3] Law as integrity provides a somewhat more accurate grid of classification through its analytical distinction among dimensions of interpretation. If we insist on classifying justices along some liberal/conservative spectrum, we must make the distinction separately for two dimensions and so create four boxes rather than two. A justice will count as conservative on the first dimension if his convictions about fit are strict: if he demands, for example, that any interpretation of constitutional doctrine match the concrete convictions of the "framers" of the Constitution or, differently, of past justices of the Supreme Court. He will count as liberal on the first dimension if his opinions about fit are more relaxed. A parallel distinction may be drawn along the substantive dimension. A justice will count as conservative if the political convictions he expresses in choosing among interpretations eligible on grounds of fit are those we associate with political conservatism: if he favors a retributivist philosophy of punishment, for example, or free enterprise in economic affairs. He will count as a liberal on this dimension if his political convictions are those liberals ordinarily have.

This new classificatory scheme is less rigid than the simple distinction between judicial liberals and conservatives. Even so, a particular justice might not fall easily into just two of the four boxes it defines. He might combine conservative positions about some aspects of fit with more relaxed opinions about others. He might think, for example, that the Constitution cannot be interpreted as prohibiting the death penalty because the framers plainly did not think they were reading the death penalty out of American jurisprudence, and yet he might refuse to accept as an argument the other way past Court decisions that held the death penalty unconstitutional under some circumstances. Another justice might reverse these interpretive premises; he might be largely uninterested in the views of the remote framers and yet anxious to preserve continuity in the chain of Supreme Court decisions on any issue. And a justice might combine traditionally liberal and conservative substantive views. Chief Justice Earl Warren, for example, apparently had egalitarian convictions about economic justice and conservative views about pornography.[4]

HISTORICISM

Framer's Intent as Speaker's Meaning

The distinction between liberal and conservative justices, therefore, is inexact and unlikely to contribute much to any serious account of constitutional adjudication. Academic scholarship has recently explored a different distinction: this divides justices into interpretivist and noninterpretivist camps. These labels are also highly misleading, however. They suggest a distinction between judges who believe constitutional decisions should be made only or mainly by interpreting the Constitution itself and others who think they should be based on extraconstitutional grounds.[5] This is an academic form of the crude popular mistake that some judges obey the Constitution and others disregard it. It ignores the philosophical character of law as interpretive. Every conscientious judge, in either of the supposed camps, is an interpretivist in the broadest sense: each tries to impose the best interpretation on our constitutional structure and practice, to see these, all things considered, in the best light they can bear. They disagree about what the best interpretation is, but it is an analytical error, a localized infection left by the semantic sting, to confuse this with a disagreement about whether constitutional adjudication should be interpretive at all. The great debates of constitutional method are debates within interpretation, not about its relevance. If one justice thinks the intentions of the framers are much more important than another does, this is the upshot of a more foundational interpretive disagreement. The former thinks that fairness or integrity requires that any sound interpretation match the framers' state of mind; the latter does not.

It is easy enough, however, to repair the academic distinction in just this way. We may use "historicist" to refer to those it calls interpretivists. A historicist, we now say, has settled on a style of constitutional adjudication that limits eligible interpretations of the Constitution to principles that express the historical intentions of the framers. He will not accept that the equal protection clause outlaws state-imposed segregation unless he is satisfied that those he counts as framers thought it did. Or, somewhat weaker, unless he is satisfied that the framers did not think the clause did not outlaw segregation. In fact the Fourteenth Amendment was proposed by lawmakers who thought they were not outlawing racially segregated education. The floor manager of the civil rights bill that preceded the amendment told the House that "civil rights do not mean that all children shall attend the same school,"[6] and the same Congress continued to segregate the schools of the District of Columbia after the Fourteenth Amendment had entered the Constitution. For the historicist, it follows that the equal protection clause does not make segregation unconstitutional.

Historicism seems, at a first look, to be only a constitutional form of the popular theory we studied in Chapter 9: the theory that statutes must be read in accordance with the intentions of their authors. If we understand it as the crude, speaker's meaning version of that theory, it makes the mental states of those who debated and enacted the Constitution decisive over how its abstract language should be read. It identifies, for each clause, a canonical moment of creation, and insists that what the framers thought then, no matter how peculiar this might seem now, exhausts the Constitution we have. In Chapter 9 we rejected the speaker's meaning version of the legislative intention theory, for reasons that hold in the constitutional theater as well. We considered a different and more attractive version: that statutes should be read so as to conform to the convictions out of which their authors voted. When Hermes explored that version he found it necessary to identify and reconcile conflicts within each legislator's convictions, by interpreting the legislator's record as a whole, and then necessary to combine the restructured convictions of different individual legislators into an overall institutional scheme of conviction, using some appropriate formula for that combination. He soon realized that he would do better to interpret a statute directly, by asking what set of convictions would provide the best justification for it rather than the best interpretation of votes for it one by one, because no formula for combining individual convictions would be appropriate unless it yielded the same result as a constructive interpretation of the statute itself.

A historicist who insists that constitutional interpretation must match the intentions of the framers will meet the same difficulties Hermes did, and if he is thoughtful he will end in the same view. He will say, first, that the Fourteenth Amendment must be read in whatever way best serves the convictions of the congressmen and other legislators who

voted for it. He will then find that these statesmen had a variety of political opinions pertinent to racial segregation.
Their dominant conviction was abstract: that the Constitution should require the law to treat all citizens as equals.
That is the conviction they actually described in the language demanding "equal protection of the laws." Many of
them had the further concrete conviction that racial segregation did not violate that requirement, but the historicist,
who is committed to keeping faith with their convictions as a
whole, must ask whether that concrete conviction was in fact
consistent with the dominant one, or was rather a misappre-
hension, understandable in the circumstances, of what the
dominant one really required. If the historicist himself believes that racial segregation is inconsistent with the conception of equality the framers accepted at a more abstract
level, he will think that fidelity to their convictions as a whole
requires holding segregation unconstitutional. (He may hold
a different view: that circumstances have changed so that although segregation was consistent with that conception in
the late nineteenth century, it is not consistent now. Then he
will also think fidelity requires declaring segregation unconstitutional.) It would be a philosophical confusion, here as in
the statutory cases we considered in Chapter 9, to deny that
the framers' convictions could have been in conflict. They
were committed to the principle that the law must treat
people as equals, and commitments are, in the language I
used in that chapter, transparent not opaque. We have good
reason to think that the framers themselves understood this,
that they did not believe that the Constitution should be
read in an opaque way, or that nothing could violate the
Fourteenth Amendment except what they thought violated
it.[7] But even if they did think that constitutions should be
read as opaque, a historicist would still have to decide
whether *that* conviction was consistent with their more abstract, and necessarily transparent, conviction that America
should henceforth treat everyone as equal before the law.[8]

So the historicist's interpretive problem is not solved but

only posed by noticing that the framers did not themselves think that their clause outlawed racially segregated schools. He must still retrieve their more abstract convictions by asking what conception of treating people as equals they are best understood as having laid down. He might try to do this for each of the framers one by one, by studying their pertinent writings and statements, if there are any, and their votes on other issues. But once again he would do better to look directly to the overall structure of the post–Civil War amendments they created together, seen as part of the more general constitutional system they left in place, and to ask what principles of equality are necessary to justify that structure. Only when he has identified and refined these principles can he sensibly decide whether, in his opinion, the framers' concrete opinion about segregation is consistent with their more abstract convictions about equality. If he decides they are not, his vow of fidelity would require him to ignore them. His historicism is subverted; he is led steadily away from relying exclusively on what the framers thought about that particular issue.

History, Fairness, and Integrity

We might find a stronger case for historicism by supposing that the historicist rejects any form of the speaker's meaning theory and follows Hercules' very different method of reading statutes. He regards the statements about racial segregation in the original legislative debates not as clues to convictions or inner mental states but as political events, and he has some political theory that makes the constitutional story better when the Constitution is read exactly as these statements declare. But what political theory would justify that bizarre conclusion? It is easy to find bad political arguments that would plainly be inadequate. The historicist might say that the historical statements of the framers must be decisive because the Constitution is law and the content of law is settled by the publicly declared intentions of its authors. That begs the question too crudely. His task is to show why the Constitution as law should be understood to be what the framers concretely thought it was, and he cannot simply assume that it should be. He might say that the declarations of the framers are decisive because they intended them to be. That is silly for two reasons: we have no evidence of this meta-intention,[9] and even if we did, enforcing it would beg the question once again. (Suppose a congressman said "oui" when asked if his statutes were valid if written in French.)

The historicist might say that democracy, on his understanding of that concept, requires that statesmen who have been selected by the people to create a constitution should have the power to decide what it means. But the abstract description of democracy, that the people must choose their governors, does not itself indicate how far the extrastatutory declarations of these governors enters the law they have made. So he must add some more concrete argument of fairness to his general appeal to democracy. He must show why democracy's assumption that the people must have roughly equal influence over legislation yields his method of deciding what the Constitution means. He can hardly hope to succeed. The framers of the original Constitution were remarkably unrepresentative of the people as a whole. They were not chosen in any way sanctioned by prior national law, and a majority of the population, including women, slaves, and the poor, was excluded from the processes that selected them and ratified the Constitution. Nor was democracy sufficiently advanced, even by the time of the post–Civil War amendments, to provide a democratic argument of fairness for taking the legislators' concrete opinions as good evidence of public opinion at the time. Quite apart from these defects, fairness cannot explain why people now should be governed by the detailed political convictions of officials elected long ago, when popular morality, economic circumstances, and almost everything else was very different. How can fairness argue that the Constitution permits individual states to practice official racial segregation, just because this was once acceptable to those in power throughout the nation, no matter what most people in most states now think?

We paid more attention in the last chapter to a different argument for taking legislative declarations into account, at least when these were made in a formal way. This is the argument from integrity in the political process, that these declarations are part of a community's political record and that the political story appears in a better light when statutes and (we may now add) constitutions are read to conform with formal declarations of purpose and conviction. But we noticed how sensitive this argument is to time. It could not be weaker than it is in the present context, when the declarations were made not just in different political circumstances but to and for an entirely different form of political life. It would be silly to take the opinions of those who first voted on the Fourteenth Amendment as reporting the public morality of the United States a century later, when the racial issue had been transformed in almost every way. It would also be perverse; it would deny that community the power to change its public sense of purpose, which means denying that it can have public purposes at all.

Stability

We should stop foisting bad arguments on the historicist and try to construct the best one we can. This is, I believe, an argument very like the main argument we considered for conventionalism as a general conception of law.[10] "Law serves its community best when it is as precise and stable as possible, and this is particularly true of foundational, constitutional law. That provides a general reason for tying the interpretation of statutes and of a constitution to some historical fact that is at least in principle discoverable and immune from shifting convictions and alliances. The historical-author test satisfies this condition better than any alternative. In its stronger version, which permits no interpretation of a constitutional provision not drawn from the concrete intentions of the historical authors, it gives constitutional law a unilateralist flavor and therefore achieves the greatest possible stability and predictability. The Constitution will not be invoked to overturn some legislative or executive decision unless historical scholarship has demonstrated that this result was intended in a concrete way. But if this unilateralist constraint is thought too restrictive, the weaker form will nevertheless provide more stability than any interpretive style that disregards concrete historical intentions altogether. No statute or decision will be overturned if it can be shown on historical grounds that the framers expected that it would not be."

Does historicism, backed by this argument from stability, offer a decent interpretation of American constitutional practice? The stronger version of historicism does not fit that practice at all. The Supreme Court has not taken a unilateralist attitude toward constitutional adjudication; it has recognized constitutional rights the framers did not contemplate. The weaker version fits the practice better just because it is weaker, and it may fit well enough to survive if the argument from stability is strong enough in substance. The Court has often applied the Constitution with results that would probably have dismayed its eighteenth- and nineteenth-century sponsors. *Brown* is one example; the capital punishment and abortion and reapportionment decisions are others. But perhaps these are not so numerous and are in the main local enough to particular Courts and periods to allow the historicist to count them as mistakes. We cannot just dismiss that claim as obviously disingenuous, as masking what is really invention rather than interpretation. For the argument from stability is quite independent of any particular view about the justice or fairness of segregation, capital punishment, and antiabortion legislation, so a judge who accepts weak historicism may well be constrained in giving effect to his other political instincts and attitudes.

We must therefore consider the argument from stability as

an argument of political morality. It makes this claim: a political community with a written constitution will be better in the long run, a fairer and more just and otherwise more successful community, if it secures stability by making the correct interpretation of that constitution depend on the concrete opinions of its authors, no matter how dated these may be, rather than on fresh, contemporary interpretive decisions that may contradict these. Is that plausible? Sometimes certainty of the law is more important than what the law is; this is true for rules of the road, for example, and perhaps for rules defining rights and obligations under negotiable commercial paper. But it is not always true. Law as integrity is sensitive to the different marginal value of certainty and predictability in different circumstances. When certainty is especially important, as in negotiable instruments, the fact that a particular rule has been recognized and applied in past cases will provide a strong argument for its place in the best interpretation of that part of the law. When certainty is relatively unimportant, its power in interpretive argument is correspondingly weaker; when I first remarked this, in Chapter 4, I cited constitutional cases as paradigms.

The historicist's political argument, that is, relies most on the importance of certainty just when that virtue is least important to good government. About some constitutional issues it does matter more that the law be settled than exactly what the law is. It matters much more that the term of a president's office be fixed and not open to fresh consideration by the Supreme Court from time to time than exactly what the term is. Certainty is of the essence, and the issue must be insulated from self-interest and short-term political opportunism. If the framers had not understood this, had not drafted their basic organizational decisions in language admitting of only one interpretation, their constitution would not have survived to be worrying jurisprudence now. Not all constitutional issues are like these, however. In some it matters a great deal that a settlement be made, but it does not always matter more than what the details of that settlement are. It is plainly very important to the working of a federal system of government that the allocation of power between national and local jurisdictions be as precise and stable as possible. But it is also important which political unit is assigned a particular power or responsibility: power to regulate a particular form of commerce, for example, or responsibility to finance public education or direct educational policy. When law as integrity interprets constitutional practice to decide how the Constitution distributes some particular responsibility among jurisdictions, it takes stability into account, but it also notices that one decision might better comport with the overall scheme of federalism the practice constructs.

There is a third class of constitutional issues whose balance is different still. Some clauses, on any eligible interpretation, recognize individual rights against the state and nation: to freedom of speech, to due process in criminal procedures, to treatment as an equal in the disposition of public resources, including education. Stability in the interpretation of each of these rights taken one by one is of some practical importance. But since these are matters of principle, substance is more important than that kind of stability. The crucial stability in any case is that of integrity: the system of rights must be interpreted, so far as possible, as expressing a coherent vision of justice. This could not be achieved by the weak form of historicism that ties judges to the concrete opinions of the historical statesmen who created each right, so far as these concrete opinions can be discovered, but asks them to use some other method of interpretation when the framers had no opinion or their opinion is lost to history. That is a formula certain to produce incoherence in the constitutional scheme it generates, because framers at different periods had different concrete views about what justice requires, and because judges using nonhistorical methods when these views cannot be retrieved will have concrete opinions different from those of any framer. Strong historicism ties judges to historical concrete intentions even more firmly: it requires them to treat these intentions as exhausting the Constitution altogether. But this is tantamount to denying that the Constitution expresses principles, for principles cannot be seen as stopping where some historical statesman's time, imagination, and interest stopped. The Constitution takes rights seriously; historicism does not.

PASSIVISM

Some Familiar Confusions

Historicism must be distinguished from a different and even more influential theory of constitutional practice that I shall call passivism. Its partisans distinguish between what they call an "active" and a "passive" approach to the Constitution. "Passive" justices, they say, show great deference to the decisions of other branches of government, which is statesmanlike, while "active" ones declare these decisions unconstitutional whenever they disapprove them, which is tyranny. Here is a representative statement and defense of the passive creed. "The great constitutional clauses our active brethren invoke to strike down what Congress or the president or some state legislature has done are framed in very general and abstract language. Everyone will have a different opinion about what they mean. Nor can their meaning be fixed in the way historicists think, by consulting the concrete intentions of framers, because the framers often had no intentions that are pertinent, and we have no reliable way of discovering the intentions they did have. In these circumstances democratic theory insists that the people themselves should decide whether the Constitution outlaws segregation or guarantees freedom of abortion or prohibits the death penalty. That means allowing state and national legislatures the last word on these issues. The people can overrule the Supreme Court only by the cumbersome and unlikely process of constitutional amendment, which anyway requires much more than a simple majority. They can overrule the legislature at the next election."[11]

But this statement of passivism muddles different issues, and we must begin our inspection by distinguishing these. It seems to speak, at once, to three different questions. The first is the enactment question. Who should make a constitution? Should the fundamental law be chosen by unelected judges appointed for life or in some more democratic fashion by legislators elected by and responsible to the people as a whole? The second is the jurisdictional question. Which institution, under the American political scheme, has authority to decide what the present Constitution, properly interpreted, actually requires? The third is the legal question. What *does* the present Constitution, properly interpreted, actually require? Some passivists think they are answering the second question; most act as if they are answering the first. But the third, the legal question, is the question they must address if their theory is to have any practical importance.

Marbury v. Madison settled the second, jurisdictional question, at least for the foreseeable future: the Supreme Court, willy nilly, must itself decide whether the Constitution prohibits states from making abortion criminal in particular circumstances. Passivism says the Court must exercise that power by adopting the legislature's answer as its own, but that advice is sound only if it follows from the right answer to the third, legal question. If the right answer to that question is that the Constitution does forbid states to make abortion criminal, then deferring to a legislature's contrary opinion would be *amending* the Constitution in just the way passivism thinks appalling. The first question, the question of enactment, depends on the third, legal question in exactly the same way. Passivists denounce judicial legislation at the constitutional level; they say democracy means that the people must make fundamental law. But the relevance of that attractive proposition presupposes, once again, a particular answer to the third, legal question. If the Constitution, properly interpreted, does not prohibit capital punishment, then of course a justice who declared that it is unconstitutional for states to execute criminals would be changing the Constitution. But if the Constitution, properly interpreted, does forbid capital punishment, a justice who *refused* to strike down state statutes providing death penalties would be changing the Constitution by fiat, usurping authority in defiance of constitutional principle. The question of law, in other words, is inescapable. We must understand passivism to declare that as a matter of law the abstract clauses of the Constitution grant citizens *no* rights except concrete rights that flow uncontroversially from the language of these clauses alone. Otherwise all its indignation about judicial usurpation, all its fervor for democracy, is irrelevant to legal practice, a turmoil of red herrings.

If strict conventionalism were the best general interpretation of American legal practice, then that austere view of constitutional rights would indeed be the correct one. Since it is controversial whether the due process clause or the equal protection clause prohibits states from making abortion criminal, for example, and there is no consensus even among constitutional lawyers how that question is to be resolved, a conventionalist must deny that as a matter of law the Constitution forbids that legislation. So a conventionalist who said that the Supreme Court nevertheless should declare antiabortion statutes unconstitutional would indeed be supposing that a nation's fundamental law should be made by appointed officials with lifetime tenure, subject to revision only by the extraordinary majorities required by the amending process. But that only adds another argument, to those we noticed in Chapter 4, why conventionalism is a poor interpretation of American law; if passivism depends on conventionalism, we have already rejected it. Under law as integrity, controversial constitutional issues call for interpretation, not amendment. Courts and legislatures, officials and citizens confront these issues under the regulative assumption that ordinarily one interpretation—one view of what free speech or equal protection or due process actually requires—provides a better justification of standing constitutional practice than any other: that is, that one interpretation is a better answer to the third question, of law. Of course, questions of the first kind, enactment questions, are appropriate in some contexts. Maybe the nation should not have the Constitution it has; maybe it should not continue to be governed by the principles that provide the best justification of its constitutional history so far. But the Constitution is undeniably clear about how these distinct enactment issues should be decided. They are issues of amendment, not interpretation, and the Constitution is clear that amendments may not be enacted except in the clumsy way it prescribes. Perhaps that was itself a mistake. Perhaps, contrary to what most Americans now think, a contemporary majority should have the power to change fundamental law, by a referendum, for example. But that is not our question either.

Can the passivist defend his austere answer to the legal question in some way other than by appealing to conventionalism? Some passivists rely on skepticism instead. The best interpretation of the abstract clauses of the Constitution, they say, even under law as integrity, is the skeptical interpretation that these neither permit nor prohibit anything beyond what follows from the strictest reading of their language alone. If that were true, then any decision the Court made about abortion, for example, would be an unacknowledged constitutional amendment. Then the enactment issue would be relevant: it might well be better, because it would be somewhat more democratic, for the Court to accept a state legislature's view about how the Constitution should be quietly amended than to impose its own contrary opinion. But does the passivist have any argument for his skepticism?

The argument he has in mind is familiar enough; we have met it before. "Someone will think one interpretation of the due process or equal protection clause better than another only because he thinks one theory of justice or equality better than another. But theories of justice and equality are only subjective; there is no right answer to which is best, only different answers."[12] If this is an appeal to external skepticism about political morality, however, it is irrelevant to constitutional practice for the reasons we studied in Chapter 2 and again in Chapter 7. And it is also self-defeating, because it assumes there is a right answer to the question *it* asks, the question of fairness about whose opinions should govern when an issue is only a matter of opinion. If the passivist's skepticism is instead global internal skepticism about morality in general, then it is entirely dogmatic, because it supplies none of the moral argument internal moral skepticism requires, and it is still self-defeating because it exempts its own moral position, that it is fairer for a legislature to make constitutional amendments than a court, from its generally scouring skepticism. If the right answer to all questions about the political rights of minorities is that there is no right answer, then how can there be a right answer to the question of whose opinions should rule us? For all its popularity, the argument from skepticism is singularly inept.

Justice, Fairness, and Majority Rule

So passivism has no short cut to the negative answer it always gives in controversial constitutional cases. It assumes that all the abstract clauses that guarantee individual rights against majoritarian decisions are properly interpreted extremely narrowly, that they forbid only what their language uncontroversially prohibits. It must defend that assumption by an interpretive argument of the kind law as integrity demands. Is that narrow reading a sound interpretation of American constitutional practice? It fits that practice somewhat better than historicism does, but it does not fit it very well: many past Supreme Court decisions, including *Brown,* could not be justified on a passivist account and would therefore have to be counted as mistakes. On the other hand, most lawyers already think that some of the decisions passivism does not fit were mistaken: the Dred Scott case,[13] in which the justices struck down the Missouri Compromise because they thought slaveowners had constitutionally protected rights in their slaves, and *Lochner*,[14] in which they said it outraged liberty for a state to limit the number of hours a baker might be employed to work at a stretch. And the passive creed has had considerable support in judicial opinions and scholarly treatises at almost every stage of constitutional history. We might well think, therefore, that passivism meets the threshold test of fit on the first dimension of interpretation; we should therefore turn to the more complex question how it fares on the other, more substantive tests. Would constitutional practice be in some way more impressive if constitutional constraints were very narrow, allowing legislatures to do almost everything the majority wanted?

That question calls for a complex judgment whose structure we studied in earlier chapters. We recognize different political virtues, which may compete with one another, in deciding which interpretation of the equal protection or due process clause, for example, would make them better in political morality. Justice is one of these virtues: an interpretation of equal protection is better, *pro tanto,* if it comes closer to realizing what justice actually requires. But fairness is another: an interpretation is also better, *pro tanto,* if it reflects convictions that are dominant or at least popular in the community as a whole than if it expresses convictions unpopular or rejected there. We can use this structure to identify arguments the passivist might make to show why his general account of the Constitution, reading its constraints on majoritarianism very narrowly, makes it a more attractive document.

Is the Constitution more just if its constraints on majoritarian government are minimal? It might be thought so for two different reasons. The first is straightforward. If someone agrees with Bentham (and with some Marxists and communitarians) that people have no rights as individuals, he might well think the Constitution better the fewer constraints it imposes on the majority's will. Or at least that any constraints should be designed to protect the democratic character of the legislative process rather than to check what the majority actually wants or requires.[15] But this straightforward argument for passivism would be unpersuasive to most Americans, who do not accept that view of justice.

The second argument from justice does not deny that individuals have rights, as a matter of justice, against the majority. It opposes constitutional constraints for the more complicated reason that over the long run legislatures are more likely to develop a sounder theory of what rights justice does require than courts trying to interpret the vague language of abstract constitutional provisions. There is an obvious objection to that claim. Legislators who have been elected, and must be reelected, by a political majority are more likely to take that majority's side in any serious argument about the rights of a minority against it; if they oppose the majority's wishes too firmly, it will replace them with those who do not. For that reason legislators seem less likely to reach sound decisions about minority rights than officials who are less vulnerable in that way. It does not follow that judges, insulated from the majority's rebuke, are the ideal people to decide about these rights. Judges have their own ideological and personal interests in the outcome of cases, and they can be tyrants too. But there is no a priori reason to think them less competent political theorists than state legislators or attorneys general.

Nor does history suggest that they are. Passivists cite *Lochner* and other cases in which the Supreme Court, wrongly, it is now agreed, appealed to individual rights to forestall or cripple desirable and just legislative programs. But we would have more to regret if the Court had accepted passivism wholeheartedly: southern schools might still be segregated, for example. Indeed, if we were to collect the

Court's decisions most generally regretted over the course of constitutional history, we would find more in which its mistake lay in failing to intervene when, as we now think, constitutional principles of justice required intervention. Americans would be prouder of their political record if it did not include, for example, *Plessy* or *Korematsu*.[16] In both these cases a decision of a majoritarian legislature was seriously unjust and also, as most lawyers now believe, unconstitutional; we regret that the Supreme Court did not intervene for justice in the Constitution's name.

So if there is a good political case for passivism, it must be found in the second line of argument we distinguished, in the idea of political fairness. But a passivist who appeals to fairness must defend two dubious claims. He must argue, first, that fairness, properly understood, demands that the majority of voters in any legislative jurisdiction be constrained, in what they can do to a minority, only by principles they themselves endorse or at least accept at the moment when the constraint is urged against them. He must argue, second, that political fairness so understood is of paramount importance in the constitutional context, that it must steadily be preferred to justice when the two are thought to conflict. These two claims, taken together, fit the general structure of the Constitution even worse than passivism's conclusions about deference fit constitutional practice, because they cannot explain clear and precise constraints like the Constitution's procedural requirements for criminal trials. If the two claims were sound, constraints would be unnecessary when the majority accepted them as proper, and unfair when it did not. Any competent interpretation of the Constitution as a whole must therefore recognize, contrary to the passivist's two claims, that some constitutional rights are designed exactly to prevent majorities from following their own convictions about what justice requires. The Constitution insists that fairness, understood as the passivist must understand it, must yield to certain fundamental rights. But once the passivist's view of the character and importance of fairness is rejected in constitutional interpretation because it cannot explain explicit constitutional rights, it cannot reappear as decisive over controversial cases that ask how far integrity requires these explicit rights to be extended to implicit rights not yet acknowledged.

Nor are the passivist's twin claims plausible in substance, as an account of what fairness should mean in an ideal constitutional structure. Fairness in the constitutional context requires that an interpretation of some clause be heavily penalized if it relies on principles of justice that have no purchase in American history and culture, that have played no part in the rhetoric of national self-examination and debate. Fairness demands deference to stable and abstract features of the national political culture, that is, not to the views of a local or transient political majority just because these have triumphed on a particular political occasion. If racial segregation offends principles of equality that are accepted over most of the nation, fairness is not violated when majorities in some states are denied title to segregate. If the nation's history generally endorses the idea of moral independence but denies that independence to homosexuals, though the distinction cannot even plausibly be justified in principle, fairness is not offended by insisting on a coherent enforcement of that idea.

We may summarize. Passivism seems, at first blush, an attractive theory about how far appointed judges should impose their will on political majorities. But when we take some care to disentangle the different issues it conflates, its intellectual foundations grow steadily weaker. It must be or contain a theory about what the Constitution, as fundamental law, already is, and that means it must be an interpretation of constitutional practice broadly understood. Passivism fits that practice only poorly and shows it in its best light only if we assume that as a matter of justice individuals have no rights against political majorities, which is foreign to our constitutional culture, or that fairness, defined in a special way that mocks the very idea of constitutional rights, is the paramount constitutional virtue. If we reject those unappealing ideas, we reject passivism. Does that mean we must accept the contrary theory, the bogeyman theory the passivists call "activism"?

Activism is a virulent form of legal pragmatism. An activist justice would ignore the Constitution's text, the history of its enactment, prior decisions of the Supreme Court interpreting it, and long-standing traditions of our political culture. He would ignore all these in order to impose on other branches of government his own view of what justice demands. Law as integrity condemns activism, and any practice of constitutional adjudication close to it. It insists that justices enforce the Constitution through interpretation, not fiat, meaning that their decisions must fit constitutional practice, not ignore it. An interpretive judgment does engage political morality, in the complex way we have been studying for several chapters. But it gives effect, not just to justice but to a variety of political virtues, some of which conflict with and check others. One of these is fairness: law as integrity is sensitive to a nation's political traditions and culture and therefore to a conception of fairness that is fit for a constitution. The alternative to passivism is not a crude activism harnessed only to a judge's sense of justice, but a more fine-grained and discriminating judgment, case by case, that gives place to many political virtues but, unlike either activism or passivism, gives tyranny to none.

We have now finished our short review of the present state of academic constitutional theory in the United States. One final observation might be wise. I have been arguing against historicism and passivism as general interpretations of American constitutional practice. I have not argued that every nation ought to have a written constitution with abstract provisions about individual rights, or that every such constitution ought to be interpreted by a court whose members are chosen in just the way Supreme Court justices are appointed. Many arrangements other than those now embedded in American legal practice are possible, and some may well be better from the point of view of ideal theory. We are faced, at this point in our more general argument, with an interpretive question of ordinary, not ideal, theory. American judges and lawyers need an interpretation of the constitutional practice they have, a successful interpretation overall, judged on the dimensions of any interpretation. Passivism and historicism cannot provide a decent interpretation. We can learn from their failure: we should be suspicious of any portmanteau, a priori, single-minded interpretive strategy for deciding what a constitution is. Once again the stage is set, by that amiable caution, for a fresh start.

HERCULES ON OLYMPUS

Hercules is promoted, in spite of the extraordinary and sometimes tedious length of his opinions in courts below. He joins the Supreme Court of the United States as Justice Hercules. Suppose *Brown*, the last of the sample cases we first met in Chapter 1, has not yet been decided. It now comes before Hercules' Court in the posture of 1953. The plaintiff schoolchildren say that the scheme of racially segregated public schools of Kansas is unconstitutional because it denies them equal protection of the law, in spite of the long history of that scheme throughout the southern states and in spite of the Court's own apparently contrary decision in a case raising the same issues of principle, *Plessy v. Ferguson*, which has been standing since 1896.[17] How does the champion of law as integrity reply to these claims?

The Constitution is, after all, a kind of statute, and Hercules has a way with statutes. He interprets each one so as to make its history, all things considered, the best it can be. This requires political judgments, but these are special and complex and by no means the same as those he would make if he were himself voting on a statute touching the same issues. His own convictions about justice or wise policy are constrained in his overall interpretive judgment, not only by the text of the statute but also by a variety of considerations of fairness and integrity. He will continue to use this strategy in his new position, but since the Constitution is a very unusual statute he will work out a special application of the strategy for constitutional cases. He will develop his strategy for statutes into a working theory of constitutional adjudication.

The Constitution is different from ordinary statutes in one striking way. The Constitution is foundational of other law, so Hercules' interpretation of the document as a whole, and of its abstract clauses, must be foundational as well. It must fit and justify the most basic arrangements of political power in the community, which means it must be a justification drawn from the most philosophical reaches of political theory. Lawyers are always philosophers, because jurisprudence is part of any lawyer's account of what the law is, even when the jurisprudence is undistinguished and mechanical. In constitutional theory philosophy is closer to the surface of the argument and, if the theory is good, explicit in it.

It is high time to repeat one of the cautions I offered earlier, however. Hercules serves our purpose because he is free to concentrate on the issues of principle that, according to law as integrity, constitute the constitutional law he administers. He need not worry about the press of time and docket, and he has no trouble, as any mortal judge inevitably does, in finding language and argument sufficiently discriminating to bring whatever qualifications he senses are necessary into even his initial characterizations of the law. Nor, we may now add, is he worried about a further practical problem that is particularly serious in constitutional cases. An actual justice must sometimes adjust what he believes to be right as a matter of principle, and therefore as a matter of law, in order to gain the votes of other justices and to make their joint decision sufficiently acceptable to the community so that it can continue to act in the spirit of a commu-

nity of principle at the constitutional level. We use Hercules
to abstract from these practical issues, as any sound analysis
must, so that we can see the compromises actual justices
think necessary as compromises with the law.

THEORIES OF RACIAL EQUALITY

We are interested now in Hercules' working theory of those
parts of the Constitution that declare individual constitutional rights against the state, and in particular in his theory
of the equal protection clause. He will begin with the abstract egalitarian idea already discussed in Chapter 8. This
holds that government must treat all its citizens as equals in
the following sense: political decisions and arrangements
must display equal concern for the fate of all. In Chapter 8
we considered how a state that respected that abstract
principle should distribute and regulate the use of private
property. We distinguished various conceptions of equality—libertarian, utilitarian, welfarist, and resource-based
conceptions—each of which supplied a somewhat different
answer to that question. We also noticed a distinction that
we must take up and elaborate here.

We distinguished between the overall, collective strategies
a government uses to secure the general interest as a matter
of policy and the individual rights it recognizes, as a matter
of principle, as trumps over these collective strategies.
Hercules now asks a neglected question of fundamental
importance for constitutional theory. How far does the
Constitution limit the freedom of Congress and the several
states to make their own decisions about issues of policy and
principle? Does the Constitution, properly interpreted, set
out a particular conception of equality that every state must
follow in its collective judgments of policy, in its general
scheme of distributing and regulating property, for example? If not, does it stipulate, in the name of equality, certain
individual rights every state must respect, as trumps over its

collective decisions of policy, whichever conception of equality the state has chosen?

These are separate questions, and the distinction is important. Hercules will answer the first in the negative. The Constitution cannot sensibly be read as demanding that the nation and every state follow a utilitarian or libertarian or resource-egalitarian or any other particular conception of equality in fixing on strategies for pursuing the general welfare. The Constitution does insist that each jurisdiction accept the abstract egalitarian principle that people must be treated as equals, and therefore that each respect *some* plausible conception of equality in each of its decisions about property and other matters of policy. (That relatively permissive constitutional standard is at least part of what constitutional lawyers call, somewhat misleadingly, the "rationality" requirement.) The second question, about individual constitutional rights over any collective justification, is a different matter. For Hercules will certainly draw this conclusion from constitutional history and practice: though the Constitution leaves each state free in matters of policy, subject only to the constraint just described, it insists that each state recognize certain rights qualifying any collective justification it uses, any view it takes of the general interest. The crucial interpretive question is then what rights these are.

Hercules is now concerned with one set of putative constitutional rights. It seems plain that the Constitution mandates some individual right not to be the victim of official, state-imposed racial discrimination. But what is the character and what are the dimensions of that right? He constructs three accounts of a right against racial discrimination. He will test each as a competent interpretation of constitutional practice under the Fourteenth Amendment.

1. *Suspect classifications.* The first account supposes that the right against discrimination is only a consequence of the more general right people have to be treated as equals according to whichever conception of equality their state pur-

sues. It supposes, in other words, that people have no distinct right not to be the victim of racial or other discrimination beyond what the rationality restraint already requires. If a state generally adopts some view of the general welfare, like that proposed by utilitarianism or equality of resources on the market model, in which gains to some are balanced against losses to others, then it meets the Constitutional standard against discrimination simply by counting everyone's welfare or choices in the same way. Race and similar grounds of distinction are special, on this account, only because history suggests that some groups are more likely than others to be denied the consideration due them, so political decisions that work to their disadvantage should be viewed with special suspicion. Even though the courts will not ordinarily review political decisions that benefit some groups more than others, unless these are shown to be "irrational" in the sense just described, it will inspect these decisions more carefully when historically mistreated minorities are disadvantaged.

Nevertheless, the standard requires only that these groups receive the right consideration in the overall balance, and a state may meet that standard even though it treats them differently from others. It might justify segregated schools, for example, by showing that integration would provide an inferior educational environment because it would outrage long-standing traditions of racial separation and that the damage to white children would then more than offset any gains to black children, even counting these gains as equally important in themselves, child by child. It might add that the facilities it has assigned to blacks, though separate, are nevertheless equal in quality. Or, even if they are not equal, that they cannot be improved except through special expense that would count the interests of each black child as more important, in the overall calculation, than the interests of each of the larger number of white children.

2. *Banned categories.* The second theory on Hercules' list insists that the Constitution does recognize a distinct right

against discrimination as a trump over any state's conception of the general interest. This is the right that certain properties or categories, including race, ethnic background, and perhaps gender, not be used to distinguish groups of citizens for different treatment, even when the distinction would advance the general interest on an otherwise permissible conception. A racially segregated school system is, on this account, unconstitutional under all circumstances.

3. *Banned sources.* The third theory recognizes a different special right against discrimination. Most conceptions of equality, including utilitarianism and resource-egalitarianism, make the public interest, and therefore proper policy, sensitive to people's tastes, preferences, and choices. A community committed to such a conception will think that certain decisions of policy are sound simply because preferences and choices are distributed in a certain way: the fact that more people want a sports stadium than an opera house, or that those who want the stadium want it much more, will justify choosing it, without any assumption that those who prefer it are worthier or their preferences more admirable. The third theory insists that people have a right, against this kind of collective justification, that certain sources or types of preferences or choices not be allowed to count in that way. It insists that preferences that are rooted in some form of prejudice against one group can never count in favor of a policy that includes the disadvantage of that group. This right, like the right proposed by the second theory, condemns the program of racially segregated education presented in *Brown*, though not quite so automatically. Segregation treats blacks differently, and history shows that the seat of the different treatment lies in prejudice. So segregation cannot be saved, according to the third account, by the kind of argument we supposed might save it under the first. It would not matter that a calculation counting all the preferences of each person as equally important, including those rooted in prejudice, might show that segregation was in the general interest, so understood.

When Hercules considers each of these theories about the force of the Fourteenth Amendment's requirement of equal protection, he will use the distinction we used in Chapter 8. He will distinguish between the academic and the practical elaboration of each theory; he will ask not only how attractive each theory is in the abstract, as it would be elaborated and applied by a sophisticated political philosopher, but how well each one could be put into practice in a community like his, as a constitutional standard courts could use effectively in deciding what legislation it disqualifies. I took the requirements of practical elaboration into account in describing the first theory. It sets out certain "suspect" classifications which, when used in legislation, raise a presumption that the interests of some group have not been taken into account in the proper way. But that presumption can be rebutted, and it is rebutted by showing that the classification does in fact give equal effect to all the preferences displayed in the community, with no distinction as to the character or source of these preferences.

The second theory, of banned categories, needs no distinct practical elaboration, because its academic elaboration is already practical enough. It sets out particular categories and insists that the constitutional right has been violated whenever the law makes distinctions among groups of citizens using any of those categories. The second theory insists (in the odd maxim often used to express it) that the Constitution is color-blind and blind also to certain other listed properties that distinguish different groups. The third theory, of banned sources, does need a distinct practical elaboration, because its fundamental principle would be extremely difficult for judges and other officials to apply directly case by case. That principle prohibits legislation that could be justified only by counting, within the overall calculation determining where the general interest lies, preferences directly or indirectly arising from prejudice. Even in theory it will often be difficult to decide which preferences these are, because people's desires usually have complex and sometimes even indeterminate sources. It will also be difficult to decide, case by case, which legislation would have been justified even if tainted preferences had not been counted in the calculation. It might be impossible to decide, for example, how far some particular parent's wish that his children be educated with other children from a similar background expresses a racially neutral view that education is always more effective in these circumstances and how far it reflects racial prejudice.

So judges who accepted the banned sources theory would have to construct a practical elaboration based on judgments about the kinds of preferences that often or typically have been generated through prejudice, and about the kinds of political decisions that in normal circumstances could not be justified were such preferences not counted as part of the justification. This practical elaboration would designate a set of "suspect" classifications much like those of the first theory, classifications that usually cause disadvantage to groups, like blacks or Jews or women or homosexuals, that have historically been the targets of prejudice; it would raise a presumption that any political decision that causes special disadvantage to these groups violates the constitutional right against discrimination. But the case necessary to rebut that presumption, according to the practical elaboration of the third theory, would be very different from the case necessary to rebut the suspicion of violation under the first theory. According to the first, the suspicion can be put to rest by showing that a calculation neutral among all preferences would justify the distinction of race. Under the third, this would not suffice: it would be necessary either to show that the classification was justified by popular preferences unstained by prejudice, or to provide some different form of justification that did not rely on preferences at all. The third theory, even when practically elaborated in this way, is also different from the second theory, of banned categories. The two come apart in confronting legislation whose purpose and effect is to benefit people who have historically been the victims of prejudice, not to harm them. The banned sources theory would distinguish between affirmative action programs designed to help blacks and Jim Crow laws designed to keep them in a state of economic and social subjugation. The banned categories theory would treat both in the same way.

DECIDING *BROWN*

Which Theory Is the Constitution's Theory?

Hercules is now ready to test these three accounts of the constitutional right against discrimination by asking how far each fits and justifies, and so provides an eligible interpretation of, American constitutional structure and practice. He will reject the first theory, which denies any special right against discrimination and insists only that the welfare or preferences of each citizen be counted in the same scale, without restriction as to source or character. Perhaps this theory would have been adequate under tests of fairness and fit at some time in our history; perhaps it would have been adequate when *Plessy* was decided. It is not adequate now, nor was it in 1954 when Hercules had to decide *Brown*. It gains little support from ideals of political fairness. The American people would almost unanimously have rejected it, even in 1954, as not faithful to their convictions about racial justice. People who supported racial segregation did not try to justify it by appealing just to the fact of their preferences, as people might support a decision for a sports stadium rather than an opera house. They thought segregation was God's will, or that everyone had a right to live with his own people, or something of that sort. And those who opposed segregation did not rest their case on unrestricted preference calculations either: they would not have thought the case for segregation any stronger if there were more racists or if racists took more pleasure in it. Hercules will think the first account inadequate in justice as well, and so he will discard it if either of the other two fit constitutional practice well enough to be eligible.

He needs to develop his working theory of constitutional adjudication only in enough detail to decide *Brown*, so he would not have to choose between banned categories and banned sources, the second and third theories on his list. Both condemn officially sponsored racial segregation in schools. Both fit the past pattern of Court decisions and the general structure of the Constitution well enough to be eligible. Both were consistent, in 1954, with ethical attitudes that were widespread in the community; neither theory fit these attitudes noticeably better than the other, because the difference between them appears only at a level of analysis popular opinion had not yet been forced to reach. America's growing sense that racial segregation was wrong in principle, because it was incompatible with decency to treat one race as inherently inferior to another, can be supported either on grounds of banned sources, that some preferences must be disregarded in any acceptable calculation of what makes the community better off on the whole, or on grounds of banned categories, that some properties, including race, must never be made the basis of legal distinction.

Hercules is therefore ready to decide, for the plaintiffs, that state-imposed racial segregation in education is unconstitutional. He knows that the congressmen who proposed the Fourteenth Amendment had a different view, which they declared in official legislative history. But for reasons we noticed in describing historicism and passivism, he does not believe that this much matters now. It cannot be evidence of any deep and dominant contemporary opinion to which he must refer, as one aspect or dimension of interpretation, for reasons of fairness. The old legislative history is no longer an act of the nation personified declaring some contemporary public purpose. Nor is this the kind of issue in which it is more important that institutional practice be settled than that it be settled in the right way. The Court had already, in earlier cases, given people reason to doubt that established patterns of racial distinction would be protected much

longer.[18] The plaintiff schoolchildren are being cheated of
what their Constitution, properly interpreted, defines as independent and equal standing in the republic; this is an in-
sult that must be recognized and removed. So if *Plessy* is
really precedent against integration, it must be overruled
now. Everything conspires toward the same decision. Racially segregated public schools do not treat black schoolchildren as equals under any competent interpretation of the
rights the Fourteenth Amendment deploys in the name of
racial equality, and official segregation is therefore unconstitutional.

Rights and Remedies

But now comes the question of remedy. Should Hercules
vote to outlaw segregated schools immediately, so that all
school districts now segregated must desegregate at once? Or
should he vote for some more gradual process of change, in
which case he will have to find some language to describe
how much delay will be permitted? Here are some arguments for delay. A school system cannot reverse major institutional structures overnight. If schools segregated in June
try to reopen as integrated in September there will be chaos,
and the education of a cohort of students, both black and
white, will be damaged or destroyed. New catchment
boundaries must be drawn, and it may be difficult to respect
the tradition of neighborhood or even territorial education;
teachers as well as pupils must be reassigned, and the personal costs of these decisions will be diverse and difficult.
Problems of backlash will be even more urgent and threatening. Long-standing racial segregation is an important part of
the lives of those who wish to maintain it; their sense of self-
identity is challenged by any substantial weakening of segregation, and these are seeds of violence as well as despair. The
problems could be ameliorated, if not entirely dissolved, by a
more stately and gradual process of change.

Someone reviewing these arguments might describe their upshot this way. "The law requires immediate dismantling of segregation, but various practical reasons of policy of the sort just described counsel against it, so Hercules must decide whether to compromise law with policy." This description is partly misleading, however; some of the reasons for delay I mentioned are practical political reasons of the sort I said Hercules would not attend to, though real justices might have to, but others do bear on the question of principle, the question of what the Constitution requires as a matter of law. Any plausible interpretation of the rights people have under the Constitution must be complex enough to speak to remedy as well as substance. So Hercules' decision about remedy is also a decision of law, a decision about the secondary rights people have to the method and manner of enforcing their primary substantive rights.[19] Hercules must decide, as a general threshold question, whether the best interpretation of the remedial practices of courts in general and the Supreme Court in particular insists that people's rights to remedy be sensitive to consequence. He will decide that it does: the point of constitutional adjudication is not merely to name rights but to secure them, and to do so in the interests of those whose rights they are.

So he must then ask which procedural decision will best protect black schoolchildren seeking an integrated education, and he may well discover that requiring overnight integration will not. But though his decision must be sensitive to consequence, it must also discriminate among consequences, and he will accordingly treat the technical and mechanical problems of integration differently from the problem of a threatened backlash, for deference to the latter would reward acts and attitudes that the Constitution outlaws and deplores. Hercules' decision, then, even about remedy, is not simply or directly consequentialist the way a flat decision of policy would be. He aims to develop an overall theory of enforcement that fits and justifies the power the

Constitution gives him, and this means a theory that does not contradict through procedure what the document demands in substance. He might arrive at the following theory or something close to it: the Court's strategies of decree must search out the most effective and immediate enforcement of substantive constitutional rights consistent with the interests of those who claim them but must not otherwise defer to or try to accommodate the interests of people who want to subvert those rights.

The Supreme Court in *Brown* settled on a formula of enforcement that, in retrospect at least, did not meet that standard.[20] It said that desegregation must proceed "with all deliberate speed," and this language proved to be a charter for obstruction and delay. It would have been better if the Court had attempted to provide a more precise schedule, even though that strategy might have jeopardized the unanimity of its decision. Much of the litigation that followed *Brown* would have been inevitable anyway, however, because the social revolution that case announced was both national and foundational and required dozens of further decisions in circumstances and on terrain very different from those of *Brown*. The most difficult problems of law appeared, in fact, not in southern states with a long history of segregation by law but in northern states, where school segregation had been achieved not by explicit racial separation but by more subtle decisions drawing school district boundaries, for example. The federal courts had to decide under which circumstances a state's failure to reverse this more subtle history of segregation was a violation of the principles announced in *Brown;* and, when it was, what orders the courts should and could make by way of remedy.

The courts developed a distinct jurisprudence of racial integration, neither entirely successful nor entirely coherent, but nevertheless largely a credit to law.[21] For a time federal judges issued and supervised decrees that brought them deep into the normal jurisdiction of school superintendents and other local officials. They demanded severe changes in school organization and set out detailed schedules for these changes; they constructed programs for busing black children to schools in white neighborhoods and vice versa. At no time in American history have their decisions seemed so different from the normal work of judges or attracted so much hostility from public and press. Some scholars, including several who approved, said their decisions marked an important change in the nature and character of the judicial office.[22] In one way these scholars were right. Judges have traditionally exercised supervisory roles ancillary to adjudication—in administering bankruptcy proceedings, for example, or antitrust or custody decrees. But the scale and detail of supervision were much greater in desegregation decrees and brought judges more firmly into the conventional domains of elected executive officers.

But under law as integrity this unusual judicial trespass on administrative functions is only the consequence, in highly special and seismic circumstances, of a perfectly traditional view of the judicial office. Hercules' thesis is at least plausible, that judges have a duty to enforce constitutional rights up to the point at which enforcement ceases to be in the interests of those the rights are supposed to protect, and this thesis provides an eligible and attractive interpretation of past constitutional practice. Its more dramatic applications in the race cases, like busing orders, can of course be challenged as mistaken applications, and this challenge will seem plausible to some lawyers at two levels. They think the Supreme Court and lower federal courts went too far in recognizing a constitutional right to an integrated education in states that had not segregated by law, and that many of the remedies the courts ordered in support of these rights, including busing, were not in blacks' interests after all. We must be careful to distinguish these dubious challenges to recent applications of Hercules' thesis from a challenge to the thesis itself.

DECIDING *BAKKE*

I will not pursue the history of *Brown*'s progeny or this defense of the more interventionist decisions that followed it, because neither story is particularly important to the constitutional wardrobe of law as integrity. We turn instead to a different problem, a child of the success rather than the failures of the revolution *Brown* began. The conscience of American business and education, and its prudence as well, was stirred by the racial wars of the 1960s, and programs collectively called affirmative action or reverse discrimination were part of their response. We can settle for a very rough description of these programs: they aimed to improve the place and number of black and other minorities in labor, commerce, and the professions by giving them some form of preference in hiring, promotion, and admission to college and professional schools. The preference was sometimes indistinct, a matter of counting a person's race or ethnic background as an advantage that could secure him a place, "all else being equal," which it never was. But sometimes the preference was both explicit and mechanical.

The medical school of the University of California at Davis, for example, used a bifurcated system for judging applicants: a quota was set apart for minority applicants who competed only among themselves for a designated number of places, with the consequence that some blacks were accepted whose test scores and other conventional qualifications were far below those of whites who were rejected. Alan Bakke was one of the latter, and it was conceded, in the litigation he provoked, that he would have been accepted had he been black. He said that this quota system was unlawful because it did not treat him as an equal in the contest for places, and the Supreme Court, justifying its decision in a divided and somewhat confused set of opinions, agreed.[23]

How would Justice Hercules have voted? The case forces him to confront the issue he found unnecessary to decide for

Brown. Is the banned categories theory a more successful interpretation of the pertinent constitutional practice, all things considered, than the banned sources theory? A practical constitutional standard enforcing the banned sources theory would designate certain racial classifications as suspect. But it would not be necessary to include in the list of suspect classifications a distinction obviously designed to aid historical victims of prejudice. Perhaps institutions that used racial quotas should have the burden, under that theory, of showing that these did not reflect covert prejudice against some other group. But Davis could have met that burden, so under the banned sources theory it would not have violated Bakke's constitutional right. It would have violated his rights according to the banned categories theory, however. The academic as well as practical elaboration of that theory is just a list of properties that must not be used to distinguish groups one of which thereby gains an advantage over the other. Race must be prominent in any such list, and Davis used racial classifications that disadvantaged whites like Bakke.

So Hercules must choose between the two theories, and he will prefer the banned sources to the banned categories theory. Though banned categories fits the decisions about racial discrimination up to *Bakke* as well as banned sources does—it fits the language used in these decisions better—it does not fit constitutional or political practice more generally. Banned categories, as it stands, is too arbitrary to count as a genuine interpretation under law as integrity. It must be supported by some principled account of why the particular properties it bans are special, and the only principle available is that people must never be treated differently in virtue of properties beyond their control. This proposition has been decisively rejected throughout American law and politics. Statutes almost invariably draw lines along natural differences of geography and health and ability: they subsidize workers who have by chance come to work in one industry or even firm rather than another, for example, and restrict licenses to drive or practice medicine to people with certain physical or mental abilities. Educational opportunities in universities and professional schools, in particular, have always and without constitutional challenge been awarded in flat violation of the supposed principle. Candidates are chosen on the basis of tests that are thought to reveal differences in natural ability, and in many schools they are also chosen to promote geographical balance in classes or even the school's athletic success. Candidates are no more responsible for their ability to score well on conventional intelligence tests or for their place of birth or skill at football than for their race; if race were a banned category because people cannot choose their race, then intelligence, geographical background, and physical ability would have to be banned categories as well. Racial discrimination that disadvantages blacks is unjust, not because people cannot choose their race, but because that discrimination expresses prejudice. Its injustice is explained, that is, by the banned sources theory, not the banned categories theory.

Suppose Bakke's lawyers argue that the banned categories strategy must be accepted for race (and perhaps for certain other special cases like ethnic background and sex as well) even though it cannot be supported by any general principle that people must never be divided according to properties they cannot control. They must not say that this special standing for race and a few other properties is just a matter of constitutional fact, that the Constitution picks out and disqualifies race and these other properties alone. For that begs the question: the correct interpretation of our constitutional practice is exactly what is now in issue, and they need an argument that justifies their claim about what the Constitution means, not an argument that begins in that claim. Suppose they say: the framers of the equal protection clause had race particularly in mind because the Fourteenth Amendment followed and was provoked by slavery and the Civil War. This is historicism, and all our former arguments against it are in point. But it is a particularly feeble form of historicism in this context. For we know that the framers of the Fourteenth Amendment did not believe they were making *any* racial discrimination in education unconstitutional, even segregation aimed at blacks, and we can hardly take their opinions as an argument that *all* racial distinction, even that designed to help blacks, is outlawed.

Suppose Bakke's lawyers now say that whatever the framers might or might not have intended, wise constitutional statecraft argues for the banned category theory for race and a few other categories alone because admissions or hiring programs that use racial classifications in any way will exacerbate racial tension and so prolong discrimination, hatred, and violence. This is exactly the kind of complex, forward-looking calculation of policy that even a weakened, sensible form of passivism would leave to the judgment of elected officials or of executives appointed by and responsible to these officials. If Congress decides that a national policy prohibiting any affirmative action is desirable, it has the power to enact a statute that will partly achieve this.[24] The Supreme Court should not take that judgment of policy upon itself.

So Hercules will reject the banned categories theory of equality, both in its general form, which cannot be made to fit, and in its special form, which is too arbitrary to count as principled. He will accept the banned sources theory as the best interpretation available,[25] then construct a suitable practical elaboration of that theory for constitutional purposes by selecting a list, open to revision as social patterns change, of "suspect" classifications whose use to disadvantage a group historically the target of prejudice is prima facie unconstitutional. The list he constructs would not outlaw affirmative action programs in principle, because these do not work to the disadvantage of any such group.

But Bakke has one more possible argument that the equal protection clause, interpreted as Hercules now understands it, does outlaw the particular quota-based form of affirmative action Davis used. The banned sources theory explicates a special right as a supplement to the general requirement of the Fourteenth Amendment, the requirement that any state's calculation of the general interest must take into account the interests of all citizens even though it disadvantages some; it must be in that sense a "rational" calculation understood as serving some acceptable conception of how people are treated as equals. Government violates this more general requirement whenever it ignores the welfare of some group in its calculation of what makes the community as a whole better off. Even though Bakke finds no help in the special right against racial discrimination Hercules recognizes, he might fall back on the general requirement. Davis argues that its quota system plausibly contributes to the general welfare by helping to increase the number of qualified black doctors. Bakke might argue to the contrary that Davis's quota system prevented it from even attending to the impact of its admissions decisions on people in his position. Hercules would decide (I believe) that this claim is confused: a quota system gives the same consideration to the full class of applicants as any other system that relies, as all must, on general classifications.[26] But reasonable judges might disagree with that part of his overall conclusion in the case.[27]

IS HERCULES A TYRANT?

We have followed Hercules through only one chain of decisions, because here as everywhere in jurisprudence detail is more illuminating than range. But the argument of the preceding chapters gives some idea of his attitudes to other constitutional issues,[28] and enough has emerged about his constitutional methods to justify a minor summary. Hercules is not a historicist, but neither is his the buccaneer style sometimes lampooned under the epithet "natural law." He does not think that the Constitution is only what the best theory of abstract justice and fairness would produce by way of ideal theory. He is guided instead by a sense of constitutional integrity; he believes that the American Constitution consists in the best available interpretation of American constitutional text and practice as a whole, and his judgment about which interpretation is best is sensitive to the great complexity of political virtues bearing on that issue.

His arguments embrace popular conviction and national tradition whenever these are pertinent to the sovereign question, which reading of constitutional history shows that history overall in its best light. For the same reason and toward the same end, they draw on his own convictions about justice and fairness and the right relation between them. He is not a passivist because he rejects the rigid idea that judges must defer to elected officials, no matter what part of the constitutional scheme is in question. He will decide that the point of some provisions is or includes the protection of democracy, and he will elaborate these provisions in that spirit instead of deferring to the convictions of those whose legitimacy they might challenge. He will decide that the point of other provisions is or includes the protection of individuals and minorities against the will of the majority, and he will not yield, in deciding what those provisions require, to what the majority's representatives think is right.

He is not an "activist" either. He will refuse to substitute his judgment for that of the legislature when he believes the issue in play is primarily one of policy rather than principle, when the argument is about the best strategies for achieving the overall collective interest through goals like prosperity or the eradication of poverty or the right balance betwen economy and conservation.[29] He would not have joined the *Lochner* majority, for example, because he would have rejected the principle of liberty the Supreme Court cited in that case as plainly inconsistent with American practice and anyway wrong and would have refused to reexamine the New York legislature's judgment on the issues of policy that then remained.[30]

Hercules, then, escapes the standard academic classifications of justices. If he fell neatly into any of the popular cate-

gories he would not be Hercules after all. Is he too conservative? Or too liberal or progressive? You cannot yet say, because your judgment would depend on how closely your
convictions matched his across the wide spectrum of different kinds of convictions an interpretation of constitutional
practice engages. I have not exposed enough of what his
convictions are, or how these would be deployed in due process cases about criminal procedure, or free speech cases, or
cases about fair electoral districting and procedures, for you
to tell. Nor have I discussed, as a distinct problem in the
constitutional context, his convictions about the role of precedent, about past decisions of the Supreme Court. You
will have some sense of this attitude from Chapter 7 and
from the fact that he was untroubled about overruling
Plessy in deciding *Brown;* but this is not the whole story because his attitude toward precedents would be more respect-
ful when he was asked to restrict the constitutional rights
they had enforced than when he was asked to reaffirm their
denials of such rights. So you must reserve your overall
political judgments for the careers of justices you know
more about.

But we have seen enough to know that one charge some
lawyers would urge against Hercules is unfair and, what is
even worse, obscurantist. Hercules is no usurping tyrant trying to cheat the public of its democratic power. When he in-
tervenes in the process of government to declare some statute
or other act of government unconstitutional, he does this in
service of his most conscientious judgment about what democracy really is and what the Constitution, parent and
guardian of democracy, really means. You may disagree
with the few judgments I have reported in his name; if I told
you more of his career on Olympus you would probably disagree with more. But if Hercules had renounced the responsibility I have described, which includes the responsibility to
decide when he must rely on his own convictions about his
nation's character, he would have been a traitor not a hero of
judicial restraint.

ELEVEN

LAW BEYOND LAW

LAW WORKS ITSELF PURE

Can Integrity Be Impure?

Sentimental lawyers cherish an old trope: they say that law works itself pure. The figure imagines two forms or stages of the same system of law, the nobler form latent in the less noble, the impure, present law gradually transforming itself into its own purer ambition, haltingly, to be sure, with slides as well as gains, never worked finally pure, but better in each generation than the last. There is matter in this mysterious image, and it adds to both the complexity and the power of law as integrity.

Can that conception recognize a purer form of the law we have? Here is an argument that it cannot. The actual, present law, for Hercules, consists in the principles that provide the best justification available for the doctrines and devices of law as a whole. His god is the adjudicative principle of integrity, which commands him to see, so far as possible, the law as a coherent and structured whole. There seems no room in this picture for the idea of law made more coherent, purer, than it actually is. If it is possible to make the system more coherent, then this more coherent system is the actual, present law, so once Hercules has worked out what the law now is, there can be no purer law latent within it. Law as integrity (we might say) *is* the idea of law worked pure.

This is too crude: the sentimental distinction does have a place within law as integrity. Our concept of law ties law to the present justification of coercive force and so ties law to adjudication: law is a matter of rights tenable in court. This makes the content of law sensitive to different kinds of institutional constraints, special to judges, that are not necessarily constraints for other officials or institutions. When judges interpret legal practice as a whole, they find reasons of different sorts, specifically applying to judges, why they should *not* declare as present law the principles and standards that would provide the most coherent account of the substantive decisions of that practice.

Strict doctrines of precedent, which require some judges to follow past decisions of other judges even when they think these are mistaken, are a familiar instance. Recall an example I used earlier: the House of Lords continues to exempt barristers from liability for negligence in certain circumstances. Integrity condemns this special treatment, and Parliament, out of integrity, should repeal it.[1] But a lower English court cannot because precedent forbids. Strict precedent varies from jurisdiction to jurisdiction, and the highest courts are ordinarily exempt. But legislative supremacy is another institutional constraint, and this normally embraces all courts. If a judge is satisfied that a statute admits of only one interpretation, then, barring constitutional impediment, he must enforce this as law even if he thinks the statute inconsistent in principle with the law more broadly seen.[2] He may think that the legislature ought to repair the inconsistency by further legislation, not only or necessarily out of a sense of justice, but because the legislature is also a guardian of integrity. But that will not affect what the law is for him.

If Hercules had decided to ignore legislative supremacy and strict precedent whenever ignoring these doctrines would allow him to improve the law's integrity, judged as a matter of substance alone, then he would have violated integrity overall. For any successful general interpretation of our legal practice must recognize these institutional constraints. Other judicial constraints are less doctrinal and more a matter of different aspects of a judge's sense of due process in court. Lord Hercules might think that exempting

barristers from the general rules of negligence law is indefensible, and he might know he has the technical power to
overrule the precedents protecting lawyers in that way. But
he might also believe it would be wrong suddenly to impose
liability on a particular barrister for acts in the past if no
court had previously signaled any change, because that barrister would have been unlikely to insure himself against
such liability. Hercules would then perhaps consider changing the law prospectively only, in the way we imagined a
pragmatist judge might in Chapter 5. But British practice is
largely innocent of that device, and he might settle for finding some other way of warning barristers through his opinion of changes to come.[3] Justice Hercules might think that
the best interpretation of the equal protection clause outlaws
distinctions between the rights of adults and those of children that have never been questioned in the community,
and yet he might think it would be politically unfair, in the
sense distinguished in Chapter 3, for the law to impose that
view on a community whose family and social practices accepted such distinctions as proper and fundamental. I do not
mean that Hercules would always, in these sorts of cases, accept substantive inconsistency to keep faith with more procedural principles, but only that the complex character of
adjudication makes it inevitable that he sometimes would.

The principle of local priority of interpretation we met in
Chapter 8 is another, more subtle kind of constraint that can
now be seen as functionally related to the institutional constraints just noticed. If a judge who accepts law as integrity
finds that two interpretations each fit the area of his immediate concern well enough to satisfy his interpretive constraints, he will expand the range of his study in a series of
concentric circles to include other areas of law and then determine which of the two better fits the expanded range. But
he will normally respect the priority of the department of
law in which his immediate problem arises; he will severely
mark down some principle as an eligible interpretation of accident law if it uproots that department of law, even if it fits

other departments well. The topology of departments is, as we saw, part of his interpretive problem, and his judgments about the boundaries of departments may be controversial and will in any case change as law develops. But special constraints apply to his judgments about boundaries: they must in principle respect settled professional and public opinions that divide law into substantial areas of public and private conduct.

Integrity and Equality

We can capitalize on earlier discussions to show the cumulative power of these various constraints, each of which appeals to integrity of process to check substantive integrity. In Chapter 8 Hercules decided that a large part of the law of unintended injury in his jurisdiction can be seen as expressing the conception of equality he thinks best from the standpoint of abstract justice, which is resource egalitarianism, and he therefore adopted that conception in constructing his interpretation of these parts of the law. In Chapter 10 he quickly rejected the suggestion that this conception of equality (or any other) is made mandatory on states by the equal protection clause of the Fourteenth Amendment. He would have to concede, moreover, that both state and nation fall very far short of what equality of resources, in even its practical elaboration, would require by way of the distribution of wealth, although some of the redistributive programs Congress and many states have adopted are steps in that direction. This concession does not threaten his view about the best interpretation of unintended injury law, because no other conception of equality fits that law nearly as well and no other would provide any better fit with the tax and redistributive programs that equality of resources fits only imperfectly.

So he must settle for an account of equality and law that is less elegant and uniform than he might have hoped. Equality of resources is his key to the law of accidents and other forms of unintended damage. But he cannot appeal to the Constitution to order Congress or state legislatures to adopt the economic and redistributive programs that equality of resources demands. Nor, given the various constraints he accepts about how far he is free to read statutes to promote his view of justice, can he read into welfare and taxation schemes provisions equality of resources would approve. Political integrity as well as justice would have been better served, he thinks, if national and local governments had more consistently accepted equality of resources as the goal of their economic programs. But he would violate integrity himself if he were to ignore the decisions they actually made.

Inclusive and Pure Integrity

Law as integrity therefore not only permits but fosters different forms of substantive conflict or tension within the overall best interpretation of law. We are now in a position to explain why. We accept integrity as a distinct political ideal, and we accept the adjudicative principle of integrity as sovereign over law, because we want to treat ourselves as an association of principle, as a community governed by a single and coherent vision of justice and fairness and procedural due process in the right relation. We have already noticed that these three component virtues—fairness and justice and process—sometimes conflict. Hercules is prevented from achieving integrity viewed from the standpoint of justice alone—coherence in the substantive principles of justice that flow throughout his account of what the law now is—because he has been seeking a wider integrity that gives effect to principles of fairness and procedural due process as well.

Justice, we said, is a matter of the right outcome of the political system: the right distribution of goods, opportunities, and other resources. Fairness is a matter of the right structure for that system, the structure that distributes influence over political decisions in the right way. Procedural due process is a matter of the right procedures for enforcing rules and regulations the system has produced. Legislative supremacy, which obliges Hercules to give effect to statutes even when these produce substantive incoherence, is a matter of fairness because it protects the power of the majority to make the law it wants. Strict doctrines of precedent, the practices of legislative history, and local priority are largely, though in different ways, matters of procedural due process because they encourage citizens to rely on doctrinal pronouncements and assumptions that it would be wrong to betray in judging them after the fact.

We can consolidate this explanation by drawing a new distinction, between two levels or kinds of integrity. The adjudicative principle that governs our law enforces *inclusive* integrity: this requires a judge to take account of all the component virtues. He constructs his overall theory of the present law so that it reflects, so far as possible, coherent principles of political fairness, substantive justice, and procedural due process, and reflects these combined in the right relation. The qualification "so far as possible" acknowledges what we have just been noticing, that proper attention to one of these virtues in an overall account of law will sometimes force compromise in the level of integrity that can be achieved in another. Hercules must fold back, into his calculations about what the law is, the best interpretation of his community's principles of fairness, which define his own powers against those of other institutions and officers, and its principles of due process, which are made pertinent by the fact that judgments of law are predicate for backward-looking attribution of blame and responsibility. So he must give effect to statutes that pull against substantive coherence and to precedents and local priorities that stand in the way of consistency over different departments of law. He will therefore be aware of a different, more abstract calculation: *pure* integrity abstracts from these various constraints of fairness and process. It invites him to consider what the law would be if judges were free simply to pursue coherence in the principles of justice that flow through and unite different departments of law.

We bow to justice, among the political virtues, by creating for it a special form of integrity. But the honor is not arbitrary. The concrete consequences of fairness and procedural due process are much more contingent than those of justice, and they are often matters of regret. We hope that our legislature will recognize what justice requires so that no practical conflict remains between justice and legislative supremacy; we hope that departments of law will be rearranged, in professional and public understanding, to map true distinctions of principle, so that local priority presents no impediment to a judge seeking a natural flow of principle throughout the law.

Our root ambition of treating ourselves as a community of principle itself recommends a special role for justice. Citizens of such a community aim to be governed justly and fairly and with due process, but the three component virtues have different meaning for them even as ideals. Fairness and due process are both, though in different ways, tied to specific institutions within the community. They assign different responsibility to different officials differently placed. Justice, on the contrary, is a matter of what the community personified, abstracting from institutional responsibilities, ought itself to achieve. So there is practical importance in isolating the question of what integrity both permits and requires seen from the standpoint of justice alone. For that question marks an agenda for the community as a whole, as prior to and shaping further questions about what institutional decisions would be necessary to achieve this.

We can now dissolve the figure sentimental lawyers celebrate, of law within and beyond law. The law we have, the actual concrete law for us, is fixed by inclusive integrity. This is law for the judge, the law he is obliged to declare and enforce. Present law, however, contains another law, which marks out its ambitions for itself; this purer law is defined by pure integrity. It consists in the principles of justice that offer the best justification of the present law seen from the perspective of no institution in particular and thus abstracting from all the constraints of fairness and process that inclusive integrity requires. This purified interpretation speaks, not to the distinct duties of judges or legislators or any other political body or institution, but directly to the community personified. It declares how the community's practices must be reformed to serve more coherently and comprehensively a vision of social justice it has partly adopted, but it does not declare which officer has which office in that grand project.

Present law gropes toward pure law when modes of decision appear that seem to satisfy fairness and process and bring law closer to its own ambition; lawyers declare optimism about this process when they say that law works itself pure. The optimism may be misplaced. A skeptical story seems better to some critics of our law: they predict the triumph of entropy instead, of law losing its overall substantive coherence in the chaos produced by selfish and disparate concentrations of political power. Which attitude—pessimism or optimism—is wise and which foolish? That depends on energy and imagination as much as foresight, for each attitude, if popular enough, contributes to its own vindication.

LAW'S DREAMS

The courts are the capitals of law's empire, and judges are its princes, but not its seers and prophets. It falls to philosophers, if they are willing, to work out law's ambitions for itself, the purer form of law within and beyond the law we have. We found in the common law of accident a conception of equality which, if allowed to run freely across the American political and economic structure, to its natural limits, would require dramatic changes in the distribution of property and other resources generally. We can find other footholds of that conception of equality in other departments of the law. We can cite, for example, the sporadic, sometimes retreating, but overall forward progress of redistribution toward handicapped people and those who are unlucky in other respects, and we can argue that this overall development is better explained by equality of resources than by other conceptions of what it means to treat people as equals. We favor this conception ourselves; now we claim that it is the goal of law purified, the community's star in its search for integrity seen from the standpoint of justice alone. What kind of argument have we begun?

Another philosopher of our law holds up a contrary, competing vision. He sees law purified as law more thoroughly utilitarian in an unrestricted sense, more consistently and accurately devoted to maximizing the uncritical satisfaction of people's overall preferences. Another describes a more communitarian vision; this supposes law purified of individual rights that corrupt the community's sense, which this vision endorses, that the only good is communal good, that lives are best lived under shared standards of what lives are best. We cannot defeat these other visions by measuring out and comparing the tracts of law that fit ours and theirs. None fits well enough to dominate present law overall; all fit well enough to claim a base within it. The argument must now move to the plane of abstract political morality; it must move toward arguments of utopian theory. But the argument still belongs to law, at least in an attenuated sense, because each contestant begins by establishing a contemporary shadow of the future he celebrates. (Neither a Marxist nor a fascist could find enough present law distinctively explained by his political philosophy to qualify for the contest.) The connection with ordinary legal argument, though attenuated, is crucial because it gives the philosophical argument a distinct yet complementary role in the larger politics of law.

Each of the contesting philosophies uses and respects integrity, and the values that support it, in this way. Each proposes to show how law can develop in the direction of justice while preserving integrity stage by stage. Each claims that his vision could be secured by the community advancing through a series of steps, none of which would be revolutionary, each of which would build on and take its place within the structure already in place. We observed this process from an external, historical point of view in our initial survey of the development of law over time in Chapter 3, and also in rejecting the claim in Chapter 4 that law is mainly a matter of convention. I said that although the content of law will be very different in one period than in another, nevertheless in a flourishing legal system even important changes can be seen as flowing from the law in place, enriching that law, changing its base, and so provoking further change.

So utopian legal politics is, in that broad way, law still. Its philosophers offer large programs that can, if they take hold in lawyers' imagination, make its progress more deliberate and reflective. They are chain novelists with epics in mind, imagining the work unfolding through volumes it may take generations to write. In that sense each of their dreams is already latent in the present law; each dream might be law's future. But the dreams are competitive, the visions are different, choices must be made—large choices by statesmen in high judicial and legislative office, smaller choices by those whose decisions are more circumscribed and immediate. No coherent program may take hold for long enough among enough people; we may be left in the hands of law's cunning after all, which is only another name for the ability of good judges to impose whatever order they can, as Hercules had to do in the chapters before this one, on a historically haphazard process. But philosophers are part of law's story even then, even when they disagree and no vision wins a dominant constituency for long, for their arguments even then remind the profession of the pressure of law beyond law, that the imperatives of integrity always challenge today's law with the possibilities of tomorrow's, that every decision in a hard case is a vote for one of law's dreams.

EPILOGUE: WHAT IS LAW?

Law is an interpretive concept. Judges should decide what the law is by interpreting the practice of other judges deciding what the law is. General theories of law, for us, are general interpretations of our own judicial practice. We rejected conventionalism, which finds the best interpretation in the idea that judges discover and enforce special legal conventions, and pragmatism, which finds it in the different story of judges as independent architects of the best future, free from the inhibiting demand that they must act consistently in principle with one another. I urged the third conception, law as integrity, which unites jurisprudence and adjudication. It makes the content of law depend not on special conventions or independent crusades but on more refined and concrete interpretations of the same legal practice it has begun to interpret.

These more concrete interpretations are distinctly legal because they are dominated by the adjudicative principle of inclusive integrity. Adjudication is different from legislation, not in some single, univocal way, but as the complicated consequence of the dominance of that principle. We tracked its impact by acknowledging the stronger force of integrity in adjudication that makes it sovereign over judgments of law, though not inevitably over the verdicts of courts, by noticing how legislation invites judgments of policy that adjudication does not, by observing how inclusive integrity enforces distinct judicial constraints of role. Integrity does not enforce itself: judgment is required. That judgment is structured by different dimensions of interpretation and different aspects of these. We noticed how convictions about fit contest with and constrain judgments of substance, and how convictions about fairness and justice and procedural due process contest with one another. The interpretive judgment must notice and take account of these several dimensions; if it does not, it is incompetent or in bad faith, ordinary politics in disguise. But it must also meld these dimensions into an overall opinion: about which interpretation, all things considered, makes the community's legal record the best it can be from the point of view of political morality. So legal judgments are pervasively contestable.

That is the story told by law as integrity. I believe it provides a better account of our law than conventionalism or pragmatism on each of the two main dimensions of interpretation, so no trade-off between these dimensions is necessary at the level at which integrity competes with other conceptions. Law as integrity, that is, provides both a better fit with and a better justification of our legal practice as a whole. I argued the claim of justification by identifying and studying integrity as a distinct virtue of ordinary politics, standing beside and sometimes conflicting with the more familiar virtues of justice and fairness. We should accept integrity as a virtue of ordinary politics because we should try to conceive our political community as an association of principle; we should aim at this because, among other reasons, that conception of community offers an attractive basis for claims of political legitimacy in a community of free and independent people who disagree about political morality and wisdom.

I argued the first claim—that law as integrity provides an illuminating fit with our legal practice—by showing how an ideal judge committed to law as integrity would decide three types of hard cases: at common law, under statutes, and, in the United States, under the Constitution. I made Hercules decide the several cases I offered as working examples in Chapter 1, and my claims of fit can be checked by comparing his reasoning with the kind of arguments that seemed appropriate to lawyers and judges on both sides of those cases. But this is too limited a test to be decisive; law students and lawyers will be able to test the illuminating power of law as integrity against a much wider and more varied experience of law at work.

Have I said what law is? The best reply is: up to a point. I have not devised an algorithm for the courtroom. No electronic magician could design from my arguments a computer program that would supply a verdict everyone would accept once the facts of the case and the text of all past statutes and judicial decisions were put at the computer's disposal. But I have not drawn the conclusion many readers think sensible. I have not said that there is never one right way, only different ways, to decide a hard case. On the contrary, I said that this apparently worldly and sophisticated conclusion is either a serious philosophical mistake, if we read it as a piece of external skepticism, or itself a contentious political position resting on dubious political convictions if we treat it, as I am disposed to do, as an adventure in global internal skepticism.

I described the nested interpretive questions a judge should put to himself and also the answers I now believe he should give to the more abstract and basic of these. I carried the process further in some cases, into the capillaries as well as the arteries of decision, but only as example and not in more detail than was needed to illustrate the character of the decisions judges must make. Our main concern has been to identify the branching points of legal argument, the points where opinion divides in the way law as integrity promises. For every route Hercules took from that general conception to a particular verdict, another lawyer or judge who began in the same conception would find a different route and end in a different place, as several of the judges in our sample cases did. He would end differently because he would take leave of Hercules, following his own lights, at some branching point sooner or later in the argument.

The question how far I have succeeded in showing what law is is therefore a distinct question for each reader. He must ask how far he would follow me along the tree of argument, given the various interpretive and political and moral convictions he finds he has after the reflection I have tried to provoke. If he leaves my argument early, at some crucial abstract stage, then I have largely failed for him. If he leaves it late, in some matter of relative detail, then I have largely succeeded. I have failed entirely, however, if he never leaves my argument at all.

What is law? Now I offer a different kind of answer. Law is not exhausted by any catalogue of rules or principles, each with its own dominion over some discrete theater of behavior. Nor by any roster of officials and their powers each over part of our lives. Law's empire is defined by attitude, not territory or power or process. We studied that attitude mainly in appellate courts, where it is dressed for inspection, but it must be pervasive in our ordinary lives if it is to serve us well even in court. It is an interpretive, self-reflective attitude addressed to politics in the broadest sense. It is a protestant attitude that makes each citizen responsible for imagining what his society's public commitments to principle are, and what these commitments require in new circumstances. The protestant character of law is confirmed, and the creative role of private decisions acknowledged, by the backward-looking, judgmental nature of judicial decisions, and also by the regulative assumption that though judges must have the last word, their word is not for that reason the best word. Law's attitude is constructive: it aims, in the interpretive spirit, to lay principle over practice to show the best route to a better future, keeping the right faith with the past. It is, finally, a fraternal attitude, an expression of how we are united in community though divided in project, interest, and conviction. That is, anyway, what law is for us: for the people we want to be and the community we aim to have.

NOTES · INDEX

.   .
NOTES
___

1. WHAT IS LAW?

1. *Brown v. Board of Educ.,* 347 U.S. 486 (1954).

2. *Priestley v. Fowler* [1837] 3 M. & W. 1.

3. See the Law Reform (Personal Injuries) Act 1948, 35 *Halsbury's Statutes of England* 548 (3rd ed.).

4. *Attorney-General v. Jonathan Cape Ltd.* [1975] 3 All E. R. 484.

5. So do law school examiners marking examination papers. Some people are made uncomfortable using "true" and "false" in this way, but they are happy to say that propositions of law can be "sound" or "unsound," or something of that sort, which for present purposes comes to the same thing. See the discussion of skepticism about law in Chapters 2 and 7.

6. I have in mind the legal "realists" discussed later in this chapter, like Jerome Frank (*Law and the Modern Mind* [New York, 1949]), and the "critical legal studies" movement discussed in Chapter 7 (see, generally, 38 *Stanford Law Review* 1–674 [1984], symposium on critical legal scholarship).

7. See, e.g., Benjamin Cardozo, *The Nature of the Judicial Process* especially at 165–80 (New Haven, 1921).

8. These possibilities are discussed in Chapters 9 and 10.

9. Oliver Wendell Holmes, "The Path of the Law," 10 *Harvard Law Review* (1897).

10. *Riggs v. Palmer,* 115 N.Y. 506, 22 N.E. 188 (1889).

11. Id. at 189.

12. There are serious enough problems in this intermediate principle, and we shall consider some of these in Chapter 9.

13. *Tennessee Valley Authority v. Hill,* 437 U.S. 153 (1978). John Oakley pointed out the value of this case as a leading example.

14. The Endangered Species Act of 1973, Pub. L. No. 93-205,

sec. 7, 87 Stat. 884, 892 (codified as amended at 16 U.S.C. sec. 1536 [1982]).

15. The Endangered Species Act Amendments of 1978, Pub. L. No. 95-632, 92 Stat. 3571 (codified as amended at 16 U.S.C. sec. 1536 [1982]).

16. *Tennessee Valley Authority v. Hill*, 437 U.S. 153, 185 (1978).

17. Id. at 196 (Powell, J. dissenting).

18. *McLoughlin v. O'Brian* [1983] 1 A.C. 410, reversing [1981] Q.B. 599.

19. *Marshall v. Lionel Enterprises Inc.* [1972] O.R. 177.

20. *Chadwick v. British Transport* [1967] 1 W.L.R. 912.

21. See, e.g., *Jaffree v. Board of School Comm'rs*, 554 F. Supp. 1104 (S.D. Ala. 1982) (district court judge refusing to follow Supreme Court precedent), *rev'd sub nom. Jaffree v. Wallace*, 705 F.2d 1526 (11th Cir. 1983), *aff'd* 605 S. Ct. 2479 (1985).

22. Practice Statement (Judicial Precedent) [1966] 1 W.L.R. 1234.

23. [1981] Q.B. 599.

24. [1983] 1 A.C. 410.

25. 163 U.S. 537 (1896).

26. *Brown v. Board of Education*, 347 U.S. (1954). The opinion consolidated cases arising from segregated schools in Topeka, Kansas; Clarendon County, South Carolina; Prince Edward County, Virginia; and New Castle County, Delaware. See 347 U.S. at 486 n.1.

27. This phrase was used in a second opinion in the case deciding matters of remedy. *Brown v. Board of Education*, 349 U.S. 294, 301 (1955).

28. See Charles Fairman, "Forward: The Attack on the Segregation Cases," 70 *Harvard Law Review* 83 (1956).

29. It is sometimes said that the goal of the theories I call semantic is not, as that name suggests, to develop theories about what the word "law" means, but rather to lay bare the characteristic and distinctive features of law as a social phenomenon. See, e.g., Ruth Gavison, "Comments on Dworkin" in *Papers of the Jerusalem Conference* (forthcoming). But this contrast is itself a misunderstanding. The philosophers I have in mind, whose theories are described in the following pages, recognize that the most distinctive aspect of law as a "social phenomenon" is that participants in institutions of law deploy and debate propositions of law and

think it matters, usually decisively, whether these are accepted or rejected. The classical theories try to explain this central and pervasive aspect of legal practice by describing the sense of propositions of law—what these mean to those who use them—and this explanation takes the form either of definitions of "law" in the older style or accounts of the "truth conditions" of propositions of law—the circumstances in which lawyers accept or reject them—in the more modern style.

30. See J. L. Austin, *The Province of Jurisprudence Determined* (H. L. A. Hart ed., New York, 1954) and *Lectures in Jurisprudence* (5th ed. 1885). See also Jeremy Bentham, *An Introduction to the Principles of Morals and Legislation* (J. H. Barns and H. L. A. Hart eds., London, 1970).

31. H. L. A. Hart, *The Concept of Law* (London, 1961).

32. For an exceptionally illuminating discussion of natural law theories and defense of a modern version, see J. Finnis, *Natural Law and Natural Rights* (New York, 1980).

33. See, e.g., Holmes, supra n. 9.

34. See Hart, supra n. 31, at 129–50, and "Positivism and the Separation of Law and Morals," 71 *Harvard Law Review* 593 (1958). Hart relies on the distinction between core and penumbra in explaining why judges must have discretion to repair gaps in statutes, and then suggests that the master rule any community uses to identify the extension of law is itself likely to have a penumbral area that can generate disputes in which "all that succeeds is success."

35. See Svetlana Alpers, *The Art of Describing* 243–44 n. 37 (London, 1983), and material cited there.

2. INTERPRETIVE CONCEPTS

1. See my *Taking Rights Seriously* 101–5 (Cambridge, Mass. and London, 1977), discussion of an unusual interpretive problem in a chess tournament.

2. In what follows I assess this assumption, that creative interpretation must be conversational interpretation, mainly by discussing an idea familiar to literary scholars: that interpreting a work of literature means recapturing the intentions of its author. But the assumption has a more general foundation in the philosophical literature of interpretation. Wilhelm Dilthey, a German

philosopher who was especially influential in shaping the debate about objectivity in the social sciences used the word *verstehen* specifically to describe the kind of understanding we achieve in coming to know what someone else means by what he says (this is a sense of comprehension, we might say, in which understanding someone involves coming to an understanding with him) rather than to describe all possible ways or modes of understanding his behavior or its mental life. (See *Meaning in History: Dilthey's Thought on History and Society* [H. P. Rickman trans. and ed., London, 1961].) He raised the question whether and how this kind of understanding is possible over cultural gaps; he found the key to this problem in "historical" consciousness: the state of mind achieved by rare and dedicated interpreters through reflection on the general structure and categories of their own lives at so high a level of abstraction that they can be supposed, at least as a methodological hypothesis, to hold across time. The contemporary masters of the continuing debate, like Gadamer and Habermas, take different directions. Gadamer thinks Dilthey's solution supposes the Hegelian apparatus Dilthey was anxious to exorcise. (See H. G. Gadamer, *Truth and Method* particularly 192–214 [Eng. trans., 2nd ed., London, 1979].) He believes the Archimedian historical consciousness Dilthey supposed possible, free from what Gadamer calls, in his special sense of the word, prejudices, is impossible, that the most we can hope to achieve is an "effective historical consciousness" that aims not to look at history from no point of view but to understand how our own viewpoint is influenced by the world we wish to interpret. Habermas criticizes Gadamer, in turn, for the latter's too-passive view that the direction of communication is one way, that the interpreter must strive to learn from and apply what he interprets on the assumption that he is subordinate to its author. Habermas makes the crucial observation (which points in the direction of constructive rather than conversational interpretation) that interpretation supposes that the author could learn from the interpreter. (See Jürgen Habermas, 1 *The Theory of Communicative Action* [T. McCarthy trans., Boston, 1984].) The long debate continues, however, mainly dominated by the assumption I describe in the text, that the only alternative to cause-and-effect understanding of social facts is conversational understanding on the model of *verstehen*.

3. See W. V. O. Quine, *Word and Object* 58–59 (Cambridge, Mass., 1960). The principle of charity is advanced and applied in a different context in Wilson, "Substance without Substrata," 12 *Review of Metaphysics* 521–39 (1959).

4. See T. Kuhn, *The Essential Tension: Selected Studies in Scientific Tradition and Change* 320–51 (Chicago, 1977); Kuhn, *The Structure of Scientific Revolution* (2nd ed., Chicago, 1970); K. Popper, *The Logic of Scientific Discovery* (New York, 1959).

5. See Gadamer, supra n. 2.

6. I owe this example to Thomas Grey.

7. Jonathan Miller emphasized the role of Jessica in his 1969 production.

8. This point is developed, in the context of interpreting statutes and the Constitution, in Chapters 9 and 10. See also *Taking Rights Seriously,* chap. 5, and my *A Matter of Principle* chap. 2 (Cambridge, Mass., 1985).

9. Stanley Cavell, *Must We Mean What We Say?* chap. 8 (New York, 1969). Compare Gadamer supra n. 2, 39–55.

10. Cavell, supra n. 9, at 228–29.

11. See T. S. Eliot, "Tradition and the Individual Talent," *Selected Essays* (New York, 1932).

12. Absent unusual circumstances. Imagine this sequence: a critic insists that, although Fellini himself did not realize this as he was filming, the right way to read *La Strada* is through the Philomel story. Then the critic adds that the film, so understood, is particularly banal. We are left with no sense of why he claims the reading he does. I do not mean that every kind of activity we call interpretation aims to make the best of what it interprets—a "scientific" interpretation of the Holocaust would not try to show Hitler's motives in the most attractive light, nor would someone trying to show the sexist effects of a comic strip strain to find a nonsexist reading—but only that this is so in the normal or paradigm cases of creative interpretation. Someone might set out to discredit a writer, of course, by trying to show the latter's work in the worst not the best light, and he will naturally present his case as an interpretation, as a claim about what that writer's work "really is." If he really does believe that no more favorable interpretation fits equally well, then his argument falls under my description. But suppose he does not, and is suppressing a more

attractive reading that is also eligible given the text. In that case his strategy is parasitic on the normal description, because he will succeed only if his audience is unaware of his true aims; only if they believe he has tried to produce the best interpretation that fits.

13. Gadamer, supra n. 2.

14. Habermas observes that social science differs from natural science for just that reason. He argues that even when we discard the Newtonian view of natural science as the explanation of theory-neutral phenomena, in favor of the modern view that a scientist's theory will determine what he takes the data to be, an important difference nevertheless remains between natural and social science. Social scientists find their data already *pre*-interpreted. They must understand behavior the way it is already understood by the people whose behavior it is; a social scientist must be at least a "virtual" participant in the practices he means to describe. He must, that is, stand ready to judge as well as report the claims his subjects make, because unless he can judge them he cannot understand them. (See Habermas, supra n. 2, at 102–11.) I argue, in the text, that a social scientist attempting to understand an argumentative social practice like the practice of courtesy (or, as I shall claim, law) must therefore participate in the spirit of its ordinary participants, even when his participation is only "virtual." Since they do not mean to be interpreting each other in the conversational way when they offer their views of what courtesy really requires, neither can he when he offers his views. His interpretation of courtesy must contest theirs and must therefore be constructive interpretation rather than conversational interpretation.

15. The idea of a social or group consciousness seems to offer an escape from a serious difficulty that is widely thought to threaten the possibility of conversational interpretation across cultures and times. How can we hope to understand what someone wrote or thought in a different culture long ago, or what his social practices and institutions meant to him? We cannot understand him unless we see the world as he does, but we cannot escape seeing it the way we already do, the way caught up in our own language and culture, and from that point of view his claims may seem silly and unmotivated. (For a version of this argument in a legal context, see Robert Gordon, "Historicism in Legal Scholarship," 90 *Yale*

Law Journal 1017, 1021 [1981].) We cannot hope to grasp what caste means to people none of whom are troubled by it, any more than we can understand someone who says he is in pain and not only doesn't mind but doesn't see why anyone should. If we can accept, however, that cultures and ages can have a kind of enduring consciousness, and that history itself has its own embracing mental life, people of one period *can* hope to understand people of another because they all participate in a common consciousness with enduring meanings they share. This ambitious idea abstracts from the conversational acts of particular people, expressing their individual interests and assumptions, into purposes and motives of larger social units, ultimately of life or mind itself.

I cannot discuss here either the ontology of group spirit or the validity of the suggestion that group spirit offers a solution to the problem of cultural isolation. (See the citations to Dilthey, Gadamer, and Habermas, supra n. 2.) It is worth noticing, however, that the problem is vicious and threatening only if conversational interpretation rather than constructive interpretation is in question. When it is appropriate to take the interpretive attitude I describe in the text toward some different culture (see the discussion of foreign and wicked legal systems in Chapter 3, for example) we try to understand it not conversationally but making of it the best, given our purposes and convictions, it can be. If we think that goal requires us to discover or adopt the actual convictions, which might not be ours, of historical actors, the problem of isolation remains. We may not be able sensibly to attribute to Shakespeare even the relatively abstract intention of arousing, among his contemporaries, a particular complex reaction to Shylock. But these problems, when they are serious, become reasons for tailoring the demands of constructive interpretation to what we can achieve, to finding some dimension of value in theater that allows us to make the best we can of *The Merchant of Venice* (or the Germanic antecedents of the common law) without doubtful speculation about states of mind closed off to us by cultural barriers. For in constructive interpretation historical intentions are not the constitutive foundations of interpretive understanding. Failure to retrieve them is not an interpretive disaster, because there are other ways, and often much better ways, of finding value in traditions we have joined.

16. For an extended discussion of this distinction, and of cre-

ative interpretation more generally, see Dworkin, "Law as Interpretation," in *The Politics of Interpretation* 287 (W. J. T. Mitchell ed., Chicago, 1983); S. Fish, "Working on the Chain Gang: Interpretation in Law and Literature," 60 *Texas Law Review* 373 (1982); Dworkin, "My Reply to Stanley Fish (and Walter Benn Michaels): Please Don't Talk about Objectivity Any More," in *The Politics of Interpretation,* at 287; S. Fish, "Wrong Again," 62 *Texas Law Review* 299 (1983). The Dworkin articles are reprinted, though the second is altered and abbreviated, in *A Matter of Principle* chaps. 6 and 7.

17. We might summarize these three stages in the observation that interpretation seeks to establish an equilibrium between the preinterpretive account of a social practice and a suitable justification of that practice. I borrow "equilibrium" from Rawls, but this account of interpretation is different from his account of reasoning about justice. He contemplates equilibrium between what he calls "intuitions" about justice and a formal theory uniting these intuitions. See John Rawls, *A Theory of Justice* 20-21, 48-50 (Cambridge, Mass., 1971). Interpretation of a social practice seeks equilibrium between the justification of the practice and its postinterpretive requirements.

18. For an important attempt to provide "defining features" of a legal system, see Joseph Raz, *The Concept of a Legal System* (2nd ed., Oxford, 1980).

19. See Derek Parfit's excellent *Reasons and Persons* (Oxford, 1984) on the identity of communities and—more controversially—personal identity.

20. Justice and other higher-order moral concepts are interpretive concepts, but they are much more complex and interesting than courtesy, and also less useful as an analogy to law. The most important difference between justice and courtesy, in this context, lies in the latent global reach of the former. People in my imaginary community use "courtesy" to report their interpretations of a practice they understand as local to them. They know that the best interpretation of their own practice would not necessarily be the best of the comparable practice of any other community. But if we take justice to be an interpretive concept, we must treat different people's conceptions of justice, while inevitably developed as interpretations of practices in which they themselves participate, as claiming a more global or transcendental authority so

that they can serve as the basis for criticizing other people's practices of justice even, or especially, when these are radically different. The leeways of interpretation are accordingly much more relaxed: a theory of justice is not required to provide a good fit with the political or social practices of any particular community, but only with the most abstract and elemental convictions of each interpreter. (For a recent discussion of the differences between justice and law in this respect, see *A Matter of Principle* chap. 10, and my exchange with Michael Walzer, *New York Review of Books,* Apr. 14, 1983.) Justice is special in another way. Since it is the most distinctly political of the moral ideals, it provides a natural and familiar element in interpretation of other social practices. Interpretations of law, as we shall see, often appeal to justice as part of the point they deploy at the interpretive stage. Interpretations of justice cannot themselves appeal to justice, and this helps to explain the philosophical complexity and ambition of many theories of justice. For once justice is ruled out as the point of a fundamental and pervasive political practice, it is natural to turn for a justification to initially nonpolitical ideas, like human nature or the theory of the self, rather than to other political ideas that seem no more important or fundamental than justice itself.

21. But the fact that Marx's political theory is so plainly not captured by this statement of the concept explains his own ambivalence, and the ambivalence of his students and critics, whether to count his theory as a theory of justice. For an intriguing account, see Stephen Lukes, *Marxism and Morality* (London, 1985).

22. Since even the preinterpretive stage requires interpretation, these boundaries around the practice are not precise or secure. So we disagree about whether one can be unjust to animals, or only cruel, and about whether relations between groups, as distinct from individuals, are matters of justice.

23. Some critics who are generally enthusiastic about this picture of interpretation try to meliorate its skeptical thrust. They rely on the idea that "critical communities" commonly develop "conventions" about what counts as a good or bad interpretation of a particular text, and they say that these conventions give individuals a sense of a constraint outside themselves, and therefore of a discovery, when they come to see the implications of these conventions for a particular work of art. See Stanley Fish, *Is There a Text in This Class?* (Cambridge, Mass., 1980). But this "solution" is

deceptive. We shall see in Chapter 4 that the idea of a convention is itself somewhat mysterious; in the present use it is lame as well. Can professional colleagues be thought to share a convention about the best way to read *Paradise Lost,* for example, when they disagree about what is the best way? If we concede that in that case they do not share a convention—that colleagues can belong to very different interpretive "communities" even though their offices are facing across a hall—then we still leave unexplained how someone can think his interpretation better than that of a colleague who belongs to a different community. For in that case he believes, not just that the conventions of the two communities are different, but that those of his community are better, the right ones to use. So the idea of conventions and professional communities is no help, and we must confront the bold position that there is "no right answer" to the question of how *Paradise Lost* should be read, that there are only different interpretations, not better and worse ones.

24. See, e.g., *Morality and Objectivity* (Ted Henderich ed., London, 1985); Bernard Williams, *Ethics and the Limits of Philosophy* (Cambridge, Mass., 1985); and Thomas Nagel, *The View from Nowhere* (forthcoming).

25. See *A Matter of Principle* chaps. 5, 6 and 7.

26. If I held the contrary view and said I really did think the superiority of rum raisin was an objective fact of the matter and not just my subjective taste, that I was describing a property of the ice cream itself, not just of my preferences, you would disagree, but our disagreement would not be some second-order disagreement about the possibility of sound aesthetic claims. It would be a contest between two aesthetic styles or attitudes: my silly view, that everyone has a reason to value the experience of rum raisin, whether or not he enjoys that experience, and your more attractive (internal) skepticism that ice cream can have aesthetic value of that sort. You would think, not that I have a defective ontology because I think ice cream contains value the way it does cream and sugar, but that I have a defective sensibility, that I have no understanding of the character of a genuine aesthetic experience.

27. When someone has a belief or conviction it makes sense to ask for its pedigree, that is, to ask for an explanation of how he came to hold it. Some explanations assume, in some part of the

story they tell, the truth of the belief or conviction, and if an explanation of this sort is accepted, the fact of the belief is itself evidence of its truth. If we can explain people's belief that grass is green only in some way that assumes that grass is green—for example, by explaining that they have seen green grass—then, obviously, the common belief is evidence of the fact. But if everyone's beliefs about some matter can be explained in some way that does not presuppose the fact, then the fact of the belief is not evidence of its truth. We think we can fully explain people's belief in witches, for example, by describing their superstitions; our explanation, no matter how far continued, would never appeal to any actual encounters people have had with witches. If so, then the fact that some people believe in witches is no evidence for their existence.

Someone might compose an internally skeptical argument about morality that begins in that observation. He argues that we can explain the fact that people hold moral beliefs without assuming the existence of special moral facts that have caused these beliefs. Our moral beliefs, he says, are caused not by encounters with special facts but by developing within a particular culture; this explains why people from different cultures hold different convictions. This plausible causal story, however, so far shows only that the fact of our moral beliefs is no evidence for their soundness, and that is hardly surprising. No one but the most enthusiastic egotist thinks the fact that he holds a particular moral opinion is itself an argument for that opinion. In any case, no one should be much troubled by being forced to abandon that view, for he abandons at most only one argument for the soundness of his moral opinions, leaving in place all the arguments he would anyway be tempted to make. The skeptic must show, not just that our moral convictions can be fully explained in ways that make no reference to any causal moral properties in the universe, but that the form the best explanation of our convictions takes in itself casts doubt on them.

Under certain circumstances discovering how we came to believe something does make us doubt it, but this is because we discover something we recognize as a *defect* in our method of instruction. If I had learned all my medieval history from a book I later discover was a work of popular fiction I would doubt everything I thought I knew. But just the bare fact that my moral

NOTES TO PAGES 91-92

convictions would be different had I been raised very differently or in very different times does not *in itself* show any defect in the culture and training and processes of reflection and observation that finally produced the convictions I now have. It may—it should—make me cautious about these convictions, force me to ask whether I have any genuine reasons for thinking as I do. It may lead me to notice connections between my community's moral assumptions and its structures of economic and other power, and noticing these connections might weaken the hold my convictions formerly had on me. All these are possible consequences of my coming to see that I am a creature of culture, but they are consequences of seeing more than *just* this, and more is necessary if the insight is to finish in any sort of internal skepticism.

The argument from causation I just described is often thought a good argument for some form of external skepticism. (See Williams, supra n. 24. The relevance of the causal argument to morality is undercut, however, by the fact that, if we believe slavery is wrong, we cannot imagine a world different from ours only in the single respect that slavery is not wrong.) But we are not concerned with the merits of external skepticism here. We are concerned with objections to the common view that one moral conviction may be better than, not merely different from, others it contradicts, that it may be the right answer and they wrong answers. The text argues that that view is itself a moral view, that it is an essential part of the moral convictions it inhabits. A moral view can be damaged only by moral argument. So the skepticism we fear is internal skepticism, and the argument from causation, by itself, has no terror. I know that my opinions would be different if I had lived in very different times. But I think the convictions I have better as well as different, and no causal explanation can force me to abandon that view, though of course a moral argument might.

3. JURISPRUDENCE REVISITED

1. The most systematic discussion of criteria essential to the existence of a legal system is found in Joseph Raz, *The Concept of a Legal System* (2nd ed., Oxford, 1980).

2. A classic of jurisprudence argues that statutes are not law. J. C. Gray, *The Nature and Sources of the Law* (Boston, 1902).

3. Some legal theories that are not, on the surface, claims about why law justifies state coercion nevertheless depend on or presuppose such claims. In Chapter 4 I try to show how familiar forms of legal positivism become more interesting when they are understood not as semantic theories but as interpretations resting on the claim that collective force is justified only when it conforms to conventional understandings. I have elsewhere tried to show how Hart's version of positivism, in particular, grows out of his conviction that special legal conventions, broadly accepted throughout the community, cure defects in the organization of political coercion that would be inevitable without these conventions. See "A Reply to Critics" in *Ronald Dworkin and Contemporary Jurisprudence* (Marshall Cohen ed., New York and London, 1984). Joseph Raz has recently developed a version of positivism, however, that explicitly denies any reliance on political convictions of any sort. (See Raz, "Authority, Law and Morality," in 68 *The Monist* 295 [July 1985].) He insists that any adequate account of the proper grounds of law must explain how law can serve as an *authority*, and he defines authority in such a way that people cannot accept law as an authority unless their tests for law wholly exclude judgments of political morality. He believes what he calls the "sources" thesis, that the grounds of law must be exclusively factual, follows from that assumption and definition. He is right that any successful interpretation of our legal practice must recognize and justify the common assumption that law can compete with morality and wisdom and, for those who accept law's authority, override these other virtues in their final decision about what they should do. (I do not mean that this assumption about the authority of law is uncontroversial; legal pragmatism denies it, as we shall see in Chapter 5.) But that condition can be met by a theory that makes judgments of morality and wisdom *part* of the grounds of law rather than law's only grounds. So it can be met by conceptions of law that reject the "sources" thesis, conceptions like those I described in Chapter 1, with reluctance, as moderate "natural law" theories. Raz thinks law cannot be authoritative unless those who accept it *never* use their own convictions to decide what it requires, even in this partial way. But why must law be blind authority rather than authoritative in the more relaxed way other conceptions assume? Some explanation is needed, and it will not do to fall back on linguistic rules, to say that this is just what

"law" or "authoritative" means under criteria for its application educated lawyers and laymen all accept. Any plausible argument must be an argument of political morality or wisdom, an argument showing why a practical distinction should be made between those justifications for coercion that are and those that are not drawn from exclusively factual sources, and why only the former should be treated as law. I consider such arguments in Chapter 4.

4. Though if I am right, they accept that concept as the right plateau for argument about the nature of law, and so frame their theories as skeptical on that plateau: they say, as a way of summarizing their conception, that there is no law.

5. Not every sociologist or political theorist who talks of popular morality and moral traditions has these relatively simple ideas in mind. Some mean to use the idea of a cultural mind I mentioned in the last chapter; others use an interpretive concept, in our sense, so that a community's moral traditions are not just a matter of the attitudes or beliefs of particular people but of the best interpretation of these. But it is the simpler, more reductive idea I mean now to distinguish from the concept of law as just described.

6. Hart argues that the choice between a narrow and a wide concept of law should be made to facilitate moral reflection. See H. L. A. Hart, *The Concept of Law* 206–7 (1961). We do better, for that purpose, to refuse to make the choice at all, as a matter of linguistic stipulation. See my remarks replying to Hart in Cohen ed., supra n. 3, at 258–60.

7. For further discussion of the issues discussed in the last several paragraphs, see Cohen ed., supra n. 3 at 256–60.

4. CONVENTIONALISM

1. The version of conventionalism I am describing here, which I later call "strict" conventionalism, may be more complex than the form in which I state it. For a society may have further legal conventions specifying how judges must decide cases when no lawmaking institution has decided the issue in play: for example, a convention that judges must decide in whatever way they believe the legislature would if the issue were before it. But a society will run out of further conventions of this sort at some point, and then

strict conventionalism must allow judges the discretion described in the text.

2. Austin's idea that law is rooted in a general habit of obedience, for example, is easily restated as an interpretation or specification of the idea that law is rooted in convention. This fact is obscured by the familiar misreading, that Austin supposes habits of obedience always to be the upshot of fear of a sanction. He is careful not to take any general position about the psychological springs of obedience; a general habit of obedience is enough to generate law for Austin, even if this habit is based in fear; but a habit developed out of love or respect for the sovereign would also be enough. Austin's account of convention in terms of habit is not a fully satisfactory theory of convention, as Hart and others have established. But it does not distort Austin's theory to treat it as a theory of convention, however unsatisfactory we find it. Hart's version of positivism is even more plainly conventional, for his rule of recognition is a rule that happens to have been accepted by almost everyone, or at least by almost all judges and other lawyers, no matter what the content of that rule may be. See H. L. A. Hart, *The Concept of Law* 97-107 (London, 1961).

3. See David Lewis, *Convention: A Philosophical Study* (Cambridge, Mass., 1969).

4. Soft conventionalism is suggested in the account of positivism given by Jules Coleman in "Negative and Positive Positivism," 11 *Journal of Legal Studies* 139 (1982), reprinted in *Ronald Dworkin and Contemporary Jurisprudence* 28 (Marshall Cohen ed., New York and London, 1984). See also E. Philip Soper, "Legal Theory and the Obligation of a Judge," in the same book, particularly at 17-20 (law can depend on controversial judgments of morality if a sovereign body declares that whatever is just is law), and David Lyons, "Principles, Positivism and Legal Theory," 87 *Yale Law Journal* 415, 422 ff. (law can depend on the correct though controversial interpretation of a fundamental document drafted in moral terms). As Coleman points out, Hart seems to reject the interpretation of his views that Soper and Lyons assume.

5. See G. Erdlich, *A Commentary on the Interpretation of Statutes* sec. 4 (1888) (citing both American and English cases); *Sutherland's Statutory Construction* sec. 46.07 (4th ed., Wilmette, Ill., 1985) (plain meaning governs unless absurdity would result); P. Langan, *Maxwell on Interpretation of Statutes* (12th ed., London, 1969)

(same). See also John W. Johnson, "The Grudging Reception of Legislative History in U.S. Courts," 1978 *Detroit C.L. Review* 413. (I owe this reference to William Nelson.)

6. Conventionalism can intelligibly be proposed as an interpretation of legal systems in autocratic or otherwise nondemocratic countries, because the officials and even the general population of such countries may sustain conventions that give autocratic power to a small group or a single tyrant. In that case, if conventionalism were accepted as the best interpretation, only the edicts of that group or tyrant would be law. But conventionalism would have much less appeal in such a society, because it would provide a less attractive account of why law so constituted justified coercion. Some divine-right theory or, in a less theistic community, a statist or goal-directed explanation would seem better. So it is no accident that positivist theories, the semantic counterparts of conventionalism, were first developed and became most popular in democracies. Bentham's account of law, which Austin popularized, seems at first sight a better fit with monarchies or other communities with a readily identifiable "sovereign." But Bentham developed that theory when democratic ideals had begun to be taken for granted, and the initial appeal of the theory, at least, was egalitarian. His theory has always been more popular in Britain and America than anywhere else.

7. One obvious exception is the practice of the Supreme Court deciding constitutional cases in the United States. The people can fundamentally alter the practice of the Court only through a constitutional amendment. This does raise special problems for democratic theory, which are considered in Chapter 10.

8. Only "roughly," because in some cases, for procedural reasons, the person or institution nominally in the position of the defendant is really the "substantial" plaintiff, that is, the person asking the state to intervene. So we should say that unilateralism provides that the substantial defendant must win unless the explicit extension of some legal convention entitles the substantial plaintiff to win. Even in this more careful form, unilateralism offers no recommendation when the distinction between substantial plaintiff and substantial defendant breaks down, as when parties dispute title to property that is not already in the possession of one or the other or that no one could possess if the courts did not

intervene in some way. But such cases are fairly rare; unilateralism would offer a decision in most hard cases.

9. Unilateralism would permit, however, a different kind of decision: that Mr. O'Brian should win the present suit because there is no established rule to the contrary, but that the judge should declare a new rule for the future so that people in Mrs. McLoughlin's position can recover in later cases, since they can then appeal to that new rule as having become part of the explicit extension through his decision. Judges do occasionally decide in this way when they are not simply making a new rule when none existed but overruling a past rule on which the winning party might have relied. This practice, called "prospective" overruling, is discussed further in Chapter 5.

10. See the discussion of the asymmetry of civil and criminal law in *Taking Rights Seriously* 100.

11. See, e.g., *Bowie v. City of Columbia*, 378 U.S. 347 (1964). British courts have been far less solicitous. See *Shaw v. Director of Public Prosecutions* [1962] A.C. 220.

12. Unilateralism would be even more effective in protecting people against unanticipated state intervention if it always assigned the plaintiff the burden of proof on factual issues.

13. Compare G. Postema, "Coordination and Convention at the Foundations of Law," 11 *Journal of Legal Studies* 165 (1982). Compare F. Hayek, *Law, Legislation and Liberty* (2 vols., Chicago, 1973, 1976).

14. See Lewis, supra n. 3.

5. PRAGMATISM AND PERSONIFICATION

1. See Guido Calabresi, *A Common Law for the Age of Statutes* (Cambridge, Mass., 1982).

2. This case for pragmatism appealed to Jonathan Swift. Gulliver reported, "It is a maxim among these lawyers that whatever hath been done before may legally be done again: and therefore they take special care to record all the decisions formerly made against common justice and the general reason of mankind. These, under the name of *precedents*, they produce as authorities to justify the most iniquitous opinions." *Gulliver's Travels* bk. 4, chap. 5 (1726). I owe this reference to William Ewald.

3. I have discussed it at some length, trying to show its connections to the other virtues, in *A Matter of Principle* chap. 3.

4. I call this virtue "procedural" due process to distinguish it from the different idea, which draws on justice as well, that is latent in the "due process" clause of the Fourteenth Amendment to the United States Constitution, as this has been interpreted by the Supreme Court in recent decades. See my "Reagan's Justice," *New York Review of Books,* Nov. 8, 1984.

5. The contrast between fairness and justice is taken up again in Chapter 6.

6. See *Baker v. Carr,* 369 U.S. 186 (1962); *Reynolds v. Sims,* 377 U.S. 533 (1964); *WMCA, Inc. v. Lomenzo,* 377 U.S. 633 (1964); *Maryland Committee for Fair Representation v. Tawes,* 377 U.S. 656 (1964); *Davis v. Mann,* 377 U.S. 678 (1964); *Roman v. Sincock,* 377 U.S. 695 (1964); *Lucas v. Forty-Fourth General Assembly,* 377 U.S. 713 (1964).

7. Compare *Candler v. Crane, Christmas & Co.,* 1951, 1 All E.R. 426, particularly the dissenting opinion of Denning, L. J., with *Hedley Byrne & Co., Ltd. v. Heller & Partners, Ltd* [1964] A.C. 465.

8. See *A Matter of Principle,* chap. 3.

9. See discussion in Chapter 6.

10. See, for useful distinctions within the general topic of group or collective responsibility, Joel Feinberg, *Doing and Deserving* chap. 9 (Princeton, 1970).

11. In Chapter 6 I discuss fraternal obligations, those members of a group have toward one another in virtue of common membership, and I argue that under certain circumstances political communities may be regarded as sponsoring fraternal obligations of that sort. I should therefore make plain that I do not regard the principles of collective responsibility we have been canvassing in this discussion as aspects of fraternal obligation that hold only when the conditions just mentioned are met. I leave open the question of how far they hold, for example, in political communities that are insufficiently egalitarian to count as fraternal associations of the kind discussed in Chapter 6.

12. Thomas Nagel, "Ruthlessness in Public life," in *Mortal Questions* 84 (Cambridge, 1979).

6. INTEGRITY

1. Justice as fairness (though not in this crude, extreme form) is the subject of Rawls's classic *A Theory of Justice* (Cambridge, Mass., 1971). See pages 197–98 and 221–24. See also his "Kantian Constructivism in Moral Theory," 77 *Journal of Philosophy* 515 (1980).

2. Utilitarian theories of democracy take this extreme position. See James Mill, "Essay on Government," in J. Lively and J. Rees, *Utilitarian Logic and Politics* (London, 1978).

3. Later in this chapter and in Chapter 10 I consider further the connection between majority will and fairness. If the nerve of political fairness is equality of political influence, some form of proportional voting provides a fairer electoral structure than simple majority vote, though as I suggest in the text, proportional voting is often not workable. In the next several pages of the text I discuss a special method for securing the kind of proportional influence fairness recommends within the normal majoritarian electoral process, a method I call the checkerboard solution. I argue that since fairness supports checkerboard solutions, we must find some other argument for rejecting them if we think them wrong.

4. See Alexander M. Bickel, *The Supreme Court and the Idea of Progress* 109–17, 151–73 (New Haven and London, 1978).

5. See *Taking Rights Seriously passim,* but particularly chaps. 5 and 7.

6. "Checkerboard" is sometimes used to describe statutes that make distinctions that are not arbitrary in this way, but rather claim a justification of policy best served by the discriminations in question. I mean to use the word only to describe statutes that display incoherence in principle and that can be justified, if at all, only on grounds of a fair allocation of political power between different moral parties.

7. This is in one way too simple a description of the model we follow. We know that principles we accept independently sometimes conflict in the sense that we cannot satisfy both on some particular occasion. We might believe, for example, that people should be free to do what they wish with their own property and also that people should begin life on equal terms. Then the question arises whether rich people should be permitted to leave their wealth to their children, and we might believe that our two prin-

ciples pull in opposite directions on that issue. Our model demands, as we shall see, that the resolution of this conflict itself be principled. A scheme of inheritance taxes might recognize both principles in a certain relation by setting rates of tax that are less than confiscatory. But we insist that whatever relative weighting of the two principles the solution assumes must flow throughout the scheme, and that other decisions, on other matters that involve the same two principles, respect that weighting as well. In any case this kind of conflict is different from the contradiction contained in the checkerboard statutes described in the text. For in these statutes one principle of justice is not outweighed or qualified by another in some way that expresses a ranking of the two. Only a single principle is involved; it is affirmed for one group and denied for another, and this is what our sense of propriety denounces.

8. See note 7. We can easily imagine other examples of compromises we would accept as not being violations of integrity, because they reflect principles of justice we recognize though we do not ourselves endorse them. People who oppose capital punishment in principle will accept a reduction in the list of crimes punished by death, provided those who are executed are morally more culpable or in some other way distinguishable according to standards generally respected in the criminal law; they will accept this much more readily than, for example, a system that allows some criminals convicted of a capital offense to escape death by drawing straws.

9. We cannot explain these constitutional compromises, as we explain the inheritance tax decision described in note 7, by arguing that the compromises give each of two independent and competing principles the proper weight. No second-order argument of principle can justify prohibiting Congress to restrict slavery before but not after a particular year. Madison said that that arrangement was "more dishonorable to the national character than saying nothing about it in the Constitution." (2 *Farrand's Debates* 415-416). I owe this reference to William Nelson. For an example of a Supreme Court decision that seems to offend integrity, see *Maher v. Roe,* 97 S.Ct. 2376, and Laurence Tribe, *American Constitutional Law* 973 n. 77 (Mineola, N.Y., 1978).

10. See generally Tribe, supra n. 9, secs. 16-6–16-7. William Nelson, in *The Fourteenth Amendment: From Political Principle to Judicial Doctrine* chaps. 8 and 9 (forthcoming), explores the commit-

ment to integrity of the framers of the Fourteenth Amendment.

11. *Roe v. Wade,* 410 U.S. 113.

12. See United States Supreme Court, *Thornburgh v. American College of Obstetricians,* Brief for the United States as Amicus Curiae, July 1985.

13. The word is unfortunate because it is etymologically masculine. I mean sorority as well, or the idea common to these latinate terms.

14. I am grateful to Jeremy Waldron for calling Kant and Rousseau to my attention in this connection.

15. See the discussion of legal rights in negligence and nuisance in Chapter 8.

16. See Rawls, *Theory of Justice* at 11-22, 118-92.

17. Id. at 333-62. See also his "Kantian Constructivism" at 569.

18. Though this name for the argument is in wide use, Rawls (and Nozick and others following them) call it the argument from the principle of fairness. I do not use the latter name because I use "fairness" in the different way described in Chapter 5 and this chapter.

19. This is an adaptation of Robert Nozick's argument against the fair play principle as the basis of political authority. See his *Anarchy, State and Utopia* 93-95 (New York, 1974).

20. Family shows that different fraternal relations are matters of choice not only to different degrees but also in different senses of choice. It also shows that fraternal reasons can be differently mixed with other sorts of reasons for recognizing various forms of obligation. Parents choose to have children but do not, in the present state of technology at least, choose the children they have. Children do not choose their parents but often have grounds for obligations to them they do not have to siblings, whom they do not choose any more than they do parents. It is therefore interesting that the class of obligations we are considering is named after the bond between siblings taken as a paradigm for the class.

21. Can we solve this puzzle about fixing the right level of concreteness for the demands of reciprocity by separating the question of when people are members of a fraternal community from the question of what each then owes others within that community? If so, it would be one question when someone is my friend, and another how I must treat him in virtue of our friendship. If this separation were sensible, we might answer the latter question

by insisting that I owe him nothing more than he thinks he owes me. But that is an incoherent solution, among its other difficulties, because he would not know what he owes me until I had decided what I owe him, and I began by not knowing this.

22. I owe this example to Donald Davidson.

23. Large questions about justice, including questions about how far justice extends beyond human beings to at least some other animals, are raised by this hasty observation, which I do not pursue.

24. I ignore the special problem of Northern Ireland here.

25. See the discussion of personification in Chapter 5.

26. This kind of concern is sometimes called "altruism." See Duncan Kennedy, "Form and Substance in Private Law Adjudication," 89 *Harvard Law Review* 1685 (1976).

27. It is not so obvious that it did. See Robert M. Cover, *Justice Accused: Antislavery and the Judicial Process* (New Haven, 1975), and my review of it in the *Times Literary Supplement*, Dec. 5, 1975.

28. *Saif Ali v. Sydney Mitchell & Co.* [1980] A.C. 198.

29. But see the discussion of the enforcement of *Brown* in Chapter 10.

30. I have elsewhere attempted to describe and defend the distinction between principle and policy; see *Taking Rights Seriously* chap. 4 and Appendix; *Ronald Dworkin and Contemporary Jurisprudence*, 263-68 (Marshall Cohen ed., New York and London, 1984). The distinction is frequently employed in *A Matter of Principle*.

31. This point is elaborated in Chapter 8.

32. This was, perhaps, the underlying issue, not made plain in the opinions, in *Gouriet v. The Union of Post Office Workers* [1977] 1 All E.R. 696 (Court of Appeal), 1978 A.C. 435 (House of Lords).

7. INTEGRITY IN LAW

1. Perhaps this is an impossible assignment; perhaps the project is doomed to produce not just an impossibly bad novel but no novel at all, because the best theory of art requires a single creator or, if more than one, that each must have some control over the whole. (But what about legends and jokes? What about the Old Testament, or, on some theories, the *Iliad?*) I need not push that question further, because I am interested only in the fact that the assignment makes sense, that each of the novelists in the chain can

have some grasp of what he is asked to do, whatever misgivings he might have about the value or character of what will then be produced.

2. See the debate cited in Chapter 2, n. 16.

3. See *A Matter of Principle* chap. 7.

4. Hercules played an important part in *Taking Rights Seriously* chap. 4.

5. See the discussion of critical legal studies later in this chapter.

6. The disagreement between Lords Edmund Davies and Scarman in *McLoughlin,* described in Chapter 1, was perhaps over just this claim. Edmund Davies's suggestions, about the arguments that might justify a distinction between compensable and noncompensable emotional injury, seemed to appeal to arguments of policy Scarman refused to acknowledge as appropriate.

7. See *Taking Rights Seriously,* chap. 4.

8. See *Thomas v. Winchester,* 6 N.Y. 397, and *MacPherson v. Buick Motor Co.,* 217 N.Y. 382, 111 N.E. 1050.

9. C. Haar and D. Fessler, *The Wrong Side of the Tracks* (New York, 1986), is a recent example of integrity working on a large canvas.

10. See, for example, Benjamin Cardozo's decision in *Hynes v. New York Central R.R. Co.,* 231 N.Y. 229.

11. These various arguments why a successful interpretation must achieve some fit with past judicial opinions as well as with the decisions themselves are discussed in Chapter 9 in the context of past legislative statements.

12. I have in mind the distinction and the special sense of fairness described in Chapter 6.

13. But see the discussion of "passivism" as a theory of constitutional adjudication in Chapter 10.

14. See the discussion of different levels of integrity in Chapter 11.

15. The disagreement between Lords Diplock and Edmund Davies, on the one hand, and Lord Dilthorne on the other, in the notorious blasphemy case *R. v. Lemon* [1979] 1 All ER 898, illustrates the importance of not ignoring this connection between changes in popular morality and the boundaries of local priority. The former insisted that the law of blasphemy be interpreted to reflect developments in other parts of criminal law; the latter that

blasphemy, for some unexplained reason, be counted an isolated domain of its own.

16. See D. Kennedy and K. Klare, "A Bibliography of Critical Legal Studies," 94 *Yale Law Journal* 461 (1984).

17. See the symposium on critical legal studies in 36 *Stanford Law Review* 1 (1984).

18. Excellent examples of historical writing in this mode include Robert Gordon, "Historicism in Legal Scholarship," 90 *Yale Law Journal* 1017 (1981), and "Critical Legal Histories," 36 *Stanford Law Review* 57 (1984). See also the historical work cited in Kennedy and Klare, supra n. 16.

19. Mark Tushnet's recent description of liberalism is representative of every account of that political theory I have seen in the literature of critical legal studies. He admits that "any summary description of the classical liberal view—the liberalism of Hobbes, Locke, and Mill and that of Dworkin and Rawls—must be a caricature." But he then offers this description, which is more a forgery. "Liberalism's psychology posits a world of autonomous individuals, each guided by his or her idiosyncratic values and goals, none of which can be adjudged more or less legitimate than those held by others. In such a world, people exist as isolated islands of individuality who choose to enter into relations that can metaphorically be characterized as foreign affairs . . . In a world of liberal individualism . . . if one person's values impel that person, for example, to seize the property of another, the victim cannot appeal to some supervening principle to which the assailant must be committed." (See Tushnet, "Following the Rules Laid Down: A Critique of Interpretivism and Neutral Principles," 96 *Harvard Law Review* 781, 783 ff., [1983].) There are several important mistakes here. First, most of Tushnet's liberals explicitly recognize that people are normally interested in one another's fates. None of their arguments depends on the preposterous assumption that people cannot share values enough to sustain a common language and other social institutions, and John Rawls, for example, has been careful to deny that assumption. See his "Kantian Constructivism in Moral Theory," 77 *Journal of Philosophy* 515 (1980), and his "Justice as Fairness: Political Not Metaphysical," 14 *Philosophy and Public Affairs* 223 (1985). (Some readers of Rawls's *A Theory of Justice* [Cambridge, Mass., 1977] make the mistake of thinking that the mutually disinterested members of the "original position" he con-

structed as an analytical device were meant to express his theory of human nature. That misreading was not encouraged by the text and is disowned in the later articles just cited.) Second, none of these "liberals" except Hobbes (why should Hobbes be counted a liberal?) adopted any form of skepticism about the possibility that one way of leading one's life can be better or more valuable than another. Mill, for example, notoriously rejected skepticism about personal values. The critical legal studies picture of liberalism confuses that form of skepticism, which most liberals reject, with the entirely different principle they accept, that claims about the relative value of personal goals do not provide competent justifications for regulative political decisions. Third, this picture of liberalism confuses *that* principle, about the neutrality of government toward conceptions of the good, with an alleged neutrality about principles of justice, which of course liberalism, because it is a theory of justice, must reject. It is absurd to say that a liberal cannot appeal to a principle of justice to explain why those whose "values" impel them to assault others should be restrained from doing so. Tushnet should not have made these mistakes about what his "classical liberals" think. He cites an article of mine as authority for his view about what I, together with his other liberals, believe. In that article I argue that the constitutive morality of liberalism "is a theory of equality that requires official neutrality amongst theories of what is valuable in life. That argument will provoke a variety of objections. It might be said that liberalism so conceived rests on skepticism about theories of the good, or that it is based on a mean view of human nature that assumes that human beings are atoms who can exist and find self-fulfillment apart from political community ... [But] liberalism cannot be based on skepticism. Its constitutive morality provides that human beings must be treated as equals by their government, not because there is no right and wrong in political morality, but because that is what is right. Liberalism does not rest on any special theory of personality, nor does it deny that most human beings will think that what is good for them is that they be active in society. Liberalism is not self-contradictory: the liberal conception of equality is a principle of political organization that is required by justice, not a way of life for individuals." See *A Matter of Principle* at 203.

20. "There are two principles competing for attention [in the

law of compensation for accidents]. The currently favored principle is admittedly individualistic. A tortfeasor's liability must be limited so as to provide some rough correlation between the degree of fault and the extent of responsibility. Accordingly, flowing from the central notion of fault, a defendant is only liable for damage that is reasonably foreseeable ... However, an exclusive reliance on such a principle might deprive entirely innocent and worthy victims of compensation. Consequently there is a competing, less dominant, but established counter-principle. This stipulates that tortfeasors are liable for any direct consequences of their actions, notwithstanding that they might not be reasonably foreseeable. Although this principle flourished and dominated for a time, it presently enjoys a more limited range of application in cases where victims, such as hemophiliacs, are particularly susceptible to injury: 'a tortfeasor must take his victim as he finds him' ... Each principle is drawn from and is empowered by two entirely different visions of a just democratic society. One rests on an individualism which represents a world consisting of independent and self-sufficient persons, confidently drawing up and robustly pursuing their own life plans. Values and tastes are relative and subjective ... The other vision flows from a collectivism that views the world as made up of interdependent and cooperating persons. Recognizing the vulnerability of individuals, it encourages greater solidarity and altruism ... Each vision represents only a partial and incomplete depiction of social life and its possibilities ... Whichever principle [anyone] opts for is simply his preference ... [he] has nothing to say by way of persuasion to anyone who disagrees with him." Allan Hutchinson, "Of Kings and Dirty Rascals: The Struggle for Democracy," 1985 *Queen's Law Journal* 273, 281–83.

Many of the mottoes popular within critical legal studies flourish in this argument. Here, for example, is the same mistaken characterization of liberal "individualism" as connected to social atomism and to the subjectivity of "values" that we noticed in note 19. Here is the familiar confusion of external and internal skepticism, yielding the familiar complaint that liberals are unaware that moral convictions are "simply" preferences, so that people have "nothing to say" to support them. (Never mind that liberals have just been taxed with that form of subjectivism.) Our present interest is in the diagnosis of contradiction: the law of accidents is said to be not only complex, because two different principles are at work, but contradictory because these cannot stand together, even as principles. But that claim rests on a crude mistake in logic: it argues in the wrong direction. It is perhaps true that someone who held the bizarre and barely comprehensible view that people are wholly "independent and self-sufficient" would be drawn to the foreseeability test of liability. (Liberals are meant to hold that bizarre view, and perhaps some liberal could be found who does. But it is hardly the view of Mill or Rawls or any of the other philosophers influential in the liberal tradition.) It is not necessarily true, for he might think that hemophiliacs need their "independent" plans protected as well, and that "robustly" self-sufficient tortfeasors should buy insurance against strict liability and take the consequences if they do not. In any case, however, that is not the issue, which is rather whether *only* someone who held that odd view could be attracted to that test. Why should a more sensible person who realizes that "the world is made up of interdependent and cooperating persons," who thrills to the appeals of "solidarity and altruism," not feel sympathy for the careless driver who has the bad luck to nick a hemophiliac as well as for the hemophiliac himself?

So the confident assignment of the two principles to two contradictory "visions" of society is procrustean and groundless. These principles are inevitable aspects of any decent response to the world's complexity. They differ only in their distribution of the risk of loss between two actors, one of whom must lose because of the acts or situation of the other, and it is implausible to suppose that someone who makes that choice differently in different kinds of circumstances, fixing the loss on the actor in some and on the victim in another, is for that reason morally schizophrenic. The problem for Hercules, faced with the set of decisions this critic describes, is in fact no more daunting than the one he faced in the text a moment ago, and it might well be more pedestrian. He constructs two principles: that people should not be held responsible for causing injury they could not reasonably foresee and that people should not be put at disadvantage, in the level of protection the law gives them, in virtue of physical disabilities beyond their control. He has no difficulty in recognizing both at work in the law of tort and more generally, and no difficulty in accepting both at the level of abstract principle. These principles are sometimes competitive, but they are not contradictory. He asks whether past decisions in cases in which they do conflict have resolved them coherently. Perhaps they have, though whatever account he accepts of that resolution will probably require him to treat some past decisions, those that fall on the wrong side of some line, as mistakes. Perhaps not: perhaps a coherent legal system must treat all cases of this kind of conflict in the same way. Then he must ask, in the way now becoming familiar, whether one of the choices the system might make between the principles is ruled out on grounds of fit; if neither is, he must decide which is superior in personal and political morality, and though others would decide differently, that in itself is no objection to his choice.

21. See the symposium on critical legal studies, supra n. 17.

8. THE COMMON LAW

1. Some lawyers have been tempted by the remarkable claim that this single principle provides all that even Hercules needs to construct a comprehensive interpretation of all parts of the law from constitutional structure to the details of rules of evidence and procedure. See generally Richard A. Posner, *The Economic Analysis of Law* (2nd ed., Boston, 1977). That imperial claim must fail, of course, if the more limited claim we shall consider, that it provides the best interpretation of unintended damage law, fails.

2. See Judge Learned Hand's formulation of this principle in *United States v. Carroll Towing Co.*, 159 F.2d 164, 173 (2d Cir. 1947).

3. See Posner, supra n. 1, at 10–12.

4. See generally Guido Calabresi, *The Cost of Accidents* (New Haven, 1970); Calabresi, "Transaction Costs, Resource Allocation and Liability Rules—A Comment," 11 *Journal of Law and Economics* 67 (1968); Ronald Coase, "The Problem of Social Cost," 3 *Journal of Law and Economics* 1 (1960). See also Guido Calabresi and A. Douglas Melamed, "Property Rules, Liability Rules, and Inalienability: One View of the Cathedral," 85 *Harvard Law Review* 1089 (1972).

5. See Calabresi and Melamed, supra n. 4, at 1089, 1096–97.

6. Notice how this argument provides support, from the eco-

nomic principle, for the "foreseeability" test used in interpretation
(5) and, in a qualified form, (6) in Chapter 7.

7. See, e.g., the debate over the economic consequences of
choosing a negligence or a strict liability basis for liability. Posner,
supra n. 1, at 137-42; Polinsky, "Strict Liability vs. Negligence in
a Market Setting," 70 *American Economic Review: Papers and Proceedings* 363 (1980); S. Shavell, "Strict Liability versus Negligence," 9
Journal of Legal Studies 1 (1980). See, more generally, "Symposium:
Efficiency as a Legal Concern," 8 *Hofstra Law Review* 485-770
(1980).

8. See, e.g., *Union Oil Co. v. Oppen,* 501 F.2d 558 (9th Cir. 1974).

9. For an earlier version of this point, and further argument
about the economic interpretation, see *A Matter of Principle* chaps.
12 and 13.

10. I mean that the argument now described is a form of utilitarian argument, not that any utilitarian argument must take this
form. Some philosophers who count themselves utilitarians insist
that the welfare or well-being they seek to maximize is very far
from being just a matter of happiness. But since it is very implausible that a wealth-maximizing scheme of law would maximize
welfare on some conception more sensitive than happiness to other
components of human flourishing, I consider for the present argument only the historically more familiar form of utilitarianism
that gives happiness a near exclusive role in fixing welfare.

11. See, e.g., R. M. Hare, *Moral Thinking: Its Levels, Methods, and
Point* (London, 1981).

12. See my "In Defense of Equality," 1 *Social Philosophy and Policy* 24 (1983).

13. See my "What Is Equality? Part 1: Equality of Welfare," 10
Philosophy and Public Affairs 185 (1981) and "Part 2: Equality of
Resources," 10 *Philosophy and Public Affairs* 283 (1981).

14. Robert Nozick saw that equality on some conceptions
would inevitably be corrupted by market transactions of almost
any sort—that is the force of his famous Wilt Chamberlin example
(see his *Anarchy, State, and Utopia* 160-64 [New York, 1974]). He
had material equality in mind, however, and it would be wrong to
suppose, I argue in the text, that every conception of equality
other than the libertarian conception would have that consequence.

15. I am mainly ignoring an important issue, which is whether and when we, as individuals, are entitled to take a generally permissive attitude toward the use we make of our own property when we believe that the public scheme is not defensible on any plausible conception of equality. Various arguments might be proposed to justify a permissive attitude even under these circumstances. Perhaps, for example, the division of responsibility discussed in the text is the best strategy for achieving a decent level of equality, under an appropriate conception, even when equality has not yet been achieved even imperfectly. Or perhaps any other strategy, which imposes more stringent moral responsibilities on individuals one by one, would lead to "victimization," that is, to moral responsibilities such that any individual who accepted these would be obligated to assume an economic position worse than the one he would occupy under a genuinely egalitarian scheme. Or perhaps most of the decisions individuals make about their property, one by one, have such diverse and unpredictable consequences that no one could sensibly undertake to make his own private decisions in such a way as to improve equality overall. See my "What Is Equality? Part 2," supra n. 13.

16. Tentative arguments for it are found in "In Defense of Equality."

17. See "What Is Equality? Part 2."

18. The qualification discussed here is sensitive to an issue I left open earlier in discussing what I called the first problem in the permissive hypothesis (see n. 15). What justifies our acting, as individuals day by day, as if the distribution of property in place has actually achieved equality of resources between us? I am now supposing that our answer in some way relies on judgments of strategy, or appeals to lack of information, in such a way that the permission does not hold in special circumstances, when someone knows that his behavior will have an immediate and predictable impact on equality of resources, that one decision he can make will improve equality without victimizing him and another will make an inequality in resources even worse.

19. See "What Is Equality? Part 2," and *A Matter of Principle* chap 17.

9. STATUTES

1. Since the political decision Hercules is now interpreting is a statute rather than a series of past judicial decisions, matters of policy are pertinent to his decision which rights the statute should be deemed to have created.

2. Nor would he find answers independent of his own convictions by looking to see what his fellow judges do, because practice differs among them. He would need to interpret their practice in the way described in the last two chapters and make essentially the same judgments about political fairness in deciding which interpretation showed judicial practice better on the whole.

3. Compare the "intention-vote" theory developed by P. Brest in "The Misconceived Quest for the Original Understanding," 60 *Boston University Law Review* 204, 212-15 (1980).

4. Of course, if there were an established and settled rule about how statutes like the Endangered Species Act were to be interpreted, a rule dictating, for example, that judges must read the statute "narrowly" to give the secretary as little power as possible, then congressmen would of course use that rule to predict what would happen to their statutes in court. If Hermes deferred to the rule, he would be doing what legislators expected but not because they expected it. The rule, that is, would explain both how Hermes decided and what judges predicted, but it would explain these independently of one another. There is no such rule, however, and Hermes is therefore interested in legislative predictions not just as matching his decision but as the ground of it. That is the option I argue would be self-defeating.

5. For an excellent account of the difficulties in determining the truth or falsity of counterfactual statements, see Nelson Goodman, "The Problem of Counterfactual Conditionals," in *Fact, Fiction and Forecast* 1-27 (4th ed., Cambridge, Mass., 1983).

6. For a discussion of opaque contexts, see W. V. O. Quine, *Word and Object,* 140-56 (Cambridge, Mass., 1960).

7. Integrity in this form might lead him to reject an interpretation that would be closer to the concrete intentions of the draftsman. See Lord Denning's dissenting opinion in *Macarthys Ltd. v. Smith* [1979] 3 All ER 325, 330. I owe this example to Sheldon Leader.

8. Though integrity, by definition, is a matter of principle,

Hercules must prefer an account of any single statute that also shows a high order of consistency in policy, for his justification does not otherwise show the legislative event in a good light. A single legislature, enacting a single statute, acts incoherently if it assigns great importance to a particular policy and so imposes severe costs and burdens in order to advance it, but yet qualifies the policy to avoid what are plainly less important costs and burdens with no corresponding gains to any other policy. *A fortiori*, of course, Hercules must respect integrity in principle. He must labor to avoid anything like a checkerboard justification that combines contradictory principles to explain different parts of the same statute. He must avoid this, if he can do so consistently with the text, even when he suspects that the statute's text was, as a matter of historical fact, a lapse in integrity, a compromise of just the sort he must try to ignore in the statute he constructs. His critics will then say he is "papering over" historical controversy. That comment, although true, is no basis for criticism; to say that the historical compromise over text compromised the real statute the text created begs the question we have been discussing throughout the chapter.

9. In the case of the United States Congress, I am assuming that the committee reports of the two chambers are not contradictory. If they are, then they must be treated as an argument about the best interpretation of the statute enacted by both chambers rather than a political decision of Congress as a whole in the sense described in the text.

10. See J. L. Austin, "Performative Utterances," in *Philosophical Papers* 223 (3rd ed., New York, 1979) and *How to Do Things with Words* (Cambridge, Mass., 1962).

11. A crucial piece of labor legislation in Britain, the Employment Protection Consolidation Act of 1978, has been repeatedly amended by both Conservative and Labour governments since its enactment. More contemporary statements of legislative purpose are better guides to even the sections of the act that were not then amended than earlier statements directly pertinent to those sections. I owe this example to Sheldon Leader.

12. The text's explanation of controversy about whether a particular phrase is "unclear" is illustrated by the controversy over the precision of the Civil Rights Act in *United Steelworkers of America v. Weber*, 443 U.S. 193 (discussed in *A Matter of Principle*

chap. 16, and the controversy over the words "restraint or coercion" in *NLRB v. Allis-Chalmers Manufacturing Co.*, 338 U.S. 175 (1967). Justice Black thought the literal meaning of these words clear, while Brennan thought them "inherently imprecise." See id. at 179.

13. See Allan Hutchison and John Wakefield, "A Hard Look at Hard Cases," 2 *Oxford Journal of Legal Studies* 86 (1982).

14. A simple chess computer program scans every legal move before it moves any piece. It draws no distinction between easy and hard cases. If the queen is *en pris,* and only one move will save her, it will nevertheless solemnly consider and reject each of the moves that lead to the queen's loss. Unlike the simple computer, I myself act differently when I think the case is an easy one. I do not consider the consequences of each move that leads to the capture of the queen; I just move her out of harm's way. This does not show that I use an antecedent distinction between easy and hard cases as a switchpoint and apply a different theory of what makes a chess move a good one in easy cases. Better players have an instinct that may alert them, in some case I treat as easy, to the possibility of a brilliant queen gambit. So they might consider, at least briefly, some moves I would not. Good players and I draw the distinction between hard and easy cases differently, not because we use different theories about what makes a move a good one, but because we have different skill in applying the single theory we share.

10. THE CONSTITUTION

1. *Marbury v. Madison,* 5 U.S. (1 Cranch) 137 (1803).

2. I offer no argument for this flat claim; a further book would be necessary to do so. It would have to take into account, among other things, that the Supreme Court's record has been spotty, that the institutions I call "majoritarian" have not always—some would say never—represented either the opinions or the interests of the majority of citizens, and that the Court has sometimes exercised the power Marshall declared to make these institutions more majoritarian than they would otherwise have been.

3. Justice John Paul Stevens recently criticized certain fellow justices as inconsistent. They are, he said, widely regarded as conservative and yet have been radically revising whole areas of

constitutional law, not just deciding each case as it arises on grounds no wider than are necessary to decide that case. See *New York Times*, Aug. 5, 1984, at A1, col. 1.

4. Compare *Roth v. United States*, 354 U.S. 476, 494–96 (1957) (Warren, C. J., concurring) (obscene materials not protected by the First Amendment) and *Jacobellis v. Ohio*, 378 U.S. 184, 199–203 (1964) (Warren, C. J., dissenting) (referring to the "right of the Nation and the States to maintain a decent society") with *Griffin v. Illinois*, 351 U.S. 12 (1956) (indigent criminal defendants may not constitutionally be required to pay for a trial transcript before obtaining appellate review), *Douglas v. California*, 372 U.S. 353 (1963) (state must provide indigent criminal defendants with counsel for appeal as of right), and *Harper v. Virginia Board of Elections*, 383 U.S. 663 (1966) (conditioning the right to vote on payment of poll tax is unconstitutional).

5. See John Hart Ely, *Democracy and Distrust: A Theory of Judicial Review* (Cambridge, Mass., 1980); M. Perry, *The Constitution, the Courts, and Human Rights: An Inquiry into the Legitimacy of Constitutional Policymaking by the Judiciary* (New Haven, 1982); R. Bork, "Neutral Principles and Some First Amendment Problems," 47 *Indiana Law Journal* 1 (1971); Thomas Grey, "Do We Have an Unwritten Constitution?" 27 *Stanford Law Review* 703 (1975).

6. Quoted in Raoul Berger, *Government by Judiciary* 118–19 (Cambridge, Mass., 1977).

7. See H. Jefferson Powell, "The Original Understanding of Original Intent," 98 *Harvard Law Review* 885 (1985).

8. I explored this distinction, between an opaque and a transparent reading of abstract constitutional provisions, in *Taking Rights Seriously* 134 ff. I compared constitutional interpretation to the problem faced by a son whose father instructed him to be fair. I said his father charged him with the *concept* of fairness, not with the particular *conception* of fairness the father happened to hold at the time he gave the instruction. See also Dworkin, *A Matter of Principle* chap. 2.

9. We have evidence they did not have this meta-intention. See Powell, supra n. 7.

10. I do not mean that historicism, on this account, is itself a conventionalist account of constitutional law. It cannot be, because we have no convention whose explicit extension includes the

proposition that the framers' concrete intentions fix constitutional law.

11. Since this argument begins in the assumption that we are committed to democracy and that our elections are democratic enough to require deference to legislative decisions, it is especially weak when the Court is asked to decide what the Constitution counts as democracy. (See Ely, supra n. 5.) A passivist therefore needs a further distinction: he needs to distinguish those constitutional provisions that protect the fairness of the political process from those meant to guarantee the justice of its results. If he believes that the right of free speech or the rights guaranteeing treatment as equals to minority groups, for example, are best interpreted as protecting the fairness of American democracy, then he has no reason to defer to the judgment of elected officials about when these rights have been violated. This qualification does not jeopardize the passive approach generally, because it does not apply to rights that are not properly understood that way, like alleged rights to an abortion or against the death penalty. A passive justice who thinks that these putative rights sound in justice rather than fairness will let elected officials decide whether the Constitution embraces them.

12. See R. Bork, "Neutral Principles and Some First Amendment Problems," 47 *Indiana Law Journal* 1, 10 (1971).

13. *Scott v. Sandford*, 60 U.S. (19 How.) 393 (1856).

14. *Lochner v. New York*, 198 U.S. 45 (1905).

15. See Ely, supra n. 5.

16. In *Korematsu*, 323 U.S. 214 (1944), the Court refused to protect Japanese Americans against unjustified internment at the beginning of World War II.

17. 163 U.S. 537 (1896).

18. See *McLaurin v. Oklahoma State Regents*, 339 U.S. 637 (1950); *Sweatt v. Painter*, 339 U.S. 629 (1950); *Sipnel v. Board of Regents*, 332 U.S. 631 (per curiam); *Missouri ex rel. Gaines v. Canada*, 305 U.S. 337 (1938).

19. For a more extended discussion of this distinction, see *A Matter of Principle* chap. 3.

20. *Brown v. Board of Education*, 349 U.S. 294 (1955).

21. See *Keyes v. School District No. 1, Denver, Colorado*, 413 U.S. 189 (1973); *Milliken v. Bradley*, 418 U.S. 717 (1974); *Milliken v.*

Bradley, 433 U.S. 267 (1977); *Dayton Board of Education v. Brinkman,* 433 U.S. 406 (1977); *Columbus Board of Education v. Penick,* 443 U.S. 449 (1979); *Dayton Board of Education v. Brinkman,* 443 U.S. 526 (1979).

22. See, e.g., Chayes, "The Role of the Judge in Public Law Litigation," 89 *Harvard Law Review* 1281 (1976); Fiss, "Foreword: The Forms of Justice," 93 *Harvard Law Review* 1 (1979).

23. *Regents of the University of California v. Bakke,* 438 U.S. 265 (1978).

24. It did not do so in the Civil Rights Act of 1964. See *A Matter of Principle* chap. 16.

25. Id. at chap. 14.

26. Id. at chap. 15.

27. See Justice Powell's opinion in *Bakke,* 438 U.S. 215.

28. See my "Reagan's Justice," *New York Review of Books,* Nov. 8, 1984, and "Law's Ambitions for Itself," 71 *University of Virginia Law Review* 73 (1985).

29. He will not substitute his judgment, that is, on constitutional grounds when his techniques of statutory construction have yielded a conclusion about what the statute properly interpreted says. His convictions about policy will, however, have a role in this latter decision, for the reasons and in the way described in Chapter 9.

30. *Lochner v. New York,* supra n. 14. The opinion in that case treats the issue as one of principle, about whether bakers and their employers have a right to contract for longer hours if they wish. Hercules would have replied that the particular interpretation of the principle of freedom of contract this asumes cannot be justified in any sound interpretation of the Constitution.

11. LAW BEYOND LAW

1. This feature of legal practice is the source of linguistic complexity. In some circumstances any accurate judgment about what the law is must in some way be indexed to refer to the level of court in which the issue is assumed to arise. Suppose a lawyer thinks that the highest court of some jurisdiction has a duty, flowing from law as integrity, to overrule a precedent and so find for the plaintiff, but that a lower court, bound by a strict doctrine

of precedent, has a duty to enforce that precedent and so decide for the defendant. He might say (this is one way to put the point) that the law for the higher court is different from the law for the lower. Or he might say (this is another) that since the highest court has the last word, the law is "really" for the plaintiff, though she must appeal to have that law recognized and enforced. The vocabulary of law, here as in the case of the wicked legal systems in Chapter 3, is flexible enough to allow us to describe the same complex structure of legal relations—rights and duties enforceable in specified circumstances—in different ways depending on audience, context, and purpose.

2. I neglect to repeat the major lesson of Chapter 9, that substantive integrity will play a great role in Hercules' decision how to read vague or ambiguous or otherwise troublesome language in this statute. I am assuming, here, that the text and context and legislative history are sufficiently crisp so that even Hercules' style of reading statutes yields the inconsistency with the rest of the law I assume in the text.

3. *Saif Ali,* cited in Chapter 6, n. 28, may prove to be an early warning of that sort. If Hercules believes integrity requires recognizing the procedural constraint in the case in which he lays down the warning, he thinks the law is for the barrister then. But once the warning has been given, that constraint is removed, so the law will not be for the barrister in a later case.

INDEX

Abortion issue, and political integrity, 178, 185, 186

Accident law. *See* Law of unintended injury

Acontextual meaning (interpretation), 17, 23, 89, 346–347, 353

Activism in constitutional interpretation: vs. passivism, 369; vs. law as integrity, 378; and Hercules, 398

Adjudication: practical politics of, 12; and inclusive integrity, 410. *See also* Judges

Adjudicative principle of integrity, 167, 176, 218–219, 337. *See also* Integrity, political

Affirmative action, 393; and antidiscrimination theories, 386–387; and *Bakke* case, 393–397

Alpers, Svetlana, 419n35

Ambiguity, and statutory interpretation, 350–353

Apportioning of costs, principle of, 269

Art, and author's intention, 55–65

Artistic interpretation, 50, 51, 53, 54, 55–58, 59–62

As-if rights, in legal pragmatism, 152–153, 154–155, 158, 161, 162

Associative (communal) obligations, 195–202; role obligations as, 195–196; conditions of, 199–201; vs. justice, 202–206; legitimacy through, 206–208; and de facto community, 209, 211–212; and rulebook community, 210, 212–213;

and community of principle, 211, 213–214, 216 (*see also* Community of principle)

Austin, J. L., 448n10

Austin, John, 32, 33–34, 109, 431n2

Authority, law as, 429n3

Automobile manufacturer, in institutional responsibility example, 169–171

Automobiles, as intention example, 100

Bakke case, 393–397

Banned categories, 383–384, 385, 386–387, 388, 394

Banned sources, 384, 385–386, 388, 394

Barrister immunity, as integrity example, 219–220, 401, 402

Bentham, Jeremy: on rights, 374–375; and legal positivism, 432n6

Berger, R., 450n6

Bickel, Alexander M., 435n4

Borderline defense, in positivists' view, 39–43

Bork, R., 450n5, 451n12

Brest, Paul, 447n3

Brown case, 29–30; as social revolution, 2, 391, 393; remedy in, 30, 389–392; and legal positivism, 37; and conventionalism, 119, 131; and integrity vs. pragmatism, 220–221; and popular morality, 250; and Fourteenth Amendment, 355; and historicism, 366; and passivism, 373–374; Hercules' interpretation of, 379–392, 399;

and banned sources theory, 384. *See also* Fourteenth Amendment

Burger, Warren, 21–22, 23, 38

Busing, school, 221, 392

Calabresi, G., 433n1, 444nn4, 5

Cardozo, Benjamin, 417n7

Cases. *See* Hard cases; Like cases; Pivotal cases

Causation, example of concept of, 32, 428n27

Cavell, Stanley, 56–57, 60

Certainty, value of, 367–368

Chain of law: and chain novel, 228–232; and character of Scrooge, 232–237; and respecting text, 238; fit/justification interplay in, 239; statutory interpretation in, 313. *See also* Rope analogy

Chayes, A., 452n22

Checkerboard laws: as political compromise, 178–184, 186; and personification of state, 187; and integrity, 217–218

Choice: communal obligation from, 197–198, 201; in political communities, 207; and public responsibility, 298–299

Christmas Carol, A, as chain novel, 232–237

Civil disobedience, and force of law, 112–113

Civil law, and unilateralism, 143

Civil suits, importance of, 1. *See also* Lawsuits

Clarity of language, and statutory interpretation, 350–353

Coherence of law, and Elmer's case, 19–20. *See also* Integrity, law as

Coleman, Jules, 431n4

Collective consciousness, 64, 422n15

Collective sympathy, principle of, 269

Command theory of law, 33–34. *See also* Positivism, legal

Common law: chain of, 238–239; conflict of rights in, 312. *See also* Emotional damages; Law of unintended injury; Precedent

Communal obligations. *See* Associative obligations

Community: and interpretive attitude, 46–47, 49; personification of, 64–65, 167–175, 186–187, 225, 296; and law as integrity, 96; in political integrity, 188–190; "bare" vs. "true," 201–202, 203–204, 207–208; political society as, 208–209; de facto model of, 209, 211–212; rule-book model of, 209–210, 212–213, 345; and love, 215; wealth of, 277 (*see also* Wealth test); pure interpretation of law directed to, 407; and attitude of law, 413

Community of principle, 211, 213–214; and legitimacy, 214–215, 216; in law as integrity, 243, 244; and integrity, 263, 404, 411; and private responsibility, 300, 309; and legislators' convictions, 328–329, 330, 336; and legislative history, 345–346; and justice, 406

Comparative cost, and equality, 301–309

Compartmentalization of law, 251–254

Compromise: *Brown* remedy as, 30; among political virtues, 176–178; and "checkerboard" laws, 178–184, 435n7; internal vs. external, 179; conventionalist acceptance of, 210; vs. comparative harm principle, 303; in legislators' intents, 323

Concept-conception distinction, 71–72; for justice, 74

Conceptions of law, 94–96; issues for, 99–101; and wicked law, 102–104, 108; on grounds and force of law, 109, 112; and legal practice, 139; and legitimacy, 190–191. *See also* Conventionalism; Integrity, law as; Pragmatism, legal

Concept of law, 92–94, 108–109; and force of law, 109–110, 190

Concept of Law, The (Hart), 34

Conflict: among political virtues, 176–178, 188; of abstract rights, 293, 296, 301, 306, 310, 312; of convictions, 330–333, 334

Consensus: in preinterpretive stage, 66; vs. convention, 135–139
Consent, legitimacy through, 192–193
Consequentialism. *See* Economic theory on unintended damage; Policy; Utilitarianism
Conservatism: of justices, 357–359; and Hercules, 398–399
Consistency: and political integrity, 219–224; and law as integrity, 227, 228
Consistency with past: and conventionalism, 130, 131, 132–135, 147; and legal pragmatism, 151, 159–160, 162, 163; and political integrity, 167, 219; and law as integrity, 227
Constitution, U.S.: and legal canon, 91; and conventionalist view, 115, 138; slavery provisions of, 184; and popular morality, 250; constraints in, 355; and role of Supreme Court, 355–356, 357; unrepresentative framers of, 364; as statute, 379; rationality requirement in, 382, 383, 397. *See also* Supreme Court
Constitutional adjudication. *See* Interpretation of Constitution
Constructive claims in law, 228
Constructive interpretation, 52–53, 54, 56, 61, 62, 65, 423n15; legal theory as, 90; vs. speaker's meaning view, 315, 336. *See also* Interpretation
Context sensitivity: of legal language, 104–105; and semantic theories, 108
Contradiction: and skeptical view of integrity, 268–269, 271, 272, 273–274; in liberalism, 274, 441n20
Convention: in Hart's theory, 34–35; vs. consensus, 135–139; coordination through, 144–146. *See also* Rules
Conventionalism, 94–95, 114–117, 410; and legal rights, 95, 152; popular view behind, 114, 115, 116, 118, 120; and positivist semantic theories, 115–116; as appeal to protected expectations, 117–120,

139–140; and legal conventions, 120–124; strict vs. soft, 124–130; and consistency with past, 130, 131, 132–135, 147; and attention to statutes or precedent, 130–132, 135; and law as integrity, 134–135, 225, 226, 261, 410, 411; and convention-consensus distinction, 135–139, 145; vs. development of law, 137–138, 157, 409; and democracy, 140, 432n6; fairness of, 140–142; as reducing surprise, 141–144; unilateral, 142–143, 146, 147, 365–366; and coordination, 144–147, 149–150, 156; and legal pragmatism, 147–150, 157, 161, 162, 264; and formal equality, 185; and rule-book model of community, 210, 212–213; and compartmentalization, 251; and easy cases, 265–266; and stability argument, 365; and passivism, 371; and rule of recognition, 431n2; and habit of obedience, 431n2
Conversational interpretation, 50, 51, 52, 53–55, 64–65, 315
Convictions: in legislative intent, 324, 327–337, 361; in constitutional interpretation, 361–362
Coordination: through conventions, 144–146; and pragmatist view, 148, 149; through retrospective rulemaking, 156–157; and legal pragmatism, 158–159
Corporations, in institutional responsibility example, 169–171
Counterfactual mental states, 325–327, 328
Courtesy: interpretive attitude toward, 47–49; constructive interpretation of, 52; intentions in 58, 59; and stages of interpretation, 66; philosophical account of, 68–73; and skepticism, 79, 81–82; as convention, 122; and judge's function, 228; vs. justice, 424n20
Cover, Robert, 438n27
Creative interpretation, 50, 51–52, 53–54, 56, 58, 62, 65, 228

Criminal cases, and importance of law, 1. *See also* Cases

Criminal law, unilateralism in, 143

Criminal process, consistency and integrity in, 224. *See also* Procedural due process

Critical legal studies, 271–274; and liberalism, 274–275, 440n19, 441n20

Davidson, Donald, 438n22

Democracy: and protected expectations, 140; and legislators' intent, 364; and constitutional passivism, 370–371, 372; and Hercules' approach, 398, 399; and legal positivism, 432n6

Dilthey, Wilhelm, 419n2

Disagreement: dilemma on, 43–44, 45–46; interpretive conception of, 46–47, 86 (*see also* Interpretation); subjective vs. objective, 76–77, 79–80, 82–83 (*see also* Skepticism); on grounds and force of law, 111, 112–113; over legal conventions, 122. *See also* Empirical disagreement; Theoretical disagreement in law

"Discovering" law, vs. theoretical disagreement, 5–6

Discrimination. *See* Racial discrimination

Distinctions: external vs. internal perspective on law, 13–14; strict vs. relaxed doctrine of precedent, 24–26; standard vs. borderline uses of "law," 39; borderline cases vs. pivotal cases, 41–42 (*see also* Easy-case problem); interpreting practice vs. acts or thoughts of participants, 63–64; meaning vs. extension, 71; concept vs. conception, 71–72; justification vs. content of rights, 106–107; weak rights vs. no rights (in wicked system), 107–108; grounds vs. force of law, 109–110, 356; explicit vs. implicit extension of convention, 123; strict vs. soft conventionalism, 124; convention vs. consensus (agreement

in conviction), 136, 145–146; arguments about vs. within rules, 137–138; paradigms vs. conventions, 138–139; "bare" vs. "true" community, 201; competition vs. contradiction in principle, 268–269; academic vs. practical elaboration of moral theory, 285–286; rights vs. collective strategies, 293, 381–382; use vs. assignment of property, 300; clear vs. unclear language, 351; inclusive vs. pure integrity, 405–406

Distinguishing of precedents, in *McLoughlin* case, 26, 27, 28

Dred Scott case, and passivism, 374

Due process. *See* Procedural due process

Duty: to obey law, 112–113; to be just, 193; to maximize wealth, 286–288. *See also* Political obligation

Earl (Judge), 18–20, 22, 36, 38, 40, 43, 130

Easy-case problem, 353, 449n14

Economic approach to law, 272

Economic theory on unintended damage, 276–280; and reasonable-person rule, 280–282; and contributory negligence, 282–283; fit of, 283–285; and wealth maximization, 286–288; and utilitarianism, 288–295

Egalitarian principle: and integrity, 222; and government, 296; and racial equality, 381; and constitutional rights, 381–382. *See also* Equality

Egalitarian theory on unintended damage, 295, 312; and public vs. private responsibility, 295–296, 299–300, 309–310; comparative cost in, 301–309

Eighth Amendment, 355, 357

Eliot, T. S., 421n11

Elmer's case, 15–20; and principle that no one should profit from own wrong, 20; and snail darter case, 21; and natural-law interpretation,

36; and legal positivism, 37; and interpretation of law, 87; and post-interpretive stage, 100; and conventionalism, 115, 122, 123, 125, 130; and legal pragmatism, 158. *See also* Statute of wills

Ely, John Hart, 450n5, 451nn11, 15

Emotional damages: and *McLoughlin* case, 24, 26–27, 240–250, 258–259 (*see also McLoughlin* case); and conventionalism, 116–117

Empirical disagreement, about law, 4, 5, 31, 33, 37. *See also* Truth and falsity

Endangered Species Act, 20; legislative history of, 22, 347; and intentions about dam construction, 23; as interpretation example, 313, 315, 321–323, 325–327, 328, 339, 340, 341, 349, 352–353. *See also* Snail darter case

Equality: and family relationships, 204–205, 402; and wealth maximization, 291–295; conceptions of, 297–299; of resources, 297–298, 299, 301–309, 312, 403–404, 407–408; and public vs. private responsibility, 299–301; skepticism about, 372–373. *See also* Egalitarian principle

Equal protection: and segregated education, 29–30, 357, 360, 362–363; and Fourteenth Amendment framers, 30, 362; and political integrity, 185; and Supreme Court role, 357; historical interpretation of, 360–361; as required of states, 381–382, 403; Hercules' approach to, 381–392, 402; and affirmative action, 395–396

Erdlich, G., 431n5

Ewald, William, 433n2

Expectations. *See* Predictability; Protected expectations

Explicit extension of convention, 123–124, 125, 126, 127, 128–129, 130, 131, 142

Extension, and meaning, 71

External skepticism, 78–85, 266–267, 272, 373, 412, 428n27

Fact, issues of, 3, 11–12

Fairman, Charles, 418n28

Fairness, 164–165; and conventionalism, 140–142; and integrity, 166, 263, 404–405; and justice, 177; in conflict with other virtues, 177–178, 188, 404; and "checkerboard" laws, 178, 179, 180, 182, 183; and equal protection, 185; in pragmatist view, 187; in community of principle, 213, 214; in law as integrity, 225, 243, 256; in Hercules' treatment of *McLoughlin*, 242, 249–250, 259; and statutory interpretation, 320, 338, 340–341, 342, 347, 349, 350; and legislative history, 342, 364–365; and historicism, 360; and passivism, 374, 376–378; vs. transient majority, 377; and activism, 378; and subject-classification theory of racial justice, 387; and pure integrity, 406

Fair play: as defense of legitimacy, 193–195; and rulebook community, 213

Family relationships, and equality, 202, 204–205, 402

Fascism, as outside present law, 408

Federal system: political integrity in, 186; and Supreme Court power, 357; certainty vs. substance of allocations in, 368; equality mandate in, 381–382, 403

Feinberg, Joel, 434n10

Fellini, Federico, intention of, 56–57

Fessler, D., 439n9

Fidelity to law: issue of, 3, 5; and plain-fact view, 7–8; and snail darter case, 23; as political obligation, 208; and historicism, 362, 363

Fifth Amendment, 355

"Finger-crossed" defense, 39, 40, 41

Finnis, John, 419n32

Fish, Stanley, 424n16, 425n23

Fiss, Owen, 452n22

Force of law: and grounds of law, 110–111; and conceptions of law, 112; and civil disobedience, 112–113; vs. integrity in adjudication, 218–219. *See also* Legitimacy

Foreseeable injuries: common-law principle on, 26-27; in Hercules' approach, 241, 245-249

Fourteenth Amendment, 29; and segregated education, 30; internal compromise outlawed by, 185; as constraint, 355; and Supreme Court role, 357; and historicism, 360, 361, 395-396; and racially segregated education, 360-361; and changed circumstances, 365; and right against discrimination, 382-392; and affirmative action, 395-397. See also Equal protection

Frank, Jerome, 417n6

Frankfurter, Felix, 358

Fraternal associations, 200-201. See also Associative obligations

Fugitive Slave Law, 111, 219

Gadamer, H. G., 55, 62, 420n2

Gaps in law: and plain-fact view, 8-9; and positivism, 37-39; and conventionalism, 115, 116-117, 118, 126, 144. See also Hard cases; "Making" law

Gavison, Ruth, 418n29

Goodman, Nelson, 447n5

Gordon, Robert, 422n15, 440n18

Gray (Judge), 17-18, 20, 21, 36, 38, 40, 43-44, 130

Gray, J. C., 428n2

Grey, Thomas, 421n6, 450n5

Grounds of law, 4, 11; truth and falsity of, 4, 6; plain-fact view of, 6-11; and semantic theories, 31-43; shared criteria for, 43-44; and force of law, 110-111, 218; and conceptions of law, 112; and civil disobedience, 112-113; in law as integrity, 225, 261-262

Group consciousness, 64, 422n15

Habermas, Jürgen, 420n2, 422n14

Hand, Learned, 1

Handicapped persons, and equality of resources, 305, 408

Happiness, in utilitarianism, 288-295

Hard cases: in plain-fact view, 10; in semantic theories, 39, 44; postinterpretive questions in, 99-100; in Nazi system, 105, 106; and interpretation, 106; conventionalist approach to, 115, 125, 128-129, 132, 139, 157; pragmatist treatment of, 158-160, 161, 163; and law as integrity, 226, 229, 255-256, 258, 265-266, 411; Hercules vs. real judges in, 264-265; and easy cases, 265-266, 353-354, 449n14; popular view of, 266; and critical legal studies, 275; market-simulating approach to, 300; and law's dreams, 410; "no right way" view of, 412. See also Gaps in law; "Making" law

Hare, R. M., 445n11

Harr, C., 439n9

Hart, H. L. A., 34-35, 109, 431n2

Hegel, G. W. F., 14

Hercules, 239-240, 276, 380-381, 411; on McLoughlin case, 240-250, 258-259, 268-271; and local priority, 251, 252-254; and compartmentalization, 252; as applying personal convictions, 259-260; as fraud, 260-263, 266; as arrogant, 263-264; as myth, 264; noncontradictory assumption by, 268; and critical legal studies, 272, 273-274, 275; statutory interpretation by, 313-314, 316-317, 330, 337-341, 342, 343, 347, 348-353, 354, 363, 379-380; and hard vs. easy cases, 354; constitutional interpretation by, 379-391, 392, 393-394, 396-399; as tyrant, 399; and pure law, 400; constraints on, 401-402; disagreement with, 412

Hermes, statutory interpretation by, 317-337, 361

Historicism in constitutional adjudication, 359-365; and stability, 365-369; and affirmative action, 395-396

History: and legal practice, 12-14; of justice, 73; of development of law, 89-90, 137-138, 157, 409; and law as integrity, 227-228; in critical legal studies, 273; legislative,

314–315, 342–347, 350, 388, 405.
See also Consistency with past
Holmes, Oliver Wendell, 14
House of Lords: confidential-records
decision by, 2–3; and precedent,
25–26; in *McLoughlin* case, 27, 38;
in conventionalist view, 115; and
barrister immunity, 220, 401
Hutchinson, Allan, 442n20, 449n13
Hyek, F., 433n13

Ideals, political. *See* Virtues, political
Inclusive integrity, 405, 406, 407,
410
Institutional identity, 68–70
Institutional responsibility, 168–171
Integrity, law as, 95–96, 216,
225–227, 254–258, 410–412; and
precedent, 118, 240, 401–402; on
making new law, 119–120; soft conventionalism as, 127–128; and conventionalism, 134–135, 225, 226,
261, 410, 411; and legal rights, 152,
312; as continuing interpretation,
226–227, 228, 239; and history,
227–228, 273; and chain of law,
228–238, 239, 313; and Hercules on
McLoughlin case, 239–250, 258–259,
268–271; local priority in, 250–254,
402–403, 405, 406; and people as
interpreters, 252; and objections
against Hercules, 259–266; and
hard vs. easy cases, 265–266; skepticism toward, 266–271; and critical
legal studies, 271–275; and accident
law, 301, 309; statutory interpretation under, 313–314, 316 (*see also*
Interpretation of statutes); and
Hercules' interpretation of statutes,
338–340, 342, 347, 349–350; and
Marshall's argument, 356; in liberal-conservative distinction, 358;
and historicism, 360; and value of
certainty, 367; and passivism, 371;
vs. activism, 378; and judicial supervision, 392; and banned categories theory, 394; and law working
itself pure, 400; and legislative supremacy, 401–402; and constraints
on equality, 403; inclusive vs. pure,

405–407; and purer law, 406–407;
and utopian dreams, 407–410. *See
also* Hercules
Integrity, personal, 166
Integrity, political, 165–166; as distinct political virtue, 166, 176–177,
178, 183–184, 188, 262–263, 411;
and legal rights, 166–167; efficiency
of, 166–167, 188–189; in legislation
and in adjudication, 167, 176,
217–219; and consistency, 167,
219–224; and personification of
community, 167–175, 186–187; in
conflict with other virtues, 176–178,
188; and "checkerboard" laws,
178–184, 186, 217–218; and U.S.
Constitution, 184–186; and community, 188–190; and legitimacy,
191–192, 193; in community of
principle, 211, 213–214, 216, 263,
404, 406, 411 (*see also* Community
of principle); sovereignty of,
217–219; and legislative convictions, 329, 336–337; stability as,
368; and equality of resources, 404,
407–408 (*see also* Resources, equality of); and judgment, 410
Intention: in conversational interpretation, 50; and constructive interpretation, 54; and social
interpretation, 54, 58, 59, 62–65;
and artistic interpretation, 55–58;
and interpretation structure, 58–59;
and aesthetic value, 59; statement
of vs. promise, 345. *See also* Purpose
Intentions of legislators: and Elmer's
case, 18–19; and snail darter case,
21–23; as issue, 100; change in attitude about, 137–138; in pragmatic
view, 158; Hercules' view on, 313,
314, 316–317, 348, 350; speaker's
meaning view of, 314–316,
317–327, 335–337, 348, 350, 352,
361; as against repeal or amendment, 318–319; and realistic alternatives, 322; and convictions, 324,
327–337, 361; and legislative history, 342–347; and time, 348–350;
and Fourteenth Amendment,
360–363, 365, 388, 396; and histor-

icism, 360–366, 367, 368–369; vs. passivism, 369

Internal skepticism, 78–86, 412; about chain novel, 230–231; toward law as integrity, 267–271; in critical legal studies, 272–274; in passivism, 373; about morality, 427n27. *See also* Skepticism

Interpretation, 50; as interpretive concept, 49; scientific, 50–51, 53; and purpose, 50–52, 56, 58–59, 62–65, 228; conversational, 51–52, 53–54, 64–65, 419n2; constructive, 52–53, 54, 56, 61, 62, 65, 90, 315, 336, 423n15; and individual acts vs. collective practices, 54–55, 63–65; artist's-intention method of, 54–62; literary, 59, 66; stages of, 65–68; vs. invention, 66, 67; assumptions or convictions in, 67–68; and institutional identity, 68–70; and concept-conception distinction, 71–72 (*see also* Conceptions of law); and paradigms, 72–73, 91–92; of justice, 73–76, 424n20 (*see also* Justice); skepticism about, 76–86, 237–238, 426n27; law as, 87–89, 90–92, 101–102, 226–227, 228, 410–411; fit and justification in, 139, 230, 231, 239, 255, 257, 410–411; of justice by citizens, 189–190, 211; of community, 203–204, 207 (*see also* Community); of political practices, 215; and law as integrity, 225–227, 228, 239 (*see also* Integrity, law as); vs. dichotomy of finding and inventing law, 228; chain novel as, 229–238; and dichotomy of freedom and constraint, 234–235; formal and substantive opinions in, 236–237; respecting of text in, 238; and Hercules in *McLoughlin*, 240–250, 258–259, 268–271 (*see also* Hercules); competitive and contradictory principles in, 241, 268–269; as fitting judicial decisions vs. opinions, 247–248, 284–285; local priority in, 250–254, 402–403, 405, 406; political convictions in, 259–260

Interpretation of Constitution: and *Brown* case, 29–30; liberalism vs. conservatism in, 357–359; historicism in, 359–369, 395–396; passivism in, 369–378, 396; activism in, 369, 378, 398; and American vs. foreign legal practice, 378–379; Hercules' approach to, 379–392, 393–394, 396–399; and individual rights, 381–382; and racial discrimination, 382–392; and remedies, 390–392; and affirmative action, 393–397. *See also* Constitution, U.S.

Interpretations of law. *See* Conceptions of law; Conventionalism; Integrity, law as; Pragmatism, legal

Interpretation of statutes, 16–17, 313–314; literal, 17–18, 99–100, 130; legislators' intentions in, 18–19, 21–23, 313, 314–327 (*see also* Intentions of legislators); in conventionalist view, 114–115, 122, 130–131; disagreement over, 122; and consistency with past, 132, 133–134; in legal pragmatist view, 148, 154–155, 162; Hercules' method for, 313–314, 316–317, 330, 337–341, 342, 343, 347, 348–353, 354, 363, 379–380; legislative history in, 314–315, 342–347; legislators' convictions in, 324, 327–337; and time, 348–350; and "unclarity" of language, 350–353. *See also* Statutes

Interpretive attitude: and disagreement, 46–47; toward courtesy, 47–49 (*see also* Courtesy); inside view of, 49, 76; and stages of interpretation, 65–68; as objective, 76–78, 79–80, 81–82; and internal skepticism, 78–79 (*see also* Internal skepticism); and foreign legal systems, 102–104, 107; and wicked law, 105–108; of conventionalism, 116; toward conventional practices, 122–123; as needing paradigms not conventions, 138–139; toward associative obligations, 197, 198, 203–204

Interpretive stage, 66; and Nazi
"law," 104
"Inventing" law, vs. theoretical disagreement, 5–6. *See also* "Making"
law
Invention vs. interpretation, 66, 67
Issues: of law, 3; of fidelity, 3, 5, 7; of
morality, 3, 7; of fact, 3, 11–12 (*see
also* Empirical disagreement; Truth
and falsity); of repair, 9; in postinterpretive stage, 99–101

Johnson, J. W., 432n5
Judges: mechanical, 8, 18; discretion
of, 9; as intuitive decision makers,
10–11; popular opinion about, 11;
in exploration of legal practice,
14–15; and doctrines of precedent,
24–26; legal realism view of, 36; interpretation by, 87, 410; and jurisprudence, 90; and force of law, 112,
218–219; and conventionalism, 115,
117, 119, 125–126, 128, 148,
157–158, 226; and protected expectations, 129–130; and consistency
with past, 132–134; and legal pragmatism, 148–149, 151–157,
158–163, 226; and political integrity, 167; and integrity in adjudication, 217, 218, 225; and law as
integrity, 226–227, 228, 238–239,
244, 245–246, 255–258; as authors
and critics, 228–229; and Hercules,
239, 264–265 (*see also* Hercules);
and explicit statement of principle,
247; statutory interpretation by,
314, 324, 333–334, 342 (*see also* Interpretation of statutes); liberal vs.
conservative, 357–359; and minority rights, 375; in school desegregation cases, 391–392; constraints on,
401–403, 410; interpretive questions
for, 412
Jurisprudence (philosophy of law):
and theoretical disagreement in
law, 6; skepticism toward, 85; in
legal arguments, 90; and grounds
vs. force of law, 111, 112; and lawyers, 380; of racial integration,
391–392; law's dreams by, 407–410

Justice, 164, 165; and law, 7, 97–98;
and natural law theory, 35–36; as
interpretive concept, 73–76,
424n20; in legal pragmatism, 151,
187; and integrity, 166, 189–190,
263, 404–405; in personal behavior,
174; fairness as, 177; in conflict
with other virtues, 177–178, 188,
404; and "checkerboard" laws,
180–183; and equal protection,
185; duty to support, 193; vs. communal obligations, 202–206; in
community of principle, 213, 214; in
law as integrity, 225, 243, 256,
262; in Hercules' treatment of
McLoughlin, 242, 249–250, 259; academic vs. practical elaboration of,
285–286, 287, 290–291; and duty to
maximize wealth, 286–288; utilitarian, 288–295 (*see also* Utilitarianism); in Hercules' interpretation
of statutes, 338; skepticism about,
372–373; and passivism, 374–376;
in pure integrity, 405–
406

Kant, Immanuel, and self-legislation,
189
Kennedy, Duncan, 438n26, 440nn16,
18
Klare, K., 440nn16, 18
Korematsu case, 376
Kuhn, Thomas, 421n4

Langen, P., 431n5
Law: empirical disagreement about,
4, 5, 31, 33, 37; grounds of, 4, 11,
112 (*see also* Grounds of law); theoretical disagreements about, 4–6, 11
(*see also* Theoretical disagreement in
law); plain-fact view of, 6–11, 15,
20, 31 (*see also* Plain-fact view of
law); and justice, 7, 97–98; vague
guidelines in, 8, 9; as social phenomenon, 12–14, 418n29; external
and internal perspectives on,
13–14; as coherent whole, 19–20;
and skepticism, 79, 85–86, 268; centrifugal and convergent forces in,
87–89; paradigms of, 88, 89, 91–92;

development of, 89–90, 137–138, 157, 409; concept of, 92–94, 108–110, 190; basic questions on, 94; conceptions of, 94–96, 99–101 (*see also* Conceptions of law); and morality, 96–98, 100, 430n5; in wicked places, 101–108, 206; chain of, 228–238, 239, 313; compartmentalization of, 250–254; economic approach to, 272; as worked pure, 400, 406–410; constraints on, 401–403, 410; empire of, 407, 413; utopian dreams of, 407–410; cunning of, 409; as authority, 429n3. *See also* Statutes

Law, theories of. *See* Conventionalism; Integrity, law as; Legal realism; Plain-fact view of law; Positivism, legal; Pragmatism, legal; Semantic theories of law

Law as integrity. *See* Integrity, law as

Law as interpretive concept, 87–89, 90–92, 410–411; and analysis of interpretation, 50; and law in wicked places, 101–102; and force of law, 111; and law as integrity, 226–227, 228; and chain of law, 228–238, 239, 313; and liberal-conservative distinction, 357–358; and interpretivist-noninterpretivist distinction, 360

Lawsuits: significance of, 1–3; issues raised in, 3; under unilateralism, 143. *See also* Cases; Hard cases

Law of unintended injury: economic theory of, 276–285, 310 (*see also* Economic theory on unintended damage); and utilitarianism, 288–295; egalitarian interpretation of, 295–309, 312; and resource egalitarianism, 297–298, 299, 301–309, 312, 403–404; antiliberalism argument from, 441–444n20

Leader, Sheldon, 448n11

Legal conventions, 114, 120–124. *See also* Conventionalism

Legal language, flexibility of, 104–105

Legal philosophy. *See* Jurisprudence

Legal positivism. *See* Positivism, legal

Legal practice: as argumentative, 13; identifying of, 90–91; conventions in, 120–124; and legal pragmatism, 158–160; and law as integrity, 225; and rise of Supreme Court, 356; constraints on, 401–403, 410; noncomputability of, 412

Legal realism, 36–37, 153, 161–162; vs. law as integrity, 228; and critical legal studies, 272

Legal rights. *See* Rights, legal

Legal theory: aspects of, 11–12; "external," 14; grounds and force of law in, 110. *See also* Theoretical disagreement in law; Theory of legislation

Legislation: in conceptions of law, 99; as communication, 315, 329, 348. *See also* Statutes

Legislation, interpretation of. *See* Intentions of legislators; Interpretation of statutes

Legislative history, 314–315; of Endangered Species Act, 22, 347; official statements of purpose in, 342–347; and passage of time, 350; and Fourteenth Amendment rights, 388; and procedural due process, 405

Legislative integrity, 167, 176, 217–218. *See also* Integrity

Legislative responsibility, 319–320, 341

Legislative supremacy: as constraint, 401; as fairness, 405; and justice, 406

Legitimacy, 190–192; through tacit consent, 192–193; and duty to be just, 193; through fair play, 193–195; through communal obligations, 206–208; and community of principle, 214–215, 216

Lewis, David, 431n3, 433n14

Liberalism: critical legal studies on, 274–275, 440n19, 441n20; of justices, 357–359; and Hercules, 398–399

Libertarianism, 297, 299, 301; and semantic sting, 73, 76

Like cases: like treatment of, 165; and political integrity, 219–224. *See also* Consistency with past; Precedent

Literal interpretation, 17–18; as issue, 99–100; as strict-conventionalist criterion, 130

Literary criticism, judge's function compared to, 228–229

Literary interpretation: author's intention in, 59; preinterpretive stage in, 66

Local priority, in interpretive judgments, 250–254, 402–403, 405, 406

Lochner case, 374, 375, 398

Lukes, Stephen, 425n21

Lyons, David, 431n4

McLoughlin case, 23–29, 38–39; and natural-law interpretation, 36; and legal positivism, 37; and protected expectations, 118; in law as integrity, 120; and legal convention, 122; and soft conventionalism, 126; and strict conventionalism, 131; and consistency with past, 133; under unilateralism, 142; and surprise, 142, 143; and legal pragmatism, 159, 162–163; and integrity, 177; and integrity vs. pragmatism, 220; and chain of law, 238–239; Hercules' treatment of, 240–250, 258–259, 268–271

Madison, James, 436n9

Majoritarian system: integrity in, 165, 177–178; and utilitarianism, 290–291; vs. constitutional rights, 356; and passivism, 373–377; in Hercules' approach, 398; and fairness, 435n3. *See also* Democracy

"Making" law: vs. theoretical disagreement, 5–6; and conventionalism, 117, 119, 126, 131–132, 142; and law as integrity, 119–120; consistency with past in, 132–133. *See also* Gaps in law; Hard cases

Marbury v. Madison, 370

Market-simulating rules, 277; in duty to maximize wealth, 286–288; in utilitarianism, 288–295; and egalitarianism, 295, 300–309

Marshall, John, 356–357

Marxism: and justice, 74, 75, 425n 21; as outside law, 408

Meaning: in interpretive attitude, 47, 50; of practice vs. individuals, 54–55, 63–65; and extension, 71

Meaning of law, 32. *See also* Semantic theories of law

Melamed, A. Douglas, 444nn4, 5

Mental states of legislators, 314, 318, 321–324, 335–336; communication of, 315; and Hercules' method, 316; counterfactual, 325–327, 328; and legislation as communication, 348; and historicism, 361. *See also* Intentions of legislators

Mill, James, 435n2

Miller, Jonathan, 421n7

Morality: in legal judgment, 1; and plain-fact view of law, 7, 8, 9; and *McLoughlin* case precedent, 28, 127; vs. policy, 28–29; and natural law theory, 35–36; skepticism toward, 78–86, 427n27; vs. taste, 82–83; and law, 96–98, 100, 430n5; vs. conventionalism, 118–119; in interpretation of conventions, 122; and soft conventionalism, 128; in legal pragmatism, 151–152, 160, 187; and political integrity, 166, 189–190; of personified community, 168–175; and political obligation, 191; associative obligations in, 196–201; in fairness of decisions, 250; and compartmentalization of law, 252; and Hercules' decision, 262; academic vs. practical elaboration of, 285–286, 287, 290–291; and duty to maximize wealth, 286–288; utilitarianism, 288–295 (*see also* Utilitarianism); promise-keeping, 344–345, 346; and Fourteenth Amendment, 365; and liberalism, 441n19. *See also* Political morality

Moral ledger, 306

Nagel, Thomas, 174, 426n24, 434n12

Natural law theories, 35–36; and morality-law connection, 98; justice-law connection in, 98, 102; and law as integrity, 263; and Hercules, 397

Nazi Germany: and rule of recognition, 35; "law" in, 102–108; and group responsibility, 172, 173

Negligence: contributory, 282–283; comparative, 283

Negligence law: and nuisance law, 253–254; interpretation of, 276, 292–293, 312 (see also Law of unintended damage)

Nelson, William, 436nn9, 10

Neurath, Otto, 111, 139

Nietzsche, Friedrich, and paradigms of justice, 75

Nihilism in law: semantic theorists' fear of, 44; and law as illusion, 101

Novel, chain, 228–232; Scrooge in, 232–237; "real" novel in, 238; and law, 239

Nozick, Robert, 437nn18, 19, 445n14

Nuisance law: and negligence law, 253–254; interpretation of, 276, 292–293, 312 (see also Law of unintended damage)

Oakley, John, 417n13

Objectivity, 82–83; and interpretive attitude, 76–78, 79–80, 81–82; and hard cases, 266; and external skepticism, 267. See also Empirical disagreement; Truth and falsity

Obligation. See Morality; Political morality; Political obligation

Obligations of community. See Associative obligations

Opaqueness of statements and convictions, 331–332, 362

Paradigms, 72–73; of justice, 75–76; of law, 88, 89, 90, 91–92; conventionalist, 121; and interpretive attitude, 138–139; conservation of species as, 341; and hard vs. easy cases, 354. See also Pivotal cases

Parental domination: as integrity example, 202, 203, 204–205; and equal protection, 402

Parfit, Derek, 424n19

Parliament, and statutory interpretation, 344

Passivism in constitutional adjudication, 369–378; issues in, 370; and fairness, 374, 376–378; and justice, 374–376; and affirmative action, 396; and Hercules, 398

Performative acts: promises as, 344–345; legislation as, 346

Perry, M., 450n5

Personification of community or state, and political integrity, 167–175, 186–187, 225, 296

Philosophy of law. See Jurisprudence

Pivotal cases: vs. "borderline" defense of positivism, 41–43; and disagreement, 45. See also Paradigms

Plain-fact view of law, 6–11; and sample cases, 15, 20, 31; and semantic/positivist theories, 31, 33, 37, 39, 40; on judges' opinions, 90; and Marshall's dictum, 356

Plessy v. Ferguson, 29–30, 118–119, 376, 379, 387, 389, 399

"Point" (purpose): and interpretation, 58–59; of law, 87–88, 94, 95, 141, 150, 356; of judicial decision, 138; of statute, 343. See also Purpose

Policy arguments: in McLoughlin case, 27–29; vs. principle, 221–224, 243–244, 310–312, 338–339, 381; and legal remedies, 390; in legislation vs. adjudication, 410. See also Economic theory on unintended damage

Polinsky, M., 445n7

Political morality: issues of, 3; and Brown case, 30; and law as integrity, 96, 239, 263; and conceptions of law, 101; and wicked law, 105, 108; vs. protected expectations, 117; and surprises, 141; vs. force of law, 218–219; and explicit announcing of principle, 247–248; and hard cases, 256, 258; and interpretation, 260, 378, 411; and statutory interpretation, 316, 319–320, 343, 345–346; in constitutional interpretation, 366–367, 374; in utopian legal politics, 408–409. *See also* Morality

Political obligation, 191; and associative obligations, 196, 201, 205–206, 216; and emigration, 207

Politics: law as, 8, 9–10; of adjudication, 12, 380–381; and borderline cases, 41; as debate, 211

Popper, Karl, 421n4

Positivism, legal, 33–35, 37–43; and justice-law connection, 98; and morality-law connection, 98; and wicked law, 102; inflexible use in, 104; and nature of law vs. force of law, 109; and law as authority, 429n3; and democracy, 432n6. *See also* Semantic theories of law

Posner, Richard, 444n1, 445n7

Postema, G., 433n13

Postinterpretive stage, 66; legal issues in, 99–101; conventionalist claims in, 116, 117; in interpretation of Constitution, 358

Powell, H. J., 452n22

Powell, Lewis, 22–23

Pragmatism, legal, 95, 151–153, 158–160, 161, 410; and justice-law connection, 98; and conventionalism, 147–150, 157, 161, 162, 264; and morality, 151–152, 160, 187; as-if strategy of, 152–153, 154–155, 158, 161, 162; and legal rights, 152–153, 154–155, 158, 160–164; and prospective rulemaking, 155–157; and development of legal culture, 157; and law as integrity, 220, 225, 226, 244, 261, 410, 411; and compartmentalization, 251; activism as, 378

Precedent: relaxed doctrine of, 24, 25–26; strict doctrine of, 24–26, 401; and convergence of interpretation, 88; in conception of law, 99; and conventionalism, 115, 121–122, 123, 130, 131–132; disagreement over interpretation of, 122; and consistency with past, 132, 133–134; changes in doctrine of, 138; in legal-pragmatist view, 148, 154–155, 158–159, 162; in Hercules'

approach, 240–250, 258–259, 337, 399, 401–402; as constraint, 401; as procedural due process, 405. *See also* Chain of law

Predictability: vs. flexibility, 146–150, 154; through compartmentalization, 252; value of, 367–368. *See also* Protected expectations

Predictive hypothesis, judge's opinion as, 36–37

Preinterpretive stage, 65–66; for justice, 75; as contingent and local, 91; for law, 91, 92; and Nazi "law," 103, 104, 105

Principle: and compromise, 179–184, 435n7; community of, 211, 213–214, 404, 406 (*see also* Community of principle); in political integrity, 221–224; vs. policy, 221–224, 243–244, 310–312, 338–339, 381; contradictory vs. competitive, 241, 268–269, 274; explicit recognition of, 247–248; in utilitarian justification, 290. *See also* Rights

Procedural due process, 166–167; in conflict with other virtues, 177–178, 404; and integrity in adjudication, 218–219; in law as integrity, 225, 243; in Hercules' interpretation, 338; in political integrity, 404–405; and pure integrity, 406

Promises: and responsibilities of public officials, 174–175; statutes as, 344–345

Property: abstract rights in, 293, 300–301 (*see also* Rights); in conceptions of equality, 296, 297–301; and equality of resources, 297–298, 299, 407; policy vs. principle on, 310–311. *See also* Law of unintended injury

Propositions of law, 3–4; grounds of, 4, 6, 11 (*see also* Grounds of law); truth or falsity of, 4–5, 32, 417n5; semantic theories on, 31, 32–44; and causation analogy, 31–32; and core vs. penumbral uses, 39–43, 419n34; and pivotal cases, 41–43; in law as integrity, 225

Protected expectations: as conventionalist ideal, 117–118, 119, 120,
129–130, 139–140; and soft conventionalism, 128; and democracy,
140; fairness of, 140–142; and predictability vs. flexibility, 143–150
Protestant attitude toward law, 413;
and integrity, 190; and compartmentalization, 252
Pure integrity, 405–407
Purpose: and interpretation, 50–52,
56, 58–59, 62–65, 228; in statutory
interpretation, 100; in legislative
history, 343–347; in Fourteenth
Amendment, 365. *See also* Intention;
"Point"

Quine, W. V. O., 421n3, 447n6
Quota system. *See* Affirmative action

Racial discrimination: and associative
obligation, 204; constitutional right
against, 382–387
Racially segregated education: and
"discovered" vs. "invented" law, 6;
and *Brown* case, 29–30, 387–389 (*see
also Brown* case); and busing, 221,
392; and Supreme Court role, 357;
and historicist interpretation,
360–361, 362–363; and fairness,
377; remedies against, 389–392;
and affirmative action, 393–397
Rationality requirement, of Constitution, 382, 383, 397
Rawls, John, 192, 193, 440n19,
424n17, 435n1, 437nn16, 17, 18
Raz, Joseph, 424n18, 428n1, 429n3
Realism, legal. *See* Legal realism
Reasonable-person rule, 280–282, 284,
306–307
Repair, 9; and positivist view, 38, 40
Resources, equality of, 297–298, 299,
301–309, 312, 403–404, 407–408
Responsibility: institutional, 168–171,
189; collective, 172–173, 175; of political officials, 173–175; principle
of, 269–270; public vs. private,
295–296, 299–300, 309–310 (*see also*
Rights, legal); legislative, 319–320,
341

Reverse discrimination. *See* Affirmative action
Rights: in simulated markets, 277; vs.
collective strategies, 292–293,
381–382; and comparative cost,
307–308, 309; and constitutional
passivism, 375, 376–378; and remedies, 390; vs. communal good, 408.
See also Principle
Rights, legal, 93, 152; and conventionalism, 95, 152; vs. other forms
of rights, 117; and legal pragmatism, 152–153, 154–155, 158,
160–164; and law as integrity, 244;
abstract (prima facie), 293, 296,
301, 306, 310, 312; judicial protection of, 356; and historicism,
368–369; against racial discrimination, 382–392; enforcement of,
390–392; as protecting fairness vs.
justice, 451n11
Rights, political: and personification
of community, 173–174; and integrity, 223; and policy, 311–312
Rope analogy: and institution of
courtesy, 69–70; and Nazi "law,"
103. *See also* Chain of law
Rousseau, Jean Jacques, and self-
legislation, 189
"Rule" of law, 93
Rulemaking, prospective vs. retrospective, 155–157
Rule of recognition, in Hart's theory,
34–35
Rules: coordination through,
145–146; in utilitarian justification,
290. *See also* Convention; Principle

Scarman, Lord, 28, 38
Scrooge, interpretation of, 232–237
Segregation. *See* Racially segregated
schools
Self-government, and political integrity, 189
Semantic sting, 45–46, 68, 70, 73, 87;
and legal system, 91; and legal
paradigms, 92; and wicked law,
103; and Hercules' decision, 262;
and constitutional adjudication,
360

Semantic theories of law, 31–37; legal positivism, 33–35, 37–43 (see also Positivism, legal); natural law theories, 35–36, 98, 102, 263, 397; legal realism, 36–37, 153, 161–162, 228, 272; defenses of, 37–43; and core vs. penumbral uses, 39–43, 419n34; and pivotal cases, 41–43; as escape from legal nihilism, 43–44; and justice, 73, 74; impossible goal of, 90; positivism-natural law contest in, 98; and wicked law, 102, 103, 108; inflexible use in, 104; and nature of law vs. force of law, 109; and conventionalism, 115–116; and consistency in principle, 135

Shavell, S., 445n7

Skepticism: and interpretation, 76–86, 237–238, 426n27; internal and external, 78–85, 266–267 (see also External skepticism; Internal skepticism); about morality, 79, 84–85, 427n27; toward law, 79, 85–86, 268; legal pragmatism as, 95, 160; toward associative institution, 203, 205; toward law as integrity, 228, 261, 266–271; about chain novel, 230–231, 237–238; in critical legal studies, 271–274; interpretive vs. historical argument in, 273; and passivism, 372–373; about hard cases, 412; and liberalism, 441n19

Skinner, B. F., 14

Slavery, and political integrity, 184

Snail darter case, 20–23; and legal positivism, 37; and strict conventionalism, 125, 131; and soft conventionalism, 125–126; as interpretation example, 313, 317, 328, 330–333, 337–338, 342, 347

Social contract theory, 192–193

Social interpretation, 50, 51, 54, 58, 59, 62–65

Social science, and interpretation, 55, 64, 68, 422n14. See also History

Society. See Community

Sociology: and legal practice, 12–14; in Brown case, 30

Soft conventionalism, 124, 125–128

Soper, Philip, 431n4

Sound-truck example, on fair play, 194

Speaker's meaning view of statutory interpretation, 314–316, 317–318; and questions of authorship, 318–320; composite intention in, 320–321, 335–337; hopes and expectations in, 321–324, 325; and legislators' conviction, 324, 327–337; canonical moment in, 348, 350; and unclarity, 352; and historicism on Constitution, 361

Stability, as historicism rationale, 365–369

State, personification of, 167–175, 186–187

State of nature, and legitimacy, 194

Statute: as document vs. law, 16–17; "checkerboard," 178–184, 186, 187, 214, 217–218; and community of principle, 214; Constitution as, 379. See also Interpretation of statutes

Statute of wills, 16, 18, 122, 132, 317, 346–347, 351, 352

Statutory interpretation. See Interpretation of statutes

Stevens, John Paul, 449n3

Subject classification account of right against discrimination, 382–383, 385, 386, 387

Supreme Court, U.S.: power of, 2, 355–357; in snail darter case, 21, 131; precedent from, 25; in Brown case, 29–30; in conventionalist view, 118–119; on vague definition of crimes, 143; abortion ruling by, 185, 186; liberals vs. conservatives on, 357–359; in historicist interpretation, 366; and Marbury v. Madison, 370; and passivism, 375–376. See also Brown case; Snail darter case

Sutherland, A., 431n5

Swift, Jonathan, 433n2

Testing cases. See Pivotal cases

Textual integrity, of statutes, 338–340, 342, 347, 349–350

Theoretical disagreement in law, 4–5, 11; vs. "inventing" law, 5–6; and plain-fact view, 6–11, 31, 37 (*see also* Plain-fact view of law); and Elmer's case, 20; and snail darter case, 23; and *Brown* case, 30; and semantic theories, 31–43 (*see also* Semantic theories of law); and shared factual criteria, 43–44, 45–46; as interpretive, 87

Theories of law. *See* Conventionalism; Integrity, law as; Legal realism; Plain-fact view of law; Positivism, legal; Pragmatism, legal; Semantic theories of law

Theory, academic vs. practical, 285

Theory of legislation: and statutory interpretation, 17, 23; change in, 137

Thought and expression, 315

Tort law, skepticism about, 268. *See also* Law of unintended injury

Traditional practices: gender interpretation of courtesy as, 72–73; and equality, 202, 204–205, 402; and racial discrimination, 383, 389. *See also* Courtesy

Transaction costs, 278–280, 287

Transparency of statements and convictions, 331–332, 363

Tribe, Laurence, 436nn9, 10

Truth and falsity: of grounds of law, 4, 6; of propositions of law, 4–5, 32, 417n5. *See also* Empirical disagreement; Objectivity

Tushnet, Mark, 440n19

Unclarity of language, and statutory interpretation, 350–353

Unilateral conventionalism (unilateralism), 142–143, 146, 147, 365–366

Utilitarianism, 288–295; and semantic sting, 73; and equality, 292–295, 297, 298; and personal responsibility, 309–310; and racial discrimination, 383, 384; in purified law, 408

Utopianism: political philosophy as, 164; in legal politics, 408–409

Values: and interpretive attitude, 47, 48; in constructive interpretation, 52–53; and artistic interpretation, 55, 57; of art, 59–62; of integrity, 188; of certainty, 367–368

Verstehen, 420n2

Virtues, political, 164–165; conflicts among, 117, 188, 404. *See also* Fairness; Integrity; Justice; Procedural due process

Wakefield, John, 449n13

Waldron, Jeremy, 437n14

Walzer, Michael, 425n20

Warren, Earl, 29–30, 359

Wealth, community: definition of, 277, 286–287; duty to maximize, 286–288; in utilitarianism, 288–295

Wealth test, 276–280; and reasonable-person rule, 280–282; and contributory negligence, 282–283; fit of, 283–285

Welfare, in utilitarianism, 288–295

Williams, Bernard, 426n24

Wittgenstein, Ludwig: and form of life, 63; rope analogy of, 69–70; on communication of thought, 315